0150316

D74217.

D1756245

This book is due for return on or before the last date shown below.

Don Gresswell Ltd., London, N.21   Cat. No. 1208

DG 02242/71

0471941115

Model Building
in
Mathematical Programming

Third Edition
Revised

H. P. WILLIAMS

Faculty of Mathematical Studies
University of Southampton

A Wiley–Interscience Publication

JOHN WILEY & SONS

Chichester · New York · Brisbane · Toronto · Singapore

Copyright © 1978, 1985, 1990, 1993 by John Wiley & Sons Ltd,
Baffins Lane, Chichester,
West Sussex PO19 1UD, England

Reprinted April 1991, Reprinted with corrections May 1993, September 1994,
October 1995, May 1997, February 1998

Other Wiley Editorial Offices

John Wiley & Sons, Inc., 605 Third Avenue,
New York, NY 10158-0012, USA

Jacaranda Wiley Ltd, 33 Park Road, Milton,
Queensland 4064, Australia

John Wiley & Sons (Canada) Ltd, 22 Worcester Road,
Rexdale, Ontario M9W 1L1, Canada

John Wiley & Sons (SEA) Pte Ltd, 37 Jalan Pemimpin #05-04,
Block B, Union Industrial Building, Singapore 129809

Library of Congress Cataloging-in-Publication Data

Williams, H.P.
    Model building in mathematical programming/H.P. Williams. – 3rd
ed. rev.
        p. cm.
    'A Wiley-Interscience publication.'
    Includes bibliographical references (p.   ).
    ISBN 0 471 94111 5 (pbk)
    1. Programming (Mathematics). 2. Mathematical models. I. Title.
T57.7.W55 1990
519.7 – dc20   89-28633
                                                                CIP

British Library Cataloguing in Publication Data

Williams, H.P. (Hilary Paul), *1943–*
    Model building in mathematical programming. – 3rd ed. rev.
    1. Mathematical programming. Applications of mathematical
    models
    I. Title.
    519.7

ISBN 0 471 94111 5 (pbk)

Typeset by Mathematical Composition Setters Ltd, Salisbury, Wiltshire
Printed and bound in Great Britain by
Biddles Ltd, Guildford and King's Lynn

To
Eileen, Anna, Alexander and Eleanor

Contents

Preface

Mathematical programmes are among the most widely used models in operational research and management science. In many cases their application has been so successful that their use has passed out of operational research departments to become an accepted routine planning tool. It is therefore rather surprising that comparatively little attention has been paid in the literature to the problems of formulating and building mathematical programming models or even deciding when such a model is applicable. Most published work has tended to be of two kinds. Firstly, case studies of particular applications have been described in the operational research journals and journals relating to specific industries. Secondly, research work on new algorithms for special classes of problems has provided much material for the more theoretical journals. This book attempts to fill the gap by, in Part 1, discussing the general principles of model building in mathematical programming. In Part 2, twenty practical problems are presented to which mathematical programming can be applied. By simplifying the problems, much of the tedious institutional detail of case studies is avoided. It is hoped, however, that the essence of the problems is preserved and easily understood. Finally, in Parts 3 and 4, suggested formulations and solutions to the problems are given together with some computational experience.

Many books already exist on mathematical programming or, in particular, linear programming. Most such books adopt the conventional approach of paying a great deal of attention to algorithms. Since the algorithmic side has been so well and fully covered by other texts it is given much less attention in this book. The concentration here is much more on the building and interpreting of models rather than the solution process. Nevertheless, it is hoped that this book may spur the reader to delve more deeply into the often challenging algorithmic side of the subject as well. It is, however, the author's contention that the practical problems and model building aspect should come first. This may then provide a motivation for finding out how to solve such models. Although desirable, knowledge of algorithms is no longer necessary if practical use is to be made of mathematical programming. The solution of practical models is now largely automated by the use of commercial package programs which are discussed in Chapter 2.

For the reader with some prior knowledge of mathematical programming, parts of this book may seem trivial and can be skipped or read quickly. Other parts are, however, rather more advanced and present fairly new material. This is particularly true of the chapters on integer programming. Indeed this book can be treated in a non-sequential manner. There is much cross-referencing to enable the reader to pass from one relevant section to another.

This book is aimed at three types of reader:

(1) It is intended to provide students in universities and polytechnics with a solid foundation in the principles of model building as well as the more mathematical, algorithmic side of the subject which is conventionally taught. For students who finally go on to use mathematical programming to solve real problems the model building aspect is probably the more important. The problems of Part 2 provide practical exercises in problem formulation. By formulating models and solving them with the aid of a computer a student learns the art of formulation in the most satisfying way possible. He can compare his numerical solution with that of other students obtained from differently built models. In this way he learns how to validate a model.

It is also hoped that these problems will be of use to research students seeking new algorithms for solving mathematical programming problems. Very often they have to rely on trivial or randomly generated models to test their computational procedures. Such models are far from typical of those found in the real world. Moreover they are one (or more) steps removed from practical situations. They therefore obscure the need for efficient formulations as well as algorithms.

(2) This book is also intended to provide managers with a fairly non-technical appreciation of the scope and limitations of mathematical programming. In addition, by looking at the practical problems described in Part 2 they may recognize a situation in their own organization to which they had not realized mathematical programming could be applied.

(3) Finally, constructing a mathematical model of an organization provides one of the best methods of understanding that organization. It is hoped that the general reader will be able to use the principles described in this book to build mathematical models and therefore learn about the functioning of systems which purely verbal descriptions fail to explain. It has been the author's experience that the process of building a model of an organization can often be more beneficial even than the obtaining of a solution. A greater understanding of the complex interconnections between different facets of an organization is forced upon anybody who realistically attempts to model that organization.

Part 1 of this book describes the principles of building mathematical programming models and how they may arise in practice. In particular linear programming, integer programming and separable programming models are described. A discussion of the practical aspects of solving such models and a very full discussion of the interpretation of their solutions is included.

Part 2 presents each of the twenty practical problems in sufficient detail to enable the reader to build a mathematical programming model using the numerical data.

Part 3 discusses each problem in detail and presents a possible formulation as a mathematical programming model.

Part 4 gives the optimal solutions obtained from the formulations presented in Part 3. Some computational experience is also given in order to give the reader some feel for the computational difficulty of solving the particular type of model.

It is hoped that the reader will attempt to formulate and possibly solve the problems for himself before proceeding to Parts 3 and 4.

All the problems can be formulated in more than one way as mathematical programming models. Possibly some are better solved by means other than mathematical programming, but this is beyond the scope of this book. It will be obvious that some problems are sufficiently precisely defined that only one optimal solution should be expected in the sense of a maximum 'profit' or minimum 'cost' (although alternative optima may still occur as discussed in Chapter 6). For other problems, however, there may be no one correct answer. The process of modelling the practical situation into a mathematical programming format may necessitate approximations and assumptions by the modeller that result in different optimal solutions. How close such solutions are to those given in Part 4 may help to indicate the value or otherwise of mathematical programming for the type of problem being considered.

By presenting twenty problems from widely different contexts the power of the technique of mathematical programming in giving a method of tackling them all should be apparent. Some problems are intentionally 'unusual' in the hope that they may suggest the application of mathematical programming in rather novel areas.

Many references are given at the end of the book. The list is not intended to provide a complete bibliography of the vast number of case studies published. Many excellent case studies have been ignored. The list should, however, provide a representative sample which can be used as a starting point for a deeper search into the literature.

Many people have both knowingly and unknowingly helped in the preparation of this book by their suggestions and opinions. In particular I would like to thank my colleagues, while I was at Sussex University, Lewis Corner, Bernard Kemp, Pat Rivett, Steven Vajda and Will Watkins who have suggested problems and references to me. Also, through my chairmanship of the Mathematical Programming Study Group of the British Operational Research Society, I have had many informal conversations with other practitioners of mathematical programming which have proved of great value. I would like especially to acknowledge the motivation and ideas provided by Martin Beale, Tony Brearley, Colin Clayman, Martyn Jeffreys, Ailsa Land and Gautam Mitra. I would also like to thank Carol Kemp for her excellent typing of the manuscript.

The second and third editions have been improved by the suggestions and help of Martin Beale, Ian Buchapan, Colin Clayman, Bob Jeroslow, Clifford Jones, Ailsa Land, Adolfo Fonseca Manjarres, Kenneth McKinnon, Heiner Müller-Merbach, Bjorn Nygreen and Richard Thomas. Also I am very grateful to my research assistant Stephen Hutcheon for help in solving the models in Part 2. Finally, I must express a great debt of gratitude to Robin Day of Edinburgh University. His deep computing knowledge and programming ability has helped me immensely.

It is very sad to record that two of the friends who have helped me most with ideas in this book, Martin Beale and Bob Jeroslow, died prematurely in 1984 and 1988, respectively.

The mathematical programming system XPRESS-MP has been implemented on a number of computing systems. Details of obtaining this, and computer programs to solve the models in this book, can be received by writing to Dash Associates Ltd, Blisworth House, Church Lane, Blisworth, Northants NN7 3BX, UK.

Winchester, England   PAUL WILLIAMS
June 1989

A reprint of this third edition has benefited from the corrections and comments of Sheena and Robert Ashford to whom I express my thanks.

Winchester, England   PAUL WILLIAMS
January 1993

PART 1

CHAPTER 1

Introduction

1.1 The Concept of a Model

Many applications of science make use of *models*. The term 'model' is usually used for a structure which has been built purposely to exhibit features and characteristics of some other objects. Generally only some of these features and characteristics will be retained in the model depending upon the use to which it is to be put. Sometimes such models are *concrete*, as is a model aircraft used for wind tunnel experiments. More often in operational research we will be concerned with *abstract* models. These models will usually be *mathematical* in that algebraic symbolism will be used to mirror the internal relationships in the object (often an organization) being modelled. Our attention will mainly be confined to such mathematical models, although the term 'model' is sometimes used more widely to include purely descriptive models.

The essential feature of a mathematical model in operational research is that it involves a set of *mathematical relationships* (such as equations, inequalities, logical dependencies, etc.) which correspond to some more down-to-earth relationships in the real world (such as technological relationships, physical laws, marketing constraints, etc.).

There are a number of motives for building such models:

(i) The actual exercise of building a model often reveals relationships which were not apparent to many people. As a result a greater understanding is achieved of the object being modelled.

(ii) Having built a model it is usually possible to analyse it mathematically to help suggest courses which might not otherwise be apparent.

(iii) Experimentation is possible with a model whereas it is often not possible or desirable to experiment with the object being modelled. It would clearly be politically difficult, as well as undesirable, to experiment with unconventional economic measures in a country if there was a high probability of disastrous failure. The pursuit of such courageous experiments would be more (though not perhaps totally) acceptable on a mathematical model.

It is important to realize that a model is really defined by the relationships which it incorporates. These relationships are, to a large extent, independent of the *data* in the model. A model may be used on many different occasions

3

with differing data, e.g. costs, technological coefficients, resource availabilities, etc. We would usually still think of it as the same model even though some coefficients had changed. This distinction is not, of course, total. Radical changes in the data would usually be thought of as a change in the relationships and therefore the model.

Many models used in operational research (and other areas such as engineering and economics) take standard forms. The mathematical programming type of model which we consider in this book is probably the most commonly used standard type of model. Other examples of some commonly used mathematical models are *simulation models, network planning models, econometric models*, and *time series models*. There are many other types of model, all of which arise sufficiently often in practice to make them areas worthy of study in their own right. It should be emphasized, however, that any such list of standard types of model is unlikely to be exhaustive or exclusive. There are always practical situations which cannot be modelled in a standard way. The building, analysing, and experimenting with such new types of model may still be a valuable activity. Often practical problems can be modelled in more than one standard way (as well as in non-standard ways). It has long been realized by operational research workers that the comparison and contrasting of results from different types of model can be extremely valuable.

Many misconceptions exist about the value of mathematical models, particularly when used for planning purposes. At one extreme there are people who deny that models have any value at all when put to such purposes. Their criticisms are often based on the impossibility of satisfactorily quantifying much of the required data, e.g. attaching a cost or utility to a social value. A less severe criticism surrounds the lack of precision of much of the data which may go into a mathematical model; e.g. if there is doubt surrounding 100 000 of the coefficients in a model, how can we have any confidence in an answer it produces? The first of these criticisms is a difficult one to counter and has been tackled at much greater length by many defenders of cost–benefit analysis. It seems undeniable, however, that many decisions concerning unquantifiable concepts, however they are made, involve an implicit quantification which cannot be avoided. Making such a quantification explicit by incorporating it in a mathematical model seems more honest as well as scientific. The second criticism concerning accuracy of the data should be considered in relation to each specific model. Although many coefficients in a model may be inaccurate it is still possible that the structure of the model results in little inaccuracy in the solution. This subject is mentioned in depth in Section 6.3.

At the opposite extreme to the people who utter the above criticisms are those who place an almost metaphysical faith in a mathematical model for decision making (particularly if it involves using a computer). The quality of the answers which a model produces obviously depends on the accuracy of the structure and data of the model. For mathematical programming models the definition of the objective clearly affects the answer as well. Uncritical faith in a model is obviously unwarranted and dangerous. Such an attitude results from a total misconception of how a model should be used. To accept the first answer produced by a mathematical model without further analysis and questioning should be very rare. A model should be used as one of a number of tools for decision making. The answer which a model produces should be subjected to close scrutiny. If it represents an unacceptable operating plan then the reasons for unacceptability should be spelled out and if possible incorporated in a modified model. Should the answer be acceptable it might be wise only to regard it as an *option*. The specification of another objective function (in the case of a mathematical programming model) might result in a different option. By successive questioning of the answers and altering the model (or its objective) it should be possible to clarify the options available and obtain a greater understanding of what is possible.

1.2 Mathematical Programming Models

It should be pointed out immediately that *mathematical programming* is very different from *computer programming*. Mathematical programming is 'programming' in the sense of 'planning'. As such it need have nothing to do with computers. The confusion over the use of the word 'programming' is widespread and unfortunate. Inevitably mathematical programming becomes involved with computing since practical problems almost always involve large quantities of data and arithmetic which can only reasonably be tackled by the calculating power of a computer. The correct relationship between computers and mathematical programming should, however, be understood.

The common feature which mathematical programming models have is that they all involve *optimization*. We wish to *maximize* something or *minimize* something. The quantity which we wish to maximize or minimize is known as an *objective function*. Unfortunately the realization that mathematical programming is concerned with optimizing an objective often leads people summarily to dismiss mathematical programming as being inapplicable in practical situations where there is no clear objective or there are a multiplicity of objectives. Such an attitude is often unwarranted since, as we shall see in Chapter 3, there is often value in optimizing some aspect of a model when in real life there is no clear cut single objective.

In this book we confine our attention to some special sorts of mathematical programming model. These can most easily be classified as *linear programming models, non-linear programming models* and *integer programming models*. We begin by describing what a linear programming model is by means of two small examples.

Example 1. A Linear Programming (LP) Model (Product Mix)

An engineering factory can produce five types of product (PROD 1, PROD 2..., PROD 5) by using two production processes: grinding and drilling.

After deducting raw material costs each unit of each product yields the following contributions to profit:

PROD 1	PROD 2	PROD 3	PROD 4	PROD 5
£550	£600	£350	£400	£200

Each unit requires a certain time on each process. These are given below (in hours). A dash indicates when a process is not needed.

	PROD 1	PROD 2	PROD 3	PROD 4	PROD 5
Grinding	12	20	—	25	15
Drilling	10	8	16	—	—

In addition the final assembly of each unit of each product uses 20 hours of a workman's time.

The factory has three grinding machines and two drilling machines and works a six-day week with two shifts of 8 hours on each day. Eight men are employed in assembly each working one shift a day.

The problem is to find how much to make of each product so as to maximize the total profit contribution.

This is a very simple example of the so-called 'product mix' application of linear programming.

In order to create a *mathematical model* we introduce variables $x_1, x_2, \ldots, x_5$ representing the numbers of PROD 1, PROD 2, ..., PROD 5 which should be made in a week. Since each unit of PROD 1 yields £550 contribution to profit and each unit of PROD 2 yields $600 contribution to profit etc., our total profit contribution will be represented by the expression:

$$550x_1 + 600x_2 + 350x_3 + 400x_4 + 200x_5. \qquad (1)$$

The *objective* of the factory is to choose $x_1, x_2, \ldots, x_5$ so as to make this expression as big as possible, i.e. (1) is the *objective function* which we wish to *maximize* (in this case).

Clearly our processing and manpower capacities, to some extent, limit the values which the x_j can take. Given that we have only three grinding machines working for a total of 96 hours a week each we have 288 hours of grinding capacity available. Each unit of PROD 1 uses 12 hours grinding. x_1 units will therefore use $12x_1$ hours. Similarly x_2 units of PROD 2 will use $20x_2$ hours. The total amount of grinding capacity which we use in a week is given by the expression on the left-hand side of (2) below:

$$12x_1 + 20x_2 \qquad + 25x_4 + 15x_5 \leqslant 288. \qquad (2)$$

(2) is a mathematical way of saying that we cannot use up more than the 288 hours of grinding available per week. (2) is known as a *constraint*. It restricts (or constrains) the possible values which the variables x_j can take.

The drilling capacity is 192 hours a week. This gives rise to the following constraint:

$$10x_1 + 8x_2 + 16x_3 \leqslant 192. \tag{3}$$

Finally, the fact that we have only a total of eight men for assembly each working 48 hours a week gives us a manpower capacity of 384 hours. Since each unit of each product uses 20 hours of this capacity we have the constraint

$$20x_1 + 20x_2 + 20x_3 + 20x_4 + 20x_5 \leqslant 384. \tag{4}$$

We have now expressed our original practical problem as a mathematical model. The particular form which this model takes is that of a *linear programming* (*LP*) *model*. This model is now a well-defined mathematical problem. We wish to find values for the variables $x_1, x_2, ..., x_5$ which make the expression (1) (the objective function) as large as possible but still satisfy the constraints (2), (3), and (4). You should be aware of why the term 'linear' is applied to this particular type of problem. Expression (1) and the left-hand sides of constraints (2), (3), and (4) are all linear. Nowhere do we get terms like x_1^2, $x_1 x_2$ or $\log x$ appearing.

There are a number of implicit assumptions in this model which we should be aware of. Firstly, we must obviously assume that the variables $x_1, x_2 ..., x_5$ are not allowed to be negative, i.e. we do not make negative quantities of any product. We might explicitly state these conditions by the extra constraints

$$x_1, x_2, ..., x_5 \geqslant 0. \tag{5}$$

In most linear programming models the non-negativity constraints (5) are implicitly assumed to apply unless we state otherwise. Secondly, we have assumed that the variables $x_1, x_2, ..., x_5$ can take fractional values, e.g. it is meaningful to make $2 \cdot 36$ units of PROD 1. This assumption may or may not be entirely warranted. If, for example, PROD 1 represented gallons of beer, fractional quantities would be acceptable. On the other hand, if it represented numbers of motor cars, it would not be meaningful. In practice the assumption that the variables can be fractional is perfectly acceptable in this type of model, if the errors involved in rounding to the nearest integer are not great. If this is not the case we have to resort to *integer programming*.

The model above illustrates some of the essential features of an LP model:

(i) There is a single linear expression (the *objective function*) to be maximized or minimized.
(ii) There is a series of *constraints* in the form of linear expressions which must not exceed ($\leqslant$) some specified value. Linear programming constraints can also be of the form '$\geqslant$' and '$=$', indicating that the value of certain linear expressions must not fall below a specified value or must exactly equal a specified value.
(iii) The set of coefficients 288, 192, 384, on the right-hand sides of the constraints (2), (3), and (4), is generally known as the *right-hand side column*.

Practical models will, of course, be much bigger (more variables and constraints) and more complicated but they must always have the above three essential features. The optimal solution to the above model is included in Section 6.3.

In order to give a wider picture of how linear programming models can arise, we give a second small example of a practical problem.

Example 2. A Linear Programming Model (Blending)

A food is manufactured by refining raw oils and blending them together. The raw oils come in two categories:

Vegetable oils	VEG 1
	VEG 2
Non-vegetable oils	OIL 1
	OIL 2
	OIL 3

Vegetable oils and non-vegetable oils require different production lines for refining. In any month it is not possible to refine more than 200 tons of vegetable oil and more than 250 tons of non-vegetable oils. There is no loss of weight in the refining process and the cost of refining may be ignored.

There is a technological restriction of hardness in the final product. In the units in which hardness is measured this must lie between 3 and 6. It is assumed that hardness blends linearly. The costs (per ton) and hardness of the raw oils are:

	VEG 1	VEG 2	OIL 1	OIL 2	OIL 3
Cost	£110	£120	£130	£110	£115
Hardness	$8 \cdot 8$	$6 \cdot 1$	$2 \cdot 0$	$4 \cdot 2$	$5 \cdot 0$

The final product sells for £150 per ton.

How should the food manufacturer make his product in order to maximize his net profit?

This is another very common type of application of linear programming although, of course, practical problems will be, generally, much bigger.

Variables are introduced to represent the unknown quantities. $x_1, x_2, ..., x_5$ represent the quantities (tons) of VEG 1, VEG 2, OIL 1, OIL 2, and OIL 3 which should be bought, refined and blended in a month. y represents the quantity of the product which should be made. Our objective is to maximize the net profit:

$$-110x_1 - 120x_2 - 130x_3 - 110x_4 - 115x_5 + 150y. \qquad (6)$$

The refining capacities give the following two constraints:

$$x_1 + x_2 \leqslant 200, \tag{7}$$

$$x_3 + x_4 + x_5 \leqslant 250. \tag{8}$$

The hardness limitations on the final product are imposed by the following two constraints:

$$8 \cdot 8 x_1 + 6 \cdot 1 x_2 + 2 x_3 + 4 \cdot 2 x_4 + 5 x_5 - 6 y \leqslant 0, \tag{9}$$

$$8 \cdot 8 x_1 + 6 \cdot 1 x_2 + 2 x_3 + 4 \cdot 2 x_4 + 5 x_5 - 3 y \geqslant 0. \tag{10}$$

Finally it is necessary to make sure that the weight of the final product is equal to the weight of the ingredients. This is done by a continuity constraint:

$$x_1 + x_2 + x_3 + x_4 + x_5 - y = 0. \tag{11}$$

The objective function (6) (to be maximized) together with the constraints (7), (8), (9), (10), and (11) make up our LP model.

The linearity assumption of LP is not always warranted in a practical problem, although it makes any model computationally much easier to solve. When we have to incorporate non-linear terms in a model (either in the objective function or the constraints) we obtain a *non-linear programming* (*NLP*) *model*. In Chapter 7 we will see how such models may arise and a method of modelling a wide class of such problems using *separable progamming*. Nevertheless, such models are usually far more difficult to solve.

Finally the assumption that variables can be allowed to take fractional values is not always warranted. When we insist that some or all of the variables in an LP model must take integer (whole number) values we obtain an *integer programming* (*IP*) *model*. Such models are again much more difficult to solve than conventional LP models. We will see in Chapters 8, 9, and 10 that IP opens up the possibility of modelling a surprisingly wide range of practical problems.

Another type of model which we discuss briefly is known as a *stochastic programming model*. This arises when some of the data are uncertain but can be specified by a probability distribution. In practice it is fairly rare for sufficient information to be known to be able to specify a distribution. Although data in many linear programming models may be uncertain, their representation by *expected* values is usually sufficient. Two other situations in which a more explicit recognition of the probabilistic nature of data may be made, but the resultant model still converted to a linear programme, are described. In Chapter 3 we mention *chance constrained* models and in Chapter 4 *two-stage models* both of which fall in the category of stochastic programming.

CHAPTER 2

Solving Mathematical Programming Models

2.1 The Use of Computers

Although very small mathematical programming models can be solved with simply a pencil and paper, by methods described in any textbook, this would never be done for practical sized models. The amount of calculation involved in solving a realistic model always necessitates the use of a computer. It can take hours of computer time and cost thousands of pounds to solve a very large model. There have, however, been major advances in the speed of computer hardware and software in recent years. It is now possible to solve many practical sized models on microcomputers. Even when a model requires solution by a mainframe computer it is often convenient to build and manipulate the model on a micro before transferring it to a mainframe.

In view of the great use which is made of computers in solving mathematical programming models we consider a few practical aspects of the use of computers here. The use of computers is rarely straightforward. It is possible to use them both efficiently and inefficiently. While the emphasis of this book is predominantly on model building, the model builder should pay some attention to this aspect.

Practical linear programming models can be very large. Most models have a few hundred constraints and variables and can be solved in a matter of minutes on most computers. A sizeable number of larger models involving thousands of constraints and variables have also been built. There also exist a few models with tens of thousands of constraints and variables. The largest linear programming model reported to date has a hundred thousand constraints. For a linear programming model the number of constraints is a fairly good indicator of its computational difficulty. As a very rough rule of thumb the time to solve a linear programming model increases by between the square and the cube of the number of constraints. By doubling the number of constraints one would therefore expect to multiply the solution time by between four and eight.

There is clearly great virtue in organizing a mathematical programming calculation as efficiently as possible on a computer. One of the major characteristics of practical models which is exploited in the calculations is *sparsity*. If one examines the coefficients in a realistically sized model one will almost always find that the great majority of them are zero. For a thousand constraint model, for example, one would probably only find that about 1% of the coefficients were non-zero. The dominant feature of sparsity in practical models is often overlooked when mathematical programming is studied theoretically through small contrived examples. Computer programs which solve practical mathematical programming models almost always make use of sparsity. Indeed, it would be doubtful if they could ever solve such models if sparsity were not exploited. Generally only the non-zero coefficients of a model will be stored in the computer. By an appropriate indexing scheme it is possible to remember the row and column of the matrix to which each coefficient belongs. Sparsity is also usually exploited in the calculation itself since arithmetic calculations involving many zeros are often more quickly done by first testing for the presence or absence of a zero before adding, subtracting, or multiplying.

Computers have limited storage and it is not always possible to store all the coefficients of a model in the computer. A number of ingenious schemes exist for storing as much of the matrix as possible. Some recent programs manage to store quite large models totally inside the computer by exploiting their sparsity. There do, however, exist many models which cannot be so stored, especially if less ingeniously designed programs are used. When this happens it is necessary to store some of the matrix on backing store such as magnetic tapes, disks or drums. A body of information stored outside the computer in this way is known as a *file*. Most commercial computer programs for solving mathematical programming problems allow for the storage of the matrix in this way. The resultant file is usually referred to as the *matrix file* or *problem file*. Another sort of file which most programs use is known as the *eta file*. This contains information used in the course of the calculation. Unlike the matrix file it changes in the course of optimization. The purpose of the eta file is outlined briefly in the next section. As with the matrix file there is great advantage to be gained from storing the information contained in the eta file inside the computer if possible. Frequently, however, there will be too much information for this to be possible. The reason it is advantageous to store information inside the computer, if possible, is that the time taken to move information in and out of a computer (input/output) is very long compared with the time required to do calculations.

Besides enabling one to do the arithmetic in the optimization of a mathematical programming problem a computer is also an efficient means of organizing and storing a model. It is possible to use the computer to store away the model (in the form of a matrix or problem file) for use at a future time. Also it is possible to store useful subsidiary information, such as the optimal solution to a particular version of the model at the same time.

A computer is also sometimes used to help one build a model. The programs to do this are known as *matrix generators* and are discussed in Section 3.5. It is often useful to get the computer to print out the optimal solution to a model in a form which makes sense in relation to the practical problem which has been modelled. Programs which do this are known as *report writers* and are discussed in Section 6.5.

The use of computers in mathematical programming is a subject in its own right and is given a full treatment in Orchard-Hays (1969) and Murtagh (1981).

2.2 Algorithms and Packages

A set of mathematical rules for solving a particular class of problem or model is known as an *algorithm*. We are interested in algorithms for solving linear programming, separable programming, and integer programming models. An algorithm can be programmed into a set of computer routines for solving the corresponding type of model assuming the model is presented to the computer in a specified format. For algorithms which are used frequently it turns out to be worth writing very sophisticated and efficient computer programs for use with many different models. Such programs usually consist of a number of algorithms collected together as a '*package*' of computer routines. Many such package programs are available commercially for solving mathematical programming models. They usually contain algorithms for solving linear programming models, separable programming models, and integer programming models. These packages are written by computer manufacturers, consultancy firms, and software houses. They are frequently very sophisticated and represent many man-years of programming effort. When a mathematical programming model is built it is usually worth making use of an existing package to solve it rather than getting diverted onto the task of programming the computer to solve the model oneself.

The algorithms which are almost invariably used in commercially available packages are: (i) the revised simplex algorithm for linear programming models; (ii) the separable extension of the revised simplex algorithm for separable programming models; (iii) the branch and bound algorithm for integer programming models.

It is beyond the scope of this book to describe these algorithms in detail. Algorithms (i) and (ii) are well described in Beale (1968). (iii) is outlined in Section 8.3 and is well described in Nemhauser and Wolsey (1988). Although the above three algorithms are not the only methods of solving the corresponding models, they have proved to be the most efficient general methods. It should also be emphasized that the algorithms are not totally independent. Hence the desirability of incorporating them in the same package. (ii) is simply a modification of (i) and would use the same computer program which would make the necessary changes in execution on recognizing a separable model. (iii) uses (i) as its first phase and then performs a tree search procedure as described in Section 8.3.

One of the advantages of package programs is that they are generally very flexible to use. They contain many procedures and options which may be used or ignored as the user thinks fit. We outline some of the extra facilities which most packages offer besides the three basic algorithms mentioned above.

Reduction

Some packages have a procedure for detecting and removing redundancies in a model and so reducing its size and hence time to solve. Such procedures usually go under the name, REDUCE, PRESOLVE, or ANALYSE. This topic is discussed further in Section 3.4.

Starting Solutions

Most packages enable a user to specify a starting solution for a model if he wishes. If this starting solution is reasonably close to the optimal solution the time to solve the model can be reduced considerably.

Simple Bounding Constraints

A particularly simple type of constraint which often occurs in a model is of the form

$$x \leqslant U,$$

where U is a constant. For example if x represented a quantity of a product to be made, U might represent a marketing limitation. Instead of expressing such a constraint as a conventional constraint row in a model, it is more efficient simply to regard the variable x as having an upper bound of U. The revised simplex algorithm has been modified to cope with such a bound algorithmically (the *bounded variable* version of the revised simplex). Lower bound constraints such as

$$x \geqslant L$$

need not be specified as conventional constraint rows either but may be dealt with analogously. Most computer packages can deal with bounds on variables in this way.

Ranged Constraints

It is sometimes necessary to place upper *and* lower bounds on the level of some activity represented by a linear expression. This could be done by *two* constraints such as

$$\sum_j a_j x_j \leqslant b_1 \quad \text{and} \quad \sum_j a_j x_j \geqslant b_2.$$

A more compact and convenient way to do this is to specify only the first constraint above together with a *range* of b_1-b_2 on the constraint. The effect of a range is to limit the *slack* variable (which will be introduced into the constraint by the package) to have an upper bound of b_1-b_2, so implying the second of the above constraints. Most commercial packages have the facility for defining such RANGES (not to be confused with ranging in sensitivity analysis, discussed below) on constraints.

Generalized Upper Bounding Constraints

Constraints representing a bound on a sum of variables such as

$$x_1 + x_2 + \cdots + x_n \leqslant M$$

are very common in many linear programming models. Such a constraint is sometimes referred to by saying that there is a generalized upper bound (GUB) of M on the set of variables $(x_1, x_2, ..., x_n)$. If a considerable proportion of the constraints in a model are of this form and each such set of variables is exclusive of variables in any other set, then it is efficient to use the so-called GUB extension of the revised simplex algorithm. When this is used it is not necessary to specify these constraints as rows of the model but treat them in a slightly analogous way to simple bounds on single variables. The use of this extension to the algorithm usually makes the solution of a model far quicker.

Sensitivity Analysis

When the optimal solution of a model is obtained there is often interest in investigating the effects of changes in the objective and right-hand side coefficients (and sometimes other coefficients) on this solution. *Ranging* is the name of a method of finding limits (ranges) within which one of these coefficients can be changed to have a predicted effect on the solution. Such information is very valuable in performing a sensitivity analysis on a model. This topic is discussed at length in Section 6.3 for linear programming models. Almost all commercial packages have a RANGE facility.

Parametric Programming

Ranging gives limits within which the effect of a change in an objective or right-hand side coefficient can be predicted. The effects of changes involving more than one coefficient or changes outside the ranges can be investigated efficiently using *parametric programming*. This topic is considered further in Section 6.4. Most packages have facilities for doing parametric programming.

Most packages have facilities not mentioned here. The facilities can be used either to obtain more information from a model or to enable the model to be solved more efficiently by exploiting its structure or the characteristics of the computer used. It is beyond the scope of this book to go further with this discussion. Commercial package programs have manuals accompanying them to make the user aware of their extra facilities (besides the basic algorithms) and to enable him to use them efficiently. It should be emphasized, however, that different packages may have different facilities. In addition some packages may be more efficient at solving particular types of model than other packages.

2.3 Practical Considerations

In order to demonstrate how a model is presented to a computer package and the form in which the solution is presented we will consider the second example given in Section 1.2. This blending problem is obviously much smaller than most realistic models but serves to show the form in which a model might be presented.

This problem was converted into a model involving five constraints and six variables. It is convenient to name the variables VEG 1, VEG 2, OIL 1, OIL 2, OIL 3, and PROD. The objective is conveniently named PROF (profit) and the constraints VVEG (vegetable refining), NVEG (non-vegetable refining), UHAR (upper hardness), LHAR (lower hardness), and CONT (continuity). The data are conveniently drawn up in the matrix presented in Table 2.1. It will be seen that the right-hand side coefficients are regarded as a column and named CAP (capacity). Blank cells indicate a zero coefficient.

Table 2.1

	VEG 1	VEG 2	OIL 1	OIL 2	OIL 3	PROD		CAP
PROF	-110	-120	-130	-110	-115	150		
VVEG	1	1					$\leqslant$	200
NVEG			1	1	1		$\leqslant$	250
UHAR	8·8	6·1	2·0	4·2	5·0	$-6·0$	$\leqslant$	
LHAR	8·8	6·1	2·0	4·2	5·0	$-3·0$	$\geqslant$	
CONT	1·0	1·0	1·0	1·0	1·0	$-1·0$	$=$	

The information in Table 2.1 would generally be presented to the computer as a file. There is a standard format for presenting such information to most computer packages. This is known as MPS (mathematical programming system) format. Other format designs exist but MPS format is the most universal. The presented data would be as in Table 2.1.

These data are divided into three main sections, the ROWS section, the COLUMNS section, and the RHS section. After naming the problem BLEND, the ROWS section consists of a listing of the rows in the model together with a designator N, L, G, or E: N stands for a *non-constraint row*—clearly the objective row must not be a constraint; L stands for a *less-than-or-equal* ($\leqslant$) constraint; G stands for a *greater-than-or-equal* ($\geqslant$) constraint; E stands for an *equality* ($=$) constraint. The COLUMNS section contains the body of the matrix coefficients. These are scanned column by column with up to two non-zero coefficients in a statement (zero coefficients are ignored). Each statement contains the column name, row names, and corresponding matrix coefficients. Finally the RHS section is regarded as a column using the same format as the COLUMNS section. The ENDATA card indicates the end of the data.

```
NAME            BLEND
ROWS
 N   PROF
 L   VVEG
 L   NVEG
 L   UHRD
 G   LHRD
 E   CONT
COLUMNS
     VEG    01  PROF     -110.000000   VVEG      1.000000
     VEG    01  UHRD        8.800000   LHRD      8.800000
     VEG    01  CONT        1.000000
     VEG    02  PROF     -120.000000   VVEG      1.000000
     VEG    02  UHRD        6.100000   LHRD      6.100000
     VEG    02  CONT        1.000000
     OIL    01  PROF     -130.000000   NVEG      1.000000
     OIL    01  UHRD        2.000000   LHRD      2.000000
     OIL    01  CONT        1.000000
     OIL    02  PROF     -110.000000   NVEG      1.000000
     OIL    02  UHRD        4.200000   LHRD      4.200000
     OIL    02  CONT        1.000000
     OIL    03  PROF     -115.000000   NVEG      1.000000
     OIL    03  UHRD        5.000000   LHRD      5.000000
     OIL    03  CONT        1.000000
     PROD       PROF      150.000000   UHRD     -6.000000
     PROD       LHRD       -3.000000   CONT     -1.000000
RHS
     RHS00001   VVEG      200.000000   NVEG    250.000000
ENDATA
```

Clearly it may sometimes be necessary to put in other data as well (such as bounds). The format for such data can always be found from the appropriate manual for a package.

Besides the data which we present in the format above it is necessary to give some instruction to the package on how to solve the model. This is done by another set of statements known as the control program. Most packages work in this way with a control program and data. The style of the control program depends on the package used although most packages work with fairly similar control programs to that presented below. For our BLEND model we used the XPRESS-MP package for solving mathematical programming models. The control program is as below:

```
INPUT
MAXIMISE
FPRINT
RANGE
FRPRINT
QUIT
```

Some of the statements relate very specifically to the computer package and will not be discussed. We mention those statements that would be used (with possibly a different name) in most packages:

INPUT tells the package to read the matrix file and store the problem in memory.

MAXIMISE tells the package to find values of the decision variables which maximize the objective function and satisfy the constraints.

FPRINT tells the package to write the solution that it has found to a disk file.

RANGE calls a procedure to find ranges for the right-hand side and objective coefficients. This topic is discussed in Section 6.3.

FRPRINT tells the package to write the results of the RANGE analysis to a disk file.

QUIT terminates execution of the package.

The purpose of the above example has only been to indicate how a model is usually presented to a computer. Full details must, of course, relate to both the package and computer used and can only be found from the appropriate manual. Solution output for this model is included in Section 6.5.

With large models the solution procedures used will probably be more complicated than is suggested by the above control program. There are many refinements to the basic algorithms which the user can exploit if he thinks it desirable. It should be emphasized that there are few hard-and-fast rules concerning when these modifications should be used. A mathematical programming package should not be regarded as a 'black box' to be used in the same way with every model on all computers. Experience with solving the same model again and again on a particular computer with small modifications to the data should enable the user to understand what algorithmic refinements prove efficient or inefficient with the model and computer installation. Experimentation with different strategies and even different packages is always desirable if a model is to be used frequently.

One computational consideration which is very important with large models will be mentioned briefly. This concerns starting the solution procedure at an intermediate stage. There are two main reasons why one might wish to do this. Firstly one might be resolving a model with slightly modified data. Clearly it would be desirable to exploit one's knowledge of a previous optimal solution to save computation in obtaining the new optimal solution. With linear and separable programming models it is usually fairly easy to do this with a package, although it is much more difficult for integer programming models. Most packages have the facility to SAVE a solution on a file. Through the control program it is usually possible to RESTORE (or REINSTATE) such a solution as the starting point for a new run. A second reason for wishing to SAVE and RESTORE solutions is that one may wish to terminate a run prematurely. Possibly the run may be taking a long time and a more urgent job has to go on the computer. Alternatively the calculations may be running into numerical difficulty and have to be abandoned. In order not to waste the (sometimes considerable) computer time already expended, the intermediate (non-optimal) solution obtained just before termination can be saved and used as a starting point for a subsequent run. It is common to save intermediate solutions at regular intervals in the course of a run. In this way the last such solution before termination is always available.

2.4 Decision Support and Expert Systems

A fairly recent trend has been to incorporate some mathematical programming algorithms in computer software designed for specific applications. Such systems are sometimes referred to as *decision support systems*. Often they are incorporated into *management information systems*. They usually perform a large number of other functions as well as, possibly, solving a model. These functions probably include accessing *data bases* and interacting with managers or decision makers in a 'user friendly' fashion. If such systems do incorporate mathematical programming algorithms, then many of the modelling and algorithmic aspects are removed from the user who can concentrate on his *specific* application. In *designing and writing* such systems, however, it is obviously necessary to automate many of the model building and interpreting procedures discussed in this book.

While decision support systems are still at an early stage of development, it seems likely that their use will grow. As they become more sophisticated they are likely to present users with possible *choices* of decision besides the simpler tasks of storing, structuring, and presenting data. Such choices may well necessitate the use of mathematical programming, although this function will be hidden from the user.

Another related development in computer applications software is that of *expert systems*. These systems also pay great attention to the *user interface*. They are, for example, sometimes designed to accept 'informal problem definitions' and, by interacting with the user help him to build up a more precise definition of his problem, possibly in the form of a model. This information is combined with 'expert' information built up in the past in order to help decision making. The computational procedures used often involve mathematical programming concepts (e.g. tree searches in integer programming as described in Section 8.3). While expert systems are beyond the scope of this book the design and writing of such systems should again depend on mathematical programming and modelling concepts.

The use of mathematical programming in artificial intelligence and expert systems in particular is described by Jeroslow (1985) and Williams (1987).

CHAPTER 3

Building Linear Programming Models

3.1 The Importance of Linearity

It was pointed out in Section 1.2 that a linear programming model demands that the objective function and constraints involve *linear* expressions. Nowhere can we have terms such as x_1^3, e^{x_1} or $x_1 x_2$ appearing. For many practical problems this is a considerable limitation and rules out the use of linear programming. Non-linear expressions can, however, sometimes be converted into a suitable linear form. The reason why linear programming models are given so much attention in comparison with non-linear programming models is that they are much easier to solve. Care should also be taken, however, to make sure a linear programming model is only fitted to situations where it represents a valid model or justified approximation. It is easy to be influenced by the comparative ease with which linear programming models can be solved compared with non-linear ones.

It is worth giving an indication of why linear programming models can be solved more easily than non-linear ones. In order to do this we will use a two-variable model as it can be represented geometrically.

$$\begin{array}{ll} \text{Maximize} & 3x_1 + 2x_2 \\ \text{subject to} & x_1 + x_2 \leqslant 4, \\ & 2x_1 + x_2 \leqslant 5, \\ & -x_1 + 4x_2 \geqslant 2, \\ & x_1, \ x_2 \geqslant 0. \end{array}$$

The values of the variables x_1 and x_2 can be regarded as the coordinates of the points in Figure 3.1.

The optimal solution is represented by point A where $3x_1 + 2x_2$ has a value of 9. Any point on the broken line in Figure 3.1 will give the objective $3x_1 + 2x_2$ this value.

Other values of the objective correspond to a line parallel to this. It should be obvious geometrically that in any two-variable example the optimal solution will always lie on the boundary of the feasible (shaded) region. Usually it will occur at a vertex such as A. It is possible, however, that the objective lines might be parallel to one of the sides of the feasible region. For example if the objective function in the above example was $4x_1 + 2x_2$ the

20

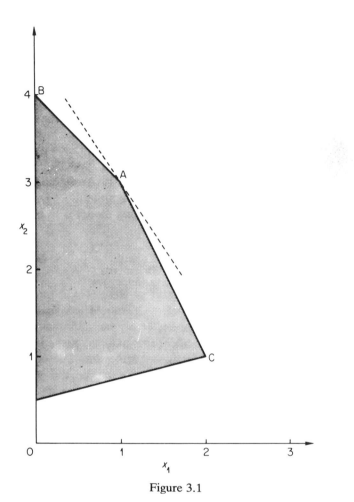

Figure 3.1

objective lines would be parallel to AC in Figure 3.1. A would then still be an optimal solution but C would be also, and any point between A and C. We would have a case of *alternative solutions*. This topic is discussed at greater length in Sections 6.2 and 6.3. Our point here, however, is to show that the optimal solution (if there is one) always lies on the boundary of the feasible region. In fact even if the case of alternative solutions does arise *there will always be an optimal solution which lies at a vertex*. This last fact generalizes to problems with more variables (which would need more dimensions to be represented geometrically). It is this fact which makes *linear* programming models comparatively easy to solve. The simplex algorithm works by only examining vertex solutions (rather than the generally infinite set of feasible solutions).

It should be possible to appreciate that this simple property of linear programming models may well not apply to non-linear programming models. For models with a non-linear objective function the objective lines in two dimensions would no longer be straight lines. If there were non-linearities in the constraints the feasible region might not be bounded by straight lines either. In these circumstances the optimal solution might well not lie at a vertex. It might even lie in the interior of the feasible region. Moreover, having found a solution it may be rather difficult to be sure it is optimal (so-called 'local optima' may exist). All these considerations are developed in Chapter 7. Our purpose here is simply to indicate the large extent to which linearity makes mathematical programming models easier to solve.

Finally it should not be suggested that a linear programming model always represents an approximation to a non-linear situation. There are many practical situations where a linear programming model is a totally respectable representation.

3.2 Defining Objectives

With a given set of constraints, different objectives will probably lead to different optimal solutions. Nevertheless it should not automatically be assumed that this will always happen. It is possible that two different objectives can lead to the same operating pattern. As an extreme case of this it can happen that the objective is irrelevant. The constraints of a problem may define a unique solution. For example the following three constraints:

$$x_1 + x_2 \leqslant 2, \tag{1}$$

$$x_1 \qquad \geqslant 1, \tag{2}$$

$$x_2 \geqslant 1. \tag{3}$$

force the solution $x_1 = x_2 = 1$ no matter what the objective is. Practical situations do arise where there is no freedom of action and only one feasible solution is possible. If the model for such a situation is at all complicated this property may not be apparent. Should different objective functions always yield the same optimal solution the property may be suspected and should be investigated since a greater understanding of what is being modelled must surely result. In fact such a discovery would result in there being no further need for linear programming.

We now assume, however, that we have a problem where the definition of a suitable objective is of genuine importance. Possible objectives that might be suggested for optimization by an organization are

Maximize profit
Minimize cost
Maximize utility
Maximize turnover
Maximize return on investment
Maximize net present value
Maximize number of employees

Minimize number of employees
Minimize redundancy
Maximize customer satisfaction
Maximize probability of survival
Maximize robustness of operating plan.

Many other objectives could be suggested. It could well be that there is no desire to optimize anything at all. Frequently a number of objectives will apply simultaneously. Possibly some of these objectives will conflict. It is, however, our contention that mathematical programming can be relevant in any of these situations, i.e. in the case of optimizing *single objectives, multiple and conflicting objectives*, or problems where there is *no optimization* of the objective.

Single Objectives

Most practical mathematical programming models used in operational research involve either maximizing profit or minimizing cost. The 'profit' which is maximized would usually be more accurately referred to as 'contribution to profit' or the cost as 'variable cost'. In a cost minimization the cost incorporated in an objective function would normally only be a *variable cost*. For example suppose each unit of a product produced cost £C. It would only be valid to assume that x units would cost £Cx if C was a *marginal cost*, i.e. the extra cost incurred for each extra unit produced. It would normally be incorrect to add in *fixed costs* such as administration or capital costs of equipment. An exception to this does arise with some integer programming models when we allow the model itself to decide whether or not a certain fixed cost should be incurred, e.g. if we do not make anything we incur no fixed cost but if we make anything at all we do incur such a cost. Normally, however, with standard linear programming models we are interested only in variable costs. Indeed a common mistake in building a model is to use average costs rather than marginal costs. Similarly when profit coefficients are calculated it is only normally correct to subtract variable costs from incomes. As a result of this the term 'profit contribution' might be more suitable.

In the common situation where a linear programming model is being used to allocate productive capacity in some sort of optimal fashion there is often a choice to be made over whether to simply minimize cost or maximize profit. Normally a cost minimization involves allocating productive capacity to meet some specified known demand at minimum cost. Such models will probably contain constraints such as

$$\sum_j x_{ij} = D_i \text{ for all } i. \tag{4}$$

or something analogous, where x_{ij} is the quantity of product i produced by process j and D_i is the demand for product i.

Should such constraints be left out inadvertently, as sometimes happens, the minimum cost solution will often turn out to produce nothing! One the other hand, if a profit maximization model is built it allows one to be more ambitious. Instead of specifying constant demands D_i it is possible to allow the model to determine optimal production levels for each product. The quantities D_i would then become variables d_i representing these production levels. Constraints (4) would become

$$\sum_j x_{ij} - d_i = 0 \text{ for all } i. \tag{5}$$

In order that the model can determine optimal values for the variable d_i they must be given suitable unit profit contribution coefficients P_i in the objective function. The model would then be able to weigh up the profits resulting from different production plans in comparison with the costs incurred and determine the optimal level of operations. Clearly such a model is doing rather more than the simpler cost minimization model. In practice it may be better to start with a cost minimization model and get it accepted as a planning tool before extending the model to be one of profit maximization.

In a profit maximization model the unit profit contribution figure P_i may itself depend upon the value of the variable d_i. The term $P_i d_i$ in the objective function would no longer be linear. If P_i could be expressed as a function of d_i a non-linear model could be constructed. An example of this idea is described by MacDonald, Cuddeford, and Beale (1974) in a resource allocation model for the health service.

A complication may arise in defining a monetary objective when the model represents activities taking place over a period of time. Some method has to be found of valuing profits or costs in the future in comparison with the present. The most usual technique is to discount future money at some rate of interest. Objective coefficients corresponding to the future will then be suitably reduced. Models where this might be relevant are discussed in Section 4.1 and are known as *multi-period* or *dynamic models*. A number of the problems presented in Part 2 give rise to such models. A further complication is illustrated by the ECONOMIC PLANNING problem of Part 2. Here decisions have to be made regarding whether or not to forego profit now in order to invest in new plant so as to make larger profits in the future. The relative desirabilities of different growth patterns lead to alternative objective functions

Multiple and Conflicting Objectives

A mathematical programming model involves a single objective function which is to be maximized or minimized. This does not, however, imply that problems with multiple objectives cannot be tackled. Various modelling techniques and solution strategies can be applied to such problems.

A first approach to a problem with multiple objectives is to solve the model a number of times with each objective in turn. The comparison of the different results may suggest a satisfactory solution to the problem or indicate further investigations. A fairly obvious example of two objectives each of which can be optimized in turn is given by the MANPOWER PLANNING problem of Part 2. Here either *cost* or *redundancy* can be minimized. The computational task of using different objectives in turn is eased if each solution is used as a starting solution to a run with a new objective as mentioned in Section 2.3.

Objectives and constraints can often be interchanged, e.g. we may wish to pursue some desirable social objective so long as costs do not exceed a specified level or alternatively we may wish to minimize cost using the social consideration as a constraint on our operations. This interplay between objectives and constraints is a feature of many mathematical programming models which is far too rarely recognized. Once a model has been built it is extremely easy to convert an objective to a constraint or vice versa. The proper use for such a model is to solve it a number of times, making such changes. An examination and discussion of the resultant solutions should lead to an understanding of the operating options available in the practical situation which has been modelled. We therefore have one method of coping with multiple objectives through treating all but one objective as a constraint. Experiments can then be carried out by varying the objective to be optimized as well as the right-hand side values of the objective/constraints.

Another way of tackling multiple objectives is to take a suitable linear combination of all the objective functions and optimize that. It is clearly necessary to attach relative weightings or utilities to the different objectives. What these weightings should be may often be a matter of personal judgment. Again it will probably be necessary to experiment with different such composite objectives in order to 'map out' a series of possible solutions. Such solutions can then be presented to the decision makers as policy options. Most commercial packages allow the user to define and vary the weightings of composite objective functions very easily. It should not be thought that this approach to multiple objectives is completely distinct from the approach of treating all but one of the objectives as a constraint. When a linear programming model is solved each constraint has associated with it a 'value' known as a *shadow price*. These values have considerable economic importance and are discussed at length in Section 6.2. If these shadow prices were to be used as the weightings to be given to the objectives/constraints in the composite approach that we have described in this paragraph, then the same optimal solution could be obtained.

When objectives are in conflict, as multiple objectives frequently will be to some extent, any of the above approaches can be adopted. Care must be taken, however, when objectives are replaced by constraints not to model conflicting constraints as such. The resultant model would clearly be infeasible. Conflicting constraints necessitate a relaxation in some or all of these constraints. Constraints become *goals* which may, or may not, be achieved. The degree of over, or under, achievement is represented in the objective function. This way of allowing the model itself to determine how to allow a certain degree of relaxation is described in Section 3.3 and is sometimes known as *goal programming*.

There is no one obvious way of dealing with multiple objectives through mathematical programming. Some or all of the above approaches should be used in particular circumstances. Given a situation with multiple objectives in which there are no clearly defined weightings for the objectives no cut-and-dried approach can ever be possible. Rather than being a cause for regret this is a healthy situation. It would be desirable if alternative approaches were adopted more often in the case of single objective models rather than a once only solution being obtained and implemented.

Minimax Objectives

The following type of objective arises in some situations

Minimize $\quad$ (Maximum $\sum_i \sum_j a_{ij}x_j$)

subject to $\quad$ conventional linear constraints.

This can be converted into a conventional linear programming form by introducing a variable z to represent the above objective. In addition to the original constraints we express the transformed model as

Minimize $\quad z$

subject to $\quad \sum_j a_{ij}x_j - z \leqslant 0$ for all i.

The new constraints guarantee that z will be *greater-than-or-equal* to each of $\sum_j a_{ij}x_j$ for all i. By minimizing z it will be driven down to the maximum of these expressions.

A special example of this type of formulation arises in goal programming and is discussed in Section 3.3.

It also arises in the formulation of zero-sum games as linear programmes.

Of course, a *maximin* objective can easily be dealt with similarly. It should, however, be pointed out that a *maximax* (or *minimin*) objective cannot be dealt with by linear programming and requires integer programming. This is discussed in Section 9.4.

Ratio Objectives

In some applications the following non-linear objective arises

Maximize $\qquad \dfrac{\Sigma_j\, a_j x_j}{\Sigma_j\, b_j x_j}$.
(or Minimize)

Rather surprisingly the resultant model can be converted into a linear programming form by the following transformations.

(i) Replace the expression $\dfrac{1}{\Sigma_j \ b_j x_j}$ by a variable t.

(ii) Represent the products $x_j t$ by variables w_j.
The objective now becomes

$$\text{Maximize} \qquad \sum_j a_j w_j.$$

(iii) Introduce a constraint

$$\sum_j b_j w_j = 1$$

in order to satisfy condition (i).
Convert the original constraints of the form

$$\sum_j d_j x_j \lesseqgtr e$$

to

$$\sum_j d_j w_j - et \lesseqgtr 0.$$

It must be pointed out that this transformation is only valid if the denominator $\Sigma_j \ b_j x_j$ is always of the same sign and non-zero. If necessary (and it is valid) an extra constraint must be introduced to avoid this. Should $\Sigma_j \ b_j x_j$ always be negative the directions of the inequalities in the constraints above must, of course, be reversed.

Once the transformed model is solved the values of the x_j variables can be found by dividing w_j by t.

An interesting application involving this type of objective arises in devising *performance measures* for certain organizations where, for example, there is no profit criterion which can be used. This is described by Charnes, Cooper and Rhodes (1978). The objective arises as a ratio of weighted *inputs* and *outputs* of the organization variables represent the weighting factors. Each organization is allowed to choose the weighting factors so as to maximize its performance ratio subject to certain constraints. Thanassoulis, Dyson and Foster (1987) use the approach to devising performance measures for local public authorities in the UK.

Non-existent and Non-optimizable Objectives

The phrase 'non-optimizable objectives' might be regarded as self-contradictory. We will, however, take the word 'objective', in this phrase, in the non-technical sense. In many practical situations there is no wish to optimize anything. Even if an organization has certain objectives (such as survival) there may be no question of optimizing them or possibly any meaning to be attached to the word 'optimization' when so applied. Mathematical programming is sometimes dismissed rather peremptorily as being concerned with optimization when many practical problems involve no optimization. Such a dismissal of the technique is premature. If the problem involves constraints, finding a solution which satisfies the constraints may be by no means straightforward. Solving a mathematical programming model of the situation with an arbitrary objective function will at least enable one to find a *feasible* solution if it exists, i.e. a solution which satisfies the constraints. The last remark is often very relevant to certain integer programming models where a very complex set of constraints may exist. It is, however, sometimes relevant to the constraints of a conventional linear programming model. The use of a (contrived) objective is also of value beyond simply enabling one to create a well-defined mathematical programming model. By optimizing an objective, or a series of objectives, in turn, 'extreme' solutions satisfying the constraints are obtained. These extreme solutions can be of great value in indicating the accuracy or otherwise of the model. Should any of these solutions be unacceptable from a practical point of view then the model is incorrect and should be modified if possible. As stated before, the validation of a model in this way is often as valuable, if not more valuable, an activity as that of obtaining solutions to be used in decision making.

3.3   Defining Constraints

Some of the most common types of constraint which arise in linear programming models are classified below.

Productive Capacity Constraints

These are the sorts of constraints which arose in the product mix example of Section 1.2. If resources to be used in a productive operation are in limited supply, then the relationship between this supply and the possible uses made of it by the different activities give rise to such a constraint. The resources to be considered could be processing capacity or manpower.

Raw Material Availabilities

If certain activities (such as producing products) make use of raw materials which are in limited supply, then this clearly should result in constraints.

Marketing Demands and Limitations

If there is a limitation on the amount of a product which can be sold, which could well result in less of the product being manufactured than would be allowed by the other constraints, this should be modelled. Such constraints may be of the form

$$x \leqslant M, \tag{6}$$

where x is the variable representing the quantity to be made and M is the market limitation.

Minimum marketing limitations might also be imposed if it was necessary to make at least a certain amount of a product to satisfy some demand. Such constraints would be of the form

$$x \geqslant L. \tag{7}$$

Sometimes (6) or (7) might be ' = ' constraints instead if some demand had to be met exactly.

The constraints (6) and (7) (or as equalities) are especially simple. When the simplex algorithm is used to solve a model such constraints are more efficiently dealt with as *simple bounds* on a variable. This is discussed later in this section.

Material Balance (Continuity) Constraints

It is often necessary to represent the fact that the sum total of the quantities going into some process equals the sum total coming out. For example in the blending problem of Section 1.2 we had to ensure that the weight of the final product was equal to the total weight of the ingredients. Such conditions are often easily overlooked. Material balance constraints such as this will usually be of the form

$$\sum_j x_j - \sum_k y_k = 0, \tag{8}$$

showing that the total quantity (weight or volume) represented by the x_j variables must be the same as the total quantity represented by the y_k variables. Sometimes some coefficients in such a constraint will not be unity but some value representing a loss or gain of weight or volume in a particular process.

Quality Stipulations

Such constraints usually arise in blending problems where certain ingredients have certain measurable qualities associated with them. If it is necessary that the products of blending have qualities within certain limits, then constraints will result. The blending example of Section 1.2 gave an example of this. Such constraints may involve, for example, quantities of nutrients in foods, octane values for petrols, strengths of materials, etc.

We now turn our attention to a number of more abstract considerations concerning constraints which we feel a model builder should be aware of.

Hard and Soft Constraints

A linear programming constraint such as

$$\sum_j a_j x_j \leqslant b \tag{9}$$

obviously rules out any solutions in which the sum over j exceeds the quantity b. There are some situations where this is unrealistic. For example, if (9) represented a productive capacity limitation or a raw material availability there might be practical circumstances in which this limitation would be overruled. It might sometimes be worthwhile or necessary to buy in extra capacity or raw materials at a high price. In such circumstances (9) would be an unrealistic representation of the situation. Other circumstances exist in which it might be impossible to violate (9). For example (9) might be a technological constraint imposed by the capacity of a pipe whose cross-section could not be expanded. Constraints such as (9) which cannot be violated are sometimes known as *hard* constraints. It is often argued that what we need are *soft* constraints which can be violated at a certain cost. If (9) were rewritten as

$$\sum_j a_j x - u \leqslant b \tag{10}$$

and u were given a suitable positive (negative) cost coefficient c for a minimization (maximization) problem we would have achieved our desired effect. b would represent a capacity or raw material availability which could be expanded to $b + u$ at a cost cu if the optimization of the model found this to be desirable. Possibly the 'surplus' variable u would be given a simple upper bound as well to prevent the increase exceeding a specified amount.

If (9) were a '$\geqslant$' constraint an analogous effect could be achieved by a 'slack' variable. Should (9) be an equality constraint it would be possible to allow the right-hand side coefficient b to be overreached or underreached by modelling it as

$$\sum_j a_j x_j + u - v = b \tag{11}$$

and giving u and v appropriately weighted coefficients in the objective function. It should be apparent that either u or v must be zero in the optimal solution. Any solution in which u and v came out positive could be adjusted to produce a better solution by subtracting the smaller of u and v from them both.

An alternative way of viewing such soft constraints is through *fuzzy sets* where a *degree of membership* corresponds to the amount by which the constraint is violated. It has, however, been shown by Dyson (1980) that formulations in terms of fuzzy set theory can be reformulated as conventional LP models with *minimax* objectives.

Chance Constraints

In some applications it is desired to specify that a certain constraint be satisfied with a given *probability*, e.g. we may wish to be 95% confident that a constraint holds. This situation is written as

$$P\left[\sum_j a_j x_j \leqslant b\right] \geqslant \beta \qquad (12)$$

where β is a probability. In practice one might expect larger values of β to correspond to higher costs which should be reflected in the objective function. This would create a more complicated model. Should no relationship between the value of β and the cost be known (as is often the case) then a rather crude, but sometimes satisfactory, approach is replace (12) by a *deterministic equivalent*. We would then replace (12) by

$$\sum_j a_j x_j \leqslant b' \qquad (13)$$

where b' is a number larger than b such that the satisfaction of (13) implies (12). This idea is due to Charnes and Cooper (1959).

Conflicting Constraints

It sometimes happens that a problem involves a number of constraints not all of which can be satisfied simultaneously. A conventional model would obviously be infeasible. The objective in such a case is sometimes stipulated to be to *satisfy all the constraints as nearly as possible*. We have the case of conflicting objectives referred to in Section 3.2 but postponed to this section.

The type of model which this situation gives rise to is sometimes known as a *goal programming* model. This term was invented by Charnes and Cooper (1961b) but the type of model which results is still a linear programming model.

Each constraint is regarded as a 'goal' which must be satisfied as nearly as possible. For example, if we wished to impose the following constraints:

$$\sum_j a_{ij} x_j = b_i \text{ for all } i, \qquad (14)$$

but wanted to allow the possibility of them not all being satisfied exactly, we would replace them by the 'soft' constraints

$$\sum_j a_{ij} x_j + u_i - v_i = b_i. \qquad (15)$$

We are clearly using the same device described before.

Our objective would be to make sure that each such constraint (14) is as nearly satisfied as possible. There are a number of alternative ways of making such an objective specific. Two possibilities are:

(i) Minimize the sum total of the deviations of the row activities $\sum_j a_{ij}x_j$ from the right-hand side values b_i.
(ii) Minimize the maximum such deviation over the constraints.

For many practical problems which of the above objectives is used is not very important.

Objective (i) can be dealt with by defining an objective function consisting of the sum of the slack (u) and surplus (v) variables in the constraints such as (15). Possibly these variables might be weighted in the objective with non-unit coefficients to reflect the relative importance of different constraints. An example of the use of such an objective is given in the MARKET SHARING problem of Part 2. The fact that this is an integer programming model does not affect the argument since such models could equally well result from linear programming models. A linear programming application arises in the CURVE FITTING problem.

Objective (ii) is slightly more complicated to deal with but can surprisingly still be accomplished in a linear programming model. An extra variable z is introduced. This variable represents the maximum deviation. We therefore have to impose extra constraints.

$$z - u_i \geqslant 0 \text{ for all } i, \tag{16}$$

$$z - v_i \geqslant 0 \text{ for all } i. \tag{17}$$

The objective function to be minimized is simply the variable z. Clearly the optimal value of z will be no greater than the maximum of u_i and v_i by virtue of optimality. Nor can it be smaller than any of u_i or v_i by virtue of the constraints (16) and (17). Therefore the optimal value of z will be both as small as possible and exactly equal to the maximum deviation of $\sum_j a_{ij}x_j$ from its corresponding right-hand side b_i. This type of problem is sometimes known as a *bottleneck problem*. Both the CURVE FITTING and MARKET SHARING problems illustrate this type of objective.

An interesting example of such a *minimax* objective is described by Redpath and Wright (1981) in an application of linear programming to deciding levels and directions for irradiating cancerous tumours. As an alternative to minimizing the *variance* of radiation across a tumour they *minimize the maximum difference* of radiation levels. This can clearly be done by computationally easier linear programming rather than quadratic programming.

Redundant Constraints

Suppose we have a constraint such as

$$\sum_j a_j x_j \leqslant b \tag{18}$$

in a linear programming model. If, in the optimal solution, the quantity $\sum_j a_j x_j$ turns out to be less than b, then the constraint (18) will be said to be *non-binding* (and have a zero shadow price). Such a non-binding constraint could just as well be left out of the model since this would not affect the optimal solution. There may well, however, be good reasons for including such *redundant constraints* in a model. Firstly, the redundancy may not be apparent until the model is solved. The constraint must therefore be included in case it turns out to be *binding*. Secondly, if a model is to be used regularly with changes in the data, then the constraint might become binding with some future data. There would then be virtue in keeping the constraint to avoid a future remodelling. Thirdly, *ranging* information, which is discussed in Section 6.3, depends on constraints which may well be redundant in the sense of not affecting the optimal solution.

It should be noted that a constraint such as (18) can be non-binding even if the quantity $\sum_j a_j x_j$ is equal to b. This happens if the removal of the constraint does not affect the optimal solution, i.e. $\sum_j a_j x_j$ must be equal to b for reasons other than the existence of constraint (18). Such non-binding constraints are recognized by their being a zero *shadow price* on the constraint in the optimal solution. Shadow prices are discussed in Section 6.2.

For '$\geqslant$' constraints analogous results hold. If (18) were such a constraint it would be non-binding if $\sum_j a_j x_j$ exceeded b but possibly still non-binding if $\sum_j a_j x_j$ equalled b.

Finally it should be pointed out that with integer programming it would not be true to say that if $\sum_j a_j x_j$ were less than b in (18) then (18) would be non-binding. (18) could well be binding and therefore not redundant. This is discussed in Section 10.3.

The advisability or otherwise of including redundant constraints in a model is discussed in Section 3.3. A quick method of detecting some such redundancies is also described.

Simple and Generalized Upper Bounds

It was pointed out that marketing constraints often take the particularly simple forms of (6) or (7). *Simple bounds* on a variable such as these are more efficiently dealt with through a modification of the simplex algorithm. Most commercial package programs use this modification. Such bounds are not therefore specified as conventional constraints but specified as simple bounds for the appropriate variables. A generalization of simple bounds known as *generalized upper bounds* also proves to be of great computational value in solving a model and therefore worth recognizing. Such constraints are usually written as

$$\sum_j x_j = b. \tag{19}$$

The set of variables x_j is said to have a generalized upper bound (GUB) of b.

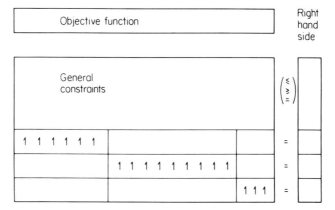

Figure 3.2

This means that the sum of these variables must be b. If (19) were a '$\leqslant$' constraint instead of an equality the addition of a slack variable would obviously convert it to the form (19). The fact that the coefficients of the variables in (19) are unity is not very important since scaling can always convert any constraint with all non-negative coefficients into this form. What is, however, important is that when a number of constraints such as (19) exist the variables in them form *exclusive sets*. A set of variables is said to belong to the GUB set if it can belong to no others. If variables are specified as belonging to GUB sets it is not necessary to specify the corresponding constraints such as (19). A further modification of the simplex algorithm copes with the implied constraint in an analogous way to simple bounding constraints. The diagrammatic representation of a model in Figure 3.2 shows three GUB-type constraints. These constraints could be removed from the model and treated as GUB sets.

There is normally only virtue in using the GUB modification of the simplex algorithm if a large number of GUB sets can be isolated. For example in the *transportation problem* which is discussed in Section 5.3 it can be seen that at least half of the constraints can be regarded as GUB sets.

The computational advantages of recognizing GUB constraints can be very great indeed with large models. A way of detecting a large number of such sets if they exist in a model is described by Brearley, Mitra, and Williams (1975).

Unusual Constraints

In this section we have concentrated on constraints which can be modelled using linear programming. It is important, however, not to dismiss 'unusual' restrictions which may arise in a practical problem as not being able to be so modelled. By extending a model to be an integer programming model it is sometimes possible to model such restrictions. For example a restriction such as

'We can only produce product 1 if product 2 is produced but neither of products 3 or 4 are produced'

could be modelled. This topic is discussed much further in Chapter 9.

3.4   How to Build a Good Model

Possible aims which a model builder has when constructing a model are: ease of understanding the model: ease of detecting errors in the model; ease of computing the solution. Ways of trying to achieve and resolve these aims are described below.

Ease of Understanding the Model

It is often possible to build a compact but realistic model when quantities appear implicitly rather than explicitly, e.g. instead of a non-negative quantity being represented by a variable y and being equated to an expression $f(x)$ by the constraint

$$f(x) - y = 0, \tag{1}$$

the variable y does not appear but $f(x)$ is substituted into all the expressions where it would appear. To build such compact models often leads to great difficulty and extra calculation in interpreting the solution. Even though a less compact model takes longer to solve it is often worth the extra time. If, however, a report writer is used, this may take care of interpretation difficulties and the use of compact models is desirable from the point of view of the third aim.

It is also desirable to use mnemonic names for the variables and constraints in a problem to ease the interpretation of the solution. The computer input to the small blending problem illustrated in Section 2.2 shows how such names can be constructed. A very systematic approach to naming variables and constraints in a model is described by Beale, Beare, and Tatham (1974).

Ease of Detecting Errrors in the Model

This aim is clearly linked to the first. Errors can be of two types: (i) clerical errors such as punching or typing and (ii) formulation errors. To avoid the first type of error it is desirable to build any but very small, models using a matrix generator or language.

There is also great value to be obtained from using a PRESOLVE or REDUCE procedure on a model for error detection. Clerical or formulation errors often result in a model being unbounded or infeasible. Such conditions can often be revealed easily by using such a procedure. A simple procedure of this kind which also simplifies models is outlined below.

Formulation can sometimes be done with error detection in mind. This point is developed in Section 6.1.

Ease of Computing the Solution

LP models can use large amounts of computer time and it is desirable to build models which can be solved as quickly as possible. This objective can conflict with the first. In order to meet the first objective it is desirable to avoid compact models. If a PRESOLVE or REDUCE procedure is applied after the model has been built, but prior to solving it, then dramatic reductions in size can sometimes be achieved. An algorithm for doing this is described by Brearley, Mitra, and Williams (1975). Karwan, Lotfi, Telgen, and Zionts (1983) provided a collection of methods for detecting redundancy. The reduced problem can then be solved and the solution used to generate a solution to the original problem.

In order to illustrate the possibility of spotting redundancies in a linear programming model we consider the following numerical example:

$$\text{Maximize} \qquad 2x_1 + 3x_2 - x_3 - x_4 \qquad (2)$$

$$\text{subject to} \qquad x_1 + x_2 + x_3 - 2x_4 \leqslant 4, \qquad (3)$$

$$-x_1 - x_2 + x_3 - x_4 \leqslant 1, \qquad (4)$$

$$x_1 \qquad\qquad + x_4 \leqslant 3, \qquad (5)$$

$$x_1, x_2, x_3, x_4 \geqslant 0. \qquad (6)$$

Since x_3 has a negative objective coefficient and the problem is one of maximization it is desirable to make x_3 as small as possible, x_3 has positive coefficients in constraints (3) and (4). As these constraints are both of the $\leqslant$ type there can be no restriction on making x_3 as small as possible. Therefore x_3 can be reduced to its lower bound of zero and hence be regarded as a redundant variable.

Having removed variable x_3 from the model, constraint (4) is worthy of examination. All the coefficients in this constraint are now negative. Therefore the value of the expression on the left-hand side of the inequality relation can never be positive. This expression must therefore always be smaller than the right-hand side value of 1 indicating that the constraint is redundant and may be removed from the problem.

The above model could therefore be reduced in size. With large models such reductions could well lead to substantial reductions in the amount of computation needed to solve the model. *Infeasibilities* and *unboundedness* can also sometimes be revealed by such a procedure. A model is said to be *infeasible* if there is no solution which satisfies all the constraints (including non-negativity conditions on the variables). If, on the other hand, there is no limit to the amount by which the objective function can be optimized, the model is said to be *unbounded*. Such conditions in a model usually suggest modelling errors and are discussed at greater length in Section 6.1.

Some package programs have procedures for reducing models in this way. Such procedures go under such names as REDUCE, PRESOLVE, ANALYSE, etc. Problem reduction can be taken considerably further. By using simple bounds on variables and considering the dual model (the dual of a linear programming model is described in Section 6.2) the above example can be reduced to nothing (completely solved). A more complete treatment of reduction is beyond the scope of this book as such reduction procedures are usually programmed and carried out automatically. It is not, therefore, always important that a model builder knows how to reduce his model, although the fact that it can be simply reduced must have implications for the situation being modelled. A much fuller treatment of the subject is given in Brearley, Mitra, and Williams (1975) and Karwan, Lotfi, Telgen, and Zionts (1983).

Substantial reduction in computing time can also, often, be achieved by exploiting the special structure of a problem. One such structure which has proved particularly valuable is generalized upper bounding (GUB) as described in Section 3.3. It is obviously desirable that the model builder detect such structure if it be present in a problem, although a few computer packages have facilities for doing this automatically through procedures such as those described by Brearley, Mitra, and Williams.

Modal Formulation

In large LP problems reduction in the number of constraints can be achieved by using *modal formulations*. If a series of constraints involves only a few variables, the feasible region for the space of these variables can be considered. For example, suppose that x_A and x_B are two of the (non-negative) variables in an LP model and they occur in the following constraints:

$$x_A + x_B \leqslant 7, \tag{7}$$

$$3x_A + x_B \leqslant 15, \tag{8}$$

$$x_B \leqslant 5. \tag{9}$$

The situation can be modelled, as demonstrated in Figure 3.3, by letting the activities for the 'extreme modes' of operation be represented by variables instead of x_A and x_B. If these variables are $\lambda_0, \lambda_1, \lambda_2, \lambda_3, \lambda_4$, we only have to specify the single constraint

$$\lambda_0 + \lambda_1 + \lambda_2 + \lambda_3 + \lambda_4 = 1. \tag{10}$$

Whenever x_A and x_B occur in other parts of the model, apart from constraints (7), (8), and (9) which are now ignored, we substitute the expressions below:

$$\text{for } x_A, \quad 2\lambda_2 + 4\lambda_3 + 5\lambda_4; \tag{11}$$

$$\text{for } x_B, \quad 5\lambda_1 + 5\lambda_2 + 3\lambda_3. \tag{12}$$

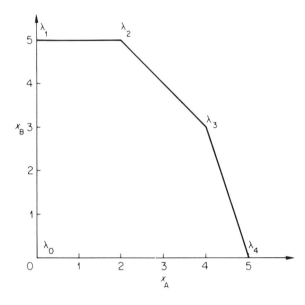

Figure 3.3

The coefficients for x_A are the 'x_A coordinates' of λ_1, λ_2, ..., etc., in Figure 3.3 and the coefficients of x_B are the 'x_B coordinates'.

In this case we have saved two constraints. The ingenious use of this idea can result in substantial savings in the number of constraints in a model.

Experiments in the use of a special case of this technique are described by Knolmayer (1982). Smith (1973) discusses the use of this approach to modelling practical problems. Modal formulations are quite common for particular processes in the petroleum industry. The REFINERY OPTIMIZA-TION model demonstrates a very simple case of this where a process has only one *mode* of operation with inputs and outputs in *fixed* proportions. In this case it is better to model the level of the process as an activity to avoid having to represent the (fixed) relationships between the inputs and outputs by constraints.

A general methodology for modelling processes with different types of input–output relations is developed by Müller-Merbach (1978).

Units of Measurement

When a practical situation is modelled it is important to pay attention to the units in which quantities are measured. Great disparity in the sizes of the coefficients in a linear programming model can make such a model difficult, if not impossible, to solve. For example, it would be stupid to measure profit in £s if the unit profit coefficients in the objective function were of the order of millions of pounds. Similarly, if capacity constraints allowed quantities in thousands of tons it would be better to allow each variable to represent a quantity in thousands of tons rather than in tons. Ideally units should be chosen so that each non-zero coefficient in a linear programming model is of a magnitude between 0·1 and 10. In practice this may not always be possible. Most commercial package programs have procedures for automatically *scaling* the coefficients of a model before it is solved. The solution is then automatically unscaled before being printed out.

3.5   The Use of Matrix Generators and Languages

A number of computer software aids exist for helping the user to *structure* and *input* his problem into a package in the form of a model. Programs to do this are known as *matrix generators* (MGs). Some such systems are more usefully thought of as special purpose high-level programming languages and are therefore known as *matrix generator languages.*

It is now recognized that the main hurdle to the successful application of a mathematical programming model is often no longer the problem of computing the solution. Rather it lies with the *interface* between the user and the computer. Some of the difficulties can be overcome by freeing the modeller from the specific needs of the package used to solve the model.

An ambitious attempt to overcome the user interface problems is described by Greenberg (1986). Other systems are described by Buchanan and McKinnon (1987) and Greenberg, Lucas and Mitra (1987). These systems pay attention to the output interface as well as the input.

A number of quite distinct approaches to building matrix generators/ languages are described below. Before doing this, however, we specify the main advantages to be gained from using them.

A More Natural Input Format

The input formats required by most packages are designed more with the package in mind than the user. As described in Secton 2.3, most commercial packages use the MPS format. This orders the model by columns in a fixed format based on the internal ordering of the matrix in the computer. This is often unnatural, tedious, and a source of clerical error. In addition this format is far from concise, requiring a separate data statement for every two coefficients in the model. The use of an MG can overcome all these disadvantages.

Debugging is Made Easier

As with computer programming the debugging and verification of a model is an important and sometimes time-consuming task. The use of a format which the modeller finds natural makes this task much easier.

Modification is Made Easier

Models are often used on a regular basis with minor modifications, or once built may be used experimentally many times with small changes of data. The separation of the data (which changes) from the structure of the model, in most MG inputs, facilitates this task.

Repetition is Automated

Large models usually arise from the combination or repetition of smaller models, e.g. multiple periods, plants, or products, as described in Section 4.1 In such circumstances there will be a lot of repetition of particular items of data and structure. Formats such as MPS demand a repetition of this data which is both inefficient and a potential source of error. MGs generally take account of such repetition very easily through the indexing of time periods, etc. This is described in Section 4.3.

Some of the distinct approaches adopted by different MGs or languages are outlined below. Fourer (1983) also provides a very good and comprehensive discussion. The methods can only be understood in detail through the manuals of the relevant systems. Clearly this is only necessary when a particular system is adopted. Fourer gives a list of available systems.

Special Purpose Generators Using a High Level Language

It is possible to write a different program, in a general language (such as FORTRAN, ALGOL, ADA, etc.), for each model one wishes to build. This approach ignores the similarities in structure which all mathematical programming models have, however diverse their application area, as well as the standard format required (e.g. MPS) which is tedious to remember and incorporate into a general program. It seems more sensible to incorporate such similarities into a specialist system such as an MG or a specialist language.

Matrix Block Building Systems

The, often huge, matrix of coefficients in a practical model always exhibits a high degree of structure. The matrix tends to consist of small dense blocks of coefficients in an otherwise very sparse matrix. These blocks are often repeats of each other and are linked together by simple matrices such as identity matrices. The systematic combination and replication of submatrices into larger matrices in this way is the method used in certain MG systems. Such systems have functions which, for example, concatenate and transpose matrices. A defect of such systems is that they still require the user to think in terms of matrices of coefficients even though they free him from some of the mechanics of assembling them.

Data Structuring Systems

Some systems allow the user to structure his model in a diagrammatic form. Flow diagrams are often particularly helpful. For example, a problem may involve flows of different raw materials into processes to give products which are then distributed via depots to customers. The MG system will allow the user to translate this representation into the system directly, avoiding algebraic notation. Such systems can be useful for *specific* applications, e.g. process industries. They do have the defect that the user needs to learn quite a lot about the system before he can use it.

Mathematical Languages

The above approaches all avoid the use of conventional notation, i.e. 'Σ' notation and *indexed* sets. Indeed an argument sometimes used in their favour is that mathematical notation is unnatural to certain users who prefer to think of their model in other ways. This may well be the case with certain established applications (e.g. the petroleum industry) where mathematical programming is so established and important for a conceptual methodology of its own to have developed. If more generality is required, then *conventional mathematical notation* provides a *language* which is widely understood as well as providing a concise way of defining many models. The fact that the notation is so widely understood by anyone with an elementary mathematical training makes learning to use such a system comparatively easy.

In order to illustrate this approach we outline one such modelling language used by the XPRESS-MP model builder MP-MODEL. Full details of its use are contained in the reference manual available from Dash Associates. MP-MODEL was used to generate all the models discussed in Parts 2, 3, and 4 of this book. Details of obtaining XPRESS-MP can be found in the Preface. It must be emphasized that this is only one such MG system. Other *purpose built* (e.g. programs in FORTRAN) systems could be used or another *general purpose* MG system could be employed. Fourer (1983) gives a list of available systems. We do suggest, however, that XPRESS-MP demonstrates an easy to understand and efficient approach. MAGIC is another such MG system (Day, 1984). Some of XPRESS-MP's features are discussed below and illustrated by the XPRESS-MP formulation of the small BLEND example of Section 2.3. In order to illustrate other features of the language the XPRESS-MP formulation of the DECENTRALIZATION model is also given in Section 13.10. Formulations in the XPRESS-MP modelling language of all the other models in Chapter 13 can be obtained on application to the author.

The XPRESS-MP Language

Particular features of XPRESS-MP are discussed in order to demonstrate desirable features in any MG system. It is emphasized that the purpose of this discussion is illustration and full details must be obtained from the appropriate manual for the system.

Indexing for Repetition

Similar variables and constraints frequently occur many times in a model. It is desirable to reflect their similarity in their names. This is done in XPRESS-MP by giving them the same *name root* but also including one or more indices in making up their name. These indices are generated automatically. In the example below the XPRESS-MP statement

$$VEG(2)$$

generates two variables VEG1 and VEG2.

For the DECENTRALIZATION example in Section 13.10 the XPRESS-MP statement

$$G(NDEPTS, NCITIES, NDEPTS, NCITIES)$$

generates 225 variables G1111, G1112, G1113, G1121, etc., when NDEPTS is set to 5 and NCITIES to 3.

For constraints the XPRESS-MP statement

$$DEPT(I = 1: NDEPTS): SUM(J = 1: NCITIES)D(I, J) = 1$$

generates five constraints named DEPT01, DEPT02, etc., involving variables named D0101, D0102, D0103, D0201, etc.

Repeated Sums

The use of 'Σ' notation is widespread in mathematical programming. In the BLEND example below the XPRESS-MP statement

$$VVEG: SUM(I = 1:2) VEG(I) < 200$$

generates a constraint

$$VEG1 + VEG2 \leqslant 200.$$

Note that for convenience '$<$' is taken to mean '$\leqslant$'.

It is possible to 'nest' repeated sums within others by the repeated use of ranges of the form $J = 1: NCITIES$ as is illustrated in Section 13.10.

Relations between Indices

Sometimes it is only desired to define constraints or include certain variables in constraints for particular combinations of indices. For example a portion of an XPRESS-MP statement from the DECENTRALIZATION example in Section 13.10 is

$$SUM(K = 1: NDEPTS, L = 1: NCITIES \mid K > I) \&$$
$$(COMM(I, K) * DIST(J, L)) * G(I, J, K, L)$$

The '&' character indicates that the statement is continued on the next line.

This will generate a sum of the variables G1121, G1122, etc. (with certain coefficients defined in the parentheses), only including variables where the third index exceeds the first.

Separating the Data from the Statements of the Model

In the BLEND example below the statements

$$\text{TABLES COST(MAXI)}$$
$$\text{DATA COST} = 110, 120, 130, 110, 115$$

define a one-dimensional array COST of length 5 when MAXI is set to 5. This array can then be used instead of numbers in defining coefficients as in the objective function definition:

$$\text{PROFIT: } -\text{SUM}(I = 1{:}2)\text{COST}(I) * \text{VEG}(I) \ \&$$
$$-\text{SUM}(I = 1{:}3)\text{COST}(I) * \text{OIL}(I - 2) \ \&$$
$$+ 150 * \text{PROD}$$

This is convenient when the *data* for a model changes frequently but the *structure* does not.

Sometimes it is convenient to read the data into arrays from a *file* instead.

Arithmetic on the Coefficients

Many of the coefficients in a model may be derived from the same figures. Rather than carry out the necessary arithmetic externally, it is often more convenient to do this within the language. An example of this is given above, where the term in parentheses,

$$(\text{COMM}(I, K) * \text{DIST}(J, L)),$$

defines a coefficient for different values of I, J, K, L using the arrays COMM and DIST.

Interactive Modelling

It is sometimes convenient to build models or portions of models interactively. Should a statement be syntactically wrong XPRESS-MP gives a message and the statement may be repeated in a corrected form. Alternatively it is possible to put all statements, or a section of statements, into a file from which XPRESS-MP reads.

Automatic Formatting

XPRESS-MP produces output in the format required by the appropriate optimization package, e.g. MPS format.

The small example below gives an XPRESS-MP program which will generate the MPS format for the BLEND model given in Section 2.3 and put it in a file named BLEND.MAT.

```
MODEL BLEND
LET MAXI = 5          ! Number of oils
TABLES
       COST(MAXI)  ! Their cost
       HARD(MAXI)  ! Their hardness

DATA
       COST(1) = 110, 120, 130, 110, 115
       HARD(1) = 8.8, 6.1, 2.0, 4.2,    5

VARIABLES
       VEG(2)         ! Vegetable oils
       OIL(3)         ! Non vegetable oils
       PROD           ! Quantity of blend produced

CONSTRAINTS

                      ! Profit
PROF: - SUM(I=1:2) COST(I)*VEG(I)                    &
      - SUM(I=3:5) COST(I)*OIL(I-2) + 150*PROD                $

                      ! Limit on total vegetable oil used
VVEG:   SUM(I=1:2) VEG(I)                              < 200

                      ! Limit on total non-vegetable oil used
NVEG:   SUM(I=1:3) OIL(I)                              < 250

                      ! Upper limit on hardness
UHRD:   SUM(I=1:2) HARD(I)*VEG(I)                 &
      + SUM(I=3:5) HARD(I)*OIL(I-2) - 6*PROD          < 0

                      ! Lower limit on hardness
LHRD:   SUM(I=1:2) HARD(I)*VEG(I)                 &
      + SUM(I=3:5) HARD(I)*OIL(I-2) - 3*PROD          > 0

                      ! Material Balance
CONT: SUM(I=1:2) VEG(I) + SUM(I=1:3) OIL(I) = PROD


GENERATE               ! Produce MPS matrix
```

CHAPTER 4

Structured Linear Programming Models

4.1 Multiple Plant, Product, and Period Models

The purpose of this section is to show how large linear programming models can arise through the combining of smaller models. Almost all very large models arise in this way. Such models prove to be more powerful as decision making tools than the submodels from which they are constructed. In order to illustrate how a multi-plant model can arise in this way we take a very small illustrative example.

Example 1. A Multi-plant Model

A company consists of two factories, A and B. Each factory makes two products, *standard* and *deluxe*. A unit of *standard* gives a profit contribution of £10, while a unit of *deluxe* given a profit contribution of £15.

Each factory uses two processes, grinding and polishing, for producing its products. Factory A has a grinding capacity of 80 hours per week and polishing capacity of 60 hours per week. For factory B these capacities are 60 and 75 hours per week respectively.

The grinding and polishing times in hours for a unit of each type of product in each factory are given in the table below:

	Factory A		Factory B	
	Standard	Deluxe	Standard	Deluxe
Grinding	4	2	5	3
Polishing	2	5	5	6

It is possible, for example, that factory B has older machines than factory A, resulting in higher unit processing times.

In addition each unit of each product uses 4 kilograms of a raw material which we refer to as *raw*. The company has 120 kilograms of *raw* available per week. To start with we will assume that factory A is allocated 75 kilograms of *raw* per week and factory B the remaining 45 kilograms per week.

Each factory can build a very simple linear programming model to maximize

46

its profit contribution. This is an obvious example of the product mix application of linear programming mentioned in Section 1.2. The resultant models are:

Factory A's Model

Maximize	Profit A	$10x_1 + 15x_2$
subject to	Raw A	$4x_1 + 4x_2 \leqslant 75,$
	Grinding A	$4x_1 + 2x_2 \leqslant 80,$
	Polishing A	$2x_1 + 5x_2 \leqslant 60,$

$$x_1, x_2 \geqslant 0,$$

where x_1 is the quantity of standard to be produced in A and x_2 is the quantity of deluxe to be produced in A.

Factory B's Model

Maximize	Profit B	$10x_3 + 15x_4$
subject to	Raw B	$4x_3 + 4x_2 \leqslant 45,$
	Grinding B	$5x_3 + 3x_4 \leqslant 60,$
	Polishing B	$5x_3 + 6x_4 \leqslant 75,$

$$x_3, x_4 \geqslant 0,$$

where x_3 is the quantity of standard to be produced in B and x_4 is the quantity of deluxe to be produced in B.

These two models can easily be solved graphically. Our purpose is not, however, to concentrate on the mechanics of solving these individual models. We do, however, give the optimal solutions below since these will be discussed later.

Optimal Solution to Factory A's Model

Profit is £225 obtained from making $11 \cdot 25$ of standard and $7 \cdot 5$ of deluxe. There is a surplus grinding capacity of 20 hours.

Optimal Solution to Factory B's Model

Profit is £$168 \cdot 75$ obtained from making $11 \cdot 25$ deluxe. There is a surplus grinding capacity of $26 \cdot 25$ hours, and a surplus polishing capacity of $7 \cdot 5$ hours.

Suppose now that a company model is built in order to maximize total profit. We will assume that the factories remain distinct and geographically separated. We will, however, no longer allocate 75 kilograms of raw to A and

45 kilograms to B. Instead we will allow the model to decide this allocation. There will now be a single raw material constraint limiting the company to 120 kilograms per week. The resultant model is given below.

Maximize	Profit	$10x_1 + 15x_2 + 10x_3 + 15x_4$
subject to	Raw	$4x_1 + 4x_2 + 4x_3 + 4x_4 \leqslant 120,$
	Grinding A	$4x_1 + 2x_2 \qquad\qquad\quad \leqslant 80,$
	Polishing A	$2x_1 + 5x_2 \qquad\qquad\quad \leqslant 60,$
	Grinding B	$\qquad\qquad 5x_3 + 3x_4 \leqslant 60,$
	Polishing B	$\qquad\qquad 5x_3 + 6x_4 \leqslant 75,$

$$x_1, x_2, x_3, x_4 \geqslant 0.$$

The Company Model

The fact that the constraints raw A and raw B of the factory models have been combined into a single constraint for the company model is of crucial significance. We are now asking the model to split the 120 kilograms of raw optimally between A and B rather than making an arbitrary allocation ourselves. As a consequence we would expect a more efficient split resulting in a greater overall company profit. This is borne out by the optimal solution.

Optimal Solution to the Company Model

Total profit is £404·15, obtained from making 9·17 of standard in A, 8·33 of deluxe in A, 12·5 of deluxe in B. There is a surplus grinding capacity in A of 26·67 hours, and a surplus grinding capacity in B of 22·5 hours.

A number of points are worth noting in comparing this solution with those for factories A and B individually:

(i) The total profit is £404·14, which is greater than the combined profit £393·75 from A and B acting independently.

(ii) Factory A only contributes £216·65 to the new total profit whereas before it produced a profit of £225. Factory B, however, now contributes £187·5 to total profit whereas before it only produced £168·75.

(iii) Factory A now uses 70 kilograms of raw and factory B 50 kilograms.

It is clear that the company model has biased production more towards factory B than before. This has been done by allocating B 50 kilograms of raw instead of 45 kilograms and so depriving A of 5 kilograms. If it had been possible to decide this 70/50 split before, it would not have been necessary to build a company model. This argument also applies to much larger, more realistic, multi-plant models. Normally, however, there will be a number of scarce resources which must be shared between plants rather than the single resource *raw* which we consider here. An optimal split would have to be found for each of these resources. Determining such splits would obviously be complex. The needs of each plant have to be balanced against how efficiently they use the scarce resources. In our example factory B's older machinery results in it being allocated less of raw than A. To start with, however, our 75/45 split was overbiased in A's favour.

The above example is intended to show how a multi-plant model can arise. It is a method of using linear programming to cope with allocation problems *between* plants as well as help with decision making *within* plants. The model which we built was a very simple example of a common sort of structure which arises in multi-plant models. This is known as a *block angular* structure. If we detach the coefficients in the company model and present the problem in a diagrammatic form we obtain Figure 4.1.

The first two rows are known as *common rows*. Obviously one of the common rows will always be the objective row. The two diagonally placed blocks of coefficients are known as *submodels*. For a more general problem with a number of shared resources and n plants we would obtain the general block angular structure shown in Figure 4.2.

$A_0, A_1, ..., B_1, B_2$, etc., are blocks of coefficients. $b_0, b_1, ...,$ etc., are columns of coefficients forming the right-hand side. The block A_0 may or may not exist but is sometimes conveniently represented. $A_0, A_1, ...,$ etc., represent the common rows. Common constraints in multi-plant models usually involve allocating scarce resources (raw material, processing capacity, manpower, etc.) across plants. They might sometimes represent transport relations between plants. For example, it might, in certain circumstances be advantageous to

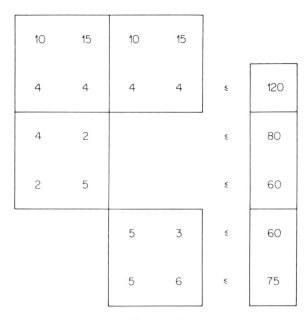

Figure 4.1

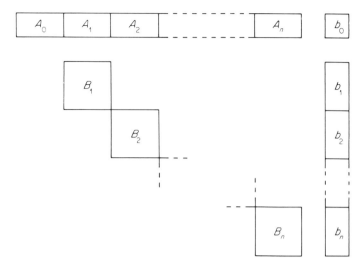

Figure 4.2

transport the product of an intermediate process from one plant to another. The model could conveniently allow for this if extra variables were introduced into the plants in question to represent amounts transported. Suppose we simply wanted to allow for transport from plant 1 to plant 2. This would be accomplished by the constraint

$$x_1 - x_2 = 0, \tag{1}$$

where x_1 is the quantity transported from 1 into 2 and x_2 is the quantity transported into 2 from 1.

Apart from constraint (1), x_1 would only be involved in constraints relating to the submodel for plant 1. Similarly x_2 would only be involved in constraints relating to plant 2. x_1 (or x_2 but not both) would probably be given cost coefficients in the objective function representing unit transport costs. Constraint (1) clearly gives another common row constraint.

Should a problem with a block angular structure have no common constraints it should be obvious that optimizing it simply amounts to optimizing each subproblem with its appropriate portion of the objective. For our simple numerical example, if there had been no raw material constraint we could have solved each factory's model separately and obtained an overall company optimum. In fact as far as the company was concerned it would have been perfectly acceptable to treat each factory as autonomous. Once we introduce common constraints, however, this will probably no longer be the case, as the small example demonstrated. The more common constraints there are, the more interconnected the separate plants must be. In Section 4.2 we discuss how a knowledge of the optimal solutions to the subproblems might be used to obtain an optimal solution to the total problem. This can be quite important computationally since such structured problems can often be very large and take a long time to solve if treated as one large model. Common sense would suggest that the number of common rows would be a good measure of how close the optimal solution to the total problem was to the sum total of the optimal solutions to the subproblems. This is usually the case. For problems with only a few common rows one might expect there to be virtue in taking account of the optimal solutions of the subproblems.

The block angular structure exhibited in Figure 4.2 does not arise only in multi-plant models. *Multi-product* models arise quite frequently in blending problems. Suppose, for example, that the blending problem which we presented in Section 1.2 represented only one of a number of products (brands) which a company manufactured. If the different products used some of the same ingredients and processing capacity then it would be possible to take account of their limited supply through a structured model. The individual blending models such as that presented in Section 1.2 would be unable to help make rational allocations of such scarce shared resources between products. For example in Figure 4.2 B_1, B_2, etc., would represent the individual blending constraints for each product. These subproblems would contain variables such as x_{ij} representing the quantity of ingredient i in product j. If ingredient i was in limited supply we would impose a common constraint:

$$\sum_j x_{ij} \leqslant \text{availability of ingredient } i. \tag{2}$$

If ingredient i used α_{ij} units of a particular processing capacity in blending product, j we would have the common constraint:

$$\sum_j \alpha_{ij}x_{ij} \leqslant \text{total processing capacity available for ingredient } i. \tag{3}$$

As with multi-plant models, multi-product models almost always arise through combining existing submodels. The submodels can be used to help make certain operational decisions. By combining such submodels into multiple models, further decisions can be brought into the realm of linear programming.

Another way in which the block angular structure of Figure 4.2 arises is in *multi-period* models. Suppose that in our blending problem of Section 1.2 we wanted to determine not just how to blend in a particular month but also how to purchase each month with the possibility of storing for later use. It would then be necessary to distinguish between *buying*, *using*, and *storing*. For each ingredient there would be three corresponding variables. These would be linked together by the relations

Amount in store at end of period $(t-1)$

+ amount bought in period t

= amount used in period t

+ amount in store at end of period t. (4)

These relations give equality constraints. The block angular structure of Figure 4.2 arises through these equality constraints providing common rows linking consecutive time periods. Each subproblem B_i consists of the original blending constraints involving only the 'using' variables. Such a multi-period model arises from the FOOD MANUFACTURE problem of Part 2. This problem is the blending problem of Section 1.2 taken over six months with different raw oil prices for different months. Full details of the formulation of this problem are given in Part 3.

It should not be thought that in a multi-period model of the kind described above each period must necessarily be of the same duration. Some periods might be of a month while later months might be aggregated together (with a corresponding increase in resources represented by righthand side coefficients). It will, however, be very likely that B_1, B_2, etc., in Figure 4.2 are the same submatrices representing the same blending constraints in each period. The corresponding rows and columns of these matrices will of course be distinguished by different names. An obvious way of doing this is suggested in Section 4.3 when the application of a matrix generator to building models is discussed.

The way in which multi-period models should be used is important. Such a model is usually run with the first period relating to the present times and subsequent periods relating to the future. As a result only the operating decisions suggested by the model for the present month are acted on. Operating decisions for future months will probably only be taken as provisional. After a further month (or the appropriate time period) has elapsed the model will be re-run with updated data and the first period applying to the new present period. In this way a multi-period model is in constant use as both an operating tool for the present and a provisional planning tool for the future.

A further point of importance in multi-period models concerns what happens at the end of the last time period in the model. If the stocks at the end of the last period which occur in constraints (4) are included simply as variables the optimal solution will almost always decide that they should be zero. From the point of view of the model this would be sensible as it would be the minimum 'cost' or maximum 'profit' solution. In a practical situation, however, the model is unrealistic since operations will almost certainly continue beyond the end of the last period and stocks would probably not be allowed to run right down. One possible way out is to set the final stocks to constant values representing sensible final levels. It could be argued that the operating plans for the final period will be very provisional anyway and any inaccuracy that far ahead not serious. This is the suggestion that is made for dealing with both the multi-period FACTORY PLANNING and FOOD MANUFACTURE problems of Part 2. An alternative approach which is sometimes adopted is to 'value' the final stocks in some way, i.e. give the appropriate variables positive 'profits' in a maximization model or negative 'costs' in a minimization model. In effect such a valuation would cause the

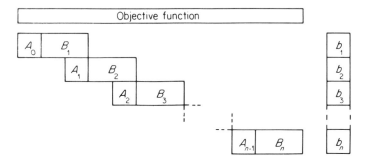

Figure 4.3

optimal solution to suggest producing final stocks to sell if it appeared profitable. Although the organization might never consider the possibility of selling off final stocks, the fact that they had been given realistic valuations would cause them to come out at sensible levels.

A description of a highly structured model which is potentially multi-period, multi-product and multi-plant is given by Williams and Redwood (1974).

Another type of structure which often arises in multi-period models is the *staircase* structure. This is illustrated in Figure 4.3.

In fact a staircase structure such as this could be converted into a block angular structure. If alternate 'steps' such as (A_0, B_1), (A_2, B_3) were treated as subproblem constraints and the intermediate 'steps' as common rows we would have a block angular structure. The block angular multi-period model which was described above could also easily be re-arranged into a staircase structure.

Another structure which sometimes arises, although less commonly than block angular and staircase structures, is shown in Figure 4.4.

In this type of model the subproblems are connected by common columns rather than rows. Such a structure is the dual to the block angular structure (the dual is defined in Section 6.2). One way in which this structure arises is as the linear programming formulation of a certain type of *stochastic programming* problem known as a *two-stage model*. Further details can be found in Dempster (1980). Two-staged models are applicable in situations where some decisions (stage 1) have to be made before other information becomes available. The result of the stage 1 decisions and the subsequent availability of extra information allows stage 2 decisions to be made. Unfortunately the relative merits of the stage 1 decisions depend on this uncertain information and the resultant stage 2 decisions. For example it may be necessary to decide production (stage 1) before demand (uncertain) is known. Then as a result of the production decisions and the subsequent actual demand stage 2 decisions must be made regarding selling any excess production at a lower price or excess production to make up a shortfall at a higher cost.

If it is realistic to consider the uncertain information as taking one of a (small) finite number of possible values with known probabilities (a discrete

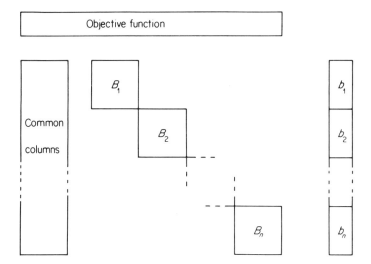

Figure 4.4

probability distribution) then a set of distinct stage 2 variables may be introduced to correspond to each uncertain value. The objective becomes one of minimizing *expected cost*. This model then becomes a linear programme.

For example suppose the production decisions are represented by stage 1 variables $x_1, x_2, \ldots, x_n$. The excess production or shortfall is represented by stage 2 variables $y_1, y_2, \ldots, y_n$, $z_1, z_2, \ldots, z_n$. These stage 2 variables will be replicated m times according to each of the possible demand levels $d_j^{(1)}, d_j^{(2)}, \ldots, d_j^{(m)}$. This gives a model of the following form

$$\text{Minimize} \qquad \sum_j c_j x_j + \sum_r p_r \left(\sum_j e_j y_j^{(r)} + \sum_j f_j z_j^{(r)} \right)$$

$$\text{subject to} \qquad \sum_j a_{ij} x_j \qquad \leqslant b_i \text{ for all production constraints } i$$

$$x_j - y_j^{(r)} + z_j^{(r)} = d_j^{(r)} \quad \text{for all } j \text{ and } r$$
$$x_j, y_j^{(r)}, z_j^{(r)} \geqslant 0$$

where p_r are given probabilities and c_j, e_j and f_j are production, excess production and shortfall costs respectively.

It is important to realise how such a model might be used. Initial decisions would be made as a result of the stage 1 variables. Only the values of those stage 2 variables would ultimately be used which corresponded to the subsequent value of the uncertain information.

The coefficients of the x_j variables form the common columns while the variables $y_j^{(r)}$ and $z_j^{(r)}$ each appear in only the rth block of the model. The combination of this structure with the block angular structure sometimes occurs giving models of the form shown in Figure 4.5.

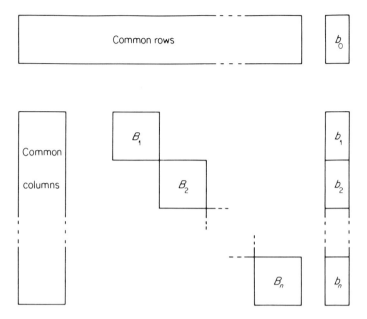

Figure 4.5

A discussion of a number of structures which arise in practice is given by Dantzig (1970).

4.2 Decomposing a Large Model

Common sense suggests that the optimal solution to a structured model should bear some relation to the optimal solutions to the submodels from which it is constructed. This is usually the case and there may, therefore, be virtue in devising computational procedures to exploit this, particularly in view of the large size of many structured models. Ways of solving a structured model by way of solutions to the subproblems forms the subject of *decomposition*. It is sometimes mistakenly thought that decomposition is the actual act of splitting a model up into submodels. Although computational procedures have been devised for doing this, decomposition concerns the solution process on a structure which is usually already known to the modeller.

The importance of decomposition is not only computational but also economic. A decomposition procedure applies to a mathematical model of a structured practical problem. If the structured model arises by way of a structured organization (such as a multi-plant model), the decomposition procedure mirrors a method of *decentralized planning*. It is for this reason that decomposition is discussed in a book on model building. The subject is best considered through this analogy with decentralized planning.

We will again consider the small illustrative problem of Section 4.1 which gave rise to the multi-plant model below.

Maximize	Profit	$10x_1 + 15x_2 + 10x_3 + 15x_4$	
subject to	Raw	$4x_1 + 4x_2 + 4x_3 + 4x_4 \leqslant 120,$	
	Grinding A	$4x_1 + 2x_2 \leqslant 80,$	
	Polishing A	$2x_1 + 5x_2 \leqslant 60,$	
	Grinding B	$5x_3 + 3x_4 \leqslant 60,$	
	Polishing B	$5x_3 + 6x_4 \leqslant 75,$	

$$x_1, x_2, x_3, x_4 \geqslant 0.$$

It was seen that splitting the 120 kilograms of *raw* between A and B in the ratio 75:45 led to a non-optimal overall solution. The optimal overall solution showed that this ratio should be 70:50. Unfortunately we had to solve the total model in order to find this optimal split. If we had a method of predetermining this optimal split we would be able to solve the individual models for factory A and B and combine the solutions to give an optimal solution for the total model. For a general block angular model as illustrated in Figure 4.2 we would need to find optimal splits in all the right-hand side coefficients in b_0 for the common rows. Algorithms for the decomposition of a block angular structure based on this principle do exist. Such methods are known as *decomposition by allocation*. One such algorithm is the method of Rosen (1964).

An alternative approach is *decomposition by pricing*. In a block angular stucture, such as our small example above where common rows represent constraints on raw material availability, we could try to seek valuations for the limited raw material. These valuations could be used as *internal prices* to be charged to the submodels. If accurate valuations could be obtained we might hope to get each submodel optimizing to the overall benefit of the total model. One such approach to this the *Dantzig–Wolfe decomposition algorithm*. A full description of the algorithm is given in Dantzig (1963). We provide a less rigorous description here paying attention to the economic analogy with decentralized planning.

To illustrate the method we again use the small two-factory example. If it were not for the raw material being in limited supply, we would have the following submodels for A and B:

Maximize	Profit A	$10x_1 + 15x_2$
subject to	Grinding A	$4x_1 + 2x_2 \leqslant 80,$
	Polishing A	$2x_1 + 5x_2 \leqslant 60,$

$$x_1, x_2 \geqslant 0;$$

Maximize	Profit B	$10x_3 + 15x_4$
subject to	Grinding B	$5x_3 + 3x_4 \leqslant 60,$
	Polishing B	$5x_3 + 6x_4 \leqslant 75,$

$$x_3, x_4 \geqslant 0.$$

These submodels should not be confused with the submodels for the same problem in Section 4.1. The raw availability constraints were included in both submodels with a suitable allocation of raw material between them. Here we are not including such constraints. Instead an attempt is made to find a suitable 'internal price' for *raw* and to incorporate this into the submodels. Suppose *raw* were to be internally priced at £p per kilogram. The objective functions for the above submodels would then become

$$\text{Profit A } (10 - 4p)x_1 + (15 - 4p)x_2 \tag{1}$$

and

$$\text{Profit B } (10 - 4p)x_3 + (15 - 4p)x_4. \tag{2}$$

In effect we have taken multiples of p times the raw material availability constraints and subtracted them from the objectives. If p is set too low we might find that the combined solutions to the submodels use more *raw* than is available in which case p should be increased. For example, if p is taken as zero (there is no internal charge for *raw*) we obtain the following optimal solutions.

Factory A's Optimal Solution with Raw Valued at 0

Profit is £250 obtained from making 17·5 standard and 5 of deluxe.

Factory B's Optimal Solution with Raw Valued at 0

Profit is £187·5 obtained from making 12·5 of deluxe.

These solutions are clearly unacceptable to the company as a whole since they demand 140 kilograms of raw which is more than the 120 kilograms available. We therefore seek some way of estimating a more realistic value for the internal price p. Whatever the value of p, A and B will have optimal solutions which are vertex solutions of the submodels presented above. Since these models only involve two variables each they can be represented graphically. This is done in Figures 4.6 and 4.7.

With the value of zero for p we can easily verify the optimal solutions above for A and B as being (17·5, 5) in Figure 4.6 and (0, 12·5) in Figure 4.7.

Any feasible solution to the total problem must clearly be feasible with respect to both subproblems (as well as additionally satisfying raw material availability limitation). The values of x_1 and x_2 in any feasible solution to the total problem must therefore be a *convex linear combination* of the vertices of the feasible region shown in Figure 4.6, i.e.

$$\binom{x_1}{x_2} = \lambda_{11}\binom{0}{0} + \lambda_{12}\binom{20}{0} + \lambda_{13}\binom{17\cdot 5}{5} + \lambda_{14}\binom{0}{12}. \tag{3}$$

$\lambda_{11}, \lambda_{12}, \lambda_{13},$ and λ_{14} are 'weights' attached to the vertices. They must be

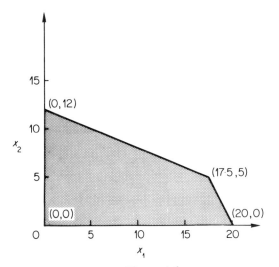

Figure 4.6

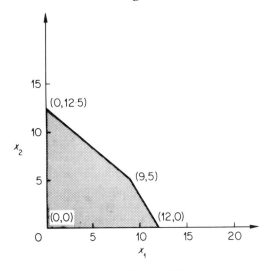

Figure 4.7

non-negative and satisfy the convexity condition

$$\lambda_{11} + \lambda_{12} + \lambda_{13} + \lambda_{14} = 1. \tag{4}$$

The vector equation (3) is a way of relating x_1 and x_2 to a new set of variables λ_{ij} by the following two equations:

$$x_1 = 0\lambda_{11} + 20\lambda_{12} + 17\cdot5\lambda_{13} + 0\lambda_{14}, \tag{5}$$

$$x_2 = 0\lambda_{11} + 0\lambda_{12} + 5\lambda_{13} + 12\lambda_{14}. \tag{6}$$

A similar argument can be applied to the second subproblem represented in

Figure 4.7. This allows x_3 and x_4 to be related to yet more variables λ_{21}, λ_{22}, λ_{23}, and λ_{24} by the following equations:

$$x_3 = 0\lambda_{21} + 12\lambda_{22} + 9\lambda_{23} + \quad 0\lambda_{24}, \tag{7}$$

$$x_4 = 0\lambda_{21} + \quad 0\lambda_{22} + 5\lambda_{23} + 12\cdot5\lambda_{24}, \tag{8}$$

$$\lambda_{21} + \quad \lambda_{22} + \lambda_{23} + \quad \lambda_{24} = 1. \tag{9}$$

λ_{2j} are 'weights' for vertices in the second subproblem while λ_{1j} are 'weights' in the first subproblem.

It is worth pointing out that what we are really doing is giving *modal formulations*, as described in Section 3.4, for each subproblem.

A slight complication arises if the feasible regions of some of the submodels are 'open', e.g. we have the situation shown in Figure 4.8.

This complication is easily dealt with and fully explained in Dantzig (1963).

We can use equations (5), (6), (7), and (8) to substitute for x_1, x_2, x_3, and x_4 in the objective and single common constraint raw of our total model. The grinding and polishing constraints of the two subproblems will be satisfied so long as the λ_{ij} are non-negative and satisfy the convexity constraints, (4) and (9). In this way our multi-plant model can be re-expressed as

Maximize

Profit $200\lambda_{12} + 250\lambda_{13} + 180\lambda_{14} \quad + 120\lambda_{22} + 165\lambda_{23} + 187\cdot5\lambda_{24}$

subject to

Raw $80\lambda_{12} + \quad 90\lambda_{13} + 48\lambda_{14} \quad + \quad 48\lambda_{22} + 56\lambda_{23} + \quad 50\lambda_{24} \leqslant 120,$

conv 1 $\lambda_{11} + \quad \lambda_{12} + \quad \lambda_{13} + \quad \lambda_{14} \qquad\qquad\qquad\qquad\qquad\qquad = 1,$

conv 2 $\lambda_{21} + \quad \lambda_{22} + \lambda_{23} + \quad \lambda_{24} = 1.$

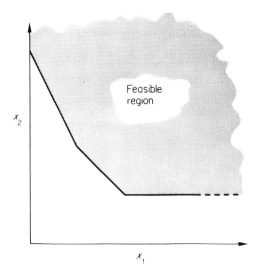

Figure 4.8

The above model is known as the *master model*. It can be interpreted as a model to find the 'optimum mix' of vertex solutions of each of the submodels. For any internal price p which is charged to A and B they will each produce vertex solutions. Such vertex solutions give rise to what are known as *proposals* since they represent 'proposed' solutions from the submodels given the provisional internal price p for raw. The proposals are the columns of coefficients in the master model corresponding to a particular vertex of a submodel. For example the proposal from the third vertex of the first subproblem is the column

$$\begin{pmatrix} 250 \\ 90 \\ 1 \\ 0 \end{pmatrix}.$$

This proposal is given a weight of λ_{13} in the master model. The role of the master model is to choose the best combination of all the proposals which have been obtained.

The master model would generally have far fewer constraints than the original model. There will be the same number of common rows as in the total model. Each submodel will, however, have been condensed down into a single convexity constraint such as conv 1 in the example above. Unfortunately the saving in constraints will generally be more than offset by a vast expansion in the number of variables. We will have a λ_{ij} variable for each vertex of each submodel. This could be an astronomic number in a realistic problem. In practice the great majority of proposals corresponding to these variables will be zero in an optimal solution. For a master model with a comparatively small number of constraints but a very large number of variables the great majority of variables will never enter a solution. We therefore resort to a practice that is used quite widely in mathematical programming. *Columns are generated in the course of optimization.* A column (proposal) is added to the master model only when it seems worthwhile. We therefore deal with only a subset of the possible proposals. Such a truncated model is known as a *restricted master model*. Proposals are added to (and sometimes deleted from) the restricted master model in the course of optimization. In general only a very small number of the potential proposals will ever be generated and added to the restricted master problem.

In order to describe how we proceed we will consider our small multi-plant model. Instead of using the master model, which we were fortunate enough to be able to obtain from geometrical considerations in so small an example, we will work with a restricted master problem. To start with we will take only the proposals corresponding to λ_{11} and λ_{13} from submodel A and λ_{21} and λ_{24} from submodel B. This choice is largely arbitrary. How it is made is not important to our discussion. In practice a number of 'good' proposals from each submodel would be used to make up the first version of the restricted master model in order to have a reasonably realistic model with some substance. Our first restricted master model is therefore:

Maximize	Profit		$250\lambda_{13}$		$+\ 187 \cdot 5\lambda_{24}$	
subject to	Raw		$90\lambda_{13}$	$+$	$50\lambda_{24}$	$\leqslant 120,$
	conv 1	$\lambda_{11} +$	λ_{13}			$=\quad 1,$
	conv 2			$\lambda_{21} +$	$\lambda_{24} =$	$1.$

When this model is optimized we can obtain a 'valuation' for the raw material. This valuation is the *marginal value* of the raw constraint in the optimal solution. Such marginal values for constraints are sometimes known as *shadow prices*. They are discussed much more fully together with their economic interpretation in Section 6.2. In fact the marginal value associated with a constraint such as raw is the rate at which this optimal profit would increase for small ('marginal') increases in the right-hand side coefficient. It is sufficient for our purpose here simply to remark that such valuations for constraints are possible. With any package programs these valuations (shadow prices) are presented with the optimal solution.

If our first restricted master model is optimized the shadow price on the raw constraint turns out to be £2·78. This can be taken as value p and used as an internal price which factories A and B are charged for each kilogram of *raw* which they wish to use. When A is charged this internal price he will reform his objective function to take account of the new charge. His new objective function comes from the expression (1) taking p as £2·78. This gives

$$\text{Profit A} \quad -1\cdot 12x_1 + 3\cdot 18x_2. \tag{10}$$

If this objective is used with the constraints of the submodel for A, we obtain the solution

$$x_1 = 0, \qquad x_2 = 12.$$

This clearly corresponds to the vertex $(0, 12)$ in Figure 4.6. The proposal corresponding to this is the column for λ_{14}. This is easily calculated to be

$$\begin{pmatrix} 180 \\ 48 \\ 1 \\ 0 \end{pmatrix}.$$

A new variable (λ_{14} but with a different name) is therefore added to the restricted master problem with this column of coefficients. This new proposal respresents factory A's new provisional production plan given the new internal charge for *raw*.

Our attention is now turned to factory B. When they are charged £2·78 per kilogram for *raw* the expression (2) gives their objective function as

$$\text{Profit B} \quad -1 \cdot 12x_3 + 3 \cdot 18x_4.$$

When this objective is optimized with the constraints of the submodel for factory B we obtain the solution

$$x_3 = 0, \qquad x_4 = 12 \cdot 5. \tag{11}$$

We have the vertex $(0, 12 \cdot 5)$ in Figure 4.7. The proposal corresponding to this is the column for λ_{24}. This proposal has already been included in our first restricted master model. We therefore conclude that even if factory B is charged at the suggested rate of £2·78 per kilogram for raw they would not suggest a new proposal (provisional production plan).

Having added only the proposal corresponding to λ_{14} to our restricted master model it now becomes

Maximize	Profit		$250\lambda_{13} + 180\lambda_{14} + 187 \cdot 5\lambda_{24}$		
subject to	Raw		$90\lambda_{13} + 48\lambda_{14} +$	$50\lambda_{24} \leqslant 120,$	
	conv 1	$\lambda_{11} +$	$\lambda_{13} + \lambda_{14}$	$= 1,$	
	conv 2			$\lambda_{21} + \lambda_{24} = 1.$	

Optimizing this model, the shadow price on *raw* turns out to be £1·67. We see that our previous valuation of £2·78 appears to have been an overestimate.

The cycle is now repeated and each factory is internally charged £1·67 per kilogram for raw. This gives the following new objectives for A and B:

$$\text{Profit A} \quad 3 \cdot 32x_1 + 8 \cdot 32x_2, \tag{12}$$

$$\text{Profit B} \quad 3 \cdot 32x_3 + 8 \cdot 32x_4. \tag{13}$$

When the objective (12) is used with the constraints of the submodel for factory A the optimal solution obtained is

$$x_1 = 17 \cdot 5, \qquad x_2 = 5.$$

This is the vertex $(17 \cdot 5, 5)$ in Figure 4.6 and gives the proposal corresponding to λ_{13}. As this proposal has already been incorporated in the restricted master problem factory A has no new proposal to offer as a result of the revised internal charge of £1·67 per kilogram for raw.

Factory B optimizes objective (13) subject to the constraints of its submodel. This results in the solution

$$x_3 = 0, \qquad x_4 = 12 \cdot 5.$$

This is the vertex $(0, 12 \cdot 5)$ of Figure 4.7 which results in the proposal corresponding to λ_{24}. As this proposal is already present in the restricted master model, factory B also has no further useful proposal to add as a result of the revised charge for raw.

We therefore conclude that factories A and B have submitted all the useful proposals that they can. The optimal solution to the latest version of the restricted master model gives the proportions in which these proposals should be used. For our example the optimal solution to this restricted master model is

$$\lambda_{13} = 0\cdot52, \qquad \lambda_{14} = 0\cdot48, \qquad \lambda_{24} = 1.$$

This enables us to calculate the optimal values for x_1, x_2, x_3, and x_4 by considering the vertex solutions of the submodels corresponding to λ_{13}, λ_{14}, and λ_{24}. We obtain

$$\begin{pmatrix} x_1 \\ x_2 \end{pmatrix} = 0\cdot52 \begin{pmatrix} 17\cdot5 \\ 5 \end{pmatrix} + 0\cdot48 \begin{pmatrix} 0 \\ 12 \end{pmatrix},$$

$$\begin{pmatrix} x_3 \\ x_4 \end{pmatrix} = 1 \begin{pmatrix} 0 \\ 12\cdot5 \end{pmatrix}.$$

This gives us the optimal solution to the total model,

$$x_1 = 9\cdot17, \qquad x_2 = 8\cdot33, \qquad x_4 = 12\cdot5,$$

giving an objective value of £404·15.

Notice, however, that we have obtained the optimal solution to the total model without solving it directly. Instead we have dealt with what would generally be much smaller models. The two types of model we have used are the *submodels* and the *restricted master model*. We further discuss the significance of these models below.

The Submodels

These contain the details relevant to the individual subproblems. For a multi-plant model such as used in our example the coefficients in the constraints only concern the particular factory, i.e. grinding and polishing times and capacities in each factory.

The Restricted Master Model

This is an overall model for the whole organization but unlike the total model it contains none of the technological detail relating to the individual subproblems. Such detail is left to the submodels. Instead the constraints for each subproblem are accounted for by a simple convexity constraint. In our example we had the constraints for factories A and B reducing to convexity constraints conv 1 and conv 2 respectively. On the other hand, the restricted master model does contain the common rows in full since its main purpose

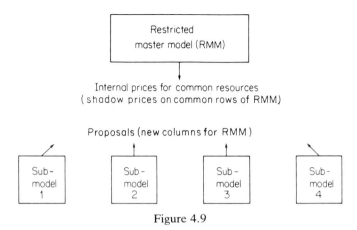

Figure 4.9

is to determine suitable valuations for the resources represented by these common rows.

By means of interactions between the submodels and the restricted master model it is possible eventually to obtain the optimal solution to the (usually much larger) total model without ever building and solving it directly. The process which we here described is represented diagrammatically in Figure 4.9.

There is considerable attraction in such a scheme since it is never necessary to build, solve, and maintain the often huge total model which would result from a large structured organization. In a multi-plant organization the individual plants would probably be geographically separated. This would make the avoidance of including all their technological details in one central model desirable. Each plant might well build and maintain their own model inside their own plant, and solve it on their own computer. The head office could maintain a restricted master model on another computer which would be linked to the computers in the individual plants. Each model could then be run independently but could supply the vital information of *proposals* and *internal prices* to the other models. It would then be possible to use a system automatically to obtain an overall optimal solution for the organization.

Decomposition has interest for economists since it clearly represents a system of decentralized planning. The existence of decomposition algorithms such as the Dantzig–Wolfe algorithm demonstrates that it is possible to devise a method of decentralized planning which achieves an optimal solution for an organization considered as a whole. This is done by allowing the sub-organizations to decide their own optimal policies, given limited control from the centre. In the case of the Dantzig–Wolfe algorithm this control takes the form of internal prices. For other methods it may take the form of allocations. An informal version of such procedures takes place in many organizations. A discussion of a large number of decomposition algorithms and their relation to decentralized planning in real life is given by Atkins (1974).

Decomposition algorithms are also of considerable computational interest since they offer a possibility of avoiding the large amount of time needed to solve large models should those models be structured. Unfortunately decomposition has only met with limited computational success. The most widely used algorithm is the Dantzig–Wolfe algorithm which applies to block angular structured models. There are many circumstances, however, in which it is more efficient to solve the total model rather than use decomposition. The main advice to someone building a structured model should not be to attempt decomposition on other than an experimental basis. As experience and knowledge grows, decomposition may well become a more reliable tool, but at present the computational experience with such methods has been disappointing. If a model is to be used very frequently, experimenting with decomposition might be considered worthwhile. The larger the model and the smaller the proportion of common rows (for block angular structures) the more valuable this is likely to be. Sometimes other aspects of the structure can be exploited to advantage. An example of this is described by Williams and Redwood (1974). Computational experiences using Dantzig–Wolfe decomposition are given by Beale, Hughes, and Small (1965) and by Ho and Loute (1981). A very full description of the computational side of decomposition is given by Lasdon (1970). Finally decomposition may commend itself for the purely organizational considerations resulting from the desirability of decentralized planning.

The use of communication networks for linking computers together makes it possible to implement a decomposition algorithm splitting the models between different computers, e.g. the master model in the head office and the submodels at individual plants. This idea has not, to the author's knowledge, yet been tried.

4.3 Using a Matrix Generator

Most structured models are so large that the manual preparation of data for input to a linear programming package would be prohibitively tedious and error prone. Since such models frequently involve a large amount of repetition the advantages of a matrix generator are obvious. For multi-plant models the structures of the individual submodels will probably be very similar, although the coefficients may well be different. This is revealed by our small two-factory example. In multi-period models the coefficients themselves may be identical across submodels. All that are needed are different names for corresponding rows and columns in corresponding submodels. A very obvious naming convention is to reserve one of the character positions in such names to indicate which submodel is referred to. In order to illustrate the value of a matrix generator in building such a structured model we have extended the XPRESS-MP formulation of the BLEND model of Section 3.5 to produce a multi-period model. The full problem is presented as the FOOD MANUFAC-TURE problem of Part 2. A suggested formulation is given in Part 3.

```
MODEL FOOD
LET MAXT = 6            ! the number of months
LET MAXI = 5            ! the number of oils
TABLES
      COST(MAXT,MAXI)   ! cost of buying oils
      HARD(MAXI)        ! hardness of each oil
      ISTORE(MAXI)      ! initial stocks of oil
      FSTORE(MAXI)      ! final stocks of oil
DISKDATA
      COST = FOOD.CST
ASSIGN
      ISTORE(I=1:MAXI) = 500
      FSTORE(I=1:MAXI) = 500
DATA
      HARD(1) = 8.8, 6.1, 2, 4.2, 5
VARIABLES
      BVEG(2,MAXT)      ! vegetable oil bought
      UVEG(2,MAXT)      ! vegetable oil used
      SVEG(2,MAXT)      ! vegetable oil stored at end of month
      BOIL(3,MAXT)      ! non-veg. oil bought
      UOIL(3,MAXT)      ! non-veg. oil used
      SOIL(3,MAXT)      ! non-veg. oil stored at end of month
      PROD(MAXT)
CONSTRAINTS

                        ! Operating profit
PROF:- SUM(T=1:MAXT,I=1:2) COST(T,I)*BVEG(I,T)        &
     - SUM(T=1:MAXT,I=1:3) COST(T,I+2)*BOIL(I,T)      &
     + SUM(T=1:MAXT) 150*PROD(T)                      &
     - SUM(T=1:MAXT,I=1:2) 5*SVEG(I,T)                &
     - SUM(T=1:MAXT,I=1:3) 5*SOIL(I,T)                $

                        ! Materials balance for raw oils
LVEG(I=1:2,T=2:MAXT): SVEG(I,T-1) + BVEG(I,T) - UVEG(I,T) = SVEG(I,T)
LVEG(I=1:2,T=1:1):     ISTORE(I) + BVEG(I,T) - UVEG(I,T) = SVEG(I,T)
LOIL(I=1:3,T=2:MAXT): SOIL(I,T-1) + BOIL(I,T) - UOIL(I,T) = SOIL(I,T)
LOIL(I=1:3,T=1:1):     ISTORE(I+2) + BOIL(I,T) - UOIL(I,T) = SOIL(I,T)

                        ! Usage limits of raw oils
VVEG(T=1:MAXT): SUM(I=1:2) UVEG(I,T) < 200
NVEG(T=1:MAXT): SUM(I=1:3) UOIL(I,T) < 250

                        ! Hardness requirement of blended product
UHRD(T=1:MAXT): SUM(I=1:2)   HARD(I)*UVEG(I,T)        &
              + SUM(I=1:3) HARD(I+2)*UOIL(I,T)   < 6*PROD(T)
LHRD(T=1:MAXT): SUM(I=1:2)   HARD(I)*UVEG(I,T)        &
              + SUM(I=1:3) HARD(I+2)*UOIL(I,T)   > 3*PROD(T)

                        ! Production volume
CONT(T=1:MAXT): SUM(I=1:2) UVEG(I,T) + SUM(I=1:3) UOIL(I,T) = PROD(T)
BOUNDS

                        ! Storage capacity of raw oils
SVEG(I=1:2,T=1:MAXT-1) < 1000
SOIL(I=1:3,T=1:MAXT-1) < 1000

                        ! Finishing stock
SVEG(I=1:2,MAXT)   = FSTORE(I)
SOIL(I=1:3,MAXT)   = FSTORE(I)

GENERATE                ! Generate MPS matrix
```

It will be seen that the variable and constraint names have an index representing the number of the period. Linking constraints (LVEG and LOIL) connect together variables for consecutive periods.

CHAPTER 5

Applications and Special Types of Mathematical Programming Model

5.1 Typical Applications

The purpose of this section is to create an awareness of the areas where linear programming (LP) is applicable. To categorize totally those industries and problems where LP can, or cannot, be used would be impossible. Some problems clearly lend themselves to an LP model. For other problems the use of an LP model may not provide a totally satisfactory solution but may be considered acceptable in the absence of other approaches. The decision of when to use, and when not to use, LP is often a subjective one depending on an individual's experience.

This section can do no more than try to give a 'feel' for those areas in which LP can be applied. In order to do this a list of industries and areas in which the technique has been applied is given. This list is by no means exhaustive but is intended to include most of the major users. A short discussion is given of the types of LP models which are of use in each area. References are given to some of the relevant published case studies. In view of the very wide use which has been made of LP it would be almost impossible to seek out every reference to published case studies. Nor would it be helpful to submerge the reader in a mass of often superfluous literature. The intention is to give sufficient references to allow the reader to follow up published case studies himself. From the references given here it should be possible to find other references if necessary. In many cases practical applications are illustrated by problems in Part 2.

Although the intention is mainly to consider *linear programming* applications in this chapter, the resultant models can very often naturally be extended by *integer programming* or *non-linear programming models*. In this way more complicated or realistic situations can often be modelled. These topics and further applications are considered more fully in Chapters 7, 8, 9, and 10.

The subject of linear programming does not have clearly defined boundaries. Other subjects impinge on, and merge with, linear programming. Two types of model which have, to some extent, been studied independently of LP are considered further in this chapter. Firstly *economic models* which are sometimes referred to as *input–output* or *Leontief models* are considered in Section 5.2. Such models can often be regarded as a special type of LP model.

Secondly, *network models* which arise frequently in Operational Research are considered in Section 5.3. Such models are, again, often usefully considered as special types of LP model. Another area which also has connections with LP is not considered in this book in view of its limited practical applicability to date. This is the *theory of games*. Game theory models can sometimes be converted into LP models (and vice versa).

The following list of applications should indicate the surprisingly wide applicability of linear programming and in consequence its economic importance.

The Petroleum Industry

This is by far the biggest user of LP. Very large models involving thousands, and occasionally tens of thousands, of constraints have been built. These models are used to help make a number of decisions starting with where and how to buy crude oil, how to ship it, and which products to produce out of it. Such 'corporate models' contain elements of *distribution, resource allocation, blending*, and possibly *marketing*. A typical example of the sort of model which arises in the industry is the REFINERY OPTIMIZATION problem of Part 2. Descriptions of the use of LP in the petroleum industry are given by Manne (1956), Catchpole (1962), and McColl (1969).

The Chemical Industry

The applications here are rather similar to those in the petroleum industry although the models are rarely as large. Applications usually involve *blending*, or *resource allocation*. An application is described by Royce (1970).

Manufacturing Industry

Linear programming is frequently used here for resource allocation. The '*product mix*' example described in Section 1.2 is an example of this type of application. Resources to be allocated are usually processing capacity, raw materials, and manpower. A multi-period problem of this type, considered in relation to the engineering industry, is the FACTORY PLANNING problem of Part 2. Other common applications of LP in manufacturing are *blending* and *blast furnace burdening* (the steel industry). Three references to the application of LP here are Lawrence and Flowerdew (1963), Fabian (1967), and Sutton and Coates (1981).

Transport

Problems of distribution can often be formulated as LP models. Two classic examples are the *transportation* and *transhipment* problems which are considered in Section 5.3 as they involve *networks*. A simple DISTRIBUTION problem of this type is presented in Part 2. An extension of this problem, DISTRIBUTION 2, involves *depot location* as well and requires integer programming. *Scheduling* problems (e.g. lorries, aircraft, tankers, trains, buses, etc.) can often be tackled through integer programming. Problems of *assignment* (trains to mines and power stations) arising in transport have also been tackled through mathematical programming. Applications of mathematical programming in distribution are described by Eilon, Watson-Gandy, and Christofides (1971) and Markland (1975).

Finance

A very early application of mathematical programming was in *portfolio selection*. This was due to Markowitz (1959). Given a sum of money to invest, the problem was how to spend it among a portfolio of shares and stocks. The objective was to maintain a certain expected rate of return from the investment but to minimize the variance of that return. The model which results is a quadratic programming model.

Agarwala and Goodson (1970) suggest how LP can be used by a government to design an *optimum tax package* to achieve some required aim (in particular an improvement in the balance of payments).

LP is increasingly being used in *accountancy*. The economic information which can be derived from the solution to an LP model can provide accountants with very useful costing information. This sort of information is described in detail in Section 6.2. A description of how LP can be used in accountancy is given by Salkin and Kornbluth (1973).

Spath, Gutgesell, and Grun (1975) describe how an LP model is applied by a mail order firm in order to minimize the total interest cost on all credits.

An interesting extension of a finance model to allow the user to set *goals* interactively (rather than objectives) and operate within the degrees of freedom permitted by the constraints is described by Jack (1985).

Agriculture

LP has been used in agriculture for *farm management*. Such models can be used to decide what to grow where, how to rotate crops, how to expand production, and where to invest. An example of such a problem is the FARM PLANNING problem of Part 2. Swart, Smith, and Holderby (1975) apply a multi-period LP model to planning the expansion of a large dairy farm. Other general references are Balm (1980) and Fokkens and Puylaert (1981).

Blending models are often applicable to agriculture problems. It is often desired to blend together livestock feeds or fertilizer at minimum cost. Glen (1980) describes a model for beef cattle ration formulation.

Distribution problems often arise in this area. The distribution of farm products, in particular milk, can be examined by the network type of LP model described in Section 5.3.

Quadratic programming has been used for determining *optimal prices* for the sale of milk in the Netherlands. This is described by Louwes, Boot, and Wage (1963). The AGRICULTURAL PRICING problem of Part 2 is based on this study. A mixed integer programming model for irrigation in a developing country is described by Rose (1973).

Health

The obvious application of mathematical programming in this area is in problems of *resource allocation*. How are scarce resources, e.g. doctors, nurses, hospitals, etc., to be used to best effect? In such problems there will obviously be considerable doubt concerning the validity of the data, e.g. how much of a nurse's time does a particular type of treatment really need? In spite of doubts concerning much of the data in such problems it has been possible to use mathematical programming models to suggest plausible policy options. McDonald, Cuddeford, and Beale (1974) describe a non-linear programming model for allocating resources in the United Kingdom health service. Revelle, Feldmann, and Lynn (1969) describe how a non-linear programming model can be used for controlling tuberculosis in an underdeveloped country.

Warner and Prawda (1972) describe a mathematical programming model for scheduling nurses. Redpath and Wright (1981) describe how linear programming is used to decide intensity and direction of beams for irradiating cancerous tumours.

Mining

A number of interesting applications of mathematical programming occur in mining. The straightforward applications are simply ones of *resource allocation*, i.e. how should manpower and machinery be deployed to best effect?

Blending problems also occur when it is necessary to mix together ores to achieve some required quality.

Two examples of mining problems are given in Part 2. The MINING problem concerns what combination of mines a company should operate in successive years. The OPENCAST MINING problem is to decide what the boundaries of an opencast mine should be. References to the application of mathematical programming in mining are Young, Fergusson, and Corbishley (1963) and Meyer (1969).

Manpower Planning

The possible movement of people between different types of job and its control by recruitment, promotion, retraining, etc., can be examined by linear programming. An example of such a problem, MANPOWER PLANNING, is given in Part 2. Applications of mathematical programming to manpower planning are described by Price and Piskor (1972), Davies (1973), Vajda (1975), Charnes *et al.* (1975), and Lilien and Rao (1975).

Food

The food industry makes considerable use of linear programming. *Blending* (sausages, meat pies, margarines, ice cream, etc.) is an obvious application often giving rise to very small and easily solved models.

Problems of *distribution* also arise in this industry giving rise to the network type models described in Section 5.3.

As in other manufacturing industries problems of *resource allocation* arise which can be tackled through linear programming.

The FOOD MANUFACTURE problem of Part 2 is an example of a multi-period blending problem in the food industry. A more complicated version of this problem is described by Williams and Redwood (1974). Jones and Rope (1964) describe another linear programming model in the food industry.

Energy

The electricity and gas supply industries both use mathematical programming to deal with problems of resource allocation. The TARIFF RATES (POWER GENERATION) problem of Part 2 involves scheduling electric generators to meet varying loads at different times of day. This problem is similar to that described by Garver (1963).

Linear programming can also be applied to *distribution* problems involving the design and use of supply networks.

Applications of mathematical programming in these areas are also described by Babayer (1975), Fanshel and Lynes (1964), Muckstadt and Koenig (1977), and Khodaverdian, Brameller, and Dunnett (1986).

Pulp and Paper

Problems of *resource allocation* in the manufacture of paper give rise to linear programming models. Such models frequently involve an element of *blending*. In addition the possibility of *recycling waste paper* has also been examined by linear programming as described by Glassey and Gupta (1974).

A totally different type of problem arising in the paper industry (and the glass industry) is the *trimloss* problem. This is the problem of arranging orders for rolls of paper of different widths so as to minimize the wastage. This problem can be tackled by linear (or sometimes integer) programming. This problem is described by Eisemann (1957). It has also been considered by Gilmore and Gomory (1961, 1963).

Advertising

The problem of spreading one's advertising budget over possible advertising outlets (e.g. television commercials, newspaper advertisements, etc.) has been approached through mathematical programming. These problems are known as *media scheduling* problems.

Authors differ over the usefulness of mathematical programming in tackling this type of problem. Selected references are Engel and Warshaw (1964), Bass and Lonsdale (1966), and Charnes *et al.* (1968). The last-mentioned reference gives a very full list of references itself.

Defence

Problems of *resource allocation* give rise to military applications of linear programming. Such an application is described by Beard and McIndoe (1970).

The siting of missile sites is described by Miercort and Soland (1971).

Other Applications

There are numerous other applications of mathematical programming. A few of the less usual ones are given here since they might otherwise go unnoticed.

Heroux and Wallace (1973) describe a multi-period linear programming model for land development.

Souder (1973) discusses the effectiveness of a number of mathematical programming models for research and development. Feuerman and Weiss (1973) show how a knapsack integer programming model can be used to help design multiple choice-type examinations. Kalvaitis and Posgay (1974) apply integer programming to the problem of selecting the most promising kind of mailing list.

Wardle (1965) applies linear programming to forestry management.

Problems of pollution control have been tackled through mathematical programming. Applications are described by Loucks, Revelle, and Lynn (1968).

Kraft and Hill (1973) describe a 0–1 integer programming model for selecting journals for a university library.

A much fuller list of papers on mathematical programming applications has been compiled by Riley and Gass (1958). The special editions of the journal *Mathematical Programming Studies* Nos 9 (1975) and 20 (1982) are devoted to applications.

5.2   Economic Models

A widely used type of national economic model is the *input–output model* representing the interrelationships between the different sectors of a country's economy. Such models are often referred to as *Leontief models* after their originator, who built such a model of the American economy. This is described by Leontief (1951). Input–output models are often regarded usefully as a special type of linear programming model.

The Static Model

The *output* from a particular industry or a sector of an economy is often used for two purposes: (i) for immediate consumption, e.g. coal to to be sold to domestic consumers; (ii) as an *input* to other industries or sectors of the economy, e.g. coal to provide power for the steel industry. Since the outputs from many industries will be able to be split in this way between (exogenous) consumption and as (endogenous) inputs into these same industries, a complex set of interrelationships will exist. The input–output type of model provides about the simplest way of representing these relationships. A number of strong (and usually oversimplified) assumptions are made regarding the inter-industry relationships. The two major assumptions are as follows:

(i) The output from each industry is directly proportional to its inputs, e.g. doubling all the inputs to an industry will double its outputs.
(ii) The inputs to a particular industry are all in fixed proportions, e.g. it is not possible to decrease one input and compensate for this by increasing another input. These fixed proportions are determined by the technology of the production process. In other words there is *non-substitutability* of inputs.

In order to demonstrate such a model we will consider a very simple example.

Example. A Three-industry Economy

We suppose that we have an economy made up of only three types of industry: coal, steel, and transport. Part of the outputs from these industries are needed as inputs to others, e.g. coal is needed to fire the blast furnaces that produce steel, steel is needed in the machinery for extracting coal, etc. The necessary inputs to produce one unit of output for each industry are given in the *input–output matrix* in Table 5.1.

It is usual in such tables to measure all units of production in monetary terms. We then see that, for example, to produce £1 in worth of coal requires £0·1 of coal (to provide the necessary power), £0·1 of steel (the steel 'used up' in the 'wear and tear' on the machinery) and £0·2 of transport (for moving the coal from the mine). In addition £0·6 of labour is required. Similarly the

Table 5.1 An input–output matrix

Inputs	Outputs		
	Coal	Steel	Transport
Coal	0·1	0·5	0·4
Steel	0·1	0·1	0·2
Transport	0·2	0·1	0·2
Labour	0·6	0·3	0·2

other columns of Table 5.1 give the inputs required (£s) for each £ of steel and each £ of transport (lorries, cars, trains, etc.).

Notice that the value of each unit of output is exactly matched by the sum of the values of its inputs.

This economy is assumed to be '*open*' in the sense that some of the output from the above three industries is used for exogenous consumption. We will assume that these 'external' requirements are (in £ millions)

Coal	20
Steel	5
Transport	25

Such a set of exogenous demands is known as a *bill of goods*.

A number of questions naturally arise concerning our economy which a mathematical model might be used to answer:

(i) How much should each industry produce in total in order to satisfy a given bill of goods?
(ii) How much labour would this require?
(iii) What should the price of each product be?

If variables x_c, x_s, and x_t are used to represent the total quantities of coal, steel, and transport produced (in a year) we get the following relationships:

$$x_c = 20 + 0 \cdot 1 x_c + 0 \cdot 5 x_s + 0 \cdot 4 x_t, \tag{1}$$

$$x_s = 5 + 0 \cdot 1 x_c + 0 \cdot 1 x_s + 0 \cdot 2 x_t, \tag{2}$$

$$x_t = 25 + 0 \cdot 2 x_c + 0 \cdot 1 x_s + 0 \cdot 2 x_t. \tag{3}$$

For example, equation (1) tells us that we must produce enough coal to satisfy external demand (£20m), input to the coal industry $(0 \cdot 1 x_c)$, input to the steel industry $(0 \cdot 5 x_s)$, and input to the transport industry $(0 \cdot 4 x_t)$.

Equations (1), (2), and (3) can conveniently be rewritten as

$$0 \cdot 9 x_c - 0 \cdot 5 x_s - 0 \cdot 4 x_t = 20, \tag{4}$$

$$-0 \cdot 1 x_c + 0 \cdot 9 x_s - 0 \cdot 2 x_t = 5, \tag{5}$$

$$-0 \cdot 2 x_c - 0 \cdot 1 x_s + 0 \cdot 8 x_t = 25, \tag{6}$$

Such a set of equations in the same number of unknowns can generally be solved uniquely. In this case we would obtain the solution

$$x_c = 56 \cdot 1, \qquad x_s = 22 \cdot 4, \qquad x_t = 48 \cdot 1.$$

The total labour requirement can then easily be obtained as

$$0 \cdot 6 \times 5 \cdot 61 + 0 \cdot 3 \times 22 \cdot 4 + 0 \cdot 2 \times 48 \cdot 1 = 50.$$

Clearly (4), (5), and (6) could be regarded as the constraints of a linear programming model. An objective function could be constructed and we could maximize it or minimize it subject to the constraints. As the model stands, however, there would be little point in doing this since there is generally only one feasible solution. The objective function would, therefore, have no influence on the solution.

Once, however, we extend this very simple type of input–output model we frequently obtain a genuine linear programming model.

The model described above is unrealistic in a number of respects. Equations (4), (5), and (6) give no real limitation to the productive capacity of the economy. It can fairly easily be shown that so long as a particular, positive, bill of goods can be produced (the economy is a 'productive' one) then these relationships guarantee that any bill of goods, however large, can be produced. This is clearly unrealistic. Firstly, we would expect there to be some limitation on productive capacity preventing more than a certain amount of output from each industry in a given period of time. Secondly, we would expect the output from an industry only to be effective as the input to another industry after a certain time has elapsed. This second consideration leads to *dynamic input–output models* which are considered below. Before doing this, however, we will consider the problem of modelling limited productive capacity in the case of a *static* model.

In our small example we assumed that once we had decided how much each industry should produce in order to meet a specified bill of goods we could provide the labour required. If labour were in short supply it might limit our productive capacity. There would then be interest in seeing what bills of goods are or are not producible in a particular period of time. Returning to our example, if we were to limit labour to 40 (£m per year) we could not produce our previous bill of goods. But what bill of goods could we produce? Answers to this question can be explored through linear programming. Variables will now represent our bill of goods:

$$\begin{array}{ll} \text{Coal} & y_c \\ \text{Steel} & y_s \\ \text{Transport} & y_t \end{array}$$

Equations (4), (5), and (6) will give the constraints

$$0 \cdot 9 x_c - 0 \cdot 5 x_s - 0 \cdot 4 x_t - y_c = 0, \tag{7}$$

$$-0 \cdot 1 x_c + 0 \cdot 9 x_s - 0 \cdot 2 x_t - y_s = 0, \tag{8}$$

$$-0 \cdot 2 x_c - 0 \cdot 1 x_s + 0 \cdot 8 x_t - y_t = 0. \tag{9}$$

The labour limitation gives the constraint

$$0 \cdot 6 x_c + 0 \cdot 3 x_s + 0 \cdot 2 x_t \leqslant 40. \tag{10}$$

Achievable bills of goods will be represented by the values of y_c, y_r, and y_t in feasible solutions to (7), (8), (9), and (10). Specific solutions can be found by introducing an objective function. For example, we might wish to maximize the total output:

$$x_c + x_s + x_t. \tag{11}$$

Alternatively we might weight some outputs more heavily than others by giving x_c, x_s, and x_t different objective coefficients. We might wish simply to maximize production in one particular sector of the economy, such as steel, and simply maximize x_s. This is clearly a situation of the type referred to in Section 3.2 in which it is of interest to experiment with a number of different objectives rather than simply concentrate on one.

We have only considered labour as a limiting factor in productive capacity. In practice there could well be other resource limitations such as processing capacity, raw material, etc. Such limitations could, of course, easily be incorporated in a model by extra constraints. Limited resources of this sort are sometimes known as *primary goods*. Primary goods only provide inputs to the economy. They are not produced as outputs as well. A major advantage of treating such models as linear programming models is that a lot of subsidiary economic information is also obtained from solving such a model. Such information is described very fully in Section 6.2. In particular, valuations are obtained for the constraints of a model. These valuations are known as *shadow prices*. For the type of model considered here we would obtain meaningful valuations for the primary goods. In this way a pricing system could be introduced into our model. This would give suitable prices for the outputs from all the industries.

Although any number of primary goods can be considered in a linear programming formulation of an input–output model it is quite common only to consider labour. In practice, particularly in the simple economies of under-developed countries, it may well not be unreasonable to consider labour as the overall limitation. If this can be done there is another less obvious advantage to be gained in the applicability of such a model. It has already been pointed out that an input–output model assumes *non-substitutability* of the inputs, i.e. it is not possible to vary the relative proportions in which all the inputs are used to produce the output of a particular industry. In practice this might well be a far from realistic assumption. For example, we might well be able to produce each unit of coal by using more power (more coal) and less machinery (less steel). To model this possibility would require a variation in the coefficients of the input–output matrix. It has been shown that if there is only one primary good (usually labour), then it will only be worthwhile to concentrate on one production process for each industry. This is the result of the *Samuelson substitution theorem* which we will not prove. Such theoretical results and a fuller description of input–output models are given in Dorfman, Samuelson, and Solow (1958). Another good reference is Shapiro (1979). The importance of this result is that we need not worry about the apparent non-substitutability limitation so long as we only have one primary good. There will be one, and only one best set of inputs (production processes) for each industry. This best production process will remain the best no matter what bill of goods we are producing. There is, of course, the problem of finding, for each industry, that production process which should be used. Once, however, this has been done, no matter what the bill of goods, we need only incorporate

Table 5.2. An input–output matrix with alternative production processes

Inputs	Outputs					
	Coal		Steel		Transport	
Coal	0·1	0·2	0·5	0·6	0·4	0·6
Steel	0·1	—	0·1	0·1	0·2	0·2
Transport	0·2	0·1	0·1	—	0·2	0·05
Labour	0·6	0·7	0·3	0·3	0·2	0·15

this one production process (column of the input–output matrix) into all future models. In fact the finding of the best production process for each industry can be done by linear programming. To illustrate how this may be done as well as illuminating the import of the Samuelson substitution theorem we will extend our small example. Table 5.2 gives two possible sets of inputs (production processes) to produce one unit of the three industries.

In practice there might be many more (possibly an infinite number) than two processes for each industry.

On the face of it we might think it advantageous to use some combination of the two processes for producing coal. The first process is more economical on coal but uses some steel as well, which the second process does not. Similarly some mixture of the two processes for producing steel and the two processes for producing transport might seem appropriate. Moreover, which processes are used might seem likely to depend upon the particular bill of goods.

We repeat, however, that our intuitive idea would be false. There will be exactly one best process for each industry and this will be used whatever bill of goods we have. Instead of the variables x_c, x_s, and x_t in our original model we can introduce variables x_{c1}, x_{c2}, x_{s1}, x_{s2}, x_{t1}, and x_{t2} to represent the total quantities of coal, steel, and transport produced by each process. Using the same bill of goods as before, instead of constraints (1), (2), and (3), we obtain

$$x_{c1} + x_{c2} = 20 + 0\cdot1x_{c1} + 0\cdot2x_{c2} + 0\cdot5x_{s1} + 0\cdot6x_{s2} + 0\cdot4x_{t1} + 0\cdot6\ x_{t2}, \quad (11)$$

$$x_{s1} + x_{s2} = 5 + 0\cdot1x_{c1} + 0\cdot0x_{c2} + 0\cdot1x_{s1} + 0\cdot1x_{s2} + 0\cdot2x_{t1} + 0\cdot2\ x_{t2}, \quad (12)$$

$$x_{t1} + x_{t2} = 25 + 0\cdot2x_{c1} + 0\cdot1x_{c2} + 0\cdot1x_{s1} + 0\cdot0x_{s2} + 0\cdot2x_{t1} + 0\cdot05x_{t2}. \quad (13)$$

These equations can be written as

$$0\cdot9x_{c1} + 0\cdot8x_{c2} - 0\cdot5x_{s1} - 0\cdot6x_{s2} - 0\cdot4x_{t1} - 0\cdot6x_{t2} = 20, \quad (14)$$

$$-0\cdot1x_{c1} - 0\cdot0x_{c2} + 0\cdot9x_{s1} + 0\cdot9x_{s2} - 0\cdot2x_{t1} - 0\cdot2x_{t2} = 5. \quad (15)$$

$$-0\cdot2x_{c1} - 0\cdot1x_{c2} - 0\cdot1x_{s1} - 0\cdot0x_{s2} + 0\cdot8x_{t1} + 0\cdot95x_{t2} = 25. \quad (16)$$

We are considering labour as the only primary good and will limit ourselves to 60 (£m). This gives the constraint

$$0\cdot6x_{c1} + 0\cdot7x_{c2} + 0\cdot3x_{s1} + 0\cdot3x_{s2} + 0\cdot2x_{t1} + 0\cdot15x_{t2} \leqslant 60. \quad (17)$$

There will generally be more than one solution to a system such as this. In order to find the 'best' solution we will define an objective function. One possible objective function would, of course, be to ignore constraint (17) and minimize the expression on the left-hand side representing labour usage. Alternatively we might specify another objective function. For this example we will do this and simply maximize total output:

$$x_{c1} + x_{c2} + x_{s1} + x_{s2} + x_{t1} + x_{t2}. \tag{18}$$

Our resultant optimal solution gives

$$x_{c1} = 64 \cdot 6,$$
$$x_{c2} = 0,$$
$$x_{s1} = 22 \cdot 6,$$
$$x_{s2} = 0,$$
$$x_{t1} = 0,$$
$$x_{t2} = 44 \cdot 6.$$

Notice that the Samuelson substitution theorem has worked in this case. One process in each industry is the best to the total exclusion of all the others. Moreover, it could be shown that these processes will be the best no matter what the bill of goods is. The optimal solution will be made up of only the variables x_{c1}, x_{s1}, and x_{t2} no matter what the right-hand side coefficients in constraints (14), (15), (16), and (17) are. We could, therefore, confine all our attention to these processes and ignore the others. It should be noted, however, that these 'best' processes are only the best because of the objective function (18) which we have chosen. If instead of maximizing output we were to choose another objective, it might be preferable to switch to another process in some cases. It will never, however, be worth 'mixing' processes. Once we consider more than a single primary good such mixing may well, however, become desirable.

The Dynamic Model

We have pointed out that our static model assumed that we could ignore time lags between an output being produced and used as an input to another (or the same) industry. This unrealistic assumption can be avoided by introducing a *dynamic model*. It has already been shown in Section 4.1 that linear programming models can often be extended to multi-period models. We can do much the same thing with the static type of input–output model. In practice some of the output from an economy will immediately be consumed (e.g. cars for private motoring) while some will go to increase productive capacity (e.g. factory machinery). Such alternative uses for the output will result in different possible growth patterns for the economy, i.e. we can live well now but neglect to invest for the future or we can sacrifice present day consumption in the interests of future wealth producing capacity. A simple example of such a problem, ECONOMIC PLANNING, leading to a dynamic input–output model is given in Part 2. Rather than discuss dynamic input–output models further here, the discussion is postponed to the specific discussion of the formulation of this problem in Part 3. A description of dynamic input–output models of this type is given by Wagner (1957).

Aggregation

To sum up the characteristics of a whole industry or sector of an economy in one column of an input–output matrix obviously requires a large amount of simplification of the real situation. It is necessary to group together many different industries into one. This *aggregation* is necessary in order to obtain a reasonable size of problem. Most input–output models are aggregated into less than 1000 industries. The problem of aggregation is obviously of paramount concern to the model builder. Unfortunately very little theoretical work has been done to indicate *mathematically* when aggregation is and is not justified. Three criteria which common sense would suggest to be good grounds for aggregating particular industries are: (i) substitutability, (ii) complementarity, and (iii) similarity of production processes. Problems of this sort are discussed more fully by Stone (1960).

In view of their sophistication and efficiency commercial mathematical programming packages provide a useful way of solving input–output models. Even if the model is of the simplest kind described above and only requires the solution of a set of simultaneous equations such packages are of use. Almost all packages contain an inversion routine which is very useful for inverting large matrices (sets of simultaneous equations). It should, however, be pointed out that input–output models are often quite dense. In this respect they are untypical of general linear programming models. As already mentioned in Section 2.1, in a thousand-constraint model one would expect only about 1% of the coefficients to be non-zero. For an input–output model this figure could well be as high as 50%. As a result input–output models can take a long time to solve on a computer and run into numerical difficulties. It is sometimes worth exploiting the special structure of an input–output linear programming model and using a special purpose algorithm. Dantzig (1955) describes how the simplex algorithm can be adapted to this purpose.

5.3 Network Models

The use of models involving networks is very widespread in operational research. Problems involving distribution, assignment, and planning (critical path analysis and PERT) frequently give rise to the analysis of networks. Many of the resultant problems can be regarded as special types of linear programming problem. It is often more efficient to use special purpose algorithms rather than the revised simplex algorithm. Nevertheless it is important for the model builder to be aware when he is dealing with a special kind of linear programming model. In order to solve his model it may be useful to adapt the simplex algorithm to suit the special structure. It may even, sometimes, be worthwhile ignoring the special structure and using a general purpose package program. Since such programs are often highly efficient and well designed their speeds outweigh the algorithmic efficiency of less well designed but more specialized programs.

It is not intended that the coverage of this topic be comprehensive. The main aim is simply to show the connection between network models and linear programming models. References are given to much fuller treatments of the subject.

The Transportation Problem

This famous type of problem first described by Hitchcock (1941) is usefully regarded as one of obtaining the minimum cost flow through a special type of network.

Suppose that a number of suppliers $(S_1, S_2, ..., S_m)$ are to provide a number of customers $(T_1, T_2, ..., T_n)$ with a commodity. The transportation problem is how to meet each customer's requirement, while not exceeding the capacity of any supplier, at minimum cost. Costs are known for supplying one unit of the commodity from each S_i to each T_j. In some cases it may not be possible to supply a particular customer T_j from a particular supplier S_i. It is sometimes useful to regard these costs as infinite in such cases. In distribution problems these costs will often be related to the distances between S_i and T_j. It is assumed that the capacity of each supplier (over some period such as a year) is known and the requirement of each customer T_j is also known. In order to describe the problem further we will consider a small numerical example.

Example 1. A Transportation Problem

Three suppliers (S_1, S_2, S_3) are used to provide four customers (T_1, T_2, T_3, T_4) with their requirements for a particular commodity over a year. The yearly capacities of the suppliers and requirements of the customers are given below (in suitable units)

Suppliers	S_1	S_2	S_3	
Capacities (per year)	135	56	93	
Customers	T_1	T_2	T_3	T_4
Requirements (per year)	62	83	39	91

The unit costs for supplying each customer from each supplier are given in Table 5.3 (in £/unit).

Table 5.3

	Customer			
Supplier	T_1	T_2	T_3	T_4
S_1	132	$—^a$	97	103
S_2	85	91	—	—
S_3	106	89	100	98

^{a}A dash indicates the impossibility of certain suppliers for certain depots or customers.

We can easily formulate this problem as a conventional linear programming model by introducing variables x_{ij} to represent the quantity of the commodity sent from S_i to T_j in a year. The resultant model is:

Minimize

$$132x_{11} + Mx_{12} + 97x_{13} + 103x_{14} + 85x_{21} + 91x_{22} + Mx_{23} + Mx_{24} + 106x_{31}$$
$$+ 89x_{32} + 100x_{33} + 98x_{34} \tag{1}$$

subject to

$$x_{11} + x_{12} + x_{13} + x_{14} \leqslant 135, (2)$$

$$x_{21} + x_{22} + x_{23} + x_{24} \leqslant 56, (3)$$

$$x_{31} + x_{32} + x_{33} + x_{34} \leqslant 93, (4)$$

$$x_{11} + x_{21} + x_{31} = 62, (5)$$

$$x_{12} + x_{22} + x_{32} = 83, (6)$$

$$x_{13} + x_{23} + x_{33} = 39, (7)$$

$$x_{14} + x_{24} + x_{34} = 91, (8)$$

$$x_{ij} \geqslant 0, \quad \text{all } i, j.$$

This model obviously has a very special structure to which we will refer later. Notice that we have included variables for non-allowed routes in the model with objective coefficients M (some very large number). This has been done simply to preserve the pattern of the model. In practice, if we were to solve the model as a linear programming problem of this form we would simply leave these variables out.

Constraints (2), (3), and (4) are known as *availability constraints*. There is one such constraint for each of the three suppliers. These constraints ensure that the total quantity out of a supplier (in a year) does not exceed his capacity. Constraints (5), (6), (7), and (8) are known as *requirement constraints*. These constraints ensure that each customer obtains his requirement. In some formulations of the transportation problem constraints (2), (3), and (4) are treated as ' = ' instead of ' ⩽ '. If the sum total of the availabilities exactly matches the sum total of the requirements then this is acceptable since all capacities must obviously be completely exhausted. In a case such as our numerical examples, however, this is not so. Total capacity (284) exceeds total demand (275). This can be coped with by introducing a dummy customer T_5 with a requirement for the excess of 9. If the cost of meeting this requirement of T_5 from each supplier S_i, is made zero we have equated total capacity to total demand with no inaccuracy in our modified model. The three constraints (2), (3), and (4) could then be made ' = '. When special algorithms are used to solve the transportation problem the employment of devices such as this is sometimes necessary. For a conventional linear programming formulation of the problem this is not necessary. For a general transportation problem with m suppliers $(S_1, S_2, ..., S_m)$ and n customers $(T_1, T_2, ..., T_n)$ there will be m availability constraints and n requirement constraints giving a total of $m + n$ constraints. If each supplier can be potentially used for each customer there will be mn variables in the linear programming model. Clearly for practical problems involving large numbers of suppliers and customers the linear programming model could be very large. This is one motive for using special algorithms.

The above problem can be looked at graphically as illustrated in Figure 5.1.

In the network of Figure 5.1 we have the suppliers S_1, S_2, and S_3 and the five customers T_1, T_2, T_3, T_4, and T_5 (including the dummy customer). S_i and T_j provide the *nodes* of the network to which we have attached the (positive) capacities or (negative) requirements. The possible supply patterns S_i to T_j provide the *arcs* of the network to which we have attached the unit supply costs. Our problem can now be regarded more abstractly as one where we wish to obtain the *minimum cost flow* through the network. The S_i nodes are

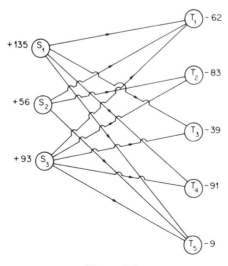

Figure 5.1

'sources' for the flow entering the system and the T_j nodes are 'sinks' where flow leaves the system. We must ensure that there is continuity of flow at each node (total flow in equals total flow out). These conditions give rise to material balance constraints of the type discussed in Section 3.3.

If x_{ij} represents the quantity of flow in the arc i to j we obtain the following constraints:

$$-x_{11} - x_{13} - x_{14} - x_{15} \qquad\qquad\qquad = -135, \quad (9)$$

$$-x_{21} - x_{22} - x_{25} \qquad\qquad = -56, \quad (10)$$

$$-x_{31} - x_{32} - x_{33} - x_{34} - x_{35} = -93, \quad (11)$$

$$x_{11} \qquad\quad + x_{21} \qquad + x_{31} \qquad\qquad = 62, \quad (12)$$

$$x_{22} \qquad + x_{32} \qquad\qquad = 83, \quad (13)$$

$$x_{13} \qquad\qquad + x_{33} \qquad = 39, \quad (14)$$

$$x_{14} \qquad\qquad + x_{34} \quad = 91, \quad (15)$$

$$x_{15} \qquad + x_{25} \qquad\qquad + x_{35} = 9. \quad (16)$$

These constraints are clearly equivalent to the constraints (2) to (8). We have, however, added the dummy customer T_5. This has resulted in the additional variables x_{15}, x_{25}, and x_{35}, and an added constraint (16), but allowed us to deal entirely with ' = ' constraints. We have also revised the signs on both sides of the availability constraints. For more general minimum cost flow problems, which we consider later, it is convenient to give negative coefficients to flows *out* of a node and positive coefficients to flows *in*. Therefore this convention has been applied here.

The transportation problem also arises in less obvious contexts than distribution. We give a numerical example below of a production planning problem.

Example 2. Production Planning

A company produces a commodity in two shifts (regular working and overtime) to meet known demands for the present and future. Over the next four months the production capacities and demands (in thousands of units producible) are

	January	February	March	April
Regular working	100	150	140	160
Overtime	50	75	70	80
Demand	80	200	300	200

The cost of production of each unit is £1 if done in regular working or £1.50 if done in overtime. Units produced can be stored before delivery at a cost of £0.30 per month per unit.

The problem is how much to produce each month to satisfy present and future demand.

It is convenient to summarize the costs in Table 5.4 (in £).

Clearly it is impossible to produce for demand of an earlier month. This is represented by a dash in the positions indicated (an infinite unit cost). The other unit costs arise from a combination of production and storage costs, e.g. production in January by overtime working for delivery in March gives a unit cost of £1·50 (production) + £0·60 (storage) = £2·10. This cost matrix is of the same form as that given for the transportation problem in Table 5.3. Although the problem here is not one of distribution it can still therefore be regarded as a transportation problem. In this case there are eight sources and five sinks including the 'surplus' demand of 45 units.

Transportation problems are obviously expressed much more compactly in a square array such as Tables 5.3 and 5.4 rather than as a linear programming matrix. This is one virtue of using a special purpose algorithm. Dantzig (1951) uses the simplex algorithm but works within this compact format. The special structure results in the algorithm taking a particularly simple form. An alternative algorithm for the transportation problem is due to Ford and Fulkerson (1956). This algorithm is usefully thought of as a special case of a general algorithm for finding the minimum cost flow through a network. Such problems are considered below and described in Ford and Fulkerson (1962).

As a result of their special structure transportation problems are particularly

Table 5.4

Production		Demand			
		January	February	March	April
January	Regular	1	1·3	1·6	1·9
	Overtime	1·5	1·8	2·1	2·4
February	Regular	—	1	1·3	1·6
	Overtime	—	1·5	1·8	2·1
March	Regular	—	—	1	1·3
	Overtime	—	—	1·5	1·8
April	Regular	—	—	—	1
	Overtime	—	—	—	1·5

easy to solve in comparison with other linear programming problems of comparable size. They also have (together with some other network flow problems) the very important property that so long as the availabilities and requirements at the sources and sinks are integral the values of the variables in the optimal solution will also be so. For example, so long as the right-hand side coefficients in the constraints (2) to (8) of the linear programming problem of Example 1 are integers, the variable values in the optimal solution will be as well. This rather surprising property of the transportation problem is computationally very important in many circumstances since it avoids the necessity of using *integer programming* to ensure that variables take integer values. As will be discussed in Chapters 8, 9, and 10 integer programming models are generally much more difficult to solve than linear programming models.

Sufficient conditions for a model to be expressible as a network flow problem are discussed in Section 10.1. The recognition of such conditions is important since it allows the use of specialized efficient algorithms and avoids the use of computationally expensive integer programming.

A further constraint that sometimes applies to transportation problems is that there are limits to the possible flow from a source to a sink. This gives rise to the *capacitated transportation problem*. There may be both lower and upper limits for the flow in each arc. For the linear programming formulation of the transportation problem (such as exemplified in Example 1 above) such limits can be accommodated by simple bounds on the variables:

$$0 \leqslant l_{ij} \leqslant x_{ij} \leqslant u_{ij}.$$

Frequently l_{ij} will be 0. Capacitated transportation problems can, like the ordinary transportation problem, be solved by straightforward extensions to the special purpose algorithms mentioned above.

Another non-distribution example of the transportation problem is described by Stanley, Honig, and Gainen (1954), who describe how the problem arises in deciding how a government should award contracts.

The Assignment Problem

This is the problem of assigning n people to n jobs so as to maximize some overall level of competence. For example person i might take an average time t_{ij} to do job j. In order to assign each person to a job and to fill each job so as to minimize total time for all tasks our problem would be:

$$\text{Minimize} \quad \sum_{i,j} t_{ij} x_{ij}$$

$$\text{subject to} \quad \sum_{i} x_{ij} = 1 \text{ for all } j, \tag{17}$$

$$\sum_{j} x_{ij} = 1 \text{ for all } i, \tag{18}$$

where

$$x_{ij} = \begin{cases} 1 & \text{if person } i \text{ is assigned to job } j, \\ 0 & \text{otherwise.} \end{cases}$$

This can obviously be regarded as a special case of the transportation problem. We can regard it as a problem with n sources and n sinks. Each source has an availability of 1 unit and each sink has a demand of 1 unit. Constraints (17) impose the condition that each job be filled. Constraints (18) impose the condition that every person be assigned a job.

It might appear that this problem demands integer programming in order to ensure that x_{ij} can only take the values 0 or 1. Fortunately, however, because this problem is a special case of the transportation problem the integrality property mentioned above holds. If we solve an assignment problem as a conventional linear programming model we can be certain that the optimal solution will give integer values to the x_{ij} (0 or 1). If marriage is regarded as an assignment problem of this kind Dantzig has suggested that the integrality property shows that monogamy leads to greatest overall happiness!

Obviously assignment problems could be solved as linear programming models although the resultant models could be very large. For example the assigning of 100 people to 100 jobs would lead to a model with 10 000 variables. It is much more efficient to use a specialized algorithm. One of the specialized algorithms for the transportation problem could obviously be applied. The most efficient method known is one allied to the Ford and Fulkerson algorithm but more specialized. This is known as the Hungarian method and is described by Kuhn (1955).

The Transhipment Problem

This is an extension of the transportation problem, due to Orden (1956). In this problem it is possible to distribute the commodity through intermediate sources and through intermediate sinks as well as from sources to sinks. In Example 1 we could allow flow (at a certain cost) between suppliers S_1, S_2, and S_3 as well as between customers T_1, T_2, T_3, and T_4. It might be advantageous sometimes to send a commodity from one supplier to another before dispatching it to the customer. Similarly it might be advantageous to send a commodity to a customer via another customer first. The transhipment problem allows for these possibilities.

If we extend Example 1 to allow the use of certain intermediate sources and sinks our graphical representation would be of the form of Figure 5.2.

Costs have now been attached to the arcs between sources and the arcs between sinks. Notice that it is sometimes possible to go either way between sources (or sinks), at not necessarily the same cost.

It is possible to convert a transhipment problem into a transportation problem. To do this the sources and sinks are considered firstly as being all sources and then as all sinks. When considered as sinks, sources have no

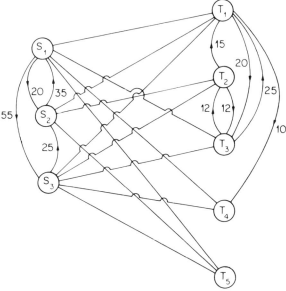

Figure 5.2

availabilities and when considered as sources, sinks have no requirements. Flow from a sink to a source is not allowed. For the transhipment extension of Example 1 illustrated in Figure 5.2 we can draw up the unit cost array of Table 5.5. 'Sources' T_1, T_2, T_3, and T_5 will have zero availabilities and 'sinks' S_1, S_2, and S_3 zero requirements.

Transhipment problems can obviously be formulated as linear programming models just as the transportation problem can. Again it is often desirable to use a specialized algorithm such as that described by Dantzig (1951) or by Ford and Fulkerson (1962).

As with transportation problems, transhipment problems can be extended

Table 5.5

| Sources | Sinks | | | | | | | |
	S_1	S_2	S_3	T_1	T_2	T_3	T_4	(T_5)
S_1	—	20	55	132	—	97	103	0
S_2	35	—	—	85	91	—	—	0
S_3	—	25	—	106	89	100	98	0
T_1	—	—	—	—	—	20	10	—
T_2	—	—	—	15	—	12	—	—
T_3	—	—	—	25	12	—	—	—
T_4	—	—	—	—	—	—	—	—
(T_5)	—	—	—	—	—	—	—	—

to capacitated transhipment problems where the arcs have upper and lower capacity limitations. These can also be solved by specialized algorithms.

An application of the transhipment problem outside the field of distribution is described by Srinivasan (1974).

The Minimum Cost Flow Problem

The transportation, transhipment, and assignment problems are all special cases of the general problem of finding a minimum cost flow through a network. Such problems may have upper and lower capacities attached to the arcs in the capacitated case. The uncapacitated case will be considered here.

Example 3. Minimum Cost Flow

The network in Figure 5.3 has two sources 0 and 1 with availabilities of 10 and 15. There are three sinks 5, 6, and 7 with requirements 9, 10, and 6 respectively. Each arc has a unit cost of flow associated with it.

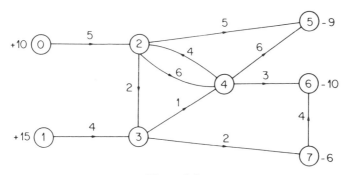

Figure 5.3

The arcs are 'directed' in the sense that only flow in the direction marked by the arrow is allowed. If flow is allowable in the opposite direction as well, this is indicated by another arc in the reverse direction. This happens in the case of the two arcs between node 2 and node 4.

The problem is simply to satisfy the requirements at the sinks by flow through the network from the sources at total minimum cost. In this case the total availability exactly equals the total requirement. This can always be made possible by the use of a dummy sink if necessary as described for the transportation problem in Example 1.

The linear programming formulation of Example 3 is:

Minimize

$$5x_{02} + 4x_{13} + 2x_{23} + 6x_{24} + 5x_{25} + x_{34} + 2x_{37} + 4x_{42} + 6x_{45} + 3x_{46} + 4x_{76}$$

subject to

$$-x_{02} \qquad\qquad\qquad\qquad\qquad\qquad\qquad\qquad = -10, \quad (19)$$

$$\qquad -x_{13} \qquad\qquad\qquad\qquad\qquad\qquad\qquad = -15, \quad (20)$$

$$x_{02} \qquad -x_{23}-x_{24}-x_{25} \qquad\qquad +x_{42} \qquad = \quad 0, \quad (21)$$

$$x_{13}+x_{23} \qquad\qquad -x_{34}-x_{37} \qquad\qquad = \quad 0, \quad (22)$$

$$x_{24} \qquad +x_{34} \qquad -x_{42}-x_{45}-x_{46} \qquad = \quad 0, \quad (23)$$

$$x_{25} \qquad\qquad +x_{45} \qquad\qquad = \quad 9, \quad (24)$$

$$x_{46}+x_{76} = \quad 10, \quad (25)$$

$$x_{37} \qquad\qquad -x_{76} = \quad 6. \quad (26)$$

In order to be systematic about this formulation it is convenient to regard each constraint as arising from the *material balance requirement* at each node. For example, at node 2 it is necessary to ensure that the total flow in ($x_{02} + x_{42}$) is the same as the total flow out ($x_{23} + x_{24} + x_{25}$). This is achieved by constraint (21). At node 7 which is a sink the total flow in (x_{37}) must again be the same as the total flow out ($x_{76} + 6$). This gives constraint (26).

The matrix of coefficients in constraints (19) to (26) of the model above is known as the *incidence matrix* of the network in Figure 5.3. It clearly has a very special structure. This structure is further discussed in Section 10.1 since, like the transportation problem, the minimum cost flow problem (whether capacitated or not) can be guaranteed to yield an optimal *integer* solution so long as the availabilities, requirements, and arc capacities are integer.

As with the other types of model so far discussed in this section it is generally more efficient to use specialized algorithms. Those due to Dantzig (1951) and Ford and Fulkerson (1962) are also applicable here.

A comprehensive survey of applications of the minimum cost network flow problem is given by Bradley (1975). Other useful references are Glover and Klingman (1977) and Jensen and Barnes (1980).

It is sometimes possible to convert a linear programming model into a form which is immediately convertible into a network flow model. A procedure for doing this, or showing such a conversion to be impossible, is given in Section 5.4.

If arcs have lower or upper bounds (or both) on their capacities, then (as with the special case of the transportation problem) it is possible to adapt the special algorithms to cope with this. It is, however, worth pointing out that such models can be converted to the uncapacitated case. This might be necessary if a program was being used which could not deal with such bounds.

Suppose the flow from node i to node j had a lower bound of l (and cost c_{ij}). An extra node i' can be added with a new arc from i to i'. If there is an external flow l *out* of i and *into* i', as shown in Figure 5.4, this provides the

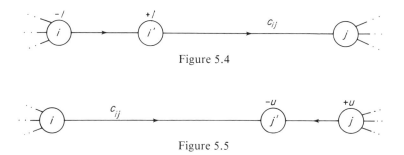

Figure 5.4

Figure 5.5

necessary restriction. Similarly Figure 5.5 demonstrates how an upper bound of u can be imposed on the flow in arc ij.

It is important to ensure that a minimum cost network flow problem is well defined. For example the unit flow costs are generally non-negative. If negative costs are allowed it is important to ensure that cost cannot be minimized indefinitely (giving an *unbounded* problem). This could happen, for example if arc 2–4 were given in a unit cost of -6 instead of $+6$. Going round the loop indefinitely would continuously reduce the cost.

A minimum cost network flow problem, DISTRIBUTION, is given in Part 2.

An extension of the problem of finding the minimum cost flow of a single commodity through a network is the problem of minimizing the cost of the flows of several commodities through a network. This is the *minimum cost multi-commodity network flow problem*. There will be capacity limitations on the flows of individual commodities through certain arcs as well as capacity limitations on the total flow of all commodities through individual arcs. For example, in the network of Figure 5.3 one commodity might flow between source 0 and sink 5 and a second commodity flow between source 1 and sinks 6 and 7. This type of problem can again be formulated as a linear programming model. The resultant model has a block angular structure of the type discussed in Section 4.1. The block angular structure makes the decomposition procedure of Dantzig and Wolfe, which is discussed in Section 4.2, applicable. In fact this leads to another linear programming formulation of the problem. This aspect of the minimum cost multi-commodity network flow problem is discussed by Tomlin (1966).

Apart from decomposition there are no special algorithms applicable to the general minimum cost multi-commodity network flow problem. The (often large) linear programming model resulting from such a problem is best solved by the standard revised simplex algorithm using a package programme.

Charnes and Cooper (1961a) formulate a traffic flow problem as a minimum cost multi-commodity network flow model.

This extension of the single-commodity network flow linear programming model to more than one commodity destroys the property that guarantees an integral optimal solution. Fractional values for the flows may result from the optimum solution to the linear programming model even if all capacities, availabilities, and requirements are integral. If the nature of the problem requires an optimal integer solution it is necessary to resort to *integer programming*.

Another important extension of the minimum cost network flow model is the *generalized network flow model*. This is sometimes known as the *network flow with gains model*. In this extension the flow in an arc may alter between the two nodes. A multiplier is then associated with each arc which gives the factor by which flow is altered. Situations which require this modification result from, for example, evaporation, wastage or application of interest rates. Glover and Klingman (1977) give applications. If it is necessary that the flows be *integer* then this can no longer be guaranteed from a linear programming solution. It is necessary to use integer programming methods. Nevertheless it is possible to exploit this simple structure to good effect in the algorithms used. Glover *et al.* (1978) describe such a method. In fact any 0−1 integer programming problem can be converted into such a generalized network model where flows must be integer. This is shown by Glover and Mulvey (1980).

The Shortest Path Problem

This is the problem of finding a shortest path between two nodes through a network. Rather surprisingly this problem can be regarded as a special case of the minimum cost flow problem.

Example 4. Finding the Shortest Path Through a Network

In the network in Figure 5.6 we wish to find the shortest path between node 0 and node 8. The lengths of each arc are marked.

We can reduce this problem to one of finding a minimum cost flow through the network by giving node 0 an availability of 1 unit (a source) and giving node 8 a requirement of 1 unit (a sink). Because of the property that minimum cost flow (as with transportation, transhipment and assignment) problems have of guaranteeing integral optimal flows, when solved as linear programming models, we can be sure that this minimal cost flow through each arc in Figure 5.6 will be 0 or 1. Exactly one of the arcs out of node 0 will therefore have a flow of 1 and exactly one of the flows into node 8 will have a flow of 1. Similarly intermediate nodes on the flow path will have exactly one arc with flow in and one with flow out. The 'cost' of the optimal flow path will give the shortest route between 0 and 8.

Although it is possible to use conventional linear programming to solve shortest path problems it would be more efficient to use a specialized algorithm. One of the most efficient such algorithms is due to Dijkstra (1959).

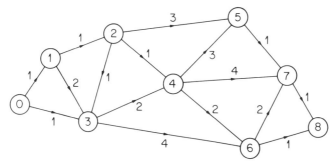

Figure 5.6

Maximum Flow Through Network

When a network has capacity limitations on the flow through arcs there is often interest in finding the maximum flow of some commodity between sources and sinks. We will again consider the network of Example 3 but our objective will now be to maximize the flows into the sources and out of the sinks rather than these quantities being given. Each arc has now been given an upper capacity which is the figure attached to it in Figure 5.7.

Example 5. Maximizing the Flow Through a Network

This problem can again be formulated as a linear programming model. The variables and constraints will be the same as those in Example 3 apart from the introduction of five new variables x_{S0}, x_{S1}, x_{5T}, x_{6T}, and x_{7T} representing the flows into sources 0 and 1 and out of sinks 5, 6, and 7. The resultant model is

Maximize $\qquad\qquad\qquad\qquad\qquad x_{S0} + x_{S1}$

subject to

$$
\begin{array}{ll}
x_{S0} \quad - x_{02} & = 0, \quad (27) \\
x_{S1} \quad - x_{13} & = 0, \quad (28) \\
x_{02} \quad - x_{23} - x_{24} - x_{25} \quad + x_{42} & = 0, \quad (29) \\
x_{13} + x_{23} \quad - x_{34} - x_{37} & = 0, \quad (30) \\
x_{24} \quad + x_{34} \quad - x_{42} - x_{45} - x_{46} & = 0, \quad (31) \\
x_{25} \quad + x_{45} \quad - x_{5T} & = 0, \quad (32) \\
x_{46} + x_{76} \quad - x_{6T} & = 0, \quad (33) \\
x_{37} \quad - x_{76} \quad - x_{7T} = 0, \quad (34)
\end{array}
$$

$x_{02} \leqslant 12, x_{13} \leqslant 20, x_{23} \leqslant 6, x_{24} \leqslant 3, x_{25} \leqslant 6, x_{34} \leqslant 7, x_{37} \leqslant 9, x_{42} \leqslant 2, x_{45} \leqslant 5, x_{46} \leqslant 8, x_{76} \leqslant 4$.

Again this type of model has the property that the optimal solution will give integer flows so long as the capacities are integer.

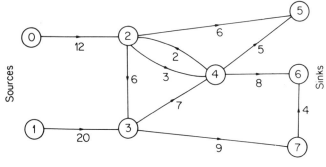

Figure 5.7

It is again more efficient to use a specialized algorithm for this type of problem. Such an algorithm is described by Ford and Fulkerson (1962).

Critical Path Analysis

This is a method of planning projects (often in the construction industry) which can be represented by a network. The arcs of the network represent *activities* occupying a duration of time, e.g. building the walls of a house, and the nodes are used to indicate the termination and beginning of activities. Once a project has been represented by such a network model the network can be analysed to answer a number of questions such as

(i) How long will it take to complete the project?
(ii) Which activities can be delayed if necessary and by how long without delaying the overall project?

Such a mathematical analysis of this kind of network is known as *critical path analysis*. The arcs for those activities in the network which cannot be delayed without affecting the overall completion time of the project can be shown to lie on a path. This *critical path* is in fact the *longest path* through the network. The problem of finding the critical path is a special kind of linear programming problem although the special structure of the problem makes a specialized algorithm appropriate.

Example 6. Finding the Critical Path in a Network

The network in Figure 5.8 represents a project of building a house. Each arc represents some activity forming part of the project. The durations (days) of the activities are attached to the corresponding arcs. The arc 4–2 marked with a broken line is a dummy activity having no duration. Its only purpose is to prevent activity 2–5 starting before activity 3–4 has finished.

In order to formulate this problem as a linear programming model we can

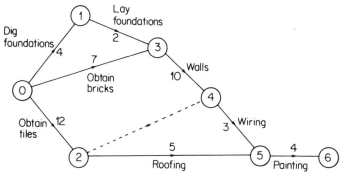

Figure 5.8

introduce the following variables:

t_0 start time for activities 0–1, 0–3, and 0–2
t_1 start time for activity 1–3
t_2 start time for activity 2–5
t_3 start time for activity 3–4
t_4 start time for activities 4–2 and 4–5
t_5 start time for activity 5–6
z finish time for the project.

Our model is then:

Minimize z

subject to

$$-t_0 + t_1 \geqslant 4, \tag{35}$$

$$-t_0 \quad + t_2 \geqslant 12, \tag{36}$$

$$-t_0 \quad + t_3 \geqslant 7, \tag{37}$$

$$-t_1 \quad + t_3 \geqslant 2, \tag{38}$$

$$-t_3 + t_4 \geqslant 10, \tag{39}$$

$$t_2 \quad - t_4 \geqslant 0, \tag{40}$$

$$-t_2 \quad + t_5 \geqslant 5, \tag{41}$$

$$-t_4 + t_5 \geqslant 3, \tag{42}$$

$$-t_5 + z \geqslant 4. \tag{43}$$

Each constraint represents a *sequencing relation* between certain activities. For example activity 3–4 cannot start before activity 1–3 has finished. This gives $t_3 \geqslant t_1 + 2$, which leads to constraint (38). Finally, since the project cannot be completed before activity 5–6 is finished we get constraint (43).

On solving this model we obtain the following results:

Project completion time $(z) = 26$ days

$$t_0 = 0,$$
$$t_1 = 4,$$
$$t_2 = 17,$$
$$t_3 = 7,$$
$$t_4 = 17,$$
$$t_5 = 22.$$

The critical path is clearly 0–3–4–2–5–6.

Building and conventionally solving the above linear programming model would be an inefficient method of finding the critical path. Special algorithms exist and there are widely used package programs for doing critical path analysis. Many extensions of the problem of scheduling a project in this way can be considered but are beyond the scope of this book. A full discussion of this subject is contained in Lockyer (1967).

One very practical extension of the problem is that of *allocating resources to the activities* in a project network. For example in the network of Figure 5.8 both activity 4–5 (wiring) and activity 2–5 (roofing) may require men (although in this contrived example they would probably be of different skills). If activity 4–5 requires three men and activity 2–5 requires six men and there are only eight men available, the optimal schedule given above is unattainable and one of those activities will have to be delayed or extended. The problem is then how to reschedule to achieve some objective. For example the objective might well be to delay the overall completion time as little as possible. Alternatively there might be a desire to 'smooth' the usage of this and other resources over time. This extension to the problem is mentioned again in Section 9.5 since it gives rise to an integer programming extension to the linear programming problem of the type above. Nevertheless integer programming would be generally far too costly in computer time to justify solving this type of problem in this way. A problem which gives rise to a very simple network is job-shop scheduling. This problem of scheduling jobs on machines can be regarded as a problem of allocating resources to activities in a network. The operations in the job shop (machining, etc.) give the activities. Sequencing relations between those operations give a (simple) network structure. The resources to be allocated are the limited machines.

All the problems described in this section (apart from the minimum cost multi-commodity network flow problem) are best tackled through specialized algorithms rather than the revised simplex algorithm available on commercial package programs. The reason for describing these problems and showing how they can, if necessary, be modelled as linear programs is that many practical problems are made up, in part, of network problems. Such problems often, however, contain additional complications which make it impossible to use a pure network model. This is where the conventional linear programming formulation becomes important. Many practical linear programming models have a very large network component. Such a feature usually makes very large models easy to solve using package programs. Some package programs have special features to take advantage of some of the network structure within a model. An example of this is the *generalized upper bound* (GUB) type of constraint which was mentioned in Section 3.3. In the linear programming formulation of the transportation problem in Example 1 constraints (2), (3), and (4) could be regarded as GUB constraints and not explicitly represented as constraints if a package with this facility was used. Alternatively (and preferably because there are more of them) constraints (5), (6), (7), and (8) could be represented as GUB constraints. The use of the GUB facility makes the solution of many network flow problems (or problems with a network flow component) particularly easy by conventional linear programming.

Another virtue in recognizing a network flow component in a linear programming model is that many variables are likely to come out at integer values in the optimal solution. It has been pointed out that this happens for all the variables in most of the network flow problems described in this section so long as the right-hand side coefficients are integers. If a model is 'not quite' of a network flow kind it is probable that the great majority of variables will still take integer values in the optimal linear programming solution. The computational difficulties of forcing all these variables to be integer by integer programming will be much reduced. This topic is discussed much more fully in Chapter 10.

There is also great virtue to be gained from remodelling a problem in order to get it into the form of a network flow model. This then opens up the possibility of using a special purpose algorithm. An example of how this can sometimes be done for a practical problem is given by Veinott and Wagner (1962). Dantzig (1969) shows how a hospital admissions scheduling program can be remodelled to give a linear programming model with a large network flow component. He then exploits this structure by use of the GUB facility. Other examples of reformulations into network flow models are Daniel (1973), Wilson and Willis (1983), and Cheshire, McKinnon and Williams (1984).

An automatic way of either converting a linear programming model to a network flow model or showing such a conversion to be impossible is given in Section 5.4. The recognition of, or conversion of, a model as a network structure relieves the need to use the computationally much more costly methods of integer programming.

In Section 6.2 the concept of the dual of a linear programming model is described. Every linear programming model has a corresponding model known as the *dual model*. The optimal solution to the dual model is very closely related to the optimal solution of the original model. In fact the optimal solution to either one can be derived very easily from the optimal solution to the other. It turns out that many practical problems give rise to a linear programming model which is the dual of a network flow model. In such circumstances it could well be worth using a specialized algorithm on the corresponding network flow model. Moreover, the dual of any of the types of network flow model mentioned here (apart from the minimum cost multi-commodity network flow model) also has the property of guaranteeing optimal integer solutions (so long as the objective coefficients of the original model are integers). The recognition of this type of model can, again, be of great practical importance for this reason. This topic is further discussed in Sections 10.1 and 10.2.

In Part 2 the OPENCAST MINING problem can be formulated as the dual of a network flow problem. The formulation is discussed in Part 3. The MINING problem of Part 2 can be formulated as an integer programming model, a large proportion of which is the dual of a network flow model. Some examples of such models are given in Williams (1982).

One famous network problem which has not been discussed in this section is the *travelling salesman problem*. This is the problem of finding a minimum distance (cost) route round a given set of cities. This problem cannot generally be solved by a linear programming model, in spite of its apparent similarity to the assignment problem. It can, however, be modelled as an integer programming extension to the assignment problem and is fully discussed in Section 9.5.

5.4   Converting Linear Programmes to Networks

The advantages of converting linear programs to minimum cost network flow models, if possible, have already been discussed in Section 5.3. They are further discussed in Section 10.1 since minimum cost network flow models have *integer* optimal solutions (so long as external flows in and out are integer). This relieves the need to use the much more costly procedures of integer programming.

We outline a method described by Baston, Rahmouni, and Williams (1991) for converting linear programs to network flow models. Another procedure, but expressed in the more abstract language of matroid theory, is given by Bixby and Cunningham (1980).

In order to illustrate the method we will take a numerical example.

$$\text{Minimize} \quad c_1x_1 + c_2x_2 + c_3x_3 + c_4x_4$$

$$\text{subject to} \quad \begin{aligned} 2x_1 \qquad\qquad\qquad + x_5 \qquad\qquad\qquad &= b_1, \\ 6x_1 \quad + 9x_3 \qquad + x_6 \qquad\qquad &= b_2, \\ -8x_1 + 4x_2 \qquad - 8x_4 \quad + x_7 \qquad &= b_3, \\ x_2 + 3x_3 - 2x_4 \qquad + x_8 \quad &= b_4, \\ x_2 + 3x_3 \qquad\qquad + x_9 &= b_5, \\ x_1, x_2, x_3, x_4, x_5, x_6, x_7, x_8, x_9 &\geqslant 0. \end{aligned}$$

Since the conversion does not depend on the objective or right-hand-side coefficients we give these in a general form. In this example we assume all the original constraints were of the '$\leqslant$' form and that *slack* variables have been added to make them equations. For '$\geqslant$' constraints *surplus* variables would be subtracted. If any of the original constraints were equations then we would add *artificial* variables (variables constrained to take the value zero). These *logical* (slack, surplus or artificial) variables will represent arcs in the network created. For the case of artificial variables these arcs will finally be deleted.

We carry out the following transformations:

(i) Scale the rows and columns in order to make the constraint coefficients 0 or ± 1 if possible.

This may not be possible; in which case the conversion to a network is not possible. In most practical problems (such as those referenced in Section 5.3) for which it is worth attempting a conversion these coefficients will already be 0 or ± 1.

In this example the resultant scaled coefficients are given below.

6	7	8	9	1	2	3	4	5	
$\frac{1}{2}c_1$	c_2	$\frac{1}{3}c_3$	$\frac{1}{2}c_4$						
1				1					$= b_1$
1		1			1				$= \frac{1}{3}b_2$
-1	1		-1			1			$= \frac{1}{4}b_3$
	1	1	-1				1		$= b_4$
	1	1						1	$= b_5$

It is also convenient to number the variables. The logical variables are numbered 1 to 5 and the original variables 6 to 9.

(ii) In this step the signs of the non-zero coefficients (± 1) are ignored. The arcs corresponding to the logical variables are arranged in the form of a *spanning tree* of the network. This spanning tree must be *compatible* with the original variables of the model in the following sense: the original variables each form a *polygon* with some of the arcs of the spanning tree. Figure 5.9 illustrates how this is possible with the example.

The arc corresponding to variable 6 forms a polygon with the arcs of the tree corresponding to variables 1, 2 and 3 since variable 6 has non-zero entries in rows 1, 2 and 3. Similarly since variable 7 has non-zero entries in rows 3, 4 and 5 arc 7 forms a polygon with arcs 3, 4 and 5. Arcs 8 and 9 are similarly compatible with the tree.

It will not always be possible to find an arrangement of the logical arcs in the form of a spanning tree which is compatible with the other arcs in the manner demonstrated above. In such a case the network conversion is

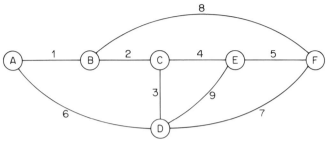

Figure 5.9

not possible. A systematic way of investigating if it is possible to construct such a spanning tree or showing it to be impossible is described by Baston, Rahmouni, and Williams.

Having created such an *undirected* network the arcs are orientated in the following manner:

(iii) For each polygon the arcs of the tree in the polygon are given a direction *opposite* to that of the non-tree arc, when going round the polygon, if the entry in the column corresponding to this arc is $+1$. If the entry is -1 the arcs are given the *same* direction.

For the example the resulting orientations are shown in Figure 5.10. Arc 6, for example, has an opposite orientation to arcs 1 and 2 (variable 6 has $+1$ coefficients in rows 1 and 2) and the same orientation to arc 3 (variable 6 has a -1 coefficient in rows 3) when going round the polygon formed by arcs 1, 2, 3 and 6. Other arcs are orientated similarly according to this rule. It may not be possible to orientate the arcs in any manner compatible with the signs of the coefficients. In such a case a (directed) network is not constructible.

(iv) The (non-tree) arcs in the network are given unit costs equal to the scaled objective coefficients of corresponding variables.

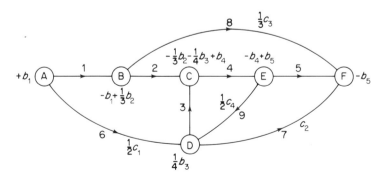

Figure 5.10

(v) Each node is given an external flow *in* equal to the sum of the scaled right-hand side coefficients of the rows corresponding to those tree arcs leaving the node less the sum of the scaled right-hand side coefficients of the rows corresponding to those tree arcs entering the node.

In the example, in Figure 5.10, node C has tree-arc 4 leaving it (row 4 has scaled right-hand side b_4) and tree-arcs 2 and 3 entering it (rows 2 and 3 have scaled right-hand sides of $\frac{1}{3}b_2$ and $\frac{1}{4}b_3$ respectively). Hence the external flow into node c is $b_4 - \frac{1}{3}b_2 - \frac{1}{4}b_3$. (A negative external flow would, of course, be regarded as a positive flow out.) The other nodes have external flows calculated in a similar manner.

The resulting directed network with its external flows gives the required minimum cost network flow model equivalent to the original linear program. When solved the values of the flows in the arcs may have to be unscaled according to the scaling factors applied.

CHAPTER 6

Interpreting and Using the Solution of a Linear Programming Model

6.1 Validating a Model

Having built a linear programming model we should be very careful before we rely too heavily on the answers which it produces. Once a model has been built and converted into the format necessary for the computer program we will wish to attempt to solve it. Assuming that there are no obvious clerical or keying errors (which are usually detected by package programs) there are three possible outcomes: (i) the model is infeasible; (ii) the model is unbounded; (iii) the model is solvable.

Infeasible Models

A linear programming model is infeasible if the constraints are self-contradictory. For example, a model which contained the following two constraints would be infeasible:

$$x_1 + x_2 \leqslant 1, \tag{1}$$

$$x_1 + x_2 \geqslant 2. \tag{2}$$

In practice the infeasibility would probably be more disguised (unless it arose through a simple keying error). The program will probably go some way towards trying to solve the model until it detects that it is infeasible. Most package progams will print out the infeasible solution obtained at the point when the program gives up.

In most situations an infeasible model indicates an error in the mathematical formulation of the problem. It is, of course, possible that we are trying to devise some plan which is technologically impossible, but more usually we are modelling a situation where we know there should be a feasible solution. The detection of why a model is infeasible can be very difficult. If we have got the infeasible solution where the program gave up we can see which constraints are unsatisfied or which variables are negative in this solution. This may enable us to find the cause of infeasibility fairly easily. It is quite possible, however, that it will not help. The cause of infeasibility may be fairly subtle. For example, it is impossible to satisfy each of the following constraints in the presence of the other two:

$$x_1 - x_2 \qquad \geqslant 1, \tag{3}$$

$$x_2 - x_3 \geqslant 1, \tag{4}$$

$$-x_1 \qquad + x_3 \geqslant 1. \tag{5}$$

It might, however, be wrong to single out any one of (3), (4), and (5) as being an infeasible constraint. What is wrong is the mutual incompatibility of all three constraints.

Assuming that we are modelling a situation which we know to be realizable, it should be possible to construct a feasible (but probably non-optimal) solution to the situation. For example, in a product mix model such as that presented in Section 1.2 we could take a previous week's mix of products (assuming no capacity has since been reduced). If our model were a correct representation of the situation, it should be possible to substitute this constructed (or known) solution into all the constraints without breaking them. Since our model admits no feasible solution, this substitution must violate some of the constraints in the model. Any constraints violated in this way must have been modelled wrongly. They are too restrictive and should be reconsidered.

Unbounded Models

A linear programming model is said to be unbounded if its objective function can be optimized without limit, i.e. for a maximization problem the objective function can be made as large as one wishes or, for a minimization problem, as small as one wishes. For example, the following trivial linear programming problem is unbounded since $x_1 + x_2$ can be made as large as we like without violating the constraint:

Maximize $\qquad x_1 + x_2 \tag{6}$

subject to $\qquad 2x_1 + x_2 \geqslant 1. \tag{7}$

While a correctly formulated infeasible model is just possible since we might be trying to attain the unattainable, a correctly formulated unbounded model is very unlikely.

As with infeasible models, most package programs print a solution to an unbounded model before the optimization is terminated on it being seen that the model is unbounded. This solution can be of help in detecting what is wrong with the model. On the other hand, detection of unboundedness may well be as difficult as the detection of infeasibility. Whereas an infeasible model has constraints which are over restrictive an unbounded model either has vital constraints unrepresented or insufficiently restrictive. Usually certain physical constraints have not been modelled. These constraints may well be so obvious as to be forgotten. A very common type of constraint to omit is a *material balance constraint* such as that described in Section 3.3. This sort of constraint is easily overlooked. If such a constraint has been inadvertently overlooked, the solution which the package program prints before giving up can be of use in detecting it. A common sense examination of this solution may reveal that things do not 'add up', e.g. we may find we are producing something without using any raw material.

In Section 6.2 we define an associated linear programming model for every model known as the *dual model*. This model can have important economic interpretations. If a model is unbounded the corresponding dual model is infeasible. It is therefore conceivable that a practical unbounded model might arise as the dual to an infeasible model where we were testing whether a certain course of action was or was not possible. Should a model be infeasible we should not assume that its dual will necessarily be unbounded. It is possible that the dual will also be infeasible.

Solvable Models

Should a linear programming model be neither infeasible nor unbounded we will refer to it as *solvable*. When we obtain the optimal solution to such a model we clearly want to know if the answer is sensible. If it is not sensible then there must be something wrong with our model. The first approach should be to examine the optimal solution critically simply using common sense. This may well reveal an obvious nonsense which should enable us to detect and correct a modelling error.

Should the solution still appear sensible we could compare the optimal objective value with what we might expect in practice. If, in a maximization problem, this value is lower than we expect, we might suspect that our model is over restrictive, i.e. some constraints are too severe. On the other hand, if the optimal objective is higher than we expect, we might suspect that our model is insufficiently restrictive, i.e. that some constraints are too weak or have been left out. For minimization problems these conclusions would obviously be reversed. To give an example, suppose we were considering a product mix application such as that considered in Section 1.2. On solving the model we would obtain a maximum profit contribution. Suppose this profit contribution was lower than what we already knew we could attain, e.g. suppose it was lower than what we obtained in a previous week (assuming there had been no subsequent cut-back in productive capacity). In this circumstance we would obviously suspect our model to be over restrictive. To find where the over severe constraints lay we could substitute our known better solution into the constraints of our model. Some of these constraints will obviously be violated and must therefore have been modelled incorrectly. Possibly we may find that there is some productive capacity which we were unaware of but is being used by the workforce. Our model, even though not yet correct, will already be proving valuable in helping to discover things we were unaware of.

Thinking again about our product mix model, suppose we find the reverse situation that the optimal objective value was greater than anything we knew we could possibly achieve. In this situation our model would obviously be under-restrictive. The approach here would be to subject the optimal solution proposed by the model to a very critical examination. This solution could be presented in an entirely non-technical manner as a proposed operating policy and the appropriate management asked to spell out why it was impossible. It should then be possible to use this information to modify constraints or add new constraints.

For situations such as the above, where we are modelling an existing situation, we obviously have the great advantage of the 'feasible' solutions suggested by the existing mode of operation. These solutions can be used to test and modify our model. For situations where we are using linear programming (or any other sort of model) to design a new situation, e.g. decide where to set up new plant, there may be no obvious 'feasible' solutions to use. Testing the model may therefore be more difficult. It is still a good approach to try to obtain good common sense solutions by rule of thumb methods. These solutions may well reveal errors in our model and show how they may be corrected.

The value of optimizing an objective should be apparent in this discussion on the validation of linear programming models. By optimizing some quantity we would expect to be using certain resources (processing capacity, raw materials manpower, etc.) to their limit. The resultant optimal solution suggested by the model would then be fairly likely to violate certain physical restrictions which had been ignored or modelled incorrectly and thereby highlight them. It is often desirable to solve the model a number of times with different (possibly contrived) objectives in order to test out as many constraints as possible. The value of optimizing an objective (and so using mathematical programming) where there is no real life objective should be apparent in *validating* and modifying a model.

It should be obvious from the foregoing discussion that the building and validation of a model should be a two-way process gradually converging on a more and more accurate representation of the situation being modelled. Unfortunately, this process is often ignored or neglected. It can be an extremely valuable activity leading to a much clearer understanding of what is being modelled. In many situations this greater understanding may be more valuable than even the optimal solution to the (validated) model.

It is often possible to build a model with error detection in mind. For example, suppose we wished to define the following constraint:

$$\sum_{j} a_j x_j \leqslant b. \tag{8}$$

If there were any danger of this constraint being too severe and making the model infeasible, we could allow it to be violated at a certain high cost by rewriting it as

$$\sum_{j} a_j x_j - u \leqslant b \tag{9}$$

and giving u a negative ('cost') coefficient in the objective function, assuming the problem to be a maximization. For a minimization problem u would be given a positive ('profit') coefficient. In this way the constraint could no longer cause the model to be infeasible but the violation of the original constraint (8) would be indicated by u appearing in the solution. For certain applications it might be argued that (9) was a more correct formulation of the constraint anyway by, for example, allowing us to 'buy in' more resources if really needed at a certain cost rather than restricting us absolutely. This topic was discussed in more detail in Section 3.3.

Another device can be used to avoid unboundedness occurring in a model. Each variable can be given a (possibly very large) finite simple upper bound in the formulation. No variable could then exceed its upper bound but any variable which rose to its bound would be open to suspicion. This might then lead one more quickly to the cause of unboundedness in the model.

Finally the desirability of using matrix generators should be re-emphasized here. By automatically generating a model the possibility of error is greatly reduced. The validation process itself is greatly simplified since the input to the matrix generator is usually presented in a much more physically meaningful form than for a linear programming package.

6.2   Economic Interpretations

It will be useful to relate the discussion in this section to a specific type of model rather than present the material more abstractly. We will use the small product mix example of Section 1.2 for this purpose. The model was:

$$
\begin{array}{lll}
\text{Maximize} & 550x_1 + 600x_2 + 350x_3 + 400x_4 + 200x_5 \\
\text{subject to} & \text{Grinding} & 12x_1 + 20x_2 \qquad\qquad\; + 25x_4 + 15x_5 \leqslant 288, \\
& \text{Drilling} & 10x_1 + \;8x_2 + 16x_3 \qquad\qquad\qquad \leqslant 192, \\
& \text{Manpower} & 20x_1 + 20x_2 + 20x_3 + 20x_4 + 20x_5 \leqslant 384, \\
& x_1, \; x_2, \; x_3, \; x_4, \; x_5 \geqslant 0.
\end{array}
$$

This problem was that of finding how much to make of five products (PROD 1, PROD 2, ..., PROD 5) subject to two processing capacity limitations (grinding and drilling) and a manpower limitation. Practical problems will, of course, usually be much bigger and more complex. The interpretation of the solution and the derivation of extra 'economic' information is, however, well illustrated by this example. Other types of application (e.g. blending) will, of course, result in different interpretations being placed on this information. It should, however, be possible to relate this information to any real life application after following the discussion applied to the small example above. The practical problems presented in Part 2 provide an excellent means of relating such information to real life situations.

If the model above is solved (by, for example, the simplex algorithm) the optimal solution turns out to be

$$x_1 = 12, \qquad x_2 = 7 \cdot 2, \qquad x_3 = x_4 = x_5 = 0,$$

giving an objective value of £10 920, i.e. we should make 12 of PROD 1, $7 \cdot 2$ of PROD 2 and none of the other products. This results in a total profit contribution (over a week) of £10 920.

It can easily be verified that the grinding and manpower capacities are fully exhausted but that there is slack drilling capacity. This information is usually given along with the rest of the solution when a package program is used.

It can fairly easily be shown (although it is beyond the scope of this book) that in a model with m linear constraints (including possibly simple upper bounds) and a linear objective one would never expect more than m of the variables to be non-zero in the optimal solution. In the example above one could therefore be sure that one need never produce more than three products.

In a problem of the above kind there is a considerable amount of extra *economic information* which might be of interest. For example, we can obtain answers to the following questions:

(i) Presumably products 3, 4 and 5 are underpriced in comparison with products 1 and 2. How much more expensive should we make them in order for it to be worth manufacturing them?

(ii) What is the value of an extra hour of grinding, drilling, or manpower capacity? Strictly speaking we are interested in the *marginal values* of each of these capacities, i.e. the effect of very small increases or decreases in capacity.

This extra information is usually presented with the ordinary solution when a package program is used. The variables have, associated with them, quantities known as *reduced costs* which can be interpreted (in this application) as the necessary price increases. Each constraint has associated with it a quantity known as the *shadow price* which can be interpreted as the marginal effect of increases (or decreases) in the capacities.

It should be emphasized that when the simplex algorithm (or one of its variants) is used to solve a model reduced costs and shadow prices arise naturally out of the optimal solution and most package programs print this information. There is, however, an alternative, and very illustrative, way of deriving this economic information which helps to clarify its true meaning. This is through another associated linear programming model known as the dual model which will now be described.

The Dual Model

We will again use the product mix problem above to illustrate this discussion.

Suppose that an accountant were trying to value each of the resources of this problem (grinding, drilling, and manpower capacities) in some way so as to give a minimal overall valuation to the factory compatible with the optimal production plan. Let us suppose that the valuations for each hour of each of the capacities were y_1, y_2, and y_3 (measured in £). His objective would be:

Minimize $\qquad\qquad$ $288y_1 + 192y_2 + 384y_3$. $\qquad\qquad$ (10)

He wishes, however, to obtain values for y_1, y_2, and y_3 which totally explain the optimal production pattern. It should be possible to impute the profit contribution obtained from each product produced to its usage of the three resources. We must make sure that the profit contribution for each unit of each product is totally 'covered' by its imputed value. For example each unit of PROD 1 has a profit contribution of £550. This must be totally accounted for by the 'value' of the 12 hours grinding capacity, 10 hours drilling capacity and 20 hours of manpower capacity used in making this unit. Since the values of an hour of each of these capacities are y_1, y_2, and y_3 (in £) we have

$$12y_1 + 10y_2 + 20y_3 \geqslant 550. \qquad\qquad (11)$$

The reason why '$\geqslant$' is used rather than '$=$' in the above constraint will not be totally obvious to start with. It should, however, become apparent later.

Similar arguments will relate the hourly values y_1, y_2, and y_3 to the unit profit contributions of each of the other products. This gives constraints (12), (13), (14), and (15) below:

$$20y_1 + \ 8y_2 + 20y_3 \geqslant 600, \qquad\qquad (12)$$

$$16y_2 + 20y_3 \geqslant 350, \qquad\qquad (13)$$

$$25y_1 \qquad\ + 20y_3 \geqslant 400, \qquad\qquad (14)$$

$$15y_1 \qquad\ + 20y_3 \geqslant 200. \qquad\qquad (15)$$

The objective (10) together with the constraints (11), (12), (13), (14), and (15) give us another linear programming model. As with most linear programming models we will implicitly assume that the variables y_1, y_2, and y_3 can only be non-negative. This new linear programming model is referred to as the *dual* of the original product mix model. In contrast the original model is usually referred to as the *primal* model.

The derivation of this model may appear somewhat contrived at first but should become more plausible once we examine its solution.

Solving this dual model by a suitable algorithm we obtain the optimal solution

$$y_1 = 6 \cdot 25, \qquad y_2 = 0, \qquad y_3 = 23 \cdot 75,$$

giving an objective value of 10 920; i.e. we should value each hour of grinding capacity at £6·25, each hour of drilling capacity at nothing and each hour of manpower capacity at £23·75. The total valuation of the factory is then £10 920.

We can immediately see some connections between this result and the optimal production plan for the original product mix model:

(i) The total valuation of the factory (over a week) is the same as the optimal objective value of the original model. This seems plausible. The total 'value' of a factory is equal to the value of its optimal productive output. It follows from the *duality theorem* of linear programming that this result will always be true.

(ii) Drilling capacity was not totally utilized in the optimal solution to the original primal model. We see that it has been given a zero valuation. This again seems plausible. Since we do not use all the capacity we have, we are not likely to place much value on it. The result here is another consequence of the duality theorem of linear programming. If a constraint is not 'binding' in the optimal primal solution the corresponding dual variable is zero in the optimal solution to the dual model. Economists would refer to the drilling capacity as a 'free good', i.e. in one sense it is not worth anything.

Let us examine the optimal solution to the dual problem further and see what it might suggest to an accountant about the production policy which the factory should pursue.

Each unit of PROD 1 contributes £550 to profit. It uses up, however, 12 hours of grinding capacity (valued at £6·25 per hour), 10 hours of drilling capacity (valued at nothing) and 20 hours of manpower capacity (valued at £23·75 per hour). The total value imputed to each unit of PROD 1 is therefore

$$£(12 \times 6·25 + 10 \times 0 + 20 \times 23·75) = £550,$$

i.e. the profit of £550 which each unit of PROD 1 contributes is exactly explained by the value imputed to it by virtue of its usage of resources. If we regarded the dual variables y_1 y_2, and y_3 as 'costs', i.e. we charged PROD 1 for its usage of scarce resources then we would come to the conclusion that PROD 1 produced zero profit. In accounting terms this does not matter since these 'costs' are purely internal accounting devices.

Similarly we find that each unit of PROD 2 has an imputed value (or extra 'cost' of

$$£(20 \times 6·5 + 8 \times 0 + 20 \times 23·75) = £600,$$

showing that the £600 contribution to profit is exactly accounted for.

For each unit of PROD 3 we get an imputed value (or extra 'cost') of

$$£(0 \times 6·25 + 16 \times 0 + 20 \times 23·75) = £475.$$

This 'cost' exceeds its profit contribution by £125. An accountant would conclude that PROD 3 would 'cost' more (in terms of usage of scarce resources) than it would contribute to profit. He would therefore suggest that PROD 3 not be manufactured. We came to the same conclusion using our original primal model.

It can easily be verified that PROD 4 and PROD 5 have 'costs' which exceed their unit profit contributions by £231·25 and £368·75 respectively and should therefore not be produced.

We are now in a position to see why the '$\geqslant$' rather than '$=$' constraints in the dual model are acceptable. If the total activity in the left-hand side (the 'cost') of a constraint in the dual model strictly exceeds the right-hand side coefficient (the profit contribution) we do not incur this excess cost by simply not manufacturing the corresponding product. This gives us a third connection between the optimal solutions to the dual and primal models:

(iii) If a product has a negative resultant 'profit' after subtracting its imputed 'costs', we do not make it. This is again a consequence of the duality theorem in linear programming. If a constraint in the dual model is not 'binding' in the optimal solution to the dual model, then the corresponding variable is zero in the optimal solution to the primal model. The symmetry between this property and property (ii) should be obvious. This result is sometimes referred to as the *equilibrium theorem*. Economically it simply means that non-binding constraints have zero valuation.

Returning to our accountant's analysis of the problem using the valuations derived from the dual model we conclude that:

(a) At most PROD 1 and PROD 2 should be manufactured (at zero 'internal profit').
(b) Drilling capacity is not a binding constraint (having a zero valuation).

(Strictly speaking the deduction of (b) is not quite valid. It is certainly true that a non-binding constraint implies a zero valuation. The converse cannot immediately be concluded, although it presents no difficulty here. This complication is referred to later.)

The accountant could therefore eliminate x_3, x_4, and x_5 from the primal problem, ignore the second (drilling) constraint and treat the remaining two constraints as equations. This gives

$$12x_1 + 20x_2 = 288, \tag{16}$$

$$20x_1 + 20x_2 = 384. \tag{17}$$

Solving this pair of simultaneous equations gives us

$$x_1 = 12 \quad \text{and} \quad x_2 = 7 \cdot 2,$$

i.e. the accountant deduces the same production plan using his valuations for the three resources as we come to from our ordinary (primal) linear programming model. In practice the derivation of these valuations (values of the dual variables) by the method we have suggested (building and solving the dual model) might be just as difficult as, or more difficult than, building and solving the original (primal) model. Our purpose is, however, to explain a useful concept. In practice one would not normally build or solve the dual model (although in some circumstances this model is easier to solve computationally and might be used for this reason).

The product mix model for which we constructed a dual model was a maximization with all constraints '$\leqslant$'. For completeness we should define the dual corresponding to a more general model. It is convenient to regard all problems as maximizations. In order to cope with a minimization we can negate the objective function and maximize it. It is also possible to convert all the constraints to ' $\leqslant$ '. We do not choose to do this as it is helpful to keep the original model close to its original form. The dual variable corresponding to a ' $\leqslant$ ' constraint was a conventional *non-negative* linear programming variable. A ' $\geqslant$ ' constraint can be dealt with by only allowing the dual variable to be *non-positive*. For an ' $=$ ' constraint we will allow the dual variable to be *unrestricted* in sign. Such a variable is sometimes known as a *free variable*.

There is a symmetry concerning duality which should be mentioned although its main interest is purely mathematical. The dual of a dual model gives the original model.

Shadow Prices

The valuations (values of the dual variables) which we have obtained by this roundabout means are in fact the *shadow prices* which we referred to in the earlier part of this section. They arise naturally, as subsidiary information, out of the optimal solution to the primal model if the simplex algorithm is used. It would, often, in fact be possible to deduce the shadow prices from simply the optimal solution values of the variables by using an argument similar to the accountancy argument which we used above. We will not, however, discuss the derivation of the shadow prices any longer since most package programs present these values in the output of the optimal solution.

It can fairly easily be seen (although we do not do so in this book) that the values of the dual variables (the shadow prices) represent the effects of small changes on the right-hand side coefficients, i.e. they are *marginal valuations*. For example, if we were to increase grinding capacity by a small amount Δ then the resultant increase in total profit (after re-arranging our optimal production plan) would be £($6 \cdot 25 \times \Delta$). Similarly the decrease in total profit by reducing grinding capacity would be £($6 \cdot 25 \times \Delta$). There will usually be limits within which Δ can lie. These limits (*ranges*) are discussed in the next section. (Strictly speaking it is possible that one or both of these limits be zero. This complication is discussed later.) It will also only be valid to interpret the shadow prices as referring to the effect of small changes on *one of the right-hand side coefficients at a time*, i.e. we could not make small changes in two right-hand side coefficients simultaneously and conclude that the effect on total profit will be the sum of the shadow prices.

Shadow prices can be of considerable value in making investment decisions. For example, each extra hour of grinding capacity is worth £6.25 per week to the factory. As long as we are permitted to increase our grinding capacity by a sufficient amount this interpretation remains valid. In the next section we will see that this capacity can be increased up to 384 hours per week (its *upper range*) with each extra unit resulting in an extra £6.25 per week. The effect of increasing capacity beyond this upper range will result in a smaller (though not immediately predictable) extra profit per unit of increase. Since we can increase grinding capacity up to 384 hours per week, enabling us to make an extra £600 of profit, we could decide whether it is worth investing in (or hiring) more grinding machines. We might compare this with the £23·75 which would result from each extra hour of manpower capacity (within the permitted range) and decide where limited funds might be invested to best effect.

The shadow price on a non-binding constraint such as that representing the drilling capacity is zero. As we might expect there is no value in increasing this capacity since we do not use all we have already.

Shadow prices are an example of '*opportunity costs*'. This is a concept which accountants are increasingly (although still too rarely) using. For example an increase in grinding capacity results in an increased *opportunity* to make more profit. Similarly a decrease in grinding capacity loses us some opportunity to make a profit. The shadow price represents the *cost* of the lost *opportunity*. Unlike some of the other costs which accountants use (such as average costs), opportunity costs are quite a sophisticated concept. They result from a careful weighing up of the demands which each product makes on the scarce resources and contributes to profit in return. As a consequence they take into account the *alternative uses* to which the resources may be put and the comparative values of these alternative uses. One would obviously expect such costs to be of more value than less sophisticated costs. Accountants are becoming increasingly interested in linear programming as a result. A good description of the application of linear programming to accountancy is given by Salkin and Kornbluth (1973).

Our discussion of the interpretation of shadow prices has been confined to our product mix application. For other applications it should be possible to deduce the correct interpretation by relating small changes in the right-hand side coefficients to the physical situation represented by the model. To help with any such interpretation we suggest meanings which might be attached to the different types of constraint described in Section 3.3.

Productive Capacity Constraints

These are the sort of constraints we have discussed above where the capacity may represent limited processing or manpower. The interpretation of the shadow prices on such constraints has been fully dealt with above.

Raw Material Availabilities

Suppose we have modelled limited raw material availabilities by constraints. Those raw materials which the model suggests be used to their limit will be represented by constraints generally (but not always) having a non-zero shadow price. This shadow price will indicate the value of acquiring more of the raw material (within the permitted ranges). Similarly it will represent the cost of cutting back on raw material. This shadow price may be very useful in helping to decide whether to purchase more of the raw material or not (at a certain cost).

Marketing Demands and Limitations

The interpretation of the shadow prices here will be the effect on the value of the objective of altering demands or limitations of the market, e.g. forcing the factory to produce more or less, or increasing or decreasing the maximum market size. Such a figure can often usefully be compared with the cost of extra sales effort. Frequently such constraints will take the form of simple upper bounds, as discussed in Section 3.3. If such simple upper bounds are treated as such in the model, they will not appear as constraints and therefore have no shadow price. The desired interpretation can, however, be obtained from the reduced cost of the bounded variable as described below.

Material Balance (Continuity) Constraints

The shadow price on such constraints may well have no useful interpretation. For example, the small blending problem (Example 2) of Section 1.2 has a material balance constraint to make sure that the weight of the final product equals the total weight of the ingredients. The right-hand side value is zero. The shadow price predicts the effect of altering this zero value. It is hard to see a useful interpretation for this. In some circumstances the shadow price on a material balance constraint may be of interest. For example we may be equating our initial (or final) stocks to some expression involving the variables of the model. The shadow price will then indicate the effect on the optimal objective value of changing these stocks. A good example of this is the FOOD MANUFACTURE model of Part 2.

Quality Stipulations

Any model which involves blending as part of the total model usually involves quality stipulations, e.g. the proportion of vitamins must not fall below a certain value or the octane rating of the petrol must not fall below some value. As an example, the blending problem in Section 1.2 has two quality constraints indicating a limitation on 'hardness'. The shadow prices of these constraints can be used to predict the effect on total revenue of relaxing or tightening up on these hardness stipulations. In some models where the right-hand side coefficient is itself a quality parameter, the interpretation is straightforward. For our small example we had a right-hand side value of 0. The upper hardness constraint is

$$8 \cdot 8x_1 + 6 \cdot 1x_2 + 2x_3 + 4 \cdot 2x_4 + 5x_6 - 6y \leqslant 0. \tag{18}$$

Suppose this right-hand side coefficient were not 0 but were Δ. We could rewrite the constraint as

$$8 \cdot 8 x_1 + 6 \cdot 1 x_2 + 2 x_3 + 4 \cdot 2 x_4 + 5 x_5 - \left(6 + \frac{\Delta}{y}\right) y \leqslant 0. \tag{19}$$

In order to interpret the effect of a relaxing or tightening of the upper hardness limitation of 6, we would have to take into account the value of y in the optimal solution. A unit increase or decrease in the hardness 6 would result in an increase or decrease of y in the right-hand side and the interpretation of the shadow price would have to be adjusted accordingly. The derivation of ranges within which the hardness parameter could validly be altered with this interpretation would be difficult since the value of y would probably alter as well.

To decide whether a small change in a right-hand side coefficient results in an *increase* or *decrease* in the optimal objective value we should decide whether the change results in a *relaxation* or a *tightening* of the problem. If we relax a problem slightly, e.g. increase the right-hand side coefficient on a '$\leqslant$' constraint or decrease the right-hand side coefficient on a '$\geqslant$' constraint, we would expect to at worse have no effect on the optimal objective value and perhaps improve it. Therefore the optimal objective value in a maximization problem would possibly get larger and in a minimization problem possibly get smaller, i.e. we would expect to do no worse, possibly to do better in view of the lessening of the restrictions. For a tightening of the constraints, e.g. reducing the right-hand side coefficients in "a" '$\leqslant$' constraint and increasing them in a '$\geqslant$' constraint, we would expect to do worse if anything, i.e. possibly degrade the optimal objective value. In the case of '$=$' constraints the improving or degrading effect of small changes in the right-hand side coefficient will probably be apparent from the meaning of the model.

Rather than formulate mathematical rules for interpreting whether the shadow price should be added or subtracted from the objective for each unit change in the corresponding right-hand coefficient it is probably better to follow the above scheme as different package programs vary in their sign conventions regarding shadow prices.

The suggested formulation of the TARIFF RATES (POWER GENERATION) problem in Part 3 causes the required rates for the sale of electricity to arise as shadow prices on demand constraints.

Reduced Costs

In our small product mix example we saw that the unit profit contributions of PROD 1 and PROD 2 are exactly accounted for by the imputed 'costs' derived from the shadow prices on each constraint. For PROD 3, PROD 4, and PROD 5, however, the imputed costs exceed the unit profit contribution. The amount by which these unit profit contributions are exceeded in each case is of interest. These quantities are the *reduced costs* of these appropriate variables. Note that any variable which comes out at a non-zero level in the optimal solution has a zero reduced cost (this result is modified if the variable has a simple upper bound; the modification is dealt with later).

For our example the reduced costs which we derived earlier for PROD 3, and could also derive for PROD 4 and PROD 5 are

PROD 3	£125
PROD 4	£231·25
PROD 5	£368·75

If we wanted to make PROD 3 we would have to increase its unit price by £125 before it was (just) worth making. This price increase would then allow the profit contribution of PROD 3 to balance the 'costs' imputed to it by way of its usage of scarce resources. Similarly the reduced costs of PROD 4 and PROD 5 indicate price increases necessary for those products. The reduced costs are usually printed out with the solution values of the variables when a package program is used and there is no necessity to calculate them by way of the shadow prices as we have done. Our purpose in using this derivation has been to indicate the correct interpretation which should be placed on reduced costs. For other applications the interpretation of reduced costs will be different. In a blending problem for example (such as that in Section 1.2) the reduced costs might represent price decreases necessary before it became worth buying and incorporating an ingredient in a blend.

The above interpretation of reduced costs can be viewed the other way round. Suppose we insisted on making a small amount of PROD 3. Since this will deny processing and manpower capacity to some of the other products (who could use it to better effect) we would expect to degrade our total profit. The amount by which this profit will be degraded for each unit of PROD 3 we make will be given by the reduced cost (£125) of PROD 3. In fact there will be a limit to the level at which PROD 3 can be made with this interpretation holding. This limit is another type of *range* which will be discussed in the next section. It is therefore possible to cost a non-optimal decision such as making PROD 3. This cost results from the lost opportunity to make other, more profitable, products. It is again an *opportunity cost*.

We should mention the slight variation in the interpretation of the reduced costs on variables with a finite *simple upper bound* as discussed in Section 3.3. If, in the optimal solution to a model, such a variable comes out at a value below its simple upper bound, there is no difficulty. The interpretation of the reduced cost will be exactly the same as that above. Suppose, however, that the variable were to come out at a value equal to its simple upper bound. This simple upper bound could well, in this case, be acting as a binding constraint. If the simple upper bound had been modelled as a conventional constraint, it would then have a non-zero shadow price which would be interpreted in the usual way. The variable would, being at a non-zero level, have a zero reduced cost. By modelling this constraint as a simple upper bound we will have lost the shadow price but it will appear as the reduced cost of the variable. The correct interpretation of this reduced cost will be the effect on the objective of forcing the variable down below its upper bound (degrading the objective) or increasing the upper bound (improving the objective).

We showed above how the shadow prices (values of the dual variables) could be used as 'accounting costs' in order to derive the optimal production plan in the product mix model. It is important to point out that such a procedure will not always work. This discussion also leads us on to an important feature of some linear programming models: *alternative optimal solutions*. Let us consider the following small linear programming model:

Maximize	$3x_1 + 1 \cdot 5x_2$	(20)
subject to	$x_1 + \quad x_2 \leqslant 4,$	(21)
	$2x_1 + \quad x_2 \leqslant 5,$	(22)
	$-x_1 + \quad 4x_2 \geqslant 2,$	(23)
	$x_1, \ x_2 \geqslant 0.$	

If the dual model is formulated with dual variables $y_1 \ y_2$, and y_3 corresponding to the three constraints, and then solved we obtain the following result:

$$y_1 = 0, \qquad y_2 = 1 \cdot 5, \qquad y_3 = 0.$$

An accountant could then use the values of y_1, y_2 and y_3 as valuations for the constraints. This would lead him to the following conclusions:

(i) The 'accounting cost' attributed to each unit of x_1 is 3, exactly equalling its objective coefficient. Similarly the 'accounting cost' attributed to x_2 is $1 \cdot 5$ exactly equalling its objective coefficient. Therefore x_1 and x_2 should both be allowed to be in the solution of the original (primal) model.

(ii) The second constraint (22) has a non-zero valuation and must therefore be binding (i.e. can be treated as an equation). It would be wrong, however (as was mentioned in applying the same procedure to the product mix example), to immediately conclude that the constraints (21) and (23) are non-binding since they have zero dual variables (shadow prices).

Suppose for the moment that we did ignore constraints (21) and (23). We deduce that x_1 and x_2 must satisfy the equation

$$2x_1 + x_2 = 5. \qquad (24)$$

This equation obviously does not determine x_1 and x_2 uniquely. It is by no means obvious how the accountant should proceed from here. In fact it is impossible to deduce a unique solution to the above model from the solution to the dual model since the original (primal) model does not possess a unique solution. This is easily seen geometrically in Figure 6.1.

Different values of the objective function (20) correspond to different lines parallel to PQ. It so happens that PQ is parallel to the edge of AC of the feasible region created by constraint (22). We therefore see that any point on

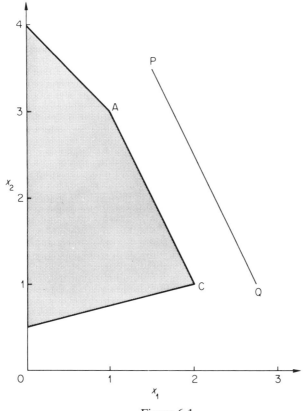

Figure 6.1

the line AC between (and including) A and C, gives an optimal solution to our model (objective $= 7 \cdot 5$).

All that our accounting information has told us (if we ignore constraints (21) and (23)) is that $2x_1 + x_2 = 5$, i.e. that we must choose points lying on (or beyond) the line AC. We still have to pay some attention to the constraints (21) and (23). If we were to treat constraint (21) as binding we would arrive at the point A. Treating (23) as binding would give us point C. As mentioned in Section 2.2, the simplex algorithm only examines vertex solutions and would therefore choose *either* the solution at A ($x_1 = 1$, $x_2 = 3$) *or* the solution at C ($x_1 = 2$, $x_2 = 1$). Most package programs indicate when there are alternative solutions. They recognize this result by noticing one of the following properties of the optimal solutions:

(i) A binding constraint with a zero shadow price.
(ii) A variable at zero level with a zero reduced cost.

In our example, if the optimal solution at A had been selected, we would note that constraint (21) was binding but had a zero shadow price. At C it would be constraint (23) that was binding with a zero shadow price.

It might seem rather unlikely that alternative solutions would arise in a practical linear programming model. In fact this is quite a common occurrence. For problems with more than two variables the situation will obviously be more complex. The characterization of all the optimal solutions (all vertex optimal solutions and various combinations of them) is often very difficult. it is, however, important to be able to recognize the phenomenon since if one optimal solution is unacceptable for some reason we have a certain flexibility to look for another solution without degrading our objective.

One of the purposes of this discussion has been to indicate that applying valuations (shadow prices) to the constraints of a linear programming model sometimes does not lead us to a unique solution (operating plan). The converse situation can also happen. We can have a unique solution (operating plan) determined by more than one set of valuations. For example, consider the following small problem:

Maximize	$3x_1 + 2x_2$	(25)
subject to	$x_1 + x_2 \leqslant 3,$	(26)
	$2x_1 + x_2 \leqslant 4,$	(27)
	$4x_1 + 3x_2 \leqslant 10,$	(28)
	$x_1, x_2 \geqslant 0.$	

Let us attach valuations y_1, y_2, and y_3 to each of the constraints (26), (27), and (28). There are a number of valuations which will lead us to the optimal solution. For example,

(i) $\quad y_1 = 1, \qquad y_2 = 1, \qquad y_3 = 0;$

(ii) $\quad y_1 = 0, \qquad y_2 = \frac{1}{2}, \qquad y_3 = \frac{1}{2}.$

Both these sets of valuations will lead us to the unique optimal solution to this problem:

$$x_1 = 1, \qquad x_2 = 2,$$

giving an objective value of 7.

In a practical problem the question which would naturally arise is how should we derive a shadow price for our scarce resources given this ambiguity, e.g. what would the value be of increasing the right-hand side value of 3 to 4? Would it be 1 or 0? This problem is again best illustrated by a diagram (Figure 6.2).

The constraints (26), (27), and (28) give rise to the lines AB, BC, and DBE respectively. Different objective values give rise to lines parallel to PQ, showing that B represents the optimal solution. The reason for the ambiguity in shadow price is that we have the 'accidental' result of three constraints going through the same point. Normally in two dimensions we would only expect two constraints to go through B. We can therefore regard either one of the constraints (26) or (28) as non-binding (having a zero valuation) in the

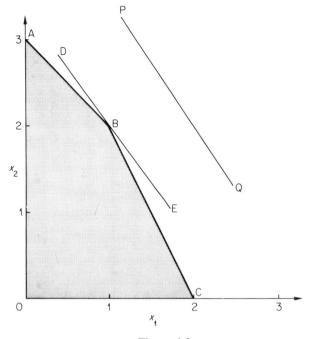

Figure 6.2

presence of the other constraint. This leads to the ambiguity in our shadow prices.

In a situation such as this it would not be correct to increase the right-hand side value of 3 in constraint (26) at all using the shadow price of 1. The *upper range* of this right-hand side value (with this shadow price) will be 3. The coefficient is already at its upper range and any further increase will not alter the objective at the rate suggested by the valuation.

In these situations the shadow price is usually defined as being the rate of change of value of the objective function with respect to the right-hand side value. Then it can be shown that the *upper shadow price* (for increases in right-hand side value) is the *minimum* of *all* the possible valuations and the *lower shadow price* (for decreases in right-hand side value) is the maximum of all the possible valuations. Defining y_1, y_2, and y_3 as shadow prices we have

upper shadow prices $\qquad y_1 = 0, \qquad y_2 = \frac{1}{2}, \qquad y_3 = 0;$

lower shadow prices $\qquad y_1 = 1, \qquad y_2 = 1, \qquad y_3 = \frac{1}{2}.$

When a computer package is used the 'shadow prices' printed out are usually only the values of the dual variables corresponding to one dual solution. They are therefore misleading if interpreted as shadow prices according to the above definition. In fact to evaluate all the alternate dual solutions, and therefore obtain the true shadow price, would generally be computationally prohibitive. It is, however, possible to evaluate *ranges* within which the valuations associated with any particular dual solution chosen are valid. For example, the upper shadow price on constraint (26) is not 1. If we take the dual solution (i) above, then the associated *upper range* on the right-hand side coefficient of 3 is also 3, showing there is no range within which this coefficient can be increased to reflect a rate-of-change increase of 1 in the objective. This example is considered again in Section 6.3, when ranges are discussed. A good discussion of the problem is given by Aucamp and Steinberg (1982).

It should be pointed out that the two complications we have just discussed are dual situations. On the one hand we had a unique dual solution leading to more than one primal solution. The first phenomenon is referred to as *alternative solutions* (in the primal model) while the second phenomenon is referred to as *degeneracy* (in the primal model).

6.3   Sensitivity Analysis and the Stability of a Model

Right-hand Side Ranges

In the last section we described how shadow prices can be useful in predicting the effect of small changes in the right-hand side coefficients on the optimal value of the objective function. It was pointed out, however, that this interpretation is only valid in a certain *range*. In this case the range is known as a *right-hand side range*. We will again use the product mix problem of Section 1.2 to illustrate our discussion. This gave the model:

$$\text{Maximize} \quad 550x_1 + 600x_2 + 350x_3 + 400x_4 + 200x_5 \tag{1}$$

$$\text{subject to} \quad 12x_1 + 20x_2 \qquad\qquad 25x_4 + 15x_5 \leqslant 288, \tag{2}$$

$$10x_1 + 8x_2 + 16x_3 \qquad\qquad\qquad \leqslant 192, \tag{3}$$

$$20x_1 + 20x_2 + 20x_3 + 20x_4 + 20x_5 \leqslant 384. \tag{4}$$

We saw that the optimal solution told us to make 12 of PROD 1 and $7 \cdot 2$ of PROD 2 and nothing of PROD 3, PROD 4, and PROD 5. This resulted in a profit of £10 920 and exhausted the grinding capacity (constraint (2)) and manpower capacity (constraint (4)).

The shadow prices on constraints (2), (3), and (4) turned out to be 6.25, 0, and $23 \cdot 75$. Increasing the grinding capacity by Δ hours per week would therefore result in a weekly increase in total profit of £$(6 \cdot 25 \times \Delta)$. Similarly, cutting back on grinding capacity by Δ hours per week would result in a weekly decrease in total profit of £$(6 \cdot 25 \times \Delta)$. We are interested in the limits within which the change Δ can take place for this interpretation to apply. For this example these ranges are:

lower range $230 \cdot 4$

upper range   384

i.e. we can increase grinding capacity by up to 96 hours a week or decrease it by up to 57·6 hours per week with the predicted effect on profit. Changes outside these ranges are unpredictable in their effect and require further analysis. The information that we have got here is, however, of some, if limited, usefulness. It tells us, for instance, that adding one grinding machine would improve profit by £(96 × 6·25) = £600 per week. We could not, however, predict the effect on total profit of taking away a grinding machine since this would take us below the lower range of the grinding capacity. It would nevertheless be correct to say that £600 is if anything an *underestimate* for the resultant decrease in profit.

It is important to restate that this interpretation of the effect on the objective of decreasing or increasing a right-hand side coefficient is only valid if one coefficient is changed at a time within the permitted ranges. The effect of changing more than one coefficient at a time, as well as changes outside the permitted ranges, are efficiently examined by *parametric programming*, which is discussed in the next section.

It is beyond the scope of this book to describe how the right-hand side ranges are calculated. Most computer packages provide these ranges with their solution output.

For completeness we will give the upper and lower ranges on the other two capacities: drilling and manpower.

The ranges on the drilling capacity of 192 hours per week are fairly trivial to obtain. Remember that we are not using all our drilling capacity. In fact we have a slack capacity of 14·4 hours. This immediately enables us to calculate the lower range by subtracting this figure from the existing capacity. Since we are not using all our drilling capacity, increasing it without limit can have no effect on the solution. The ranges are therefore

$$\text{lower range} \qquad 177·6$$
$$\text{upper range} \qquad \infty$$

Within these ranges there will be no change at all in the objective (or optimal solution) since the shadow price on the (non-binding) drilling constraint is zero.

The ranges on the manpower capacity of 384 hours per week are again non-trivial to calculate. They turn our to be

$$\text{lower range} \qquad 288$$
$$\text{upper range} \qquad 406·1$$

For changes within these ranges the objective changes by £23·75 for each unit of change. For example an extra man (48 hours per week) improves profit by (23·75 × 48) = £1140 per week. This might prove quite valuable information when compared with the fact that an extra grinding machine is worth only £600 per week.

The meaning of right-hand side ranges is well illustrated geometrically using

120

a two-variable example:

Maximize $\qquad\qquad\qquad 3x_1 + 2x_2$ $\qquad\qquad$ (5)

subject to $\qquad\qquad\qquad x_1 + x_2 \leqslant 4,$ $\qquad\qquad$ (6)

$\qquad\qquad\qquad\qquad 2x_1 + x_2 \leqslant 5,$ $\qquad\qquad$ (7)

$\qquad\qquad\qquad\quad -x_1 + 4x_2 \geqslant 2,$ $\qquad\qquad$ (8)

$\qquad\qquad\qquad\qquad\quad x_1, \; x_2 \leqslant 0.$

Geometrically we have the situation in Figure 6.3. The optimal solution is represented by the point A, giving an objective value of 9. The shadow price on constraint (6) turns out to be 1.

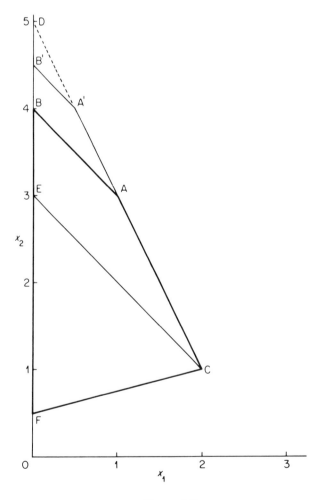

Figure 6.3

If constraint (6) is relaxed by increasing the right-hand side coefficient from 4 to 4·5 we move the boundary AB of the feasible region to A'B'. The resultant increase in the objective is $1 \times 0·5 = 0·5$. We can continue to increase the right-hand side coefficient to 5 when this boundary of the feasible region shrinks to the point D. There is clearly no virtue in further increasing the right-hand side coefficient since the point D will continue to represent the optimal solution. The *upper range* on the right-hand side coefficient in constraint (6) therefore is obviously 5.

If constraint (6) is tightened by decreasing the right-hand side coefficient, the boundary AB of the feasible region progressively moves down until it becomes CE. This happens when the right-hand side coefficient is 3. Any decreases in this coefficient between 4 and 3 result in a degradation of the objective by 1 (the shadow price) for each unit of decrease. The value 3 is the *lower range*. For decreases in coefficient values below 3 the optimal objective value will decrease at a greater rate. This rate will not immediately be predictable from our knowledge of the solution at A. For decreases down to 3 the optimal objective value is represented by points on the line AC. Decreases below 3 give points on the line CF.

So far we have only suggested using right-hand side ranges together with shadow prices to investigate the effect which changes on the right-hand side coefficients have on the optimal objective value. Such investigations sometimes give rise to the expression *post-optimal analysis*. Another purpose to which such information can be put is in investigating the sensitivity of the model to the right-hand side data. This forms part of a subject known as *sensitivity analysis*.

We will consider this new use to which right-hand side ranging information can be put in relation to the product mix model. Suppose we were rather doubtful about the accuracy of the grinding capacity of 288 hours per week (constraint (2)). In practice it is quite likely that such a figure would be open to doubt since machines could well be down for maintenance or repair for durations which were not wholly predictable. How confident should we be in suggesting that the factory dispenses with making PROD 3, PROD 4, and PROD 5 and only concentrates on PROD 1 and PROD 2? From our range information we can immediately say that this should remain the optimal policy as long as the true capacity figure does not lie outside the limits 230·4 to 384. Although the policy (in terms of what is, and is not, made) does not change within these limits, the levels at which PROD 1 and PROD 2 are made (and the resultant profit) obviously will change. This information is therefore of limited, but nevertheless sometimes significant, usefulness. Obviously if there is doubt about one capacity figure there will probably also be doubt about others and ranging information can only strictly be applied when one change only is made. Nevertheless such information does give some indication of the sensitivity of the solution to accuracy in the right-hand side data. If, for example, the ranges on the right-hand side coefficient in constraint (2) had been very close, say 287 to 288·5, we would have to be very careful in applying our suggested solution since it clearly would depend very critically on the accuracy of the grinding capacity figure.

It should be pointed out that the sensitivity analysis interpretation of the easily obtained ranges of $177 \cdot 6$ and ∞ on the non-binding drilling constraint is rather stronger. As long as this capacity lies within these figures not only will our optimal solution be no different, but the levels of the variables in that optimal solution will be unchanged as well.

Changing the right-hand side coefficient on a binding constraint within the permitted ranges does of course alter the values of the variables in the optimal solution (as well as the objective value). The rates at which the values of the variables change are quite easily obtained using most package programs. Such values are known as *marginal rates of substitution* and discussed below. Before doing this, however, we will consider other types of ranging information to be obtained from a linear programming model.

Objective Ranges

It is often useful to know the effects of changes in the objective coefficients on the optimal solution. Suppose we change an objective coefficient (e.g. a unit profit contribution or cost). How will this affect the value of the objective function. In an analogous manner to right-hand side ranges we can define *objective ranges*. If a single objective coefficient is changed within these ranges then the optimal solution values of the variables will not change (although the optimal value of the objective may change). This is a rather stronger result than in the right-hand side ranging case where the solution values could change. The result is not altogether intuitive. If a particular item became more profitable or costly we might expect to bias our solution towards or away from that item. In fact our solution will not change at all as long as we remain within the permitted ranges. The situation is well described geometrically by means of the two-variable model we used before:

Maximize	$3x_1 + 2x_2$	(9)
subject to	$x_1 + x_2 \leqslant 4,$	(10)
	$2x_1 + x_2 \leqslant 5,$	(11)
	$-x_1 + 4x_2 \geqslant 2,$	(12)
	$x_1, \ x_2 \geqslant 0.$	

This gives rise to Figure 6.4. The optimal solution ($x_1 = 1$, $x_2 = 3$, objective $= 9$) is represented by the point A. The line PQ represents the points giving an objective value of 9.

Suppose that the objective coefficient 3 of variable x_1 were to increase. The steepness of the line PQ would increase (in a negative sense) but A would still represent the optimal solution as long as PQ did not rotate (around A) in a clockwise direction beyond the direction AC. When the objective coefficient of

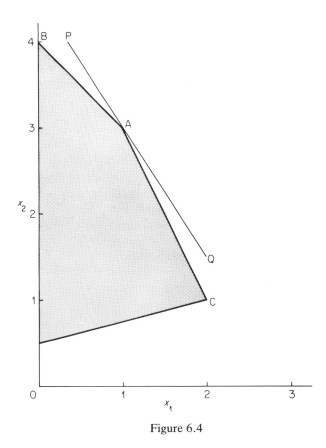

Figure 6.4

x_1 became 4 the objective line would coincide with the line AC. This provides us with an upper range of 4 for this coefficient. Similarly a lower range is provided by decreasing this coefficient until the objective line coincides with AB. This gives a lower range of 2. Note that as long as the objective coefficient of x_1 remains within the range 2 to 4, the optimal solution values of the variables will be unchanged and represented by point A. This is the slightly unintuitive result mentioned before. The optimal objective value does of course change if we alter this coefficient within its ranges. Since x_1 has a value of 1 in the optimal solution, each unit of increase or decrease in its objective coefficient will obviously provide an increase or decrease of 1 in the objective value.

Ranges on the objective coefficient of 2 for x_2 can be discovered in a similar manner.

We will now return to our product mix example and present the objective ranges for that problem. To describe how these ranges are calculated in a problem which cannot be represented geometrically is beyond the scope of this book. Most package programs do, however, provide this information. Our main concern is with the correct interpretation rather than the derivation.

For PROD 1 the ranges on the objective coefficient are

lower range	£500
upper range	£600

This means that if we vary the objective coefficient of PROD 1 within these limits the values of the variables in our optimal solution will not change. We should still continue to produce 12 of PROD 1, 7·2 of PROD 2, and nothing else. As remarked before, such a result is often difficult for people with little understanding to accept. We might expect there to be a gradual and continuous shift towards making more of PROD 1, the more expensive we make it. In fact the production plan should not alter at all until PROD 1 produces a unit profit contribution of more than £600. When this happens there will be a new optimal production plan (almost certainly involving more of PROD 1) the investigation of which would require further analysis. The same restrictions apply to the interpretation of objective ranges as applied in the case of right-hand side ranges. Our interpretation is only valid within the permitted ranges and if only one change is made in an objective coefficient. This clearly limits the value of this information somewhat. *Parametric programming* provides an efficient means of investigating the effects of more than one change, possibly outside the ranges.

Although the optimal solution values of the variable do not change within the ranges, the objective value obviously will. For each £1 that we add to the price of PROD 1 we obviously improve the objective by £12 since the optimal solution involves producing 12 of PROD 1.

Similarly objective ranges can be obtained for PROD 2. These turn out to be

lower range	£550
upper range	£683·3

For PROD 3, PROD 4, and PROD 5, which should not be made in the optimal production plan, the derivation of objective ranges is simple. We have already seen that PROD 3 must be increased in price by £125 (its reduced cost) before it is worth making. This gives us its upper range. Since it is already too cheap to be worth making a reduction in price cannot affect the solution. The objective ranges for PROD 3 are therefore

lower range	$-\infty$
upper range	£475

For PROD 4 we have

lower range	$-\infty$
upper range	£631·25

For PROD 5 we have

lower range	$-\infty$
upper range	£568·75

Objective ranges can be put to a similar use to that which right-hand side ranges are put in sensitivity analysis. If there were doubt surrounding the true profit contribution of £550 from PROD 1, we could be sure of our production plan as long as we knew that this figure was between £500 and £600. The width or narrowness of the objective ranges enables one to obtain a good feel for the sensitivity of the solution to changes (or errors in the objective data). In fact this interpretation is rather stronger than is the case with right-hand side ranges. Not only will the optimal production policy not change if a coefficient is altered within its permitted ranges; the values of the variable quantities in that plan will not alter either.

Ranges on Interior Coefficients

It is also possible to obtain ranges for other coefficients in a linear programming model. Sometimes these may provide valuable information in much the same way that right-hand side and objective ranges do. Generally, however, such information is far less useful. When a model is built often the only data which are changed are the objective and right-hand side coefficients (taken together these are sometimes referred to as the *rim* of the model). In consequence many package programs do not provide the facility for obtaining ranges on coefficients other than in the rim. When such information is obtainable its interpretation and use is very similar to that in the case of right-hand side and objective ranges.

We must now consider the complication which we described in Section 6.2 when there was ambiguity concerning the valuations (shadow prices) of the constraints. This ambiguity also extends to the ranging information. Alternative sets of valuations corresponding to a unique optimal solution lead to alternative sets of ranges. We will repeat the small example we used before:

Maximize $\quad\quad\quad\quad\quad\quad\quad 3x_1 + 2x_2$ $\quad\quad\quad\quad\quad\quad\quad\quad$ (13)

subject to $\quad\quad\quad\quad\quad\quad x_1 + x_2 \leqslant 4,$ $\quad\quad\quad\quad\quad\quad$ (14)

$\quad\quad\quad\quad\quad\quad\quad\quad 2x_1 + x_2 \leqslant 5,$ $\quad\quad\quad\quad\quad\quad$ (15)

$\quad\quad\quad\quad\quad\quad\quad\quad 4x_1 + 3x_2 \leqslant 10,$ $\quad\quad\quad\quad\quad\quad$ (16)

$\quad\quad\quad\quad\quad\quad\quad\quad\quad x_1, \, x_2 \geqslant 0.$

There are a number of possible valuations for the constraints which give rise to the optimal solution. We presented the following two where y_1, y_2, and y_3 are the dual values on constraints (14), (15), and (16) respectively:

$\quad\quad\quad$ (i) $\quad\quad y_1 = 1, \quad\quad y_2 = 1, \quad\quad y_3 = 0;$

$\quad\quad\quad$ (ii) $\quad\quad y_1 = 0, \quad\quad y_2 = \frac{1}{2}, \quad\quad y_3 = \frac{1}{2}.$

(i) arises when we regard constraints (14) and (15) only as binding; (ii) arises when we regard constraints (15) and (16) only as binding.

Table 6.1 gives the right-hand side ranges within which the set (i) can be used as shadow prices.

126

Table 6.1

Constraint	Lower range	Upper range
(14)	2	3
(15)	3	4
(16)	10	∞

Each range extends on one side of the right-hand side coefficient only. For example constraint (14) has an upper range of 3 indicating that it would be incorrect to use a shadow price of 1 on this constraint to predict the effect of *increasing* the right-hand side coefficient. It would, however, be correct to use this as a shadow price to predict the effect of *decreasing* this coefficient. Similar arguments apply to the other two constraints. For constraint (16) we can increase the right-hand side coefficient of 10 indefinitely without affecting the optimal solution or objective value (shadow price of 0). We cannot, however, decrease this coefficient at all without altering the objective. This last result is obvious from studying Figure 6.2 of Section 6.2.

The clue to changes in the right-hand side coefficients in the other directions are given by the set of valuations (ii) together with their corresponding ranges. These ranges are given in Table 6.2. For example, increasing the right-hand side coefficient of 3 has no effect (shadow price of 0) on the objective whereas decreasing this coefficient does have an effect (shadow price of 1). Similarly the second set of ranges on the other constraints are in opposite directions indicating the ranges of interpretation of the second set as shadow prices.

We have demonstrated how *two-valued shadow prices* can exist for constraints with different marginal values for decreasing or increasing a right-hand side coefficient. In solving a practical model using a package program the user will only be presented with one set of 'shadow prices' corresponding to his optimal solution. Which set of dual values this is will be very arbitrary and depend upon the manner in which the model was solved. Solving the same model with exactly the same data could well result in a different set of dual values. The clue to the limited (one-sided) interpretation which he can place on these shadow prices lies in the right-hand side ranges. If some of these ranges lie on one side of their corresponding right-hand side coefficient only, then this limits the shadow price to being interpreted for changes in one direction only. To investigate the effects of changes in the opposite direction alternate sets of

Table 6.2

Constraint	Lower range	Upper range
(14)	3	∞
(15)	4	5
(16)	8	10

dual values and their corresponding ranges should be sought. Alternatively *parametric programming* could be used as discussed in the next section.

It may well seem to the reader that a disproportionate amount of attention has been paid, in both this and the last section, to the apparently rather trivial complication concerning alternative valuations (shadow prices) for the constraints of a linear programming model. As has already been pointed out, however, this complication is a very common occurrence in practical linear programming models. It is well known in the computational side of linear programming as the phenomenon of *degeneracy*. We have here been concerned with the economic interpretations concerning degenerate solutions. In view of the difficulty which many people have in understanding this, we have given it considerable attention.

A further, rather different, final point should be made concerning the uniqueness of the ranging information from a model. The inclusion or exclusion of redundant constraints from a model will obviously not affect the optimal solution. This could well, however, affect the values of the ranges. Figure 6.3 and its associated model illustrate this point. Constraint (8) gives rise to the edge CF of the feasible region. The ignoring of constraint (8) would obviously not affect the optimal solution represented by the point A. In this sense constraint (8) is redundant and might never have been modelled in the first place in a practical situation if its redundancy had been obvious. The presence or absence of constraint (8) will, however, obviously affect the value of the lower right-hand side range on constraint (6). With constraint (8) present this lower range is 3. If constraint (8) were removed it would be $2 \cdot 5$.

Marginal Rates of Substitution

We have seen that there is a certain flexibility in altering a right-hand side coefficient of a model. As long as we remain within the permitted range the effect on the objective value is governed (for each unit of change) by the shadow price of the constraint. This change in the objective value occurs because the values of the variables in the optimal solution change. The relatives rates at which they change are given by the *marginal rates of substitution*. It is beyond the scope of this book to describe how these figures can be calculated but they are obtainable from the solution output of most package programs. A small geometric example will illustrate the meaning which should be attached to these figures. Our example is the same as that used before:

Maximize $\quad\quad\quad\quad 3x_1 + 2x_2$

subject to $\quad\quad\quad\quad x_1 + \ x_2 \leqslant 4,$ $\quad\quad\quad$ (17)

$\quad\quad\quad\quad\quad\quad 2x_1 + \ x_2 \leqslant 5,$ $\quad\quad\quad$ (18)

$\quad\quad\quad\quad\quad\quad -x_1 + 4x_2 \geqslant 2,$ $\quad\quad\quad$ (19)

$\quad\quad\quad\quad\quad\quad x_1, \ x_2 \geqslant 0.$

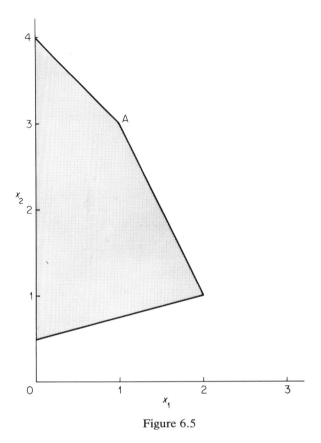

Figure 6.5

The feasible region is represented by Figure 6.5. The optimal solution is represented by point A ($x_1 = 1$, $x_2 = 3$, objective = 9).

We have already seen that the right-hand side coefficient of 4 on constraint (17) can be changed within the range 3–5, causing the objective to change by 1 (the shadow price on constraint (17)) for each unit of change. The values of the variables (x_1 and x_2) will also obviously change. Their rates of change, per unit increase in this right-hand side coefficient, are

$$x_1 \quad -1$$
$$x_2 \quad +2$$

i.e. x_1 will get smaller by one and x_2 will get larger by two for each unit of increase. Decreasing the right-hand side coefficient will obviously produce the opposite effect.

Such figures can be very valuable in many applications. For example, they might indicate how a production plan should alter as a certain resource becomes scarcer or more plentiful. In a blending application they could indicate the rate at which one ingredient should be substituted for another as it became more plentiful.

The same limitations apply to the interpretation of marginal rates of substitution as apply to shadow prices. We can only consider one change at a time within the permitted ranges. If a range is one-sided we can only apply the marginal rates of substitution for changes in one direction. A different set of marginal rates of substitution will exist (although will require more computation to derive) for changes in the opposite direction.

Building Stable Models

We have shown that quite a lot of useful information can be obtained to suggest how sensitive the optimal solution to a linear programming model is to changes (or inaccuracies) in the data. In many practical situations *stable solutions* are more valuable than *optimal solutions*. Having obtained an optimal solution to a model we might be very reluctant to change our operating plan if only small changes occurred in certain parameters, e.g. capacities or costs. To some extent we can incorporate this reluctance in our model.

Suppose we were to run out of a particular resource (e.g. processing capacity, raw material, manpower, etc.). It might well be that in practice we would buy in more in this resource at a cost until this increased cost became prohibitive. As was pointed out in Section 6.1, this situation can easily be modelled. For example, suppose the following constraint represented a resource limitation:

$$\sum_j a_j x_j \leqslant b. \tag{20}$$

The alternative representation

$$\sum_j a_j x_j - u = b. \tag{21}$$

would allow the resource's availability to be expanded at a cost per unit of c if u was given this objective cost (profit of $-c$) in the objective function. Sometimes (21) is referred to as a 'soft constraint' in contrast to the 'hard constraint' (20) since (21) does not provide the total barrier that (20) does.

Computer Output

In order to demonstrate how the information described in this section and Section 6.2 might be presented, output for the product mix problem is given here. This output comes from the solution of the model by the XPRESS-MP package. Fuller information is given in the XPRESS-MP reference manual.

The first set of output comes from the FRPRINT and FPRINT procedures of the package. This is in two sections. First, the ROWS of the model are listed by name together with their slack values in the optimal solution. This indicates those capacities which are fully utilized (zero slack) and those which are not. The *dual values* for the constraints are also given here together with the original right-hand side values (RHS). Secondly, the variables (COLUMNS) in the model are listed by name together with their *solution values and reduced costs*. The objective coefficients (INPUT COST) which were specified for the model are also given.

The next set of output comes from the FRPRINT procedure, which gives the results of the RANGE procedure. First, information is given for the constraints (ROWS) in the problem. Those at their upper bound (UL) or lower bound (LL) are binding. Those which are basic (BS) are not binding and may have a positive SLACK (or surplus) activity. The value of the left-hand side is given by the ACTIVITY. If the total activity in a constraint were to be forced up or down the objective value would change. Within the *ranges* given by the LOWER ACTVTY and UPPER ACTVTY the cost per unit change up or down is given by UNIT COST UP and UNIT COST DN respectively. For those at their lower or upper limits this will correspond to their dual values. Also given is the name of the variable which leaves the optimal solution (goes to one of its bounds) when a right-hand side coefficient reaches its *lower* or *upper activity*. When the outgoing variable name is that of a row of the model (e.g. DRILLING), the implication is that the corresponding constraint becomes binding (it ceases to have any slack capacity).

Secondly, information is given for the variables (COLUMNS) in the problem. One which is at its lower bound (usually zero) has an entry of LL and one which is at a level specified by an upper bound is denoted UL. A variable which is basic and may have a value between its bounds is denoted BS. Its optimal value is given by the ACTIVITY. If its value were to be forced up or down the objective value would change. As for the constraints, within the limits given by the LOWER ACTVTY and UPPER ACTVTY the cost per unit change up or down is given by UNIT COST UP and UNIT COST DN respectively. For variables at their lower or upper limits the information given is largely a repeat of that given with the FPRINT output. It has already been pointed out that the *objective ranges* for such variables are derivable from their reduced costs. For example, PROD03 takes a value of zero in the optimal solution and has a reduced cost (UNIT COST UP) of 125. Therefore the original objective coefficient (INPUT PRFT) of 350 has an upper range (UPPER PRFT) of 475 and a lower range (LOWER PRFT) of $-$infinity which is here represented by $-1 \cdot 000000E + 30$, i.e. -10^{30}. When the coefficient is increased or decreased to a range the variable leaving the solution is given together with the new value of the original variable (LOWER ACTVTY and UPPER ACTVTY). For basic variables the ranges given for the objective coefficients are again the UPPER and LOWER PRFT and the value that the original variable takes when the coefficient is at the ends of the range is again given by the LOWER and UPPER ACTVTY.

```
        Problem Statistics
        Matrix PRODMIX
        Objective PROFIT
        RHS RHS00001
        Problem has      4 rows and      5 structural columns

        Solution Statistics
        Maximisation performed
        Optimal solution found after     3 iterations
        Objective function value is  10920.00000
```

Rows Section

Number		Row	At	Value	Slack Value	Dual Value	RHS
N	1	PROFIT	BS	10920.00000	-10920.00000	.000000	.000000
L	2	GRINDING	UL	288.000000	.000000	6.250000	288.000000
L	3	DRILLING	BS	177.600000	14.400000	.000000	192.000000
L	4	MANPOWER	UL	384.000000	.000000	23.750000	384.000000

Columns Section

Number		Column		At	Value	Input Cost	Reduced Cost
C	5	PROD	01	BS	12.000000	550.000000	.000000
C	6	PROD	02	BS	7.200000	600.000000	.000000
C	7	PROD	03	LL	.000000	350.000000	125.000000
C	8	PROD	04	LL	.000000	400.000000	231.250000
C	9	PROD	05	LL	.000000	200.000000	368.750000

Rows Section

Vector Number	Activity Slack	Lower actvty Upper actvty	Unit cost DN Unit cost UP	Lower prft	Limiting Process	AT
N PROFIT	10920.00000	10560.00000	1.000000		GRINDING	UL
BS 1	-10920.00000	10920.00000	1.00000E+30			
L GRINDING	288.000000	230.399993	6.250000		PROD 02	LL
UL 2	.000000	384.000000	-6.250000		PROD 01	LL
L DRILLING	177.600000	147.692306	34.259258		PROD 04	LL
BS 3	14.400000	192.000000	25.000000		GRINDING	UL
L MANPOWER	384.000000	288.000000	23.750000		PROD 01	LL
UL 4	.000000	406.153839	-23.750000		DRILLING	UL

Columns Section

Vector Number	Activity Input prft	Lower actvty Upper actvty	Unit cost DN Unit cost UP	Lower prft Upper prft	Limiting Process	AT
C PROD 01	12.000000	.000000	50.000000	500.000000	PROD 03	LL
BS 5	550.000000	19.200000	50.000000	600.000000	GRINDING	UL
C PROD 02	7.200000	.000000	50.000000	550.000000	GRINDING	UL
BS 6	600.000000	14.400000	83.333335	683.333312	PROD 03	LL
C PROD 03	.000000	-4.800000	-125.000000	-1.00000E+30	PROD 02	LL
LL 7	350.000000	4.800000	125.000000	475.000000	PROD 01	LL
C PROD 04	.000000	-2.133333	-231.250000	-1.00000E+30	DRILLING	UL
LL 8	400.000000	4.430769	231.250000	631.250000	PROD 02	LL
C PROD 05	.000000	-1.556757	-368.750000	-1.00000E+30	DRILLING	UL
LL 9	200.000000	19.200000	368.750000	568.750000	PROD 02	LL

6.4 Further Investigations Using a Model

The previous two sections described how a lot of useful information could be derived concerning the effects on the optimal solution of changes in the coefficients of a linear programming model. Such information was, however, limited in value by the fact that (i) only one coefficient could be changed at a time; (ii) that coefficient could only be changed within certain ranges. *Parametric programming* is a convenient method of investigating the effects of more radical changes. It is beyond the scope of this book to describe how the method works. There is virtue, however, in describing how such investigations can be organized and presented to a computer package. Parametric programming is computationally quick and therefore provides a cheap means of determining how the optimal solution changes with alterations in objective and right-hand side coefficients. It is useful to illustrate the description again by means of a numerical example. We will again use the product mix model introduced in Section 1.2. In the last section we saw how the right-hand side coefficients could be varied individually within their permitted ranges. Suppose that instead we wished to investigate the possibility of increasing both grinding capacity and manpower simultaneously. Parametric programming on the right-hand side allows us to carry out such an investigation as long as the coefficients increase (or decrease) by constant relative amounts. For example, we could investigate the effect of employing an extra man on assembly for each new grinding machine bought. Each increase of 96 hours per week in grinding capacity will therefore be accompanied by an increase of 48 hours per week in manpower capacity. If θ new grinding machines are bought, the right-hand side vector of coefficients would become

$$\begin{pmatrix} 288 \\ 192 \\ 384 \end{pmatrix} + \theta \begin{pmatrix} 96 \\ 0 \\ 48 \end{pmatrix}.$$

Parametric programming allows one to specify a *change column* such as

$$\begin{pmatrix} 96 \\ 0 \\ 48 \end{pmatrix}$$

and *limits* within which θ can vary. The procedure will then allow θ to vary between these limits and calculate the value of the objective function at various intervals. For example, the parameter θ was allowed to vary between 0 (the original capacities) and 10 (when the new capacities become 1248, 192, and 864 respectively).

Such information can be very valuable in examining the effect of expansions or contractions in the availability of different resources. The result is well expressed graphically, as is done for the example we have just discussed in Figure 6.6.

Analogous to parametric programming on the right-hand side is parametric programming on the objective function. For example, in the product mix model, if we wished to increase the prices of all products by the same amount simultaneously, we would specify a *change row*:

$$(1, \quad 1, \quad 1, \quad 1, \quad 1).$$

A parameter θ would be allowed to vary between specified limits adding θ times this row to the row of objective coefficients. The effect on the optimal objective view would again be mapped out. An example of the use of parametric programming on the objective is given for the FOOD MANUFACTURE model in Part 2.

Most packages have facilities for parametric programming. It is necessary to incorporate a change column or change row in the data for the model and specify limits for the parameter in the control program. A parametric procedure is also called in the control program usually after the SOLUTION procedure. Such parametric procedures usually go under such names as PARAOBJ and PARARHS. Full details of how to use such facilities would obviously be given in the appropriate manual. Some packages also have a

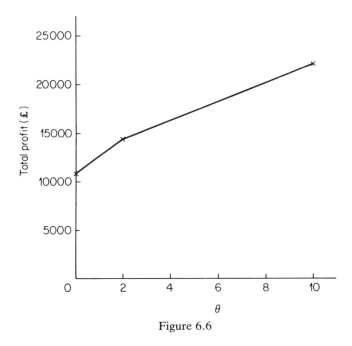

Figure 6.6

facility for doing parametric programming on the objective and right-hand side coefficients simultaneously, i.e. on the so called 'rim' of the model.

6.5   Presentation of the Solutions

This chapter has described a lot of useful information which can be derived from linear programming models. It is often easy to lose sight of the difficulty which non-specialists may have in relating such information to the real life situation which has been modelled. Obscure presentation of information derived from a linear programming model can lead to complete rejection of the technique. Computer output is often obscure since a package program is designed to solve any model no matter what the application is. The output must obviously, therefore, relate to the mathematical aspects of the model. One way of overcoming the difficulty is for an intermediate person (possibly the model builder) to convert the computer output into a written report which can easily be understood. For models which are run frequently this can be a cumbersome and slow process. Many organizations have computer programs which read the solution output from the linear programming package and convert it into a form which relates to the application. Computer programs which do this are known as *report writers*. Clearly a report writer program must be related to the application. As a consequence such programs are usually purpose written for the type of model solved. Frequently they are written by the organization using the model rather than by the producer of the package. A high level language such as FORTRAN is usually used. It is necessary for the program to read the solution output from the package. With most packages it is quite easy to do this by getting the package to write its output on to a file. Many practitioners would argue in favour of such purpose-built report writers. There do, however, exist general purpose report writers which sometimes accompany particular packages. Sometimes these report writers can be used satisfactorily for the application required.

Report writers are often considered in conjunction with matrix generators which were discussed in Section 3.5. A matrix generator relates the *input* for a linear programming model to the practical problem while a report writer so relates the *output*.

We give the computer output to the blending example introduced in Section 1.2. This output should be fairly easy to understand when considered in conjunction with the original statement of the problem (Example 2 of Section 1.2) and the format of its presentation to the package (Section 2.3).

```
Problem Statistics
Matrix BLEND
Objective PROF
RHS RHS00001
Problem has      6 rows and      6 structural columns

Solution Statistics
Maximisation performed
Optimal solution found after      4 iterations
Objective function value is   17592.59259

Rows Section
     Number      Row    At      Value     Slack Value   Dual Value        RHS
  N      1   PROF     BS    17592.59259   -17592.59259      .000000      .000000
  L      2   VVEG     UL      200.000000        .000000    29.629630   200.000000
  L      3   NVEG     UL      250.000000        .000000    46.666667   250.000000
  L      4   UHRD     UL          .000000        .000000     3.703704      .000000
  G      5   LHRD     BS     1350.000000    1350.000000      .000000      .000000
  E      6   CONT     EQ          .000000        .000000  -172.222222      .000000

Columns Section
     Number   Column   At      Value     Input Cost   Reduced Cost
  C      7   VEG  01   BS      159.259259   -110.000000      .000000
  C      8   VEG  02   BS       40.740741   -120.000000      .000000
  C      9   OIL  01   LL          .000000   -130.000000    11.851852
  C     10   OIL  02   BS      250.000000   -110.000000      .000000
  C     11   OIL  03   LL          .000000   -115.000000     7.962963
  C     12   PROD      BS      450.000000    150.000000      .000000

Rows Section
     Vector    Activity   Lower actvty Unit cost DN  Lower prft  Limiting AT
     Number      Slack    Upper actvty Unit cost UP              Process

N PROF      17592.59259   16428.57299     1.000000                VVEG    UL
BS    1    -17592.59259   17592.59155  1.00000E+30

L VVEG        200.000000    160.714294    29.629629                VEG   02 LL
UL    2           .000000  4500.000000   -29.629629                VEG   01 LL

L NVEG        250.000000     11.111115    46.666667                VEG   01 LL
UL    3           .000000    311.111114   -46.666667                VEG   02 LL

L UHRD            .000000   -430.000000     3.703704                VEG   01 LL
UL    4           .000000    110.000000    -3.703704                VEG   02 LL

G LHRD       1350.000000    920.000000     3.703704                UHRD    UL
BS    5      1350.000000   1350.000000  1.60000E+31

E CONT            .000000    -18.333333  -172.222229                VEG   02 LL
EQ    6           .000000     71.666664   172.222229                VEG   01 LL
```

```
Columns Section
      Vector     Activity    Lower actvty Unit cost DN  Lower prft  Limiting AT
      Number     Input prft  Upper actvty Unit cost UP  Upper prft  Process

  C VEG   01    159.259259  -340.740753   10.000000   -120.000000 UHRD      UL
  BS       7    -110.000000  200.000000   14.545455    -95.454544 OIL    01 LL

  C VEG   02     40.740741  -162.962966   14.545455   -134.545455 OIL    01 LL
  BS       8    -120.000000  200.000000   10.000000   -110.000000 UHRD      UL

  C OIL   01       .000000  -195.454544  -11.851852 -1.00000E+30 VEG    01 LL
  LL       9    -130.000000   50.000000   11.851852   -118.148147 VEG    02 LL

  C OIL   02    250.000000  -287.500000    7.962963   -117.962966 OIL    03 LL
  BS      10    -110.000000  250.000000 1.28000E+32  1.28000E+32

  C OIL   03       .000000  -137.500000   -7.962963 -1.00000E+30 VEG    02 LL
  LL      11    -115.000000  250.000000    7.962963   -107.037040 OIL    02 LL

  C PROD        450.000000   410.714294   29.629629    120.370368 VVEG      UL
  BS      12    150.000000   450.000000 1.28000E+32  1.28000E+32
```

In order to show the advantage of a report writer, the information is presented again through a purpose-built report writer for the application. The output should be self-explanatory.

```
DATE:        1 JANUARY  1993

                OPTIMAL SOLUTION TO BLEND PROBLEM

                TOTAL REVENUE   $17593

                MANUFACTURE       450    TONS OF PROD

                        USE       159    TONS OF VEG1

                        USE        41    TONS OF VEG2

                        USE       250    TONS OF OIL2

                HARDNESS OF PROD  6.0 UNITS

      ***********************************************************

              PRICE REDUCTION NECESSARY BEFORE PURCHASE

                      OIL1          $12/TON

                      OIL3          $8/TON

      ***********************************************************

              MARGINAL VALUE OF EXTRA REFINING CAPACITY

                VEGETABLE OILS        $30/TON

              NON-VEGETABLE OILS      $47/TON

      ***********************************************************
```

CHAPTER 7

Non-linear Models

7.1 Typical Applications

It has already been pointed out that many mathematical programming models contain variables representing activities which compete for the use of limited resources. For a linear programming model to be applicable the following must apply:

(i) There must be constant returns to scale.
(ii) Use of a resource by an activity is proportional to the level of the activity.
(iii) The total use of a resource by a number of activities is the sum of the uses by the individual activities.

These conditions clearly applied in the product mix example of Section 1.2 and the result was the linear programming model given there. All the expressions in that model are *linear*. Nowhere do we get expressions such as x_1^2, $x_1 x_2$, $\log x_1$, etc. Suppose, however, that the first of the above conditions did not apply. Instead of each unit of PROD 1 produced contributing £550 to profit we suppose that the unit profit contribution depends on the quantity of PROD 1 produced. If this unit profit contribution *increases* with the quantity produced we are said to have *increasing returns to scale*. For *decreases* in the unit profit contribution there are said to be *decreasing returns to scale*. These two situations together with the case of a *constant return to scale* are illustrated in Figures 7.1, 7.2, and 7.3 respectively.

In our product mix model each unit of PROD 1 produced contributes £550 to profit. This gives rise to a term $550x_1$ in the objective function. The whole objective function is made up of the sum of similar terms and is said to be *linear*. As an example of increasing returns to scale we could suppose that the unit profit contribution depended on x_1 and was $550 + 2x_1$. This would give rise to the *non-linear* term $2x_1^2$ in the objective function. We would now have a non-linear model, although the constraints would still be linear expressions. In practice the non-linear term might not be known explicitly and might simply be represented graphically as in Figure 7.1 or Figure 7.2.

As an example of decreasing returns to scale we could suppose that the unit profit contribution was $550/(1 + x_1)$. This would give rise to the *non-linear* term $550x_1/(1 + x_1)$ in the objective function.

The above two cases of non-linearities in the objective function arose

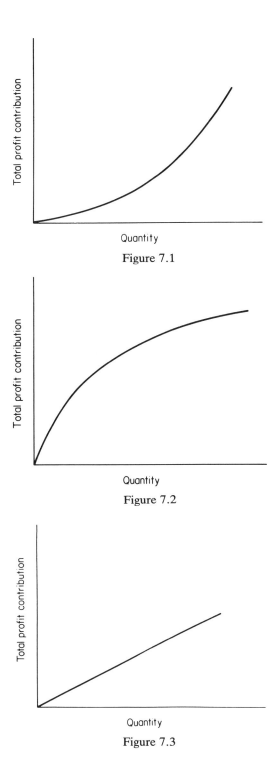

Figure 7.1

Figure 7.2

Figure 7.3

through profit margins being affected by increasing or decreasing unit costs arising from increased production. In a similar way unit profit margins will be altered if unit selling price is affected by the volume of production. It frequently happens, in practice, that the unit price which a product can command increases with the demand for it. In this case it may be convenient to treat unit selling price as a variable to be determined by the model. For example if the quantity to be produced is x, the unit cost is c and the unit selling price is $p(x)$, which depends on x, we have

$$\text{profit contribution} = (p(x) - c)x = p(x)x - cx.$$

The term $p(x)x$ introduces a non-linearity into the objective function. An obvious first approximation is to take $p(x)$ as a linear function of x. If this is done quadratic terms are introduced into the objective function, resulting in a *quadratic programming* model. An example of such a model results from the AGRICULTURAL PRICING problem of Part 2.

A, sometimes, rather more accurate way to reflect the relationship between $p(x)$ and x is through a *price elasticity*. We have the following definition of the *price elasticity of demand for a good x*:

$$E_x = \frac{\text{percentage change in quantity of } x \text{ demanded}}{\text{percentage change in } p(x)}.$$

It is possible to regard E_x as constant for the range of values of x and $p(x)$ considered. The above definition then leads to

$$p(x) = \frac{k}{x^{1/E_x}},$$

where k is the price above which demand is reduced to unity.

For a particular volume of production x, $p(x)$ gives the unit price at which this level will exactly balance the demand. The resultant non-linear term in the objective function will be

$$p(x)x = kx^{1 - (1/E_x)}.$$

A way in which price elasticities are incorporated in a non-linear programming model of the British national health service is described by McDonald, Cuddeford, and Beale (1974).

So far we have described how mathematical programming models with non-linear objective functions can arise. Non-linear terms also, sometimes, arise in the constraints of a mathematical programming model.

For example, in a blending problem (such as that described in the second example of Section 1.2) a quality (such as hardness) might not depend linearly on the ingredient proportions. Restrictions on such qualities would then give rise to non-linear constraints.

One type of model which has received a certain amount of attention, where non-linearities occur in the constraints, is the *geometric programming* type of model. Here the non-linear expressions are all polynomials. For example we might have the following constraint:

$$x_1 x_2 x_3 + 2x_2^2 x_3 \leqslant 32.$$

Such models do arise often in engineering problems. They are, however, fairly rare in managerial applications. A full treatment of the subject is given by Duffin, Peterson, and Zener (1968).

Non-linear programming models are usually far more difficult to solve than correspondingly sized linear models. It is, however, often possible to solve an approximation to the model through either linear programming or an extension of linear programming known as separable programming. Which case is applicable depends upon an important classification of non-linear models into *convex* and *non-convex* problems. This distinction is explained in the next section.

7.2   Local and Global Optima

Non-linear programming can be divided usefully into *convex programming and non-convex programming*.

Definition

A *region* of space is said to be convex if the portion of the straight line between any two points in the region also lies in the region.

For example, the area shaded in Figure 7.4 is a convex region in two-dimensional space. On the other hand, the area shaded in Figure 7.5 is a

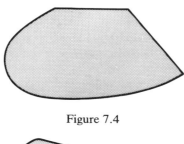

Figure 7.4

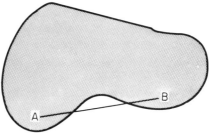

Figure 7.5

non-convex region since A and B are both points within the region yet the line AB between them does not lie entirely in the region.

Definition

A *function $f(x)$* is said to be convex if the set of points (x, y) where $y \geqslant f(x)$ forms a convex region.

For example, the function x^2 is convex, as is demonstrated by Figure 7.6 since the shaded area is a convex region. On the other hand, the function $2 - x^2$ is non-convex, as is demonstrated by Figure 7.7.

It should be intuitive that the concepts of convex and non-convex regions and functions apply in as many dimensions as required.

Definition

A *mathematical programming* model is said to be convex if it involves the *minimization of a convex function* over a convex feasible region.

Clearly minimizing a convex function is equivalent to maximizing the negation of a convex function. Such a maximization problem will also therefore be convex.

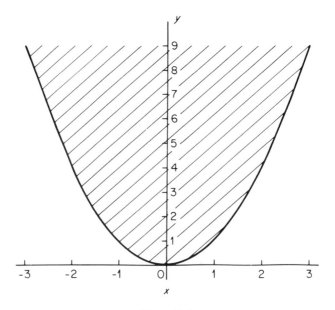

Figure 7.6

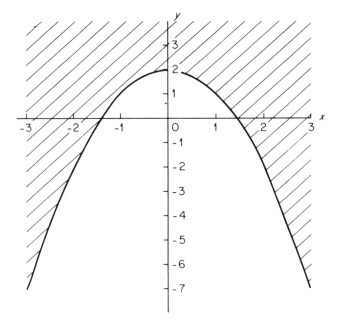

Figure 7.7

Example 1. A Convex Programming Model

Minimize $\quad x_1^2 - 4x_1 - 2x_2$

subject to $\quad x_1 + x_2 \leqslant 4,$

$\qquad\qquad 2x_1 + x_2 \leqslant 5,$

$\qquad\qquad -x_1 + 4x_2 \geqslant 2,$

$\qquad\qquad\qquad x_1, x_2 \geqslant 0.$

The function $x_1^2 - 4x_1 - 2x_2$ is represented in Figure 7.8 and easily seen to be convex.

This model is represented geometrically in Figure 7.9 with different objective values represented by the curved lines which arise from contours of the surface in Figure 7.8. Clearly the optimal solution is represented by point A.

It should be obvious that linear programming (LP) is a special case of convex programming. All LP models can be expressed as minimizations, if necessary, of linear functions. A linear function obviously satisfies the definition of a convex function. Moreover, the feasible region defined by a set of linear constraints can easily be shown to be convex.

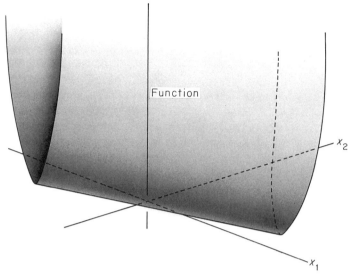

Figure 7.8

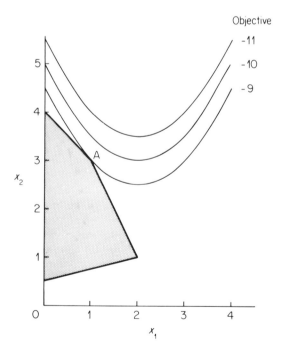

Figure 7.9

Example 2. A Non-convex Programming Model

Minimize $-4x_1^3 + 3x_1 - 6x_2$

subject to $x_1 + x_2 \leqslant 4,$

                      $2x_1 + x_2 \leqslant 5,$

                $-x_1 + 4x_2 \geqslant 2,$

                       $x_1, x_2 \geqslant 0.$

The function $-4x_1^3 + 3x_1 - 6x_2$ is represented in Figure 7.10 and seen to be non-convex, although of course the feasible region of the above model is still convex.

The model is represented geometrically in Figure 7.11.

Again different objective values give rise to the curved lines which are contours of the surface in Figure 7.10. Clearly the optimal solution is at C. For a larger problem, however, we would not have the geometrical intuition which we have here. As far as many algorithms (including the separable programming algorithm) are concerned, the point A would also appear as an optimal solution. At A the curved line representing this objective value of -19 deviates away from the feasible region in both directions. This would be taken as evidence in a convex (including linear) programming model that A were the optimal solution. Figure 7.9 demonstrates how the objective contours for a convex problem curve away from the feasible region. For our non-convex example, however, Figure 7.11 demonstrates how the objective contours curve in towards the feasible region and may re-enter it. This, in fact, happens in the example here. The fact that the objective contour passing through A deviates away from the feasible region at A in both directions cannot, therefore, be

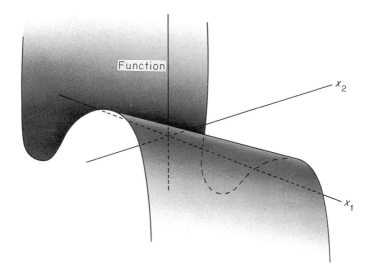

Figure 7.10

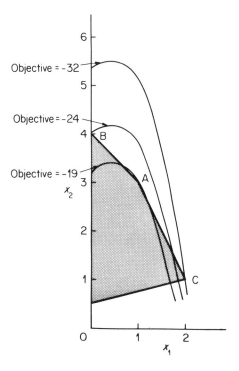

Figure 7.11

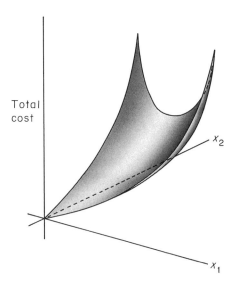

Figure 7.12

taken as evidence that it will not re-enter it. In fact, as we can see, it is possible to move out to a better (smaller) objective contour passing through B. Even then we can move out to a still better objective contour passing through C. Points A and B represent what are known as *local optima*. Many computational procedures (such as separable programming) can guarantee no more than local optima. Clearly what is really required is a true *global optimum* such as that represented by point C in Figure 7.11. A fairly graphic way of describing the situation is to consider the problem of a mountaineer on a range of mountains in a thick fog. It is easy for him to determine when he is at a local optimum, i.e. a mountain peak. The ground will begin to drop in height whichever way he walks. This does not guarantee, however, that there is not another, higher mountain peak, hidden in the fog. The situation of the mountaineer is similar to that of many non-linear programming algorithms.

The possibility of local optima arising from non-convex programming models when certain algorithms are used is what makes such models much more difficult to solve than convex programming models. With a convex programming model any optimum found must be a global optimum. To find a guaranteed global optimum to a non-convex model requires more sophisticated algorithms than the separable programming algorithm described in the next section. A satisfactory, though often computationally expensive, way of tackling such problems is through *integer programming* as described in Section 9.3.

A good illustration of the distinction between convex and non-convex programming models is given by the non-linear programming models mentioned in Section 7.1, which arise when there are *diseconomies of scale*

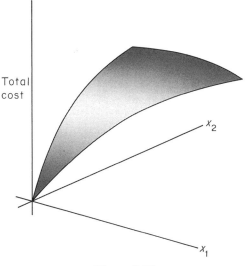

Figure 7.13

and *economies of scale*. The former type of model is convex and the latter non-convex. To see why this is so we first consider the type of cost function which arises when we have diseconomies of scale. This is illustrated in Figure 7.12. If x_1 and x_2 represent quantities of two products to be made, diseconomies of scale will result in the total cost rising faster and faster with increasing values of x_1 and x_2. The result is clearly a convex cost function (to be minimized).

For the case of economies of scale we have the situation represented in Figure 7.13. x_1 and x_2 again represent quantities of two products to be made. As x_1 and x_2 increase, decreasing unit costs result in the total cost rising less and less quickly. The result is clearly a non-convex cost function (to be minimized).

7.3 Separable Programming

Definition

A *separable* function ·is a function which can be expressed as the sum of functions of a single variable.

For example, the function

$$x_1^2 + 2x_2 + e^{x_3}$$

is separable since each of terms x_1^2, $2x_2$ and e^{x_3} is a function of a single variable. On the other hand, the function

$$x_1 x_2 + \frac{x_2}{1 + x_1} + x_3$$

is not separable since the terms $x_1 x_2$ and $x_2/(1 + x_1)$ are each functions of more than one variable.

The importance of separable functions in a mathematical programming model lies in the fact that they can be approximated to by *piecewise linear functions*. It is then possible to use separable programming to obtain a global optimum to a convex problem or possibly only a local optimum for a non-convex problem.

Although the class of separable functions might seem to be a rather restrictive one it is often possible to convert mathematical programming models with non-separable functions into ones with only separable functions. Ways in which this may be done are discussed in Section 7.4. In this way a surprisingly wide class of non-linear programming problems can be converted into separable programming models.

In order to convert a non-linear programming model into a suitable form for separable programming it is necessary to make piecewise linear approximations to each of the non-linear functions of a single variable. As will become apparent, it does not matter whether the non-linearities are in the objective function or the constraints or both. To illustrate the procedure we will consider the non-linear model given in Example 1 of Section 7.2. The only non-linear term occurring in the model is x_1^2. A piecewise linear approximation to this function is illustrated in Figure 7.14.

It is easy to see that x_1 can never exceed $2 \cdot 5$ from the second constraint of the problem. The piecewise linear approximation to x_1^2 need, therefore, only be considered for values of x_1 between 0 and $2 \cdot 5$. The curve between 0 and C has been divided into three straight line portions. This inevitably introduces some inaccuracy into the problem. For example, when x_1 is $1 \cdot 5$ the transformed model will regard x_1^2 as $2 \cdot 5$ instead of $2 \cdot 25$. Such inaccuracy can obviously be reduced by a more refined grid involving more straight line portions. For our purpose, however, we will content ourselves with the grid indicated in Figure 7.14. If such inaccuracy is considered serious, one approach would be to take the value of x, obtained from the optimal solution, refine the grid in the neighbourhood of this value, and re-optimize. Some package programs allow one to do this automatically a number of times, all within one computer run.

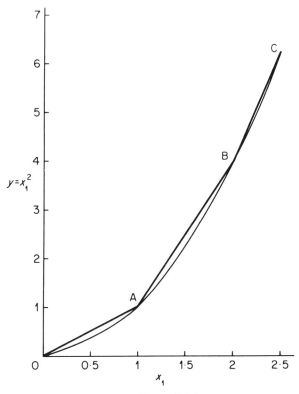

Figure 7.14

Our aim is to eliminate the non-linear term x_1^2 from our model. We can do this by replacing it by the single (linear) term y. It is now possible to relate y to x_1 by the following relationships:

$$x_1 = 0\lambda_1 + 1\lambda_2 + 2\lambda_3 + 2 \cdot 5 \ \lambda_4, \tag{1}$$

$$y = 0\lambda_1 + 1\lambda_2 + 4\lambda_3 + 6 \cdot 25\lambda_4, \tag{2}$$

$$\lambda_1 + \lambda_2 + \lambda_3 + \lambda_4 = 1. \tag{3}$$

The λ_i are new variables which we introduce into the model. They can be interpreted as 'weights' to be attached to the vertices 0, A, B, and C. It is, however, necessary to add another stipulation regarding the λ_i:

$$\text{at most two adjacent } \lambda_i \text{ can be non-zero.} \tag{4}$$

The stipulation (4) guarantees that corresponding values of x_1 and y lie on one of the straight line segments 0A, AB, or BC. For example if $\lambda_2 = 0 \cdot 5$ and $\lambda_3 = 0 \cdot 5$ (other λ_i being zero) we could get $x_1 = 1 \cdot 5$ and $y = 2 \cdot 5$. Clearly ignoring stipulation (4) would incorrectly allow the possibility of values x_1 and y off the piecewise straight line 0ABC.

(1), (2), and (3) give rise to constraints which can be added to our original model (Example 1 of Section 7.2). The term x_1^2 is replaced by y. This results in the following model:

Minimize $\quad y - 4x_1 - 2x_2$

subject to
$$
\begin{aligned}
x_1 + x_2 &\leqslant 4, \\
2x_1 + x_2 &\leqslant 5, \\
-x_1 + 4x_2 &\geqslant 2, \\
-x_1 \qquad + \lambda_2 + 2\lambda_3 + 2 \cdot 5 \ \lambda_4 &= 0, \\
-y \qquad + \lambda_2 + 4\lambda_3 + 6 \cdot 25 \ \lambda_4 &= 0, \\
\lambda_1 + \lambda_2 + \lambda_3 + \lambda_4 &= 1, \\
y, x_1, x_2, \lambda_1, \lambda_2, \lambda_3, \lambda_4 &\geqslant 0.
\end{aligned}
$$

It is important to remember that stipulation (4) must apply to the set of variables λ_i. A solution in which, for example, we had $\lambda_1 = \frac{1}{3}$ and $\lambda_3 = \frac{2}{3}$ would not be acceptable since this results in the wrong relationship between x_1 and $y(x_1^2)$. In general stipulation (4) cannot be modelled using linear programming constraints. It can, however, be regarded as a 'logical condition' on the variables λ_i and be modelled using integer programming. This is described in Section 9.3. Fortunately in our example here no difficulty arises over stipulation (4). This is because the original model was *convex*. Suppose, for example, we were to take as the set of values $\lambda_1 = 0 \cdot 5$, $\lambda_2 = 0 \cdot 25$, $\lambda_3 = 0 \cdot 25$, and $\lambda_4 = 0$. This clearly breaks stipulation (4). From the relations (1) and (2) it clearly leads to the point $x_1 = 0 \cdot 75$ and $y = 1 \cdot 25$ on Figure 7.14. This is above the piecewise straight line. Since our objective involves minimizing $y(x_1^2)$, we would expect to get a better solution by taking $x_1 = 0 \cdot 75$ and $y = 0 \cdot 75$ when we drop on to the piecewise straight line. In view of the (convex) shape of the graph we cannot obtain values for the λ_i which give us points below the piecewise straight line. Therefore we must always obtain corresponding values of x_1 and y which lie on one of the line segments by virtue of optimality. Stipulation (4) is therefore guaranteed in this case. We can therefore solve our transformed model by linear programming and obtain a satisfactory optimal solution. It is not even necessary to resort to the separable extension of the simplex algorithm which is discussed below. This happens, however, only because our problem is convex.

For a non-convex problem stipulation (4) would generally not be satisfied automatically. In order to guarantee that it be satisfied we could resort to the separable programming modification of the simplex algorithm. In order to demonstrate the difficulty that a non-convex problem presents we will make a piecewise linear approximation to the non-linear term x_1^3 in the non-convex model of Example 2 in Section 7.2. This is demonstrated in Figure 7.15.

This gives us the relationships

$$x_1 = 0\lambda_1 + \quad 0\cdot5\lambda_2 + 1\lambda_3 + \quad 1\cdot5\lambda_4 + \quad 2\cdot5\lambda_5,$$
$$y \ = 0\lambda_1 + 0\cdot125\lambda_2 + 1\lambda_3 + 3\cdot375\lambda_4 + 15\cdot625\lambda_5.$$

As before the λ_i variables can be interpreted as 'weights' attached to the vertices in Figure 7.15.

The λ_i variables must again satisfy the stipulation that at most two adjacent λ_i are non-zero. This time this stipulation is not automatically guaranteed by optimality. Suppose, for example, that we were to obtain the set of values $\lambda_2 = 0\cdot4$, $\lambda_3 = 0\cdot5$, and $\lambda_4 = 0\cdot1$. This would give $x_1 = 0\cdot85$ and $y = 1\cdot3375$. The point with these coordinates lies above the piecewise line in Figure 7.15.

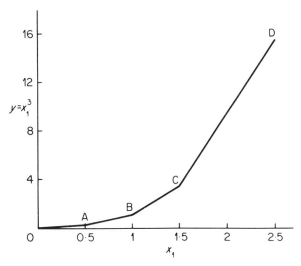

Figure 7.15

As our objective function, to be minimized, is dominated by the term $-4x_1^3$, our optimization will tend to maximize y. This will tend to take us away from the piecewise line rather than down on to it. In this (non-convex) case it is therefore necessary to use an algorithm which does not allow more than two adjacent λ_i to be non-zero.

The *separable programming* extension of the simplex algorithm due to Miller (1963) never allows more than two adjacent λ_i into the solution. As a result it restricts corresponding values of x_1 and y to the coordinates of points lying on the desired piecewise straight line.

Unfortunately with non-convex problems, such as Example 2 of Section 7.2, which was modelled above, restricting the values of λ_i to at most two adjacent ones being non-zero does not guarantee any more than a local optimum. We could easily end up at points A or B on Figure 7.11 rather than C.

In both our examples the non-linear functions of a single variable appeared in the objective function. Should such non-linear functions also appear in the constraints the analysis is just the same. They are replaced by linear terms and a piecewise linear approximation made to the non-linear function. Variables λ_i are then introduced in order to relate the new term to the old.

It may not always be easy to decide whether a problem is convex or not. For known convex problems (such as, for example, problems which are linear apart from diseconomies of scale) consisting only of separable functions, piecewise linear approximations are all that are needed. It is not necessary here to use the separable programming algorithm. For problems which are non-convex (such as, for example, problems with economies of scale) or where it is not known whether or not they are convex, linear programming is not sufficient. Separable programming can be used but no more than a local optimum can be guaranteed. It is often possible to solve such a model a number of times using different strategies to obtain different local optima. The best of these may then have some chance of being a global optimum. Such computational considerations are, however, beyond the scope of this book, but are sometimes described in manuals associated with particular packages. The only really satisfactory way of being sure of avoiding local optima when a problem is not known to be convex is to resort to integer programming which is generally much more costly in computer time. This is discussed in Sections 9.2 and 9.3.

Before finishing this section an alternative way of modelling a piecewise linear approximation to a separable function will be described. The formulation method just described is usually known as the λ-*form* for separable programming where variables λ_i are interpreted as weights attached to the vertices in the piecewise straight line. There is an alternative formulation known as the δ-*form*. In order to demonstrate the δ-form we will reconsider the piecewise linear approximation to the function $y = x_1^2$ shown in Figure 7.4. This approximation is redrawn in Figure 7.16.

Variables δ_1, δ_2, and δ_3 are introduced to represent *proportions* of the intervals 0P, PQ, and QR which are used to make up the value of x_1. We then get

$$x_1 = \delta_1 + \delta_2 + 0 \cdot 5\delta_3, \qquad (5)$$

where

$$0 \leqslant \delta_1, \delta_2 \, \delta_3 \leqslant 1$$

Since 0P and PQ are each of length 1, the coefficients of δ_1 and δ_2 in equation (5) are 1. The coefficient of δ_3 is $0 \cdot 5$, reflecting the length of the interval QR.
  Similarly

$$y = \delta_1 + 3\delta_2 + 2 \cdot 25\delta_3, \qquad (6)$$

where the coefficients of δ_1, δ_2, and δ_3 are now the lengths of the intervals 0S, ST and TU.

  In order to ensure that x_1 and y are the coordinates of points on the piecewise lines 0C we must make the following stipulation:

> if any δ_i is non-zero, all the preceding δ_i must take
> the value 1 and all the succeeding δ_i must take the value 0. $\qquad (7)$

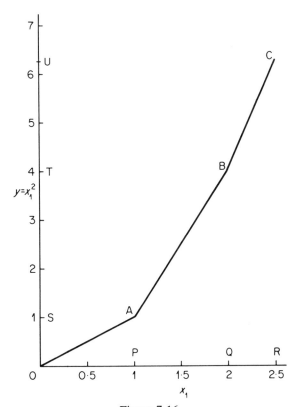

Figure 7.16

Stipulation (7) clearly ensures that x_1 and y truly represent distances along their respective axes.

The above δ-form for separable programming is usually considered to be computationally more efficient. As a result many packages are designed to work with this formulation. The variables δ_i are given simple upper bounds of 1, thus exploiting the bounded variable version of the simplex algorithm. The possibility of local optima, however, with non-convex problems still remains.

7.4 Converting a Problem to a Separable Model

The restriction of only allowing non-linear functions to be separable might seem to impose a severe limitation on the class of problems which can be tackled by separable programming. Rather surprisingly it is possible to convert a very large class of non-linear programming problems into separable models. When non-separable functions occur in a model it is often possible to transform the model into one with only separable functions.

A very common non-separable function which occurs in practice is the product of two or more variables. For example, if a term such as $x_1 x_2$ occurs the model is not immediately a separable one since this is a non-linear function of more that one variable. The model is easily converted into a separable form, however, by the following transformation:

(i) Introduce two new variables u_1 and u_2 into the model.
(ii) Relate u_1 and u_2 to x_1 and x_2 by the relations

$$u_1 = \tfrac{1}{2}(x_1 + x_2), \tag{1}$$

$$u_2 = \tfrac{1}{2}(x_1 - x_2). \tag{2}$$

(iii) Replace the term $x_1 x_2$ in the model by

$$u_1^2 - u_2^2.$$

It is easy to see by elementary algebra that $u_1^2 - u_2^2$ is the same as the product $x_1 x_2$ as long as (1) and (2) are added to the model in the form of equality constraints. The model now contains non-linear functions u_1^2 and u_2^2 of single variables and is therefore separable. These non-linear terms can be dealt with by piecewise linear approximations. It is important to remember that u_2 might need to take negative values. When the possible ranges of values for u_1 and u_2 are considered it may be necessary to either translate u_2 by an appropriate amount or treat it as a 'free' variable. A 'free' variable in linear programming is one which is not restricted to non-negative values.

Should the product of more than two variables occur in a model (as might happen for example in a geometric programming model) then the above procedure could be repeated successively to reduce the model to a separable form.

An alternative way of dealing with product terms in a non-linear model is to use logarithms. We will again consider the example where a product $x_1 x_2$ of two variables occurs in a model although the method clearly generalizes to larger products. The following transformation can be carried out:

(i) Replace $x_1 x_2$ by a new variable y.
(ii) Relate y to x_1 and x_2 by the equation

$$\log y = \log x_1 + \log x_2. \tag{3}$$

(3) gives a non-linear equality constraint to be added to the model. The expression in this constraint is, however, separable since we only have non-linear functions $\log y$, $\log x_1$, and $\log x_2$ of single variables.

Care must be taken, however, when this transformation is made to ensure that neither x_1 nor x_2 (and consequently y) ever take the value 0. If this were to happen their logarithms would become $-\infty$. It may be necessary to translate x_1 and x_2 by certain amounts to avoid this ever happening.

The use of logarithms to convert a non-linear model to a suitable form does, however, sometimes lead to computational problems. Beale (1975) suggests that this can happen if both a variable and its logarithm occur together in the same model. If these are likely to be of widely different orders of magnitude numerical inaccuracy may lead to computational difficulties.

Non-linear functions of more than one variable (such as product terms) can be dealt with in yet another way by generalizing a piecewise linear approximation to more dimensions. A more complex relationship then has to be specified between the λ_i. As with non-convex separable models this is only really satisfactorily dealt with through *integer programming* and is described in Section 9.3.

Many other non-linear functions of more than one variable can be reduced to non-linear functions of a single variable by the addition of extra variables and constraints. Ingenuity is often required but the range of non-linear programming problems which can be made separable in this way is vast. Such transformations do, however, often greatly increase the size of a model and hence the time to solve it.

CHAPTER 8

Integer Programming

8.1 Introduction

A suprisingly wide class of practical problems can be modelled using integer variables and linear constraints. Sometimes such a model consists solely of integer variables. That is a *pure integer programming* (PIP) *model*. More commonly there are both conventional continuous variables together with integer variables present. Such a model is said to be a *mixed integer programming* (*MIP*) *model*.

The wide applicability of integer programming (IP) (sometimes known as discrete programming) as a method of modelling is not obvious. Clearly we can think of situations where it is only meaningful to make integral quantities of certain goods, e.g. cars, aeroplanes, or houses, or use integral quantities of some resource, e.g. men. In these cases we might use an IP model instead of an LP model. Although such obvious applications of integer programming do occur they are not common. In fact in such situations it is often more desirable to use conventional LP and round off the optimal solution values to the nearest integers.

The obvious type of application described above obscures the real power of IP as a method of modelling. Most practical IP models restrict the integer variables to two values, 0 or 1. Such 0–1 variables are used to represent 'yes or no' decisions. Logical connections between such decisions can often be imposed using linear constraints. Such methods of modelling are described in the following chapters.

Before discussing the building of IP models something must be said about the way in which they are solved. Mathematically IP models involve many times as much calculation in solution as similar sized LP models. The difficulty of integer problems compared with (continuous) problems involving real or rational numbers is well known in other branches of mathematics. While an LP model involving thousands of constraints and variables can almost certainly be solved in a reasonable amount of time using a modern computer and package program, a similar situation does not hold for IP models. There is a considerable danger in building an IP model only to find no way of solving it in a reasonable time. Ways of avoiding this unfortunate and embarrassing experience are described in the next two chapters. In view of this danger as well as the computational difficulty of IP, Section 8.3. is devoted to methods of solving IP models. That section purposely only outlines in any detail the most successful method of solving IP models, the branch and bound method. It is felt necessary that a model builder should have, at least, this minimum of understanding as he can often influence the exact way in which the calculation proceeds to great advantage. Moreover, this most successful method to date of solving IP models receives surprisingly little attention in the theoretical mathematical programming books possibly because of its lack of mathematical sophistication.

8.2   The Applicability of Integer Programming

The purpose of this section is to classify loosely the different types of problem for which IP models may be built. Inevitably there is a certain amount of overlap in this classification where particular applications do not fit neatly into any category. Many practical problems will combine aspects from a number of categories. By this loose classification it is hoped to convey a feeling for the type of problem to which IP is applicable. In some ways the name 'discrete programming' conveys what this sort of problem is rather better. One of the reasons why IP has not been applied anywhere near as widely as it might to practical situations is the failure to recognize when a problem can be cast in this mould. This section is purposely rather superficial. Little indication is given of the way in which particular problems may be formulated as IP models. This is left to the next chapter or in particular cases to the detailed formulations of Part 3 of this book.

A precise definition of those situations which can be formulated by IP models is given by Meyer (1975) and Jeroslow (1987).

Problems with Discrete Inputs and Outputs

This class of problems includes the most obvious IP applications mentioned earlier where it is only possible to make *whole numbers of products* or *use integral units of a resource*. Economists sometimes refer to such problems as having 'lumpy' inputs or outputs. To see why IP is sometimes necessary here, consider the following very small (and contrived) model:

Maximize $x_1 + x_2$
subject to
$$-2x_1 + 2x_2 \geqslant 1,$$
$$-8x_1 + 10x_2 \leqslant 13,$$
$$x_1, x_2 \geqslant 0.$$

If the variables represent quantities of two different goods to be made it is important to be clear if these outputs should be integral, e.g. represent indivisible goods such as aeroplanes. Should this not be the case and they represent divisible goods such as gallons of beer we would be content with treating the problem as an LP model and taking the (continuous) optimum which is

$$x_1 = 4, \qquad x_2 = 4\tfrac{1}{2}. \tag{1}$$

On the other hand, restricting the variables to be integer forces us to accept the integer optimum, which is

$$x_1 = 1, \qquad x_2 = 2. \tag{2}$$

It is very difficult to see how one could arrive at the solution (2) from the continuous optimum (1). Rounding the values in (1) to the nearest integers gives an infeasible solution. In some circumstances such as this it is therefore necessary to solve such a problem as an IP model. This is obviously likely to happen when the values of the variables will be small (say less than 5). For most problems of this type, however, the values of the variables are likely to be much larger than this and the errors involved in rounding the LP fractional solution will not be serious. Indeed solving such a problem as an IP model could well take a great deal of time in view of the many combinations of integer solutions which could be considered. An extreme case of this was once seen where a national agricultural IP model was built. On examination this model was found to be an IP model only because there were an integral number of cows, hens, pigs, etc., in the country considered!

Similar considerations to those above apply to problems where the inputs rather than (or as well as) the outputs are discrete. Frequently such an input will be manpower capacity which, if sufficiently large, may be treated as continuous (infinitely divisible).

An application which is quite common occurs when an input (usually a processing capacity or a resource) only occurs at certain discrete values. Apart from this the model may be a conventional LP model. For example, processing capacity might be measured in machine hours per week. By buying extra machines it might be possible to expand processing capacity. It will, however, only be correct to allow this capacity to expand in steps equal to the machine hours per week resulting from extra whole machines. IP can be used to model this type of situation. A related situation to this is presented in the FACTORY PLANNING 2 problem in Part 2.

Another particular type of problem in this category where IP must be used is the *knapsack problem*. This is an IP problem with a single constraint. A particular instance where it might arise is in stocking a warehouse. The problem is: given a limited warehouse capacity, stock the warehouse with goods (of different volumes) to maximize some objective (such as the total value of goods in the warehouse). It will generally not be possible to use the LP solution to this problem, which is trivial and simply involves stacking the warehouse to capacity with the most valuable good per unit volume, thereby ignoring the discrete nature of the goods. Extensions of the knapsack problem arise where extra simple upper bounding constraints also apply to the variables of the problem. It is again usually necessary to use IP rather than LP to obtain a meaningful solution. Knapsack problems do arise in practice but they occur most commonly as subproblems which have to be solved as part of a much larger LP or IP problem.

Problems with Logical Conditions

It frequently happens that it is desired to impose extra conditions on an LP model. These conditions are sometimes of a logical nature which cannot be modelled by conventional LP. For example an LP model might be used to decide how much to make of each of the possible products in a factory subject to capacity limitations (the *product mix* application). It might be desirable to add an extra condition such as 'If product A is made then product B or C must be made as well'. By introducing some extra integer variables into the model together with extra constraints, conditions such as this can easily be imposed. The resultant model is a mixed integer problem. Any such *logical condition* as that above can be imposed on an LP model using IP. This is illustrated in the FOOD MANUFACTURE 2 problem. In addition that problem also illustrates another common use of IP to extend an LP model, *limiting the number of ingredients in a blend*.

The correct formulation of logical conditions sometimes involves considerable ingenuity and can be done a number of different ways. Methods of approaching such a formulation systematically are described in Chapter 9.

Combinatorial Problems

Many operational research problems have the characteristic of a very large number of feasible solutions (often an astronomic number) arising from different orders of carrying out operations or of allocating items or people to different positions. Such problems are loosely referred to as 'combinatorial'. It is useful to further subdivide this category into *sequencing problems* and *allocation problems*. A particularly difficult type of sequencing problem arises in *job-shop scheduling* where an optimal ordering of operations on different machines in a job-shop is desired. IP gives a method of modelling this type of situation. There are a number of possible formulations. Unfortunately IP has not proved a very successful way of tackling this problem to date.

Another very well known sequencing problem is the *travelling salesman problem*. This is the problem of finding the optimal order in which to visit a set of cities and return home covering minimum distance. There are other problems which take the same form. For example, the problem of sequencing operations on a machine so as to minimize total set-up cost takes this form. Obviously the set up cost for an operation will depend on the preceding operation and can be regarded as the 'distance' between operations. The travelling salesman problem is again a very difficult type of problem for which different IP formulations have been attempted.

A very straightforward allocation problem is given in Part 2. This is the MARKET SHARE problem. The problem involves allocating customers to divisions in a company for their services. Although the formulation is comparatively straightforward, problems like this are not always easy to solve. Problems of a very similar form arise in *project selection* and *capital budget allocation*.

The class of allocation problems includes two problems already mentioned for which IP is not needed. It has been pointed out in Section 5.3 that in the *transportation problem* it is not necessary to impose an integrality requirement. The LP optimal solution will automatically be integer because of the structure of the problem. As the *assignment problem* can be regarded as a special case of the transportation problem, this property holds for it also. Fortunately these two problems, although apparently IP problems, can therefore be treated as LP problems and solved fairly easily. Other apparently IP problems also have this property or can be formulated to have this property with great computational advantage. This topic is treated further in Sections 10.1 and 10.2. A complicated extension of the assignment problem is the *quadratic assignment problem*. This problem occurs where the 'cost of an assignment' is not independent of other assignments. The resulting problem can be regarded as an assignment problem with a quadratic objective function. The quadratic terms can be converted into linear expressions reducing the problem to an IP problem. The quadratic assignment problem is one of the most difficult combinatorial problems known in mathematical programming. Fairly small problems can be tackled by reducing the problem to a linear IP model. The DECENTRALIZATION example of Part 2 is a special sort of quadratic assignment problem. The quadratic assignment problem is discussed further in Section 9.5.

A practical problem which arises and can be regarded as falling into the allocation category is the *assembly line balancing* problem. This is the problem of assigning workers to tasks on a production line to achieve a given production rate. It is possible to formulate this problem as an IP problem and solve it fairly easily. The usual formulation results in a special sort of IP model known as a *set partitioning problem*. This type of problem is discussed further in Section 9.5.

Another set partitioning problem is the *aircrew scheduling problem*. This is the problem of assigning aircrews to sets of flights (rotations or rosters). In practice this type of problem frequently involves an enormous number of potential rosters and is difficult to solve as an IP problem in consequence. This is discussed further in Section 9.5.

Problems of *logical design* involving switching circuits or logical gates can be tackled through IP. Unfortunately such problems often turn out to be very large when formulated in this way and so difficult to solve. A small problem of this kind, LOGICAL DESIGN, is given in Part 2.

The *political districting* problem is also a set partitioning problem when regarded as an IP problem. This is the problem of designing constituencies or electoral districts in order to, as near as possible, equalize political representation. IP has been used in the USA to solve practical problems of this nature.

A fairly common application of IP is to the *depot location problem*. This is the problem of deciding where to locate depots (or warehouses or even factories) in order to supply customers. Two sorts of costs may enter the problem, the capital costs of building the depots and the distribution costs resulting from particular sitings of the depots. This sort of problem can be modelled using IP. Frequently the resultant model is a mixed integer problem. The DEPOT LOCATION problem of Part 2 is an example.

Non-linear Problems

As was mentioned in Chapter 7, non-linear problems can sometimes be treated as IP problems with advantage. If the problem can be expressed in a separable programming form it can be solved using either separable programming as described in Section 7.3 or by IP. Should the problem be convex (this term is explained in Section 7.2) it may be treated by LP and no difficulty arises. On the other hand, special methods have to be used for non-convex problems where separable programming has the disadvantage of producing possibly local optima (this is again explained in Section 7.2). IP overcomes this difficulty and produces a true (global) optimal solution, although possibly with considerably more expenditure in computer time. Problems to which this method is relevant have already been mentioned in Chapter 7. They include problems involving *economies of scale, quadratic programming problems* and *geometric programming problems* as well as much more general non-linear programming problems.

The way in which such problems can be converted into a separable form is described in Chapter 7. How to convert the resultant separable problems into an IP form is described in Chapter 9. There is, however, an alternative way of approaching such problems by integer programming. This is through the use of special ordered sets of variables. A number of package programs have facilities for dealing with IP problems in this way to considerable computational advantage. The concept of special ordered sets and how they may be applied to non-linear problems (as well as other types of problem) is described by Beale and Tomlin (1969).

A very common application of IP is the *fixed charge problem*. This occurs when the cost of an activity involves a threshold set-up cost as well as the usual costs which rise in proportion to the level of the activity. In this way the problem can be regarded as non-linear. For example, if it is decided to produce any amount of a product at all it may be necessary to set up a piece of machinery. This set up cost is independent of the quantity produced. It is not possible to model this situation using conventional LP but it can be modelled very easily using IP. This is described in Example 1 of Section 9.1.

Network Problems

Many problems in operational research involve networks. A lot of these problems can be modelled using LP or IP. Those problems which give rise to LP models have already been considered in Section 5.3.

It has already been pointed out in Section 5.3 that the problem of finding the critical path in a PERT network can be viewed as an LP problem. A secondary problem often arises in practice. This is the problem of *resource allocation on a PERT network*. It may be necessary to alter the order in which certain activities (arcs) are carried out in view of the limited resources available, e.g. we cannot simultaneously build the walls and lay the floors in a house if there are not enough workmen available. The problem of optimally allocating these limited resources to the arcs of the PERT network so as to (for example) minimize the total completion time for a project can be formulated as an IP problem. Although an IP model is a method of tackling this problem, it is not to be recommended except in very simple cases. The computational difficulties of solving a complex problem of this kind by IP can be very great. In practice non-rigorous heuristic means are used to obtain useful but non-optimal solutions.

Many IP problems arise in *graph theory*. A well known problem to which IP is relevant is the *four-colour problem*. It has recently been proved that at most four colours are needed to colour every country on a map differently from its neighbouring countries. For any map, IP could be used to find the minimum number of colours necessary. The above problem can be represented as the problem of colouring the vertices of a graph so that vertices jointed by an edge are coloured differently. Other colouring problems arise in graph theory. For example, it is possible to devise problems involving colouring the edges of a graph. Although many such problems exist and can be solved using IP, such considerations are largely beyond the scope of this book. The concern here is mainly with practical problems. Graph theory and integer programming has been extensively treated elsewhere, for example by Christofides (1975).

The above five categories encompass most of the different types of problem which arise to which IP is applicable. In practice most problems which one meets fall into the second category. They are LP problems on which it is desired to impose extra conditions. These extra conditions are frequently of a logical type. One therefore extends the LP model by adding integer variables and extra constraints. The extra constraints applied to the integer variables sometimes have a combinatorial flavour. Sometimes these extra constraints serve the purpose of modelling non-linearities in an otherwise LP model.

Pure integer programming models arise less frequently in practice. They are usually combinatorial problems. The comparatively large number of combinatorial problems listed above should not disguise that fact that the majority of practical IP models are in the second category and may arise as extensions to almost any application of LP. Combinatorial problems do arise in practice, however, and are sometimes satisfactorily solved through IP. Great care must be exercised, however, when applying IP to such problems. While IP offers an apparently attractive way of modelling a combinatorial problem, experience has shown that such models can be very difficult to solve. It is often desirable to experiment with small scale versions of the problem before embarking on a large model. There are also good and bad ways of formulating such problems from the point of view of ease of solution. This is discussed in Section 10.1. Also it is hoped that the comparative solution times given with the solutions to the models in Part 4 will be indicators of the difficulty of certain types of model.

8.3   Solving Integer Programming Models

This section is in no way intended to be a full description of integer programming algorithms. Instead it is an attempt to indicate different ways in which IP models may be solved and suggest how a model builder may use existing packages in an efficient manner. Some references to fuller expositions of the algorithmic side of IP are given.

The main approaches to solving IP problems are categorized below. Unlike LP with the simplex algorithm, no one good IP algorithm has emerged. Different algorithms prove better with different types of problem, often by exploiting the structure of special classes of problem. It seems unlikely that a universal IP algorithm will ever emerge. If it did it would open up the possibility of solving a very wide class of problems. Some of these problems (such as the travelling salesman problem and the quadratic assignment problem) have defied many attempts to find powerful algorithms for their solution. There is now even some theoretical evidence resulting from the theory of computational complexity to suggest that a 'universal' IP algorithm is unlikely. The most successful algorithm so far found to solve practical general IP problems is the branch and bound method described below. Considering its apparent crudeness the success of this method is surprising. Almost all commercial packages offering a mixed integer programming facility use the algorithm. In fact the algorithm is little more than an approach to solving IP problems. There is great flexibility in the way it can be used. This is one of the reasons why it is briefly described in a book on model building. Using the branch and bound method in a way suited to the problem can show dramatic improvements over less intelligent strategies.

Most methods of solving IP problems fall into one of four broad categories. There is some overlap between the categories and some particularly successful approaches to large problems have exploited features of a number of methods.

Cutting Planes Methods

These methods can be applied to general MIP problems. They usually start by solving an IP problem as if it were an LP problem by dropping the integrality requirements. If the resultant LP solution (the continuous optimum) is integer, this solution will also be the integer optimum. Otherwise extra constraints (cutting planes) are systematically added to the problem, further constraining it. The new solution to the further constrained problem may or may not be integer. By continuing the process until an integer solution is found or the problem shown to be infeasible the IP problem can be solved.

Although cutting plane methods may appear mathematically fairly elegant, they have not proved very successful on large problems.

The original method of this sort is described by Gomory (1958). Further references are given with the exposition in Chapter 5 of Garfinkel and Nemhauser (1972).

Enumerative Methods

These are generally applied to the special class of 0–1 PIP problems. In theory there are only a finite (though extremely large) number of possible solutions to a problem in this class. Although it would be prohibitive to examine all these possibilities, by use of a tree search it is possible to examine only some solutions and systematically rule out many others as being infeasible or non-optimal. Such methods together with their variants and extensions have proved very successful with certain types of problem and not very successful on others. Commercial package programs do exist for such methods but are not widely used.

The best known of these methods is Balas' additive algorithm described by Balas (1965). Other methods are given by Geoffrion (1969). A good overall exposition is given in Chapter 4 of Garfinkel and Nemhauser (1972).

Pseudo-Boolean Methods

Attempts have been made to exploit the obvious analogy between Boolean algebra and 0–1 PIP problems. A number of algorithms have been developed. As with other algorithms they work well on some types of problem but less well on others. This approach is entirely unlike any other for solving IP problems. The constraints of a problem are expressed not as equations or inequalities but through Boolean algebra. In some cases this can give a very concise statement of the constraints but in others it is large and unwieldy. As far as the author is aware no commercial packages capable of accepting practical problems use any of these methods.

These approaches have been developed by Hammer and are described in Hammer and Rudeanu (1968), Granot and Hammer (1972), and Hammer and Peled (1972).

It should not be thought that the specialized 0–1 PIP algorithms are only of relevance to 0–1 PIP problems. Methods have been developed for partitioning a MIP problem with 0–1 variables into its continuous and integer portions. It then becomes necessary, at stages in the optimization, to solve a 0–1 PIP problem as a subproblem. Clearly these specialized algorithms might be applicable. Any discussion of this topic is beyond the scope of this book. The main reference to this partitioning method is Benders (1962).

Branch and Bound Methods

It is these methods which have proved most successful in general on practical MIP problems. Such methods are also sometimes classed as enumerative but we choose to distinguish them from the enumerative methods described earlier.

As with cutting plane methods, the IP problem is first solved as an LP problem by relaxing the integrality conditions. If the resultant solution (the continuous optimum) is integer the problem is solved. Otherwise we perform a tree search. The procedure is best understood by reference to a concrete example. Afterwards we will more rigorously describe the general method. A MIP model with the following dimensions was solved: 71 constraints, 25 continuous variables, and 40 0–1 (integer) variables. The 0–1 variables will be referred to in the description and are denoted by δ_{it} and γ_{it} where $i = 1, 2, 3, 4$, and $t = 1, 2, 3, 4, 5$. The problem was a maximization.

It should be noted that this problem is not entirely general since the integer variables are 0–1. The modification to cope with general integer variables is, however, very slight and is explained afterwards in the general description of the method.

Initially the associated LP problem was solved yielding an objective value of 159·13, but some of the integer variables came out at fractional values. This continuous optimum of the problem therefore had to be further restricted. It is convenient to view the subsequent solution process diagrammatically as a tree in Figure 8.1. The nodes of the tree each represent an LP problem and are numbered sequentially in the order in which the problems are examined. At each node the optimal objective value of the corresponding LP problem is given. To start with we have the original LP problem at node 1. The optimization goes through the following stages:

(a) On solving the corresponding LP problem one of the integer variables which has come out at a fractional value is chosen. (This variable is known as the *branching variable.*) In this case we chose the variable γ_{25} which was at value 0·87. Since γ_{25} must be at the value 0 or 1 in any integer solution we have one of the following two possibilities: either $\gamma_{25} = 0$ or $\gamma_{25} = 1$.

(b) Both of the possibilities are considered by creating two new *subproblems.* For the first subproblem, represented by node 2, we append the constraint $\gamma_{25} = 0$ and for the second subproblem we append $\gamma_{25} = 1$. The LPs corresponding to these subproblems are solved. Both give fractional solutions with objective values of 154·1 and 158·77 respectively. As would be expected, constraining the original LP model in either way leads to a deterioration in the optimal objective value.

One of the resultant subproblems is chosen for development. Which we choose is, to some extent, arbitrary, although heuristics can be used as mentioned below. For this example we choose node 3 for further development and follow procedure (a) again. In this case variable δ_{25} is chosen for branching producing two new subproblems at nodes 4 and 5. Both of these problems produce fractional solutions when solved as LPs. Developing nodes and branching as demonstrated in Figure 8.1, we eventually produce a problem, at node 25, which is so constrained that the integer variables all come out at integer values.

It is important to note the successive deterioration in the optimal objective values as we progressively further constrain the problem going down the tree.

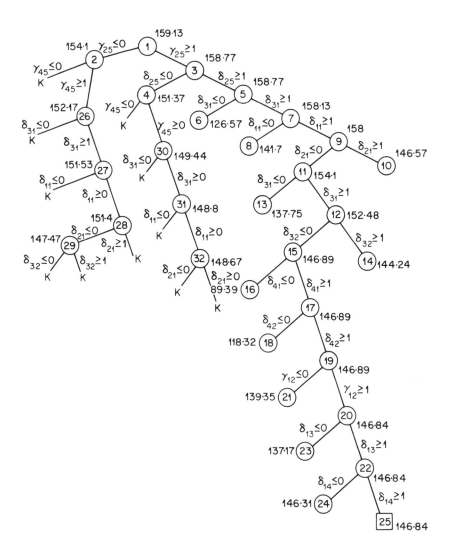

Figure 8.1

(c) Having reached an integer solution (but not necessarily an optimal one) at node 25 we save the solution and note its objective value of 146·84. This is clearly the best known integer solution so far obtained. Obviously there are no more variables left to branch on at this node so we can terminate the branch. Since the objective value can get no better as we go down a branch of the tree we can *drop* any nodes where the objective value of the LP problem is worse (smaller) than 146·84. Nodes 6, 8, 10, 13, 14, 16, 18, 21, 23, and 24 need not be developed any further for this reason and are therefore dropped.

(d) We now choose a node which is still a candidate for development (known as a *waiting node*). Nodes 2 and 4 are the current waiting nodes. Choosing node 2 we branch on variable γ_{45}. In the course of optimizing the subproblem in which the constraint $\gamma_{45} = 0$ is imposed, the objective function deteriorates below 146·84. Therefore the LP associated with this subproblem is not solved to optimality and the node is not represented on the tree in Figure 8.1. The symbol K is used to indicate this.

Proceeding in this manner through nodes 26, 27, 28, and 29, all branches are dropped. The only remaining waiting node is 4, which is developed into nodes 30, 31, and 32 until all branches are dropped. Since there are no more waiting nodes the solution found at node 25 is optimal.

A number of arbitrary choices were made in the above procedure:

(i) We chose the integer variable, with fractional value, which had the largest objective coefficient as the *branching variable* at each node.
(ii) We have always developed the *waiting node* whose associated LP problem has largest objective value.

These choices have purposely been made to demonstrate the principle of branch and bound. It is much better to make these choices more intelligently. This is discussed below. We now describe the steps of the general procedure for solving a MIP problem by the branch and bound method.

Step 1. Choose a Waiting Node

The LP problem corresponding to this node is solved. The result will be one of the following:

(i) The problem is infeasible.
(ii) The optimal value of the objective is worse than the best integer solution already known.
(iii) The problem gives an integer solution.
(iv) The problem gives a fractional solution.

If (i) or (ii) occur the problem may be ignored and we return to Step 1. If (iii) occurs the result may be a useful integer solution. Should it be the first integer solution found, or be better than any other integer solution found, it is stored as the best integer solution to date. Otherwise we return to Step 1. If (iv) occurs we proceed to Step 2.

Initially the only waiting node will be the node corresponding to the continuous problem which is numbered as node 1.

Step 2. Choose a Branching Variable x

This will be an integer variable with a fractional value in the optimal solution to the current LP problem. Suppose the current value of x is $N + f$, where N is an integer and $0 < f < 1$. Since x is an integer variable, we may impose either of the following extra constraints on the current LP problem:

$$x \leqslant N \tag{1}$$

or

$$x \geqslant N + 1. \tag{2}$$

N.B. For the example described above x was always a 0–1 variable. In this case (1) and (2) reduce to $x = 0$ and $x = 1$ respectively, i.e. the 0–1 variable becomes fixed at one of its possible values.

The whole procedure terminates when there are no more waiting nodes. When this happens the best integer solution found is the integer optimum. Should no integer solution have been found, the IP problem has been shown to be infeasible.

As long as all the integer variables have finite upper and lower bounds there is only a finite number of possible branches and the procedure must eventually terminate.

There is considerable flexibility in the way this procedure is performed. A number of choices have to be made.

At Step 1 we have to choose from a number of waiting nodes. This may be done in a number of ways. For the problem described above we chose the node whose LP solution had the best objective value. Other strategies can be used, however.

At Step 2 we have to choose from a number of integer variables with fractional values in the current LP solution. The way in which this choice is made can have a dramatic effect on the time taken to solve the problem. For the problem described above we took the variable with highest objective coefficient. More sophisticated *penalty calculations* can be performed to choose the branching variable. The best approach is probably to use a knowledge of the practical problem for which the model was built. It is generally better to branch on a variable representing a major investment decision rather than on a variable representing a decision of lesser importance. For example a 0–1 variable, representing a decision whether to build a factory or not, is probably more important than a variable representing a decision whether to supply a certain customer or not. By giving a priority ordering to the variables in the model it is possible to choose branching variables in order of importance.

Many variations and elaborations on the above procedures often prove very valuable. One such is to specify a 'cut-off' value so that nodes with objective values worse than this figure can terminate a branch. This 'cut-off' value takes the place of the objective value of the best known integer solution (until an integer solution with an objective value better than the 'cut-off' value is found). In this way large sections of the tree search are avoided. It must be emphasized strongly that the person using a package to solve an IP problem by the branch and bound method has great control over the solution strategy adopted. For preference, this person is the model builder himself, who can use his knowledge of the problem to direct the tree search in a physically meaningful manner.

The above description is only a brief sketch of the branch and bound method. Its purpose is to indicate to the model builder the importance of relating the solution strategy to the problem considered. In order to emphasize this point the problem used above with the solution tree in Figure 8.1 was chosen from the problems in Part 2. It is the MINING problem. A more intelligent solution strategy using a knowledge of the problem is suggested in Part 3 with the suggested formulation of the problem. By giving the variables a priority ordering the problem is solved more easily. The resultant solution tree is given with the solution in Part 4. It is interesting to compare this solution tree with that in Figure 8.1, bearing in mind the physical interpretation of the variables given in Part 3.

A very good discussion of efficient solution strategies to use with the branch and bound method on practical models is given by Forrest, Hirst, and Tomlin (1974). Geoffrion and Marsten (1972) put the branch and bound method, together with enumeration methods, which also use a tree search, into a general framework which makes the basic principles easy to understand. References to the various forms of the branch and bound method are given in that paper.

A comprehensive survey of integer programming packages is given by Land and Powell (1979).

CHAPTER 9

Building Integer Programming Models I

9.1   The Uses of Discrete Variables

When integer variables are used in a mathematical programming model they may serve a number of purposes. These are described below.

Indivisible (Discrete) Quantities

This is the obvious use mentioned at the beginning of Chapter 8 where we wish to use a variable to represent a quantity which can only come in whole numbers such as aeroplanes, cars, houses or men.

Decision Variables

Variables are frequently used in integer programming (IP) to indicate which of a number of possible decisions should be made. Usually these variables can only take the two values, zero or one. Such variables are known as zero–one (0–1) variables. For example, $\delta = 1$ indicates that a depot should be built and $\delta = 0$ indicates that a depot should not be built. We will usually adopt the convention of using the Greek letter 'δ' for 0–1 variables and reserving Latin letters for continuous (real or rational) variables.

It is easy to ensure that a variable, which is also specified to be integer, can only take the two values 0 or 1 by giving the variable a simple upper bound (SUB) of 1. (All variables are assumed to have a simple lower bound of 0 unless it is stated to the contrary).

Although decision variables are usually 0–1, they need not always be. For example we might have $\gamma = 0$ indicates that no depot should be built; $\gamma = 1$ indicates that a depot of type A should be built; $\gamma = 2$ indicates that a depot of type B should be built.

Indicator Variables

When extra conditions are imposed on a linear programming (LP) model, 0–1 variables are usually introduced and 'linked' to some of the continuous variables in the problem to indicate certain states. For example, suppose that x represents the quantity of an ingredient to be included in a blend. We may well wish to use an indicator variable δ to distinguish between the state where $x = 0$ and the state where $x > 0$. By introducing the following constraint we can force δ to take the value 1 when $x > 0$:

$$x - M\delta \leqslant 0. \tag{1}$$

M is a constant coefficient representing a known upper bound for x.

Logically we have achieved the condition

$$x > 0 \rightarrow \delta = 1, \tag{2}$$

where ' $\rightarrow$ ' stands for 'implies'.

In many applications (2) provides a sufficient link between x and δ (e.g. Example 1 below). There are applications (e.g. Example 2 below), however, where we also wish to impose the condition

$$x = 0 \rightarrow \delta = 0. \tag{3}$$

(3) is another way of saying

$$\delta = 1 \rightarrow x > 0. \tag{4}$$

Together (2) and (3) (or (4)) impose the condition

$$\delta = 1 \leftrightarrow x > 0, \tag{5}$$

where ' $\leftrightarrow$ ' stands for 'if and only if'.

It is not possible totally to represent (3) (or (4)) by a constraint. On reflection this is not suprising. (4) gives the condition 'if $\delta = 1$ the ingredient represented by x must appear in the blend'. Would we really want to distinguish in practice between no usage of the ingredient and, say, one molecule of the ingredient? It would be much more realistic to define some threshold level m below which we will regard the ingredient as unused. (4) can now be rewritten as

$$\delta = 1 \rightarrow x > m. \tag{6}$$

This condition can be imposed by the constraint

$$x - m\delta \geqslant 0. \tag{7}$$

Example 1. The Fixed Charge Problem

x represents the quantity of a product to be manufactured at a marginal cost per unit of C_1. In addition, if the product is manufactured at all there is a setup cost of C_2. The position is summarized as follows:

$$x = 0, \quad \text{total cost} = 0;$$
$$x > 0, \quad \text{total cost} = C_1 x + C_2.$$

The situation can be represented graphically as in Figure 9.1.

Clearly the total cost is not a linear function of x. It is not even a continuous

170

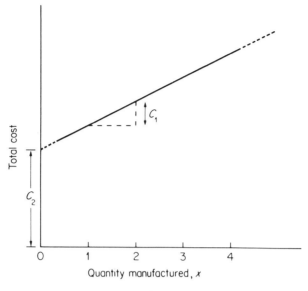

Figure 9.1

function as there is a discontinuity at the origin. Conventional LP is not capable of handling this situation.

In order to use IP we introduce an indicator variable δ so that if any of the product is manufactured $\delta = 1$. This can be achieved by constraint (1) above. The variable δ is given a cost of C_2 in the objective function giving the following expression for the total cost:

$$\text{total cost} = C_1 x + C_2 \delta.$$

By the introduction of $0-1$ variables such as δ and extra constraints such as (1), to link these variables to the continuous variables such as x, fixed charges can be introduced into a model if the δ variables are given objective coefficients equal to the fixed charges.

It is worth pointing out that this is a situation where it is not generally necessary to model the condition (3). This condition will automatically be satisfied at optimality if the objective of the model has the effect of minimizing cost. Although a solution $x = 0$, $\delta = 1$ does not violate the constraints it is clearly non-optimal since $x = 0$, $\delta = 0$ will not violate the constraints either but will result in a smaller total cost.

It would certainly not be invalid to impose condition (3) explicitly by a constraint such as (6) (as long as m was sufficiently small). In certain circumstances it might even be computationally desirable.

Example 2. Blending

(This example is relevant to the FOOD MANUFACTURE 2 problem in Part 2.)

x_A represents the proportion of ingredient A to be included in a blend; x_B represents the proportion of ingredient B to be included in a blend.

In addition to the conventional quality constraints (for which LP can be used) connecting these and other variables in the model it is wished to impose the following extra condition: *if A is included in the blend B must be included also*.

IP must be used to model this extra condition. A $0-1$ indicator variable δ is introduced which will take the value 1 if $x_A > 0$. This is linked to variable x_A by the following constraint of type (1):

$$x_A - \delta \leqslant 0. \qquad (8)$$

Here the coefficient M of constraint (1) can conveniently be taken as 1 since we are dealing with proportions.

We are now in a position to use the new $0-1$ variable δ to impose the condition

$$\delta = 1 \rightarrow x_B > 0. \qquad (9)$$

In order to impose this condition of (4) we must choose some proportionate level m (say $1/100$) below which we will regard B as out of the blend. This gives us the following constraint:

$$x_B - 0 \cdot 01\delta \geqslant 0. \qquad (10)$$

We have now imposed the extra condition on the LP model by introducing a $0-1$ variable δ with two extra constraints (8) and (10).

Notice that here (unlike Example 1) it was necessary to introduce a constraint to represent a condition of type (4). The satisfaction of such a condition could not be guaranteed by optimality. An extension of the extra condition which we have imposed might be the following: *if A is included in the blend B must be included also and vice versa*. This requires two extra constraints which the reader might like to formulate.

It should be pointed out that any constant coefficient M can be chosen in constraints of type (1) so long as M is sufficiently big not to restrict the value of x to an extent not desired in the problem being modelled. In practical situations it is usually possible to specify such a value for M. Although theoretically any sufficiently large value of M will suffice there is computational advantage in making M as realistic as possible. This point is explained further in Section 10.1 of Chapter 10. Similar considerations apply to the coefficient m in constraints of type (7).

It is possible to use indicator variables in a similar way to show whether an inequality holds or does not hold. First, suppose that we wish to indicate whether the following inequality holds by means of an indicator variable δ:

$$\sum_j a_j x_j \leqslant b.$$

The following condition is fairly straightforward to formulate. We will therefore model it first:

$$\delta = 1 \rightarrow \sum_j a_j x_j \leqslant b. \tag{11}$$

(11) can be represented by the constraint

$$\sum_j a_j x_j + M\delta \leqslant M + b, \tag{12}$$

where M is an upper bound for the expression $\sum_j a_j x_j - b$. It is easy to verify that (12) has the desired effect, i.e. when $\delta = 1$ the original constraint is forced to hold and when $\delta = 0$ no constraint is implied.

A convenient way of constructing (12) from condition (11) is to pursue the following train of reasoning. If $\delta = 1$ we wish to have $\sum_i a_j x_j - b \leqslant 0$, i.e. if $(1 - \delta) = 0$ we wish to have $\sum_j a_j x_j - b \leqslant 0$. This condition is imposed if

$$\sum_j a_j x_j - b \leqslant M(1 - \delta),$$

where M is a sufficiently large number. In order to find how large M must be we consider the case $\delta = 0$ giving $\sum_j a_j x_j - b \leqslant M$.

This shows that we must choose M sufficiently large that this does not give an undesired constraint. Clearly M must be chosen to be an upper bound for the expression $\sum_j a_j x_j - b$. Re-arranging the constraint we have obtained with the variables on the left we obtain (12).

We will now consider how to model the reverse of constraint (11), i.e.

$$\sum_j a_j x_j \leqslant b \rightarrow \delta = 1. \tag{13}$$

This is conveniently expressed as

$$\delta = 0 \rightarrow \sum_j a_j x_j \nleqslant b, \tag{14}$$

i.e.

$$\delta = 0 \rightarrow \sum_j a_j x_j > b. \tag{15}$$

In dealing with the expression $\sum_j a_j x_j > b$ we run into the same difficulties that we met with the expression $x > 0$. We must rewrite

$$\sum_j a_j x_j > b \quad \text{as} \quad \sum_j a_j x_j \geqslant b + \varepsilon,$$

where ε is some small tolerance value beyond which we will regard the constraint as having been broken. Should the coefficients a_j be integers as well as the variables x_j, as often happens in this type of situation, there is no difficulty as ε can be taken as 1.

(15) may now be rewritten as

$$\delta = 0 \rightarrow -\sum_j a_j x_j + b + \varepsilon \leqslant 0. \tag{16}$$

Using an argument similar to that above we can represent this condition by the constraint

$$\sum_j a_j x_j - (m - \varepsilon)\delta \geqslant b + \varepsilon, \tag{17}$$

where m is a lower bound for expression

$$\sum_j a_j x_j - b.$$

Should we wish to indicate whether a '$\geqslant$' inequality such as

$$\sum_j a_j x_j \geqslant b$$

holds or not by means of an indicator variable δ, the required constraints can easily be obtained by transforming the above constraint into a '$\leqslant$' form. The corresponding constraints to (12) and (17) above are

$$\sum_j a_j x_j + m\delta \geqslant m + b, \tag{18}$$

$$\sum_j a_j x_j - (M + \varepsilon)\delta \leqslant b - \varepsilon, \tag{19}$$

where m and M are again lower and upper bounds respectively on the expression

$$\sum_j a_j x_j - b_i.$$

Finally, to use an indicator variable δ for an '$=$' constraint such as

$$\sum_j a_j x_j = b$$

is slightly more complicated. We can use $\delta = 1$ to indicate that the '$\leqslant$' and '$\geqslant$' cases hold simultaneously. This is done by stating both (12) and (18) together.

If $\delta = 0$ we want to force *either* the '$\leqslant$' or the '$\geqslant$' constraint to be broken. This may be done by expressing (17) and (19) with two variables δ' and δ'' giving

$$\sum_j a_j x_j - (m - \varepsilon)\delta' \geqslant b + \varepsilon, \tag{20}$$

$$\sum_j a_j x_j - (M + \varepsilon)\delta'' \leqslant b - \varepsilon. \tag{21}$$

The indicator variable δ forces the required condition by the extra constraint

$$\delta' + \delta'' - \delta \leqslant 1. \tag{22}$$

In some circumstances we wish to impose a condition of type (11). Alternatively we may wish to impose a condition of type (13) or impose both conditions together. These conditions can be dealt with by the linear constraints (12) or (17) taken individually or together.

Example 3

Use a 0–1 variable δ to indicate whether or not the following constraint is satisfied:

$$2x_1 + 3x_2 \leqslant 1.$$

(x_1 and x_2 are non-negative continuous variables which cannot exceed 1.)
We wish to impose the following conditions:

$$\delta = 1 \rightarrow 2x_1 + 3x_2 \leqslant 1, \tag{23}$$

$$2x_1 + 3x_2 \leqslant 1 \rightarrow \delta = 1. \tag{24}$$

Using (12) M may be taken as 4 ($= 2 + 3 - 1$). This gives the following constraint representation of (23):

$$2x_1 + 3x_2 + 4\delta \leqslant 5. \tag{25}$$

Using (17) m may be taken as -1 ($= 0 + 0 - 1$). We will take ε as $0 \cdot 1$. This gives the following constraint representation of (24):

$$2x_1 + 3x_2 + 1 \cdot 1\delta \geqslant 1 \cdot 1. \tag{26}$$

The reader should verify that (25) and (26) have the desired effect by substituting 0 and 1 for δ.

In all the constraints derived in this section it is computationally desirable to make m and M as realistic as possible.

9.2 Logical Conditions and Zero–One Variables

In Section 9.1 it was pointed out that 0–1 variables are often introduced into an LP (or sometimes an IP) model as decision variables or indicator variables. Having introduced such variables it is then possible to represent logical connections between different decisions or states by linear constraints involving these 0–1 variables. It is at first sight rather surprising that so many different types of logical condition can be imposed in this way.

Some typical examples of logical conditions which can be so modelled are given below. Further examples are given by Williams (1977).

(a) If no depot is sited here then it will not be possible to supply any of the customers from the depot.

(b) If the library's subscription to this journal is cancelled then we must retain at least one subscription to another journal in this class.

(c) If we manufacture product A we must also manufacture product B or at least one of products C and D.

(d) If this station is closed then both branch lines terminating at the station must also be closed.

(e) No more than five of the ingredients in this class may be included in the blend at any one time.

(f) If we do not place an electronic module in this position then no wires can connect into this position.

(g) Either operation A must be finished before operation B starts or vice versa.

It will be convenient to use some notation from Boolean algebra in this section. This is the so called set of *connectives* given below:

'$\vee$'   means 'or' (this is inclusive, i.e. A or B or both).
'.'   means 'and'.
'$\sim$'   means 'not'.
'$\rightarrow$'   means 'implies' (or 'if...then').
'$\leftrightarrow$'   means 'if and only if'.

These connectives are used to connect propositions denoted by P, Q, R, etc., $x > 0$, $x = 0$, $\delta = 1$, etc.

For example, if P stands for the proposition 'I will miss the bus' and Q stands for the proposition 'I will be late', then $P \rightarrow Q$ stands for the proposition 'If I miss the bus then I will be late'. $\sim P$ stands for the proposition 'I will not miss the bus'.

As another example suppose that X_i stands for the proposition 'Ingredient i is in the blend' (i ranges over the ingredients A, B and C). Then $X_A \rightarrow (X_B \vee X_C)$ stands for the proposition 'If ingredient A is in the blend then ingredient B or C (or both) must also be in the blend'. This expression could also be written as $(X_A \rightarrow X_B) \vee (X_A \rightarrow X_C)$.

It is possible to define all these connectives in terms of a subset of them. For example they can all be defined in terms of the set $\{\vee, \sim\}$. Such a subset is known as a complete set of connectives. We do not choose to do this and will retain the flexibility of using all the connectives listed above. It is important, however, to realize that certain expressions are equivalent to expressions involving other connectives. We give all the equivalences below which are sufficient for our purpose.

To avoid unnecessary brackets we will consider the symbols '$\sim$', '.', '$\vee$' and '$\rightarrow$' as each being more binding than their successor when written in this order. For example

$$(P . Q) \vee R \text{ can be written as } P . Q \vee R$$

$$P \rightarrow (Q \vee R) \text{ can be written as } P \rightarrow Q \vee R$$

$$\sim \sim P \text{ is the same as } P \tag{1}$$

$$P \to Q \text{ is the same as } \sim P \vee Q; \tag{2}$$

$$P \to Q . R \text{ is the same as } (P \to Q).(P \to R) \tag{3}$$

$$P \to Q \vee R \text{ is the same as } (P \to Q) \vee (P \to R) \tag{4}$$

$$P . Q \to R \text{ is the same as } (P \to R) \vee (Q \to R) \tag{5}$$

$$P \vee Q \to R \text{ is the same as } (P \to R).(Q \to R) \tag{6}$$

$$\sim (P \vee Q) \text{ is the same as } \sim P . \sim Q \tag{7}$$

$$\sim (P . Q) \text{ is the same as } \sim P \vee \sim Q \tag{8}$$

(7) and (8) are sometimes known as De Morgan's laws.

Although Boolean algebra provides a convenient means of expressing and manipulating logical relationships, our purpose here is to express these relationships in terms of the familiar equations and inequalities of mathematical programming. (In one sense we are performing the opposite process to that used in the pseudo-Boolean approach to 0–1 programming mentioned in Section 8.3.)

We will suppose that indicator variables have already been introduced in the manner described in Section 9.1 to represent the decisions or states which we want logically to relate.

It is important to distinguish propositions and variables at this stage. We will use X_i to stand for the proposition $\delta_i = 1$ where δ_i is a 0–1 indicator variable. The following propositions and constraints can easily be seen to be equivalent:

$$X_1 \vee X_2 \text{ is equivalent to } \delta_1 + \delta_2 \geqslant 1; \tag{9}$$

$$X_1 . X_2 \text{ is equivalent to } \delta_1 = 1, \delta_2 = 1; \tag{10}$$

$$\sim X_1 \text{ is equivalent to } \delta_1 = 0 \text{ (or } 1 - \delta_1 = 1); \tag{11}$$

$$X_1 \to X_2 \text{ is equivalent to } \delta_1 - \delta_2 \leqslant 0; \tag{12}$$

$$X_1 \leftrightarrow X_2 \text{ is equivalent to } \delta_1 - \delta_2 = 0. \tag{13}$$

To illustrate the conversion of a logical condition into a constraint we will consider an example.

Example 1. Manufacturing

If either of products A or B (or both) are manufactured, then at least one of products C, D, or E must also be manufactured.

Let X_i stand for the proposition 'Product i is manufactured' (i is A, B, C, D, or E). We wish to impose the logical condition

$$(X_A \vee X_B) \to (X_C \vee X_D \vee X_E). \tag{14}$$

Indicator variables are introduced to perform the following functions: $\delta_i = 1$ if and only if product i is manufactured; $\delta = 1$ if the proposition $X_A \vee X_B$ holds. The proposition $X_A \vee X_B$ can be represented by the inequality

$$\delta_A + \delta_B \geqslant 1. \tag{15}$$

The proposition $X_C \vee X_D \vee X_E$ can be represented by the inequality

$$\delta_C + \delta_D + \delta_E \geqslant 1. \tag{16}$$

Firstly we wish to impose the following condition:

$$\delta_A + \delta_B \geqslant 1 \rightarrow \delta = 1. \tag{17}$$

Using (19) of Section 9.1 we impose this condition by the constraint

$$\delta_A + \delta_B - 2\delta \leqslant 0. \tag{18}$$

Secondly we wish to impose the condition

$$\delta = 1 \rightarrow \delta_C + \delta_D + \delta_E \geqslant 1. \tag{19}$$

Using (18) of Section 9.1 this is achieved by the constraint

$$-\delta_C - \delta_D - \delta_E + \delta \leqslant 0. \tag{20}$$

Hence the required extra condition can be imposed on the original model (LP or IP) by the following:

(i) Introduce 0–1 variables δ_A, δ_B, δ_C, δ_D, and δ_E and link them to the original (probably continuous) variables by constraints of type (1) and (7) of Section 9.1. It is not strictly necessary to include constraints of type (7) for the variables δ_A and δ_B since it is not necessary to have the conditions (4) of Section 9.1 in these cases.

(ii) Add the additional constraints (18) and (20) above.

This is not the only way to model this logical condition. Using the Boolean identity (6) above it is possible to show that condition (14) can be re-expressed as

$$[X_A \rightarrow (X_C \vee X_D \vee X_E)] \cdot [X_B \rightarrow (X_C \vee X_D \vee X_E)]. \tag{21}$$

The reader should verify that an analysis similar to that above results in the constraint (20) together with the following two constraints in place of (18):

$$\delta_A - \delta \leqslant 0; \tag{22}$$

$$\delta_B - \delta \leqslant 0. \tag{23}$$

Both ways of modelling the condition are correct. There are computational advantages in (22) and (23) over (18). This is discussed further in Section 10.1 of Chapter 10.

It is sometimes suggested that polynomial expressions in 0–1 variables are useful for expressing logical conditions. Such polynomial expressions can always be replaced by linear expressions with linear constraints, possibly with a considerable increase in the number of 0–1 variables. For example the constraint

$$\delta_1 \delta_2 = 0 \tag{24}$$

represents the condition

$$\delta_1 = 0 \lor \delta_2 = 0. \tag{25}$$

More generally, if a product term such as $\delta_1 \delta_2$ were to appear anywhere in a model the model could be made linear by the following steps:

(i) Replace $\delta_1 \delta_2$ by a 0–1 variable δ_3.
(ii) Impose the logical condition

$$\delta_3 = 1 \leftrightarrow \delta_1 = 1 \cdot \delta_2 = 1 \tag{26}$$

by means of the extra constraints

$$
\begin{aligned}
-\delta_1 \quad\;\; + \delta_3 &\leqslant 0, \\
-\delta_2 + \delta_3 &\leqslant 0, \\
\delta_1 + \delta_2 - \delta_3 &\leqslant 1.
\end{aligned}
\tag{27}
$$

An example of the need to linearize products of 0–1 variables in this way arises in the DECENTRALIZATION problem in Part 3. Products involving more than two variables can be progressively reduced to single variables in a similar manner.

It is even possible to linearize terms involving a product of a 0–1 variable with a continuous variable. For example the term $x\delta$, where x is continuous and δ is 0–1, can be treated in the following way:

(i) Replace $x\delta$ by a continuous variable y.
(ii) Impose the logical conditions

$$
\begin{aligned}
\delta = 0 &\rightarrow y = 0, \\
\delta = 1 &\rightarrow y = x
\end{aligned}
\tag{28}
$$

by the extra constraints

$$
\begin{aligned}
y - M\delta &\leqslant 0, \\
-x + y \quad\;\; &\leqslant 0, \\
x - y + M\delta &\leqslant M.
\end{aligned}
\tag{29}
$$

where M is an upper bound for x (and hence also y).

Other non-linear expressions (such as ratios of polynomials) involving 0–1 variables can also be made linear in similar ways. Such expressions tend to occur fairly rarely and are not therefore considered further. They do, however, provide interesting problems of logical formulation using the principles described in this section and can provide useful exercises for the reader.

The purpose of this section together with Example 1 has been to demonstrate a method of imposing logical conditions on a model. This is by no means the only way of approaching this kind of modelling. Different rule of thumb methods exist for imposing the desired conditions. Experienced modellers may feel that they could derive the constraints described here by easier methods. It has been the author's experience, however that:

(i) Many people are unaware of the possibility of modelling logical conditions with 0−1 variables.

(ii) Among those people who realize that this is possible many find themselves unable to capture the required restrictions by 0−1 variables with logical constraints.

(iii) It is very easy to model a restriction incorrectly. By using concepts from Boolean algebra and approaching the modelling in the above manner it should be possible satisfactorily to impose the desired logical conditions.

A system for automating the formulation of logical conditions within standard predicates and implemented within the language PROLOG is described by McKinnon and Williams (1989).

9.3 Special Ordered Sets of Variables

Two very common types of restriction arise in mathematical programming problems for which the concept special ordered set of type 1 (SOS1) and special ordered set of type 2 (SOS2) have been developed. This concept is due to Beale and Tomlin (1969).

An SOS1 is a set of variables (continuous or integer) within which exactly one variable must be non-zero.

An SOS2 is a set of variables within which at most two can be non-zero. The two variables must be adjacent in the ordering given to the set.

It is perfectly possible to model the restrictions that a set of variables belongs to an SOS1 set or an SOS2 set using integer variables and constraints. The way in which this can be done is described below. There is great computational advantage to be gained, however, from treating these restrictions algorithmically. The way in which the branch and bound algorithm can be modified to deal with SOS1 and SOS2 sets is beyond the scope of this book. It is described in Beale and Tomlin.

Some examples are given on how SOS1 sets and SOS2 sets can arise.

Example 1. Depot Siting

A depot can be sited at any one of the positions A, B, C, D, or E. Only one depot can be built.

If 0−1 indicator variables δ_i are used to perform the following purpose: $\delta_i = 1$ if and only if the depot is sited at i (i is A, B, C, D, or E), then the set of variables $(\delta_1, \delta_2, \delta_3, \delta_4, \delta_5)$ can be regarded as an SOS1 set.

The SOS1 condition together with the constraint

$$\delta_1 + \delta_2 + \delta_3 + \delta_4 + \delta_5 = 1 \tag{1}$$

guarantees integrality and it is not necessary to stipulate that the δ_i be integral. Only if the sites have a natural ordering is there great advantage to be gained in the SOS formulation.

Example 2. Capacity Extension

The capacity C of a plant can be extended in *discrete* amounts by increasing levels of investment I.

If the set of variables $(\delta_0, \delta_1, \delta_2, \delta_3, \delta_4, \delta_5)$ is regarded as an SOS1 set then we can model

$$C = C_1\delta_1 + C_2\delta_2 + C_3\delta_3 + C_4\delta_4 + C_5\delta_5, \tag{2}$$

$$I = I_1\delta_1 + I_2\delta_2 + I_3\delta_3 + I_4\delta_4 + I_5\delta_5 \tag{3}$$

$$\delta_0 + \delta_1 + \delta_2 + \delta_3 + \delta_4 + \delta_5 = 1. \tag{4}$$

It is not necessary to treat the δ_i as integer variables since the SOS1 condition together with (4) forces integrality. Conceptually it is important to regard a SOS set as an *entity*. We can then regard C as a quantity which is a *discrete* function of I. This can be regarded as a *generalization of a* 0–1 *variable* to more than two discrete values. Such a generalization is often more useful than the conventional general integer variable.

Although the most common application of SOS1 sets is to modelling what would otherwise be 0–1 integer variables with a constraint such as (4), there are other applications.

The most common application of SOS2 sets is to modelling non-linear functions as described by the following example.

Example 3. Non-linear Functions

In Section 7.3 the concept of a separable set was introduced in order to make a piecewise linear approximation to a non-linear function of a single variable. Using the λ-convention for such a separable formulation we obtained the following convexity constraint:

$$\lambda_1 + \lambda_2 + \cdots + \lambda_n = 1. \tag{5}$$

In addition, in order that the coordinates of x and y should lie on the piecewise linear curve in Figure 7.15, it was necessary to impose the following extra restriction:

$$At\ most\ two\ adjacent\ \lambda s\ can\ be\ non\text{-}zero. \tag{6}$$

Instead of approaching this restriction through separable programming with the danger of local rather than global optima as described in Section 7.2, we can use an SOS2. The restriction (6) need not be modelled explicitly. Instead we can say that the set of variables $(\lambda_1, \lambda_2, ..., \lambda_n)$ is an SOS2.

The formulation of a non-linear function in Example 3 demands that the non-linear function be *separable*, i.e. the sum of non-linear functions of a single variable. It was demonstrated in Section 7.4 how models with non-separable functions may sometimes be converted into models where the non-linearities are all functions of a single variable. While this is often possible, it can be cumbersome, increasing the size of the model considerably as well as the computational difficulty. An alternative is to extend the concept of a SOS set to that of a *chain of linked SOS sets*. This has been done by Beale (1980). The idea is best illustrated by a further example.

Example 4. Non-linear Functions of Two or More Variables

Suppose $z = g(x, y)$ is a non-linear function of x and y.

We define a grid of values of (x, y) (not necessarily equidistant) and associate non-negative 'weightings' λ_{ij} with each point in the grid as shown in Figure 9.2.

If the values of (x, y) at the grid points are denoted by (X_s, Y_k) we can approximate the function $z = g(x, y)$ by means of the following relations:

$$x = \sum_s \sum_k X_s \lambda_{sk} \tag{7}$$

$$y = \sum_s \sum_k Y_k \lambda_{sk}, \tag{8}$$

$$z = \sum_s \sum_k g(X_s, Y_k) \lambda_{sk}, \tag{9}$$

$$\sum_s \sum_k \lambda_{sk} = 1. \tag{10}$$

In addition it is necessary to impose the following restriction on the λ variables:

$$\text{At most four neighbouring } \lambda s \text{ can be non-zero.} \tag{11}$$

This last condition is clearly a generalization of an SOS2 set. We can impose condition (11) in the following way. Let

$$\xi_s = \sum_k \lambda_{sk}, \qquad \eta_k = \sum_s \lambda_{sk}$$

for all s, k. $(\xi_1, \xi_2, \xi_3, ...)$ and $(\eta_1, \eta_2, \eta_3, ...)$ are each taken as SOS2 sets. The SOS2 condition for the first set allows λ_s to be non-zero in at most two neighbouring rows in Figure 9.2. For the second set the SOS2 condition allows

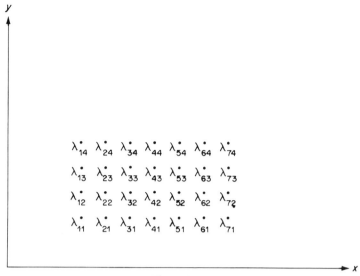

Figure 9.2

λ_s to be non-zero in at most two neighbouring columns. For example we might have $\xi_2 = 1/3$, $\xi_3 = 2/3$, $\eta_5 = 1/4$, $\eta_6 = 3/4$.

The values of ξ and η above could arise from $\lambda_{25} = 1/6$, $\lambda_{26} = 1/6$, $\lambda_{35} = 1/12$, $\lambda_{36} = 7/12$, all other λ_s being zero. They could, however, also arise from other values of the λ_s e.g. $\lambda_{25} = 1/4$, $\lambda_{26} = 1/12$, $\lambda_{36} = 2/3$ with all other λ_s being zero.

In order to get round this non-uniqueness we can restrict the non-zero λ_s to vertices of a triangle (such as in the second instance above). A lengthy way of doing this is to impose the extra constraints:

$$\zeta_t = \sum_s \lambda_{s,t+s} \tag{12}$$

and treat the ζ_t as a further SOS2 set.

If, however, we are content to restrict the x (or y) to grid values (i.e. not interpolate in that direction) then the problem does not arise. Indeed we can also avoid introducing the sets ξ_s so long as within each set λ_{sk}, with the same s, the member which is non-zero has the same index k. The sets λ_{sk} are then known as a *chain* of *linked SOS* sets as described by Beale (1980) and the restriction can be dealt with algorithmically.

Some of the problems presented in Part 2 can be formulated to take advantage of special ordered sets. In particular, DECENTRALIZATION and LOGIC DESIGN can exploit SOS1.

While it is desirable to treat SOS sets algorithmically if this facility exists in the package being used, the restrictions which they imply can be imposed using 0−1 variables and linear constraints. This is now demonstrated.

Suppose $(x_1, x_2, ..., x_n)$ is an SOS1 set. If the variables are not 0–1 we introduce 0–1 indicator variables $\delta_1, \delta_2, ..., \delta_n$ and link them to the x_i variables in the conventional way by constraints:

$$x_i - M_i \delta \leqslant 0, \qquad i = 1, 2, ..., n, \tag{13}$$

$$x_i - m_i \delta \geqslant 0, \tag{14}$$

where M_i and m_i are constant coefficients being upper and lower bounds respectively for x_i.

The following constraint is then imposed on the δ_i variables:

$$\delta_1 + \delta_2 + \cdots + \delta_n = 1. \tag{15}$$

If the x_i variables are 0–1 we can immediately regard them as the δ_i variables above and only need impose the constraint (15).

To model an SOS2 set using 0–1 variables is more complicated. Suppose $(\lambda_1, \lambda_2, ..., \lambda_n)$ is an SOS2 set. We introduce 0–1 variables $\delta_1, \delta_2, ..., \delta_{n-1}$ together with the following constraints:

$$
\begin{array}{llll}
\lambda_1 & & -\delta_1 & \leqslant 0, \\
\lambda_2 & & -\delta_1 - \delta_2 & \leqslant 0, \\
\lambda_3 & & -\delta_2 - \delta_3 & \leqslant 0, \\
& \ddots & \ddots & \vdots \\
\lambda_{n-1} & & -\delta_{n-2} - \delta_{n-1} \leqslant 0, \\
\lambda_n & & -\delta_{n-1} \leqslant 0, \\
\end{array}
\tag{16}
$$

and

$$\delta_1 + \delta_2 + \cdots + \delta_{n-1} = 1. \tag{17}$$

This formulation suggests the relationship between SOS1 and SOS2 sets since (17) could be dispensed with by regarding the δ_i as belonging to an SOS1 set as long as the δ_i each have an upper bound of 1.

9.4   Extra Conditions Applied to Linear Programming Models

Since the majority of practical applications of IP give rise to mixed integer programming models where extra conditions have been applied to an otherwise LP model, this subject will be considered further in this section. A number of the commonest applications will briefly be outlined.

Disjunctive Constraints

Suppose that for an LP problem we do not require all the constraints to hold simultaneously. We do, however, require at least one subset of constraints to hold. This could be stated as

$$R_1 \vee R_2 \vee ... \vee R_N, \tag{1}$$

184

where R_i is the proposition 'The constraints in subset i are satisfied' and constraints $1, 2, ..., N$ form the subset in question. (1) is known as a *disjunction of constraints*.

Following the principles of Section 9.1 we will introduce N indicator variables δ_i to indicate whether the R_i are satisfied. In this case it is only necessary to impose the conditions

$$\delta_i = 1 \rightarrow R_i. \tag{2}$$

This may be done by constraints of type (12) or (18) (Section 9.1) taken singly or together according to whether R_i are '$\leqslant$', '$\geqslant$', or '$=$' constraints. We can then impose condition (1) by the constraint

$$\delta_1 + \delta_2 + \cdots + \delta_N \geqslant 1. \tag{3}$$

An alternative formulation of (1) is possible. This is discussed in Section 10.2 and is due to Jeroslow and Lowe (1984), who report promising computational results in Jeroslow and Lowe (1985).

A generalization of (1) which can arise is the condition

At least k of $(R_1, R_2, ..., R_N)$ must be satisfied. (4)

This is modelled in a similar way but using the constraint below in place of (3):

$$\delta_1 + \delta_2 + \cdots + \delta_N \geqslant k. \tag{5}$$

A variation of (4) is the condition

At most k of $(R_1, R_2, ..., R_N)$ must be satisfied. (6)

To model (6) using indicator variables δ_i it is only necessary to impose the conditions

$$R_i \rightarrow \delta_i = 1. \tag{7}$$

This may be done by constraints of type (17) or (19) (Section 9.1) taken together or singly according to whether R_i is a '$\leqslant$', '$\geqslant$', or '$=$' constraint. Condition (6) can then be imposed by the constraint

$$\delta_1 + \delta_2 + \cdots + \delta_N \leqslant k. \tag{8}$$

Disjunctions of constraints involve the logical connective '$\vee$' ('or') and necessitate IP models.

It is worth pointing out that the connective '.' ('and') can obviously be coped with through conventional LP since a conjunction of constraints simply involves a series of constraints holding simultaneously. In this sense one can regard 'and' as corresponding to LP and 'or' as corresponding to IP.

Non-convex Regions

As an application of disjunctive constraints we will show how restrictions corresponding to a non-convex region may be imposed using IP. It is well

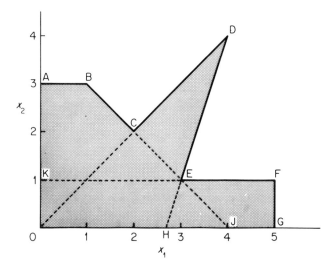

Figure 9.3

known that the feasible region of an LP model is convex. (Convexity is defined in Section 7.2 of Chapter 7.) There are circumstances, however, in non-linear programming problems where we wish to have a non-convex feasible region. For example, we will consider the feasible region ABCDEFGO of Figure 9.3. This is a non-convex region bounded by a series of straight lines. Such a region may have arisen through the problem considered or represent a piecewise linear approximation to a non-convex region bounded by curves.

We may conveniently think of the region ABCDEFGO as made up of the union of the three convex regions ABJO, ODH, and KFGO, as shown in Figure 9.3. The fact these regions overlap will not matter.

Region ABJO is defined by the constraints

$$x_2 \leqslant 3,$$
$$x_1 + x_2 \leqslant 4. \tag{9}$$

Region ODH is defined by the constraints

$$-x_1 + x_2 \leqslant 0,$$
$$3x_1 - x_2 \leqslant 8. \tag{10}$$

Region KFGO is defined by the constraints

$$x_2 \leqslant 1,$$
$$x_1 \leqslant 5. \tag{11}$$

We will introduce indicator variables δ_1, δ_2, and δ_3 to use in the following conditions:

$$\delta_1 = 1 \rightarrow (x_2 \leqslant 3) . (x_1 + x_2 \leqslant 4), \tag{12}$$

$$\delta_2 = 1 \rightarrow (-x_1 + x_2 \leqslant 0) . (3x_1 - x_2 \leqslant 8), \tag{13}$$

$$\delta_3 = 1 \rightarrow (x_2 \leqslant 1) . (x_1 \leqslant 5). \tag{14}$$

(12), (13), and (14) are respectively imposed by the following constraints:

$$
\begin{aligned}
x_2 + \quad \delta_1 &\leqslant 4, \\
x_1 + x_2 + 5\delta_1 &\leqslant 9,
\end{aligned}
\tag{15}
$$

$$
\begin{aligned}
-x_1 + x_2 + 4\delta_2 &\leqslant \quad 4, \\
3x_1 - x_2 + 7\delta_2 &\leqslant 15,
\end{aligned}
\tag{16}
$$

$$
\begin{aligned}
x_2 + 3\delta_3 &\leqslant 4, \\
x_1 &\leqslant 5.
\end{aligned}
\tag{17}
$$

It is now only necessary to impose the condition that at least one of the set (9), (10), or (11) must hold. This is done by the constraint

$$\delta_1 + \delta_2 + \delta_3 \geqslant 1. \tag{18}$$

It would also be possible to cope with a situation in which the feasible region was disconnected in this way.

There is an alternative formulation for a connected non-convex region, such as that above, so long as the line joining the origin to any feasible point lies entirely within the feasible region. Seven 'weighting' variables $\lambda_A, \lambda_B, \ldots, \lambda_G$ are associated with the vertices $A, B, \ldots, G$ and incorporated in the following constraints:

$$\lambda_B + 2\lambda_C + 4\lambda_D + 3\lambda_E + 5\lambda_F + 5\lambda_G - x_1 = 0, \tag{19}$$

$$3\lambda_A + 3\lambda_B + 2\lambda_C + 4\lambda_D + \lambda_E + \lambda_F - x_2 = 0, \tag{20}$$

$$\lambda_A + \lambda_B + \lambda_C + \lambda_D + \lambda_E + \lambda_F + \lambda_G \leqslant 1 \tag{21}$$

The λ variables are then restricted to form an SOS2. Notice that this is a generalization of the use of a SOS2 set to model a piecewise linear function such as that represented by the line ABCDEFG. In that case constraint (21) would become an equation, i.e. the λs would sum to 1. For the example here we simply relax this restriction to give a '$\leqslant$' constraint.

Limiting the Number of Variables in a Solution

This is another application of disjunctive constraints. It is well known that in LP the optimal solution need never have more variables at a non-zero value then there are constraints in the problem. Sometimes it is required, however, to restrict this number still further (to k). To do this requires IP. Indicator variables δ_i are introduced to link with each of the n continuous variables x_i in the LP problem by the condition

$$x_i > 0 \rightarrow \delta_1 = 1. \tag{22}$$

As before this condition is imposed by the constraint

$$x_i - M_i\delta_i \leqslant 0, \tag{23}$$

where M_i is an upper bound on x_i.

We then impose the condition that at most k of the variables x_i can be non-zero by the constraint

$$\delta_1 + \delta_2 + \cdots + \delta_n \leqslant k.$$

A very common application of this type of condition is in limiting the number of ingredients in a blend. The FOOD MANUFACTURE 2 example of Part 1 is an example of this. Another situation in which the condition might arise is where it is desired to limit the range of products produced in a product mix type LP model.

Sequentially Dependent Decisions

It sometimes happens that we wish to model a situation in which decisions made at a particular time will affect decisions made later. Suppose, for example, that in a multi-period LP model (n periods) we have introduced a decision variable γ_t into each period to show how a decision should be made in each period. We will let γ_t represent the following decisions: $\gamma_t = 0$ means the depot should be permanently closed down; $\gamma_t = 1$ means the depot should be temporarily closed (this period only); $\gamma_t = 2$ means the depot should be used in this period. Clearly we would wish to impose (among others) the conditions

$$\gamma_t = 0 \rightarrow (\gamma_{t+1} = 0).(\gamma_{t+2} = 0)...(\gamma_n = 0). \tag{24}$$

This may be done by the following constraints:

$$\begin{aligned} -2\gamma_1 + \gamma_2 &\leqslant 0, \\ -2\gamma_2 + \gamma_3 &\leqslant 0, \\ \ddots \ \vdots \quad \\ -2\gamma_{n-1} + \gamma_n &\leqslant 0. \end{aligned} \tag{25}$$

In this case the decision variable γ_t can take three values. More usually it will be a 0–1 variable.

A case of sequentially dependent decisions arises in the MINING problem of Part 2.

Economies of Scale

It was pointed out in Chapter 7 that economies of scale lead to a non-linear programming problem where the objective is equivalent to minimizing a non-convex function. In this situation it is not possible to reduce the problem

188

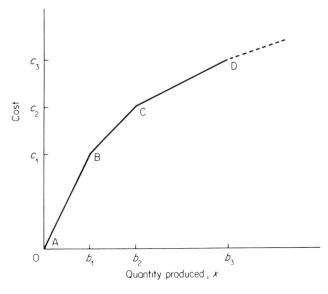

Figure 9.4

to an LP problem by piecewise linear approximations alone. Nor is it possible to rely on separable programming since local optima might result.

Suppose for example that we have a model where the objective is to minimize cost. The amount to be manufactured of a particular product is represented by a variable x. For increasing x the unit marginal costs decrease.

Diagrammatically we have the situation shown in Figure 9.4. This may be the true cost curve or be a piecewise linear approximation.

The unit marginal costs are successively

$$\frac{c_1}{b_1} > \frac{c_2 - c_1}{b_2 - b_1} > \frac{c_3 - c_2}{b_3 - b_2} \dots .$$

Using the λ-formulation of separable programming as described in Chapter 7, we introduce $n + 1$ variables λ_i ($i = 0, 1, 2, \dots, n$) which may be interpreted as 'weights' attached to the vertices A, B, C, D, etc. We then have

$$x = b_1\lambda_1 + b_2\lambda_2 + \dots + b_n\lambda_n, \tag{26}$$

$$\text{cost} = c_1\lambda_1 + c_2\lambda_2 + \dots + c_n\lambda_n. \tag{27}$$

The set of variables ($\lambda_0, \lambda_1, \dots \lambda_n$) is now regarded as a special ordered set of type 2. If IP is used, a global optimal solution can be obtained.

It is also, of course, possible to model this situation using the δ-formulation of separable programming.

Discrete Capacity Extensions

It is sometimes unrealistic to regard an LP constraint (usually a capacity constraint) as applying in all circumstances. In real life it is often possible to violate the constraint at a certain cost. This topic has already been mentioned in Section 3.3. There, however, we allowed this constraint to be relaxed continuously. Often this is not possible. Should the constraint be successively relaxed it may be possible that it can only be done in finite jumps, e.g. we buy in whole new machines or whole new storage tanks.

Suppose the initial right-hand side (RHS) value is b_0 and that this may be successively increased to $b_1, b_2, ..., b_n$.

We have

$$\sum_j a_j x_j \leqslant b_i; \tag{28}$$

also

$$\text{cost} = \begin{cases} 0 & \text{if } i = 0, \\ c_i & \text{otherwise,} \end{cases}$$

where $0 < c_1 < c_2 \cdots < c_n$.

This situation may be modelled by introducing 0–1 variables δ_0, δ_1, δ_2, etc., to represent the successive possible RHS values applying. We then have

$$\sum_j a_j x_j - b_0 \delta_0 - b_1 \delta_1 - \cdots - b_n \delta_n \leqslant 0. \tag{29}$$

The following expression is added to the objective function:

$$c_1 \delta_1 + c_2 \delta_2 + \cdots + c_n \delta_n. \tag{30}$$

The set of variables $(\delta_0, \delta_1, ..., \delta_n)$ may be treated as an SOS1 set. If this is done then the δ_i can be regarded as continuous variables having a generalized upper bound of 1, i.e. the integrality requirement may be ignored.

Maximax Objectives

Suppose we had the following situation:

Maximize $\left(\text{Maximum}_i \left(\sum_j a_{ij} x_j \right) \right)$

subject to   conventional linear constraints.

This is analogous to the *minimax* objective discussed in Section 3.2 but unlike that case it cannot be modelled by linear programming.

We can, however, treat it as a case of a disjunctive constraint and use integer programming. The model can be expressed as:

Maximize z

subject to $\sum_j a_{1j} x_j - z = 0$ *or* $\sum_j a_{2j} x_j - z = 0$ *or* ... etc.

9.5   Special Kinds of Integer Programming Model

The purpose of this section is to describe some well known special types of IP model which have received considerable theoretical attention. By describing the structure of these types of model it is hoped that the model builder may be able to recognize when he has such a model. Reference to the extensive literature and computational experience on such models may then be of value.

It should, however, be emphasized that most practical IP models do not fall into any of these categories but arise as MIP models often extending an existing LP model. The considerable attention that has been paid to the IP problems described below should not disguise their limited but nevertheless sometimes significant practical importance.

Set Covering Problems

These problems derive their name from the following type of abstract problem.

We are given a set of objects which we number as the set $S = (1, 2, 3, ..., m)$. We are also given a class $\mathscr{S}$ of subsets of S. Each of these subsets has a cost associated with it.

The problem is to 'cover' all members of S at minimum cost using members of $\mathscr{S}$.

For example, suppose $S = (1, 2, 3, 4, 5)$ and $\mathscr{S} = ((1, 2), (1, 3, 5), (2, 4, 5), (3), (1), (4, 5))$ and all members of $\mathscr{S}$ have cost 1.

A cover for S would be $(1, 2)$, $(1, 3, 5)$, and $(2, 4, 5)$.

In order to obtain the minimum cost cover of S in this example we could build a 0–1 PIP model. The variables δ_i have the following interpretation:

$$\delta_i = \begin{cases} 1 & \text{if the } i\text{th member of } \mathscr{S} \text{ is in the cover,} \\ 0 & \text{otherwise} \end{cases}$$

Constraints are introduced to ensure that each member of S is covered. For example, in order to cover the member 1 of S we must have at least one of the members $(1, 2)$, $(1, 3, 5)$, or (1) of $\mathscr{S}$ in the cover. This condition is imposed by constraint (1) below. The other constraints ensure a similar condition for the other members of S.

If the objective is simply to minimize the number of members of S used in the cover, the resultant model is as follows:

$$\begin{array}{lll} \text{Minimize} & \delta_1 + \delta_2 + \delta_3 + \delta_4 + \delta_5 + \delta_6 & \\ \text{subject to} & \delta_1 + \delta_2 \qquad\quad + \delta_5 \qquad \geq 1, & (1) \\ & \delta_1 \quad\; + \delta_3 \qquad\qquad\qquad \geq 1, & (2) \\ & \delta_2 \quad\; + \delta_4 \qquad\qquad \geq 1, & (3) \\ & \delta_3 \qquad\qquad + \delta_6 \geq 1, & (4) \\ & \delta_2 + \delta_3 \qquad\qquad + \delta_6 \geq 1. & (5) \end{array}$$

Alternatively the variables could be given non-unit cost coefficients in the objective.

This model has a number of important properties:

Property 1 The problem is a minimization and all constraints are '$\geqslant$'.
Property 2 All RHS coefficients are 1.
Property 3 All other matrix coefficients are 0 or 1.

As a result of the abstract set covering application described above, all 0–1 PIP models with the above three properties are known as *set covering problems*.

Generalizations of the problem exist. If property 2 is relaxed and we allow larger positive integers than 1 for some RHS coefficients we obtain the *weighted set covering problem*. An interpretation of this is that some of the members of S are to be given greater 'weight' in the covering than others, i.e. they must be covered a certain number of times.

Another generalization that sometimes occurs is when we relax property 2 above but also relax property 3 to allow matrix coefficients 0 or ± 1. This gives rise to the *generalized set covering problem*.

The best known application of set covering problems is to aircrew scheduling. Here the members of S can be regarded as 'legs' which an airline has to cover and the members of $\mathscr{S}$ are possible 'rosters' (or rotations) involving particular combinations of flights. A common requirement is to cover all legs over some period of time using the minimum number of crews. Each crew is assigned to a roster.

A comprehensive list of applications of set covering problems is given by Balas and Padberg (1975).

Special algorithms do exist for set covering problems. Two such algorithms are described in Chapter 4 of Garfinkel and Nemhauser (1972).

Set covering problems have an important property which often makes them comparatively easy to solve by the branch and bound method. It can be shown that the optimal solution to a set covering problem must be a vertex solution in the same sense as for LP problems. Unfortunately this vertex solution will not generally be (but sometimes is) the optimal vertex solution to the corresponding LP model. It will, however, often be possible to move from this continuous optimum to the integer optimum in comparatively few steps.

The difficulty of solving set covering problems usually arises not from their structure but from their size. In practice models frequently have comparatively few constraints but an enormous number of variables. There is often considerable virtue in generating columns for the model in the course of optimization.

Set Packing Problems

These problems are closely related to set covering problems. The name again derives from an abstract problem which we will first describe.

We are given a set of objects which we number as the set $S = (1, 2, 3, ..., m)$.

We are also given a class $\mathscr{S}$ of subsets of S each of which has a certain value associated with it.

The problem is to 'pack' as many of the members of $\mathscr{S}$ into S as possible to maximize total value but for there to be no overlap.

For example, suppose $S = (1, 2, 3, 4, 5, 6)$ and $\mathscr{S} = ((1, 2, 5), (1, 3), (2, 4), (3, 6), (2, 3, 6))$. A pack for S would be $(1, 2, 5)$ and $(3, 6)$.

Again we could build a 0–1 PIP model to help solve the problem. The variables δ_i have the following interpretation:

$$\delta_i = \begin{cases} 1 & \text{if the ith member of $\mathscr{S}$ is in the pack,} \\ 0 & \text{otherwise.} \end{cases}$$

Constraints are introduced to ensure that no member of S is included in more than one member of $\mathscr{S}$ in the pack, i.e. there shall be no overlap. For example, in order that the member 2 shall not be included more than once we cannot have more than one of $(1, 2, 5)$, $(2, 4)$, and $(2, 3, 6)$ in the pack. This condition gives rise to the constraint (7) below. The other constraints ensure similar conditions for the other members of S.

The objective here is to maximize the number of members of S we can 'pack in'. For this example the model is:

$$
\begin{array}{llr}
\text{Maximize} & \delta_1 + \delta_2 + \delta_3 + \delta_4 + \delta_5 & \\
\text{subject to} & \delta_1 + \delta_2 \leqslant 1, & (6) \\
& \delta_1 + \delta_3 + \delta_5 \leqslant 1, & (7) \\
& \delta_2 + \delta_4 + \delta_5 \leqslant 1, & (8) \\
& \delta_3 \leqslant 1, & (9) \\
& \delta_1 \leqslant 1, & (10) \\
& \delta_4 + \delta_5 \leqslant 1. & (11)
\end{array}
$$

(Constraints (9) and (10) are obviously redundant.)

Like the set covering problem this model has a number of important properties:

Property 4 The problem is a maximization and all constraints are '$\leqslant$'.
Property 5 All RHS coefficients are 1.
Property 6 All other matrix coefficients are 0 or 1.

An interesting observation is that the LP problem associated with a set packing problem with objective coefficients of 1 is the dual of the LP problem associated with a set covering problem with objective coefficients of 1. This result is of little obvious significance as far as the optimal solutions to the IP problems are concerned since there may be a 'duality gap' between these solutions. This term is explained in Section 10.3. Although a set packing problem with objective coefficients of 1 is the 'dual' of a set covering problem with objective coefficients of 1 in this sense it should be realized that the set S

which we wish to cover with members of $\mathscr{S}$ is not the same as the set S which we wish to pack with members of another class of subsets $\mathscr{S}$. The two examples used above to illustrate set covering and set packing problems are so chosen as to be dual problems in this sense, but the set S and class of subsets $\mathscr{S}$ are different.

As with the set covering problem there are generalizations of the set packing problem obtained by relaxing some of the properties 4, 5, and 6 above. If property 5 is relaxed and we allow positive integral RHS coefficients greater than 1, we obtain the *weighted set packing problem*. If we relax property 5 as above together with property 6 to allow matrix coefficients of 0 or ± 1, we obtain the *generalized set packing problem*.

A special sort of packing problem is known as the *matching problem*. This problem can be represented by a graph in which the objects S to be packed are *nodes*. Each subset from S consists of two members of S and is represented by an *arc* of the graph whose end points represent the two members of S. The problem then becomes one of matching (or pairing) as many vertices as possible together. Extensive work on this problem has been done by Edmonds (1965).

Set packing problems are equivalent to the class of set partitioning problems which we consider next. Applications and references will be described there.

Set Partitioning Problems

In this case we are, as before, given a set of objects which we number as the set $S = (1, 2, 3, ..., m)$ and a class $\mathscr{S}$ of subsets of S.

The problem this time is both to cover all the members of S using members of $\mathscr{S}$ and also to have no overlap. We, in this sense, have a covering and packing problem combined. There is no useful purpose in distinguishing between maximization and minimization problems here. Both may arise.

As an example we will consider the same S and $\mathscr{S}$ used in the example to describe the set covering problem. The difference is that we must now impose stricter conditions to ensure that each member of S is in exactly one member of the partition (or cover and pack combined). This is done by making the constraints (1), (2), ..., (5) ' = ' instead of ' $\geqslant$ ', giving

$$\delta_1 + \delta_2 + \quad\quad + \delta_5 \quad\quad = 1, \tag{12}$$

$$\delta_1 \quad\quad + \delta_3 \quad\quad = 1, \tag{13}$$

$$\delta_2 \quad\quad + \delta_4 \quad\quad = 1, \tag{14}$$

$$\delta_3 \quad\quad + \delta_6 = 1, \tag{15}$$

$$\delta_2 + \delta_3 \quad\quad + \delta_6 = 1. \tag{16}$$

For example, a feasible partition of S consists of $(1, 2)$, (3), and $(4, 5)$.

An easily understood way in which the set partitioning problem can arise is again in aircrew scheduling. Suppose that we did not allow aircrews to travel as passengers on other flights. It would then be necessary that each member of S (a leg) be covered by exactly one member of $\mathcal{S}$ (a roster). We would then have a set partitioning problem in place of the set covering problem.

Another application of the set partitioning problem is to *political districting*. In this problem there is usually an extra constraint fixing the total number of political districts (or constituencies). The objective is usually to *minimize the maximum deviation* of the electorate in a district from the average electorate in a district. This *minimax* objective can be dealt with in the way described in Section 3.3. A reference to tackling the problem by IP is Garfinkel and Nemhauser (1970).

We will now show the essential equivalence between set partitioning and set packing problems. If we introduce slack variables into each of the ' $\leqslant$ ' constraints of a set packing problem we obtain ' $=$ ' constraints. These slack variables can only take the values 0 or 1 and could therefore be regarded with all the other variables in the problem as 0–1 variables. The result would clearly be a set partitioning problem.

To show the converse is slightly more complicated. Suppose we have a set partitioning problem. Each constraint will be of the form

$$a_1\delta_1 + a_2\delta_2 + \cdots + a_n\delta_n = 1. \tag{17}$$

We introduce an extra 0–1 variable δ into constraint (17) giving

$$a_1\delta_1 + a_2\delta_2 + \cdots + a_n\delta_n + \delta = 1. \tag{18}$$

If the problem is a minimization, δ can be given a sufficiently high positive cost M in the objective to force δ to be zero in the optimal solution. For a maximization problem, making M a negative number with a sufficiently high absolute value has the same effect. Instead of introducing δ explicitly into the objective function we can substitute the expression below derived from (18):

$$1 - a_1\delta_1 - a_2\delta_2 - \cdots - a_n\delta_n. \tag{19}$$

There is no loss of generality in replacing (18) by the constraint

$$a_1\delta_1 + a_2\delta_2 + \cdots + a_n\delta_n \leqslant 1. \tag{20}$$

If similar transformations are performed for all the other constraints the set partitioning problem can be transformed into a set packing problem.

Hence we obtain the result that set packing problems and set partitioning problems can easily be transformed from one to the other. Both types of problem possess the property mentioned in connection with the set covering problems, that the optimal solution is always a vertex solution to the corresponding LP problem.

The set partitioning (or packing) problem is generally even easier to solve than the set covering problem. It is easy to see from the small numerical example that a set partitioning problem by using ' $=$ ' constraints is more constrained than the corresponding set covering problem. Likewise the corresponding LP problem is more constrained. It will be seen in Section 10.1

that constraining the corresponding LP problem to an IP problem as much as possible is computationally very desirable.

A comprehensive list of applications and references to the set packing and partitioning problems is given by Balas and Padberg (1975). Chapter 4 of Garfinkel and Nemhauser (1972) treats these problems very fully and gives a special purpose algorithm.

In view of its close similarity to set partitioning and packing problems it is rather suprising that the set covering problem has some important differences. Although the set covering problem is an essentially easy type of problem to solve it is distinctly more difficult than the former problems. It is possible to transform a set partitioning (or packing) problem into a set covering problem by introducing an extra 0–1 variable with a negative coefficient in (17) and performing analogous substitutions to those described above. The reverse transformation of a set covering problem to a set partitioning (or packing) problem is not, however, generally possible, revealing the distinctness of the problems.

The Knapsack Problem

A PIP model with a single constraint is known as a knapsack problem. Such a problem can take the form:

Maximize $p_1\gamma_1 + p_2\gamma_2 + \cdots + p_n\gamma_n$

subject to $a_1\gamma_1 + a_2\gamma_2 + \cdots + a_n\gamma_n \leqslant b,$ (21)

where $\gamma_1, \gamma_2, ..., \gamma_n \geqslant 0$ and take integer values.

The name 'knapsack' arises from the rather contrived application of a hiker trying to fill his knapsack to maximum total value. Each item he considers taking with him has a certain value and a certain weight. An overall weight limitation gives the single constraint.

An obvious extension of the problem is where there are additional upper bounding constraints on the variables. Most commonly these upper bounds will all be 1 giving a 0–1 *knapsack problem*.

Practical applications occasionally arise in *project selection* and *capital budgeting allocation* problems if there is only one constraint. The problem of *stocking a warehouse* to maximum value given that the goods stored come in indivisible units also gives rise to an obvious knapsack problem.

The occurrence of such immediately obvious applications is, however, fairly rare. Much more commonly the knapsack problem arises in LP and IP problems where one generates the columns of the model in the course of optimization. Since such techniques are intimately linked with the algorithmic side of mathematical programming they are beyond the scope of this book. The original application of the knapsack problem in this way was to the *cutting stock problem*. This is described by Gilmore and Gomory (1963, 1965).

In practice knapsack problems are comparatively easy to solve. The branch and bound method is not, however, an efficient method to use. If it is desired to solve a large number of knapsack problems (e.g. when generating columns for an LP or IP model), it is better to use a more efficient method. Dynamic programming proves an efficient method of solving knapsack problems. This method and further references are given in Chapter 6 of Garfinkel and Nemhauser (1972).

The Travelling Salesman Problem

This problem has received a lot of attention largely because of its conceptual simplicity. The simplicity with which the problem can be stated is in marked contrast to the difficulty of solving such problems in practice.

The name 'travelling salesman' arises from the following application.

A salesman has to set out from home to visit a number of customers before finally returning home. The problem is to find the order in which he should visit all the customers if he is to minimize the total distance covered.

Generalizations and special cases of the problem have been considered. For example, sometimes it is not necessary that the salesman return home. Often the problem itself has special properties, e.g. the distance from A to B is the same as the distance from B to A. The *vehicle routing problem* can be reduced to a travelling salesman problem. This is the problem of organizing deliveries to customers using a number of vehicles of different sizes. The reverse problem of picking up deliveries (e.g. letters from the post office boxes) given a number of vehicles (or postmen) can also be treated in this way.

Job sequencing problems in order to minimize set-up costs can be treated as travelling salesman problems where the 'distance between cities' represents the 'set-up cost between operations'. A not very obvious (nor probably practical) application of this sort is to sequencing the colours which will be used for a single brush in a series of painting operations. Obviously the transition between certain colours will require a more thorough cleaning of the brush than a transition between other colours. The problem of sequencing the colours to minimize the total cleaning time gives rise to a travelling salesman problem.

The travelling salesman problem can be formulated as an IP model in a number of ways. We present one such formulation here. Any solution (not necessarily optimal) to the problem will be referred to as a 'tour'.

Suppose the cities to be visited are numbered $0, 1, 2, \ldots, n$. 0–1 integer variables δ_{ij} are introduced with the following interpretation:

$$\delta_{ij} = \begin{cases} 1 & \text{if the tour goes from } i \text{ to } j \text{ direct.} \\ 0 & \text{otherwise.} \end{cases}$$

The objective is simply to minimize $\Sigma_{i,j} \, c_{ij} \delta_{ij}$, where c_{ij} is the distance (or cost) between i and j.

There are two obvious conditions which must be fulfilled:

> Exactly one city must be visited immediately after city i.   (22)

Exactly one city must be visited immediately before city j.　　(23)

Condition (22) is achieved by the constraints

$$\sum_{\substack{j=0 \\ i \neq j}}^{n} \delta_{ij} = 1, \qquad i = 0, 1, \ldots, n. \tag{24}$$

Condition (23) is achieved by the constraints

$$\sum_{\substack{i=0 \\ i \neq j}}^{n} \delta_{ij} = 1, \qquad j = 0, 1, \ldots, n. \tag{25}$$

As the model has so far been presented we have an assignment problem as described in Section 5.3. Unfortunately the constraints (24) and (25) are not sufficient. Suppose, for example, we were considering a problem with eight cities ($n = 7$). The solution drawn in Figure 9.5 would satisfy all the conditions (24) and (25).

Clearly we cannot allow subtours such as those shown here.

The problem of adding extra constraints so as to avoid subtours proves quite difficult. In practice it is often desirable to add these constraints in the course of optimization as subtours arise. Here we will describe a method of adding sufficient constraints to the original model to prevent subtours ever arising.

Extra variables u_i are added to the problem for $i = 1, 2, \ldots, n$. These variables may be regarded as continuous (although they will take integer values in the optimal solution). The physical interpretation of the variables u_i need not concern us immediately. Extra constraints are now added of the form below:

$$u_i - u_j + n\delta_{ij} \leqslant n - 1, \tag{26}$$

where $i, j = 1, 2, \ldots, n$ and $i \neq j$.

In order to show that the extra constraints (26) have the desired effect we have to show: (a) that constraints (26) rule out any subtours; and (b) that the constraints (26) are not over restrictive, i.e. that total tours will not violate (26).

In order to demonstrate (a) we will refer to the example in Figure 9.5. Here $n = 7$. We will consider those constraints (26) relating to the subtour *not*

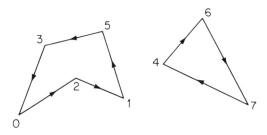

Figure 9.5

containing city 0. This gives

$$u_4 - u_6 + 7\delta_{46} \leqslant 6, \tag{27}$$

$$u_6 - u_7 + 7\delta_{67} \leqslant 6, \tag{28}$$

$$u_7 - u_4 + 7\delta_{74} \leqslant 6. \tag{29}$$

Clearly δ_{46}, δ_{67}, and δ_{74} all take the value 1 in the 'solution' of Figure 9.5. Adding (27), (28), and (29) together gives

$$21 \leqslant 18. \tag{30}$$

As this inequality is obviously false the 'solution' shown in Figure 9.5 cannot satisfy the new constraints (26).

A similar argument could be applied to any other subtour not containing city 0. The crux of the formulation is, however, that we have no variable u_0 and therefore no constraint (26) involving $i = 0$ or $j = 0$. It is not therefore possible to complete the similar constraints to (27), (28), and (29) round any tour or subtour containing city 0. Therefore if no subtours exist, the total tour must contain city 0, and the above argument does not apply.

We will now demonstrate (b) more rigorously and show that total tours are definitely not ruled out by our new constraints (26). The following interpretation can now be applied to the variables u:

u_i = sequence number in which city i is visited.

For example, we will consider the total tour shown in Figure 9.6 for the small example. Here the variables u_i would take the following values:

$$u_2 = 1,$$
$$u_1 = 2,$$
$$u_4 = 3,$$
$$u_7 = 4,$$
$$u_6 = 5,$$
$$u_5 = 6,$$
$$u_3 = 7.$$

It is easy to see that this total tour does not violate the constraints (26).

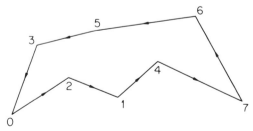

Figure 9.6

The size of the IP model generated in this formulation should be noted. We are considering a problem with $n + 1$ cities. This model has the following dimensions:

$n(n + 1)$	δ_{ij} variables,
n	u_i variables,
$n + 1$	constraints of type (24),
$n + 1$	constraints of type (25),
$n(n - 1)$	constraints of type (26).

By adding constraints (26) to avoid subtours we enormously expand the number of constraints in a realistic problem. For example, if our problem involves 100 cities we have a model with over 10 000 constraints.

A comprehensive survey of the problem giving a number of alternative formulations is Lawler *et al.* (1985). Eilon, Watson-Gandy, and Christofides (1971), describe how the vehicle scheduling problem can be reduced to a travelling salesman problem.

Special algorithms have been developed for the travelling salesman problem. One of the most successful is that of Held and Karp (1971).

The Quadratic Assignment Problem

This is a generalization of the assignment problem described in Section 5.3. Whereas that problem could be treated as an LP problem and was therefore comparatively easy to solve, the quadratic assignment problem is a genuine IP problem and often very difficult to solve.

Like the assignment problem we will consider the problem as related to two sets of objects S and T. S and T both have the same number of members which will be indexed 1 to n. The problem is to assign each member of S to exactly one member of T in order to achieve some objective. There are two sorts of conditions we must fulfil:

Each member of S must be assigned to exactly one member of T.   (31)

Each member of T must have exactly one member of S assigned to it. (32)

0–1 variables δ_{ij} can be introduced with the following interpretations:

$$\delta_{ij} = \begin{cases} 1 & \text{if } i \text{ (a member of } S\text{) is assigned to } j \text{ (a member of } T\text{),} \\ 0 & \text{otherwise.} \end{cases}$$

Conditions (31) and (32) are imposed by the following two types of constraint:

$$\sum_{j=1}^{n} \delta_{ij} = 1, \qquad i = 1, 2, ..., n \tag{33}$$

$$\sum_{i=1}^{n} \delta_{ij} = 1, \qquad j = 1, 2, ..., n. \tag{34}$$

The objective is more complex than with the assignment problem. We have cost coefficients c_{ijkl} which have the following interpretations. c_{ijkl} is the cost incurred by assigning i (a member of S) to j (a member of T) at the same time as assigning k (a member of S) to l (a member of T). This cost will clearly be incurred only if $\delta_{ij} = 1$ and $\delta_{kl} = 1$, i.e. if the product $\delta_{ij}\delta_{kl} = 1$. The objective then becomes a quadratic expression in 0–1 variables:

Minimize

$$\sum_{\substack{i,j,k,l=1 \\ k>i}}^{n} c_{ijkl}\delta_{ij}\delta_{kl}. \tag{35}$$

The condition $k > i$ on the indices prevents the cost of each pair of assignments being counted twice. It is very common for the coefficients c_{ijkl} to be derived from the product of other coefficients t_{ik} and d_{jl} so that

$$c_{ijkl} = t_{ik}d_{jl}. \tag{36}$$

In order to understand this rather complicated model it is worth considering two applications.

Firstly we will consider S to be a set of n factories and T to be a set of n cities. The problem is to locate one factory in each city and to minimize total communication costs between factories. The communication costs depend on (i) the frequency of communication between each pair of factories, and (ii) the distances between the two cities where each pair of factories is located.

Clearly some factories will have little to do with each other and can be located far apart at little cost. On the other hand, some factories may need to communicate a lot. The cost of communication will depend on the distance apart. In this application we can interpret the coefficients t_{ik} and d_{jl} in (36) as follows; t_{ik} is the frequency of communication between factories i and k (measured in appropriate units); d_{jl} is the cost per unit of communication between cities j and l (clearly this will be related to the distance between j and l). Obviously the cost of communication between the factories i and k, if they are located in cities j and l, will be given by (36). The total cost is therefore represented by the objective function (35).

Another application concerns the placement of n electronic modules in n predetermined positions on a backplate. S represents the set of modules and T represents the set of positions on the backplate. The modules have to be connected to each other by a series of wires. If the objective is to minimize the total length of wire used we have a quadratic assignment problem similar to the above model. The coefficients t_{ik} and d_{jl} have the following interpretations: t_{ik} is the number of wires which must connect module i to the module k, and d_{jl} is the distance between position j and position l on the backplate. Many modifications of the quadratic assignment problem described above exist. Frequently conditions (31) and (32) are relaxed, to allow more than one member of S (or possibly none) to be assigned to a member of T, where S and

T may not have the same number of members. A modified problem of this sort is the DECENTRALIZATION example in Part 2.

One way of tackling the quadratic assignment problem is to reduce the problem to a linear 0–1 PIP problem. It is necessary to remove the quadratic terms in the objective function. A way of transforming products of 0–1 variables into linear expressions in an IP model was described in Section 9.2. For fairly small models such a transformation is possible but for larger models the result can be an enormous expansion in the number of variables and constraints in the model. The solution of a practical problem of this sort by using a similar type of transformation is described by Beale and Tomlin (1972).

A survey of practical applications as well as other methods of tackling the problem is given by Lawler (1974). He also shows how a different formulation of the travelling salesman problem to that given here leads to a quadratic assignment problem. It should be pointed out, however, that although a travelling salesman problem is often difficult to solve a quadratic assignment problem of comparable dimensions is usually even harder.

CHAPTER 10

Building Integer Programming Models II

10.1 Good and Bad Formulations

Most of the considerations of Section 3.4 concerning linear programming (LP) models will also apply to integer programming (IP) models and will not be reconsidered here. There are, however, some important additional considerations which must be taken account of when building IP models. The primary additional consideration is the much greater computational difficulty of solving IP models over LP models. It is fairly common to build an IP model only to find the cost of solving it prohibitive. Frequently it is possible to reformulate the problem, giving another, easier to solve, model. Such reformulations must often be considered in conjunction with the solution strategy to be employed. It will be assumed throughout that the branch and bound method described in Section 8.3 of Chapter 8 is to be used.

In some respects there is much greater flexibility possible in building IP models than in building LP models. The flexibility results in a greater divergence between good and bad models of a practical problem. The purpose of this section is to suggest ways in which good models may be constructed.

It is convenient to consider variables and constraints separately. There is often the possibility of using many or few variables and many or few constraints in a model. The considerations governing this will be considered.

The Number of Variables in an IP Model

We will confine our attention here to the number of integer variables in an IP model since this is often regarded as a good indicator of the computational difficulty.

Suppose we had a 0–1 IP model (either mixed integer or pure integer). If the model had n 0–1 variables this would indicate 2^n possible settings for the variables and hence 2^n potential nodes hanging at the bottom of the solution tree. In total there would be $2^{n+1} - 1$ nodes in such a tree. One might therefore expect the solution time to go up exponentially with the number of 0–1 variables. For quite modest values of n, 2^n is very large, e.g. 2^{100} is greater than one million raised to the power 5. The situation is not of course anywhere as bad as this, since many of the 2^n potential nodes will never be examined.

The branch and bound method rules out large sections of the potential tree from examination as being infeasible or worse than solutions already known. It is, however, worth pausing to consider the fact that one may sometimes solve 100 0–1 variable IP problems in a few hundred nodes. This represents only about $0 \cdot 00 \ldots 01$ per cent of the potential total where there are 28 zeros after the decimal point. In view of this very surprising efficiency that the branch and bound method exhibits over the potential amount of computation, the number of 0–1 variables is often a very poor indicator of the difficulty of an IP model. We will, however, suggest one circumstance in which the number of such variables might be usefully reduced, later in this section. Before doing that we will indicate ways in which the number of integer variables in a model might be increased to good effect.

It is convenient here to describe a well known device for expanding any general integer variable in a model to a number of 0–1 variables. Suppose γ is a general (non-negative) integer variable with a known upper bound of u (an upper bound is required for all integer variables in an IP model if the branch and bound method is to be used), i.e.

$$0 \leqslant \gamma \leqslant u.$$

γ may be replaced in this model by the expression

$$\delta_0 + 2\delta_1 + 4\delta_2 + 8\delta_3 + \cdots + 2^r\delta_r, \tag{1}$$

where the δ_i are 0–1 variables and 2^r is the smallest power of 2 greater than or equal to u.

It is easy to see that the expression (1) can take any possible integral value between 0 and u by different combinations of values for the δ_i variables. Clearly the number of 0–1 variables required in an expansion like this is roughly $\log_2 u$. In practice u will probably be fairly small and the number of 0–1 variables produced not too large. If, however, this device were employed on a lot of the variables in the model the result might be a great expansion in model size. Generally there will be little virtue in an expansion of this sort except to facilitate the use of some specialized algorithm applying only to 0–1 problems. This is beyond the scope of this book.

Although there is some virtue in keeping an LP model compact, any such advantages that this may imply for the corresponding IP model are usually drowned by other much more important considerations. Using the branch and bound method there is sometimes virtue in introducing extra 0–1 variables as useful variables in the branching process. Such 0–1 variables represent 'dichotomies' in the system being modelled. To make such dichotomies explicit can be valuable, as is demonstrated in the following example due to Jeffreys (1974).

Example 1

One new factory is to be built. The possible decisions are represented by 0–1

204

variables $\delta_{n,b}$, $\delta_{n,c}$, $\delta_{s,b}$, and $\delta_{s,c}$:

$$\delta_{n,b} = \begin{cases} 1 & \text{if the factory is in the north and uses} \\ & \text{a batch process,} \\ 0 & \text{otherwise;} \end{cases}$$

$$\delta_{n,c} = \begin{cases} 1 & \text{if the factory is in the north and uses} \\ & \text{a continuous process,} \\ 0 & \text{otherwise;} \end{cases}$$

$$\delta_{s,b} = \begin{cases} 1 & \text{if the factory is in the south and uses} \\ & \text{a batch process,} \\ 0 & \text{otherwise;} \end{cases}$$

$$\delta_{s,c} = \begin{cases} 1 & \text{if the factory is in the south and uses} \\ & \text{a continuous process,} \\ 0 & \text{otherwise.} \end{cases}$$

The condition that only one factory be built can be represented by the constraint

$$\delta_{n,b} + \delta_{n,c} + \delta_{s,b} + \delta_{s,c} = 1. \tag{2}$$

It is not possible, using constraint (2), to express the dichotomy 'either we site the factory in the north or we site it in the south' by a single 0–1 variable. Since this is clearly an important decision, it would be advantageous to have a 0–1 variable indicating the decision. By adding an extra 0–1 variable δ to represent this decision, together with the extra constraints

$$\delta_{n,b} + \delta_{n,c} - \delta = 0, \tag{3}$$

$$\delta_{s,b} + \delta_{s,c} + \delta = 1, \tag{4}$$

this is possible, δ is a valuable variable to have at our disposal since use can be made of it as a variable to branch on in the tree search. The dichotomy 'either' we use a batch process or we use a continuous process' could also be represented by another 0–1 decision variable in a similar way.

Another use of extra integer variables in a model is to specify the slack variable in a constraint, made up of only integer variables, as itself being integer. For example, if all the variables, coefficients, and right-hand side are integer in the constraint

$$\sum_j a_j x_j \leqslant b, \tag{5}$$

we can put in a slack variable u and specify this variable to be integer, giving

$$\sum_j a_j x_j + u = b. \tag{6}$$

Normally such a slack variable would be inserted by the mathematical programming package used but treated only as a continuous variable. There is advantage in treating u as an integer variable and giving it priority in the branching process. When u is the variable branched on, constraint (6) will have the effect of a cutting plane and restrict the feasible region of the corresponding LP problem. This idea is due to Mitra (1973).

To summarize there is often advantage in increasing rather than decreasing the number of integer variables in a model especially if these extra variables are made use of in the tree search strategy. Such ideas can be used to advantage in some of the IP problems given in Part 2.

In some circumstances, however, there is advantage to be gained in reducing the number of integer variables. A case of this is illustrated in the following example. Here the problem exhibits a symmetry which can be computationally undesirable

Example 2

As part of a larger IP model the following variables are introduced.

$$\delta_{ij} = \begin{cases} 1 & \text{if lorry } i \text{ is sent on trip } j \\ 0 & \text{otherwise} \end{cases}$$

where $i = \{1, 2, 3\}$, $j = \{1, 2\}$. The lorries are indistinguishable in terms of running costs, capacities, etc.

Clearly corresponding to each possible integer solution, e.g.

$$\delta_{11} = 1, \quad \delta_{22} = 1, \quad \delta_{32} = 1, \tag{7}$$

there will be symmetric integer solutions, e.g.

$$\delta_{12} = 1, \quad \delta_{21} = 1, \quad \delta_{32} = 1. \tag{8}$$

As the branch and bound tree search progresses each symmetric solution may be obtained at a separate node.

A better formulation involving less integer variables and avoiding the symmetry could be devised using the following integer variables:

$$n_i = \text{number of lorries sent on trip } j.$$

The solutions (7) and (8) above would now be indistinguishable as the solution

$$n_1 = 1, \quad n_2 = 2. \tag{9}$$

The Number of Constraints in an IP Model

It was pointed out in Chapter 3 that the difficulty of an LP model is very dependent on the number of constraints. Here we will show that in an IP model this effect is often completely drowned by other considerations. In fact an IP model is often made easier to solve by expanding the number of constraints.

In an LP model we are searching for vertex solutions on the boundary of the

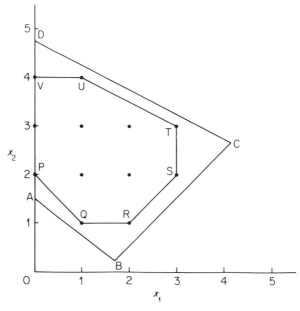

Figure 10.1

feasible region. For the corresponding IP model we are interested in integer points which may well lie in the interior of the feasible region. This is illustrated in Figure 10.1. ABCD is the feasible region of the LP problem but we must confine our attention to the lattice of integer points. For an IP model the corresponding LP model is known as the LP *relaxation*.

In this diagram we are supposing both x_1 and x_2 to be integer variables. For mixed integer problems we are interested in points in an analogous diagram to Figure 10.1, some of whose coordinates are integer, but where other coordinates are allowed to be continuous. Clearly this situation is difficult to picture in a few dimensions. Suppose, however, that there were a further continuous variable x_3 to be considered in Figure 10.1. This would give rise to a coordinate coming out at right angles to the page. Feasible solutions to the mixed integer problem would consist of lines parallel to the x_3 axis coming out of the page from the integer points in Figure 10.1. These lines would have, of course, to lie inside the three-dimensional feasible region of the corresponding LP problem.

Ideally we would like to reformulate the IP model so that the feasible region of the corresponding LP model became PQRSTUV. This is known as the *convex hull of feasible integer points* in ABCD. It is the smallest convex set containing all the feasible integer points. If it were possible to reformulate the IP problem in this way we could solve the problem as an LP problem since the integrality requirement would automatically be satisfied. Such a formulation, where the LP relaxation gives the convex hull of IP solutions, is known as *sharp*.

Each vertex (and hence optimal solution) of the new feasible region PQRSTUV is an integer point. Unfortunately in many practical problems the effort required to obtain the convex hull of integer points would be enormous and far outweigh the computation needed to solve the original formulation of the IP problem. There are, however, important classes of problems where:

(i) The straightforward formulation results in an IP model where the feasible region is already the convex hull of integer points.
(ii) The problem can fairly easily be reformulated to give a feasible region corresponding to the convex hull of integer points.
(iii) By reformulating it is possible to reduce the feasible region of the LP problem to nearer that of the convex hull of integer points.

We will consider each of these classes of problem in turn.

Case (i) concerns some problems which have already been considered in Section 5.3. Although superficially these problems might appear to give rise to PIP models, the optimal solution of the corresponding LP problem always results in integer values for the integer variables. It is not therefore necessary to treat the model as any other than an LP problem. Problems falling into this category include the *transportation problem*, the *minimum cost network flow problem*, and the *assignment problem*. It is sometimes possible to recognize when an IP model has a structure which guarantees that the corresponding LP model will have an integer optimal solution. Clearly it is very useful to be able to recognize this property since the high computational cost of integer programming need not be incurred. Consider the following LP model: maximize $\mathbf{c}'\mathbf{x}$, subject to $A\mathbf{x} = \mathbf{b}$ and $\mathbf{x} \geqslant 0$.

Here we assume that slack variables have been added to the constraints, if necessary, to make them all equalities. For the above model to yield an optimal solution with all variables integer for every objective coefficient vector $\mathbf{c}$ and integer right-hand side $\mathbf{b}$ the matrix A must have a property known as *total unimodularity*.

Definition

A matrix A is totally unimodular if every square sub-matrix of A has its determinant equal to 0 or ± 1.

The fact that this property guarantees that there will be an integer optimal solution to the LP model (for any $\mathbf{c}$ and integer $\mathbf{b}$) is proved in Garfinkel and Nemhauser (1972, p. 67). Unfortunately the above definition of total unimodularity is of little help in detecting the property. To evaluate the determinant of every square sub-matrix would be prohibitive. There is, however, a property (which we call P) which is easier to detect and which guarantees total unimodularity. It is, however, only a sufficient condition, not a necessary condition. Matrices without property P may still be totally unimodular.

Property P

(1) Each element of A is 0, 1 or -1.
(2) No more than two non-zero elements appear in each column.
(3) The rows can be partitioned into two subsets P_1 and P_2 such that: (a) if a column contains two non-zero elements of the same sign, one element is in each of the subsets: (b) if a column contains two non-zero elements of opposite sign, both elements are in the same subset.

A particular case of the property P is when subset P_1 is empty and P_2 consists of all the rows of A. Then for the property to hold we must have all columns consisting of either one non-zero element ± 1 or two non-zero elements $+1$ and -1.

As an example of this property holding we can consider the small transportation problem of Section 5.3:

$$
\begin{aligned}
-x_{11} - x_{13} - x_{14} - x_{15} &= -135, \\
-x_{21} - x_{22} - x_{25} &= -56, \\
-x_{31} - x_{32} - x_{33} - x_{34} - x_{35} &= -93, \\
x_{11} \quad\quad + x_{21} \quad\quad + x_{31} &= 62, \\
+ x_{22} \quad\quad + x_{32} &= 83, \\
x_{13} \quad\quad + x_{33} &= 39, \\
x_{14} \quad\quad + x_{34} &= 91, \\
x_{15} \quad\quad + x_{25} \quad\quad + x_{35} &= 9.
\end{aligned}
\tag{10}
$$

Each column clearly contains a $+1$ and a -1, showing the property to hold and hence guaranteeing total unimodularity. There is often virtue in trying to reformulate a model in order to try to capture this easily detected property. The automation of such reformulation (where possible) was described in Section 5.4. In case (ii) below the dual situation is illustrated.

Although the property above refers to a partitioning of the rows of a matrix A into two subsets, the partitioning could equally well apply to the columns. If A is totally unimodular, its transpose A' must also be totally unimodular. Again a particular instance of this property guaranteeing total unimodularity is when each row of the matrix A of an LP model contains a $+1$ and a -1.

Finally it should be pointed out that total unimodularity is a strong property that guarantees integer optimal solutions to an LP problem for all c and integer b. Many IP models for which the matrix A is not totally unimodular frequently (although not always) produce integer solutions to the optimal solution of the corresponding LP problem. In particular this often happens with the set packing, partitioning, and covering problems discussed in Section 9.5. There are good reasons why this is likely to happen for these types of problem. Such considerations are, however, fairly technical and beyond the scope of this book. They are discussed in Chapter 8 of Garfinkel and Nemhauser (1972). Properties of A which guarantee integer LP solutions for a specific right-hand side **b** are discussed by Padberg (1974) for the case of the set partitioning problem.

The discussion of total unimodularity above applies only to PIP models. Clearly there are corresponding considerations for MIP models, where integer values for the integer variables in the optimal LP solution are guaranteed. Such considerations are, however, very difficult and there is little theoretical work as yet which is of value to practical model builders.

Case (ii) above concerns problems where, with a little thought, a reformulation can result in a model with the total unimodularity property. Consider a generalization of the constraint (18) of Section 9.2:

$$\delta_1 + \delta_2 + \dots \delta_n - n\delta \leqslant 0, \tag{11}$$

where δ_i and δ are 0–1 variables.

This kind of constraint arises fairly frequently in IP models and represents the logical condition

$$\delta_1 = 1 \lor \delta_2 = 1 \lor \dots \lor \delta_n = 1 \rightarrow \delta = 1. \tag{12}$$

Sometimes this condition is more easily thought of as the logical equivalent condition

$$\delta = 0 \rightarrow \delta_1 = 0 . \delta_2 = 0 \dots \delta_n = 0. \tag{13}$$

It was shown in Section 9.2 that by a different argument constraint (18) of that section can be reformulated using two constraints. A similar reformulation can be applied here, giving the n constraints

$$
\begin{aligned}
\delta_1 - \delta &\leqslant 0, \\
\delta_2 - \delta &\leqslant 0, \\
&\vdots \\
\delta_n - \delta &\leqslant 0,
\end{aligned}
\tag{14}
$$

Should all the constraints in the model be similar to the constraints of (14) then the dual problem has the property P described above which guarantees total unimodularity. There is, therefore, great virtue in such a reformulation since the high computational costs associated with an IP problem over an LP problem is avoided. An example of a reformulation of a problem in this way is described by Rhys (1970). He also demonstrates another advantage of the reformulation as yielding a more meaningful economic interpretation of the shadow prices. This topic is considered in Section 10.3. A practical example of a formulation such as that described above is given in Part 3 where the formulation of the OPENCAST MINING problem is discussed.

Constraint (11) above shows the possibility of sometimes reformulating a PIP problem that is not totally unimodular in order to make it totally unimodular. There is also virtue in reformulating an already totally unimodular problem which we do not know to be totally unimodular if by so doing we convert it into a form where property P applies. Examples of this are given by Veinott and Wagner (1962) and Daniel (1973). As with case (i) the above discussion of case (ii) only applies to PIP problems. Again it must be possible (although difficult) to generalize these ideas to MIP problems.

Case (iii) concerns problems where there is either no obvious totally unimodular reformulation or where the problem gives a MIP model. In cases (i) and (ii) we were reducing the feasible region to the convex hull of feasible integer points, even though this was not obvious from the algebraic treatment given. It is sometimes possible to go part way towards this aim. Suppose for example (as might frequently happen in a MIP model) that only some of the constraints were of the form (11). By expanding these constraints into the series of constraints (14) we would reduce the size of the LP feasible region. Even though the existence of other constraints in the problem might result in some integer variables taking fractional values in the LP optimal solution this solution should be 'nearer' the integer optimal solution than would be the case with the original model. The term 'nearer' is purposely vague. A reformulation such as this might result in the objective value at node 1 of the solution tree (for example Figure 8.1) being closer to the objective value of the optimal integer solution when found. On the other hand, it might result in there being less fractional solution values in the LP optimum. Whatever the result of the reformulation one would normally expect the solution time for the reformulated model to be less than for the original model. Constraints involving just two coefficients $+1$ and -1 also arise in models involving sequentially dependent decisions as described in Section 9.4. Such constraints are always to be desired even if their derivation results in an expansion of the constraints of a model. An example of this is the suggested formulation in Part 3 for the MINING problem.

It is worth indicating in another way why a series of constraints such as (14) is preferable to the single constraint (11). Although (11) and (14) are exactly equivalent in an IP sense they are certainly not equivalent in an LP sense. In fact (11) is the sum of all the constraints in (14). By adding together constraints in an LP problem one generally weakens their effect. This is what happens here. (11) admits fractional solutions which (14) would not admit. For example the solution

$$\delta_1 = \tfrac{1}{2}, \quad \delta_2 = \delta_3 = \tfrac{1}{4}, \quad \delta = 1/n, \quad \text{all other } \delta_i = 0 \tag{15}$$

satisfies (11) but breaks (14) (for $n \geqslant 3$).

Hence (14) is more effective at ruling out unwanted fractional solutions.

The ideas discussed above are relevant to the FOOD MANUFACTURE 2 problem which gives rise to a MIP model and to the DECENTRALIZATION and LOGICAL DESIGN problems which give rise to PIP models.

Some of the material so far presented in this section was first published by Williams (1974). A discussion of some very similar ideas applied to a more complicated version of the DECENTRALIZATION problem is given in Beale and Tomlin (1972).

It is also relevant here to discuss the value of the coefficient 'M' when linking indicator variables to continuous variables by constraints such as (1), (12),

(19), (21) of Section 9.1. These types of constraints usually (but not always) arise in MIP models.

We will consider the simplest way in which such a constraint arises when we are using a 0–1 variable δ to indicate the condition below on the continuous variable x:

$$x > 0 \rightarrow \delta = 1. \tag{16}$$

This condition is represented by the constraint

$$x - M\delta \leqslant 0. \tag{17}$$

So long as M is a true upper bound for x condition (16) is imposed, however large we make M. There is virtue, however, in making M as small as possible without imposing a spurious restriction on x. This is because by making M smaller we reduce the size of the feasible region of the LP problem corresponding to the MIP problem. Suppose, for example, we took M as 1000 when it was known that x would never exceed 100. The following fractional solution would satisfy (17):

$$x = 70, \qquad \delta = \tfrac{1}{2}, \tag{18}$$

but would violate (17) if M were taken as 100. There are other good reasons for making M as realistic as possible. For example, if M were again taken as 1000 the following fractional solution would satisfy (17):

$$x = 5, \qquad \delta = 0 \cdot 005. \tag{19}$$

A small value of δ such as this might well fall below the tolerance which indicates whether a variable were integer or not. If it did δ would be taken as 0 giving the spurious integer solution

$$x = 5, \qquad \delta = 0. \tag{20}$$

If, however, M was made smaller this would be less likely to happen. Finally the inadvisability of having coefficients of widely differing magnitudes, as mentioned in Section 3.4, makes a small value of M desirable.

It is also sometimes possible to split up a constraint using a coefficient M in an analogous fashion to the way in which (11) was split up into (14). This is demonstrated by the following example.

Example 3

$$\delta = \begin{cases} 1 & \text{if the depot is built,} \\ 0 & \text{otherwise.} \end{cases}$$

If the depot is built it can supply customer i with a quantity up to M_i, $i = 1$, $2, \ldots, n$. If the depot is not built, none of these customers can be supplied with anything.

$$x_i = \text{quantity supplied to customer } i.$$

These conditions can be imposed by the following constraint:

$$x_1 + x_2 + \cdots + x_n - M\delta \leqslant 0, \tag{21}$$

where $M = M_1 + M_2 + \cdots + M_n$.

On the other hand, the following constraints are superior as the corresponding LP problem is more constrained:

$$\begin{aligned} x_1 - M_1\delta &\leqslant 0, \\ x_2 - M_2\delta &\leqslant 0, \\ &\vdots \\ x_n - M_n\delta &\leqslant 0. \end{aligned} \tag{22}$$

To summarize this section the main objectives of an IP formulation should be as follows:

(1) To use integer variables which can be put to a good purpose in the branching process of the branch and bound method. If necessary, introduce extra 0–1 variables to create meaningful dichotomies.
(2) To make the LP problem corresponding to the IP problem as constrained as possible.

A final objective not yet mentioned in this section is

(3) To use special ordered sets as described in Section 9.3 if it is possible and the computer package used is capable of dealing with them.

Further ways of reformulating IP models in order to ease their solution are described in the next section.

Before a large IP model is built it is often a very good idea to build a small version of the model first. Experimentation with different solution strategies and possibly with reformulation can give valuable experience before embarking on the much larger model.

Sometimes, by examining the structure of a model, it is possible to make observations that lead one to a tightening of the constraints. A dramatic example of this (even when the application was unknown) is described by Daniel (1978), resulting in the solution of a reformulated model in 171 nodes where previously the tree search had been abandoned after 4757 nodes.

The automatic reformulation of IP models in order to tighten the LP relaxation is described by Crowder, Johnson, and Padberg (1983) and Van Roy and Wolsey (1984).

10.2 Simplifying an Integer Programming Model

In the last section it was shown that it is often possible to reformulate an IP model in order to create another model which is easier to solve. This is sometimes made possible by considering the practical situation being modelled. In this section we will be concerned with rather less obvious transformation of an IP model. Again the aim will be to make the model easier to solve.

Tightening Bounds

In Section 3.4, part of the procedure of Brearley, Mitra, and Williams (1975) for simplifying LP models was outlined. The full application of that procedure involves removing redundant simple bounds in an LP model. It is not, however, generally worthwhile removing redundant bounds on an integer variable. Instead it is better to tighten the bounds if possible. The argument for doing this is similar to some of the reformulation arguments used in the last section. By tightening bounds the corresponding LP problem may be made more constrained resulting in the optimal solution to the LP problem being closer to the optimal IP solution. In order to illustrate the procedure a small example from Balas (1965) will be used. This example was also used in the description of the procedure given by Brearley, Mitra, and Williams.

Example 1

Minimize $\quad 5\delta_1 + 7\delta_2 + 10\delta_3 + 3\delta_4 + \delta_5$

subject to $\quad \delta_1 - 3\delta_2 + 5\delta_3 + \delta_4 - \delta_5 \geqslant 2,$ $\qquad$ (R1)

$\qquad\qquad -2\delta_1 + 6\delta_2 - 3\delta_3 - 2\delta_4 + 2\delta_5 \geqslant 0,$ $\qquad$ (R2)

$\qquad\qquad - \delta_2 + 2\delta_3 - 2\delta_4 - \delta_5 \geqslant 1.$ $\qquad$ (R3)

The δ_i are all 0–1 variables.

(1) By constraint (R3)

$$2\delta_3 \geqslant 1 + \delta_2 + \delta_4 + \delta_5 \geqslant 1.$$

Hence

$$\delta_3 \geqslant \tfrac{1}{2}.$$

Since δ_3 is an integer variable this implied lower bound may be tightened. In this case (since δ_3 is 0–1) δ_3 may be set to 1 and removed from the problem.

(2) By constraint (R2)

$$6\delta_2 \geqslant 3 + 2\delta_1 + 2\delta_4 - 2\delta_5 \geqslant 1.$$

Hence

$$\delta_2 \geqslant \tfrac{1}{6}.$$

Similarly the lower bound of δ_2 may be tightened to 1 so fixing δ_2 at 1.

(3) By constraint (R3)

$$\delta_4 \leqslant -\delta_5 \leqslant 0.$$

Hence

$$\delta_4 \leqslant 0.$$

Therefore δ_4 can be fixed at 0.

(4) By constraint (R3), $\delta_5 \leqslant 0$. Therefore δ_5 can be fixed at 0.

(5) All the constraints now turn out to be redundant and may be removed. The only remaining variable is δ_1 which must obviously be set to 0.

This example is obviously an extreme case of the effect of tightening bounds in an IP model since this procedure alone completely solves the problem.

Simplifying a Single Integer Constraint to Another Single Integer Constraint

Consider the integer constraint

$$4\gamma_1 + 6\gamma_2 \leqslant 9, \tag{1}$$

where γ_1 and γ_2 are general integer variables. By looking at this constraint geometrically in Figure 10.2 it is easy to see that it may also be written as

$$\gamma_1 + 2\gamma_2 \leqslant 2, \tag{2}$$

In Figure 10.2 the original constraint (1) indicates the feasible points must lie to the left of AB. By shifting the line AB to CD no integer points are excluded from, and no new integer points are included in, the feasible region. CD gives rise to the new constraint (2).

Clearly there are advantages in using (2) rather than (1) since the feasible region of the corresponding LP problem has been reduced. While constraints such as (1) involving general integer variables do not arise very frequently such constraints can occur involving only 0–1 variables. We will therefore confine

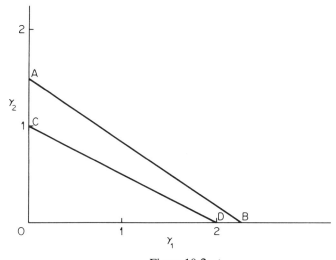

Figure 10.2

our attention to the 0–1 case. Should more general integer variables be involved it is, of course, always possible to expand them into 0–1 variables as described in Section 10.1. Our problem will now be, given a constraint such as

$$a_1\delta_1 + a_2\delta_2 + \cdots + a_n\delta_n \leqslant a_0, \tag{3}$$

where the δ_i are 0–1 variables, to re-express it as an equivalent constraint

$$b_1\delta_1 + b_2\delta_2 + \cdots + b_n\delta_n \leqslant b_0, \tag{4}$$

where (4) is more constrained than (3) in the corresponding LP problem. There is no loss of generality in assuming all the coefficients of (3) and (4) to be non-negative since should a negative coefficient a_i occur in (3) the corresponding variable δ_i may be complemented by the substitution

$$\delta_i = 1 - \delta_i',$$

making the new coefficient of δ_i' positive.

Clearly '$\geqslant$' constraints can be converted to '$\leqslant$'. Equality constraints are most conveniently dealt with by converting them into a '$\leqslant$' together with a '$\geqslant$' constraint. The result will be two simplified constraints in place of the original single ' $=$ ' constraint.

The simplification of a pure 0–1 constraint such as (3) in order to produce (4) can itself be formulated and solved as an LP problem. Rather than present the technical details of the procedure here a specific problem, OPTIMIZING A CONSTRAINT is given in Part 2. The formulation and discussion in Part 3 should make the general procedure clear.

If the original constraint to be simplified involved general integer, rather than 0–1 integer, variables and it is desired to replace it by a constraint in the same variables, then it will be necessary to restrict the new coefficients of the 0–1 form. For example, suppose we had a general integer variable γ ($\leqslant 7$). If its original coefficient were a in the 0–1 form of the constraint, we would have the term

$$a\gamma_1 + 2a\gamma_2 + 4a\gamma_3, \tag{5}$$

with $\gamma_1 + 2\gamma_2 + 4\gamma_3$ representing variable γ, where γ_1, γ_2 and γ_3 are 0–1 variables. The resultant simplification would produce an equivalent term

$$b_1\gamma_1 + b_2\gamma_2 + b_3\gamma_3. \tag{6}$$

In order for this term to be replaceable by a term $b\gamma$ we would have to ensure that

$$b_3 = 2b_2, \qquad b_2 = 2b_1, \tag{7}$$

giving $b = b_1$.

Using the LP formulation described for the 0–1 example in Part 2 it would be necessary to impose conditions such as (7) as *extra* LP constraints for the general integer case.

The effort of trying to simplify single integer constraints in this way will often not be worthwhile. In many models these constraints represent logical conditions and are already in their simplest form as single constraints. Applications where such simplification could possibly prove worthwhile are project selection and capital budgeting problems. It also proves worthwhile to simplify single constraints in this way in the MARKET SHARING problem presented in Part 2.

The simplification of a single 0–1 constraint into another single 0–1 constraint considered here has been described by Bradley, Hammer, and Wolsey (1974).

Simplifying a Single Integer Constraint to a Collection of Integer Constraints

We will again confine our attention to pure 0–1 constraints given that general integer variables can be expanded, if necessary, into 0–1 variables.

It may often be advantageous to express a single 0–1 constraint as a collection of 0–1 constraints. We have already seen this in Section 10.1, where constraint (11) was re-expressed as the constraints (14). Here we present a general procedure for expanding any pure 0–1 constraint into a collection of constraints. Ideally we would like to be able to re-express the constraint by a collection of constraints defining the convex hull of feasible 0–1 solutions. In order to make this clear we present an example.

Example 2

$$3\delta_1 + 3\delta_2 - 2\delta_3 + 2\delta_4 + 2\delta_5 \leqslant 4. \tag{5}$$

δ_i are 0–1 variables.

The convex hull of 0–1 solutions which are feasible according to (5) is given by the constraints

$$\delta_1 + \delta_2 - \delta_3 + \delta_4 \leqslant 1, \tag{6}$$

$$\delta_1 + \delta_2 - \delta_3 + \delta_5 \leqslant 1, \tag{7}$$

$$\delta_1 + \delta_2 + \delta_4 + \delta_5 \leqslant 2, \tag{8}$$

$$2\delta_1 + \delta_2 - \delta_3 + \delta_4 + \delta_5 \leqslant 2, \tag{9}$$

$$\delta_1 + 2\delta_2 - \delta_3 + \delta_4 + \delta_5 \leqslant 2, \tag{10}$$

together with the trivial constraints $\delta_i \geqslant 0$ and $\delta_i \leqslant 1$.

Unfortunately no practical procedure has yet been devised for obtaining constraints defining the convex hull of integer solutions corresponding to a single 0–1 constraint. The faces which form the boundary of the feasible region defined by an LP problem are known as 'facets'. For two-variable problems these facets are one-dimensional lines and can easily be visualized in a diagram such as Figure 10.2. With three-variable problems the facets are two-dimensional planes. For n-variable problems these facets are $(n-1)$-

dimensional hyperplanes. Hammer, Johnson, and Peled (1975) give a table of the facets of the convex hulls for all 0–1 constraints involving up to five variables. In order to use this table it is first necessary to simplify the constraint to another single constraint using the procedure mentioned above. It is also possible to obtain the convex hull for particular types of constraint involving more than five variables. The expansion of constraint (11) into constraints (14) in Section 10.1 is obviously an instance of this. Although a general procedure for producing the convex hull constraints for a single 0–1 constraint does not yet exist, Balas (1975) gives a procedure for producing some of the facets of the convex hull. Hammer, Johnson, and Peled (1975) and Wolsey (1975) also give similar procedures. They are able to obtain those facets represented by constraints containing only coefficients 0 and ±1. For example the procedure would obtain the constraints (6), (7), and (8) of Example 2 above.

We now describe this procedure of Balas. Consider the following pure 0–1 constraint:

$$a_1\delta_1 + a_2\delta_2 + a_3\delta_3 + \cdots + a_n\delta_n \leqslant a_0. \tag{11}$$

As before there is no loss of generality in considering a '$\leqslant$' constraint with all coefficients non-negative.

Definition

A subset $\{i_1, i_2, \ldots, i_r\}$ of the indices $1, 2, \ldots, n$ of the coefficients in (11) will be called a *cover* if $a_{i_1} + a_{i_2} + \cdots a_{i_r} > a_0$.

Clearly it is not possible for all the δ_i, corresponding to indices i within a cover, to be 1 simultaneously. This condition may be expressed by the constraint

$$\delta_{i_1} + \delta_{i_2} + \cdots + \delta_{i_r} \leqslant r - 1. \tag{12}$$

Definition

A cover $\{i_1, i_2, \ldots, i_r\}$ is said to be a *minimal cover* if no proper subset of $\{i_1, i_2, \ldots, i_r\}$ is also a cover.

Definition

A minimal cover $\{i_1, i_2, \ldots, i_r\}$ can be extended in the following way:

(i) Choose the largest coefficient a_{i_j} where i_j is a member of the minimal cover.

(ii) Take the set of indices $\{i_{r+1}, i_{r+2}, \ldots, i_{r+s}\}$ not in the minimal cover corresponding to coefficients $a_{i_{r+k}}$ such that $a_{i_{r+k}} \geqslant a_{i_j}$.

(iii) Add these set of indices to the minimal cover giving $\{i_1, i_2, \ldots, i_{r+s}\}$. This new cover is known as an *extended cover*.

If $\{i_1, i_2, \ldots, i_r\}$ is a minimal cover it can be augmented to give an extended cover $i_1, i_2, \ldots, i_{r+s}$. The constraint (12) corresponding to the minimal cover can correspondingly be extended to

$$\delta_{i_1} + \delta_{i_2} + \cdots + \delta_{i_{r+s}} \leqslant r - 1. \tag{13}$$

Definition

If a minimal cover gives rise to an extended cover which is not a proper subset of any other extended cover arising from a minimal cover with the same number of indices, the original minimal cover is known as a *strong cover*.

Balas shows that if an extended cover arises from a strong cover then the constraints such as (13) encompass all the facets of the convex hull of feasible 0–1 points of (11) which have coefficients 0 or 1.

It is obviously fairly easy to devise a systematic and computationally quick method of generating all strong covers corresponding to a 0–1 constraint and therefore obtaining facet constraints such as (13). In this way any facet of the convex hull of feasible 0–1 points of a constraint can be defined when the facet is represented by a constraint involving only coefficients 0 and ± 1. Two examples are presented in order to make the process clear.

Example 3

This is the same as Example 2, only we here show how the constraints (6), (7), and (8) involving only coefficients 0 and ± 1 are obtained. It is more convenient to write constraint (5) with positive coefficients as

$$3\delta_1 + 3\delta_2 + 2\delta_3' + 2\delta_4 + 2\delta_5 \leqslant 6, \tag{14}$$

where $\delta_3' = 1 - \delta_3$.

The minimal covers of constraint (14) are

$$\{1, \quad 2, \quad 3\}, \tag{15}$$
$$\{1, \quad 2, \quad 4\}, \tag{16}$$
$$\{1, \quad 2, \quad 5\}, \tag{17}$$
$$\{1, \quad 3, \quad 4\}, \tag{18}$$
$$\{1, \quad 3, \quad 5\}, \tag{19}$$
$$\{1, \quad 4, \quad 5\}, \tag{20}$$
$$\{2, \quad 3, \quad 4\}, \tag{21}$$
$$\{2, \quad 3, \quad 5\}, \tag{22}$$
$$\{2, \quad 4, \quad 5\}, \tag{23}$$

These minimal covers can be augmented to produce the extended covers

$$\{1, \quad 2, \quad 3\} \quad \text{from (15),} \tag{24}$$

$$\{1, \quad 2, \quad 4\} \quad \text{from (16),} \tag{25}$$

$$\{1, \quad 2, \quad 5\} \quad \text{from (17),} \tag{26}$$

$$\{1, \quad 2, \quad 3, \quad 4\} \quad \text{from (18) and (21),} \tag{27}$$

$$\{1, \quad 2, \quad 3, \quad 5\} \quad \text{from (19) and (22),} \tag{28}$$

$$\{1, \quad 2, \quad 4, \quad 5\} \quad \text{from (20) and (23),} \tag{29}$$

Since (24), (25), and (26) are proper subsets of (27), (29), and (28) respectively, the first three minimal covers (15), (16), and (17) are not strong covers. The remaining minimal covers (18) to (23) are, however, strong covers and their extensions (27), (28), and (29) give rise to the following facet constraints:

$$\delta_1 + \delta_2 + \delta_3' + \delta_4 \qquad \leqslant 2, \tag{30}$$

$$\delta_1 + \delta_2 + \delta_3' \qquad + \delta_5 \leqslant 2, \tag{31}$$

$$\delta_1 + \delta_2 \qquad + \delta_4 + \delta_5 \leqslant 2. \tag{32}$$

Replacing δ_3' by $1 - \delta_3$ gives the three facet constraints (6), (7), and (8) in Example 2.

Example 4

$$\delta_{n+1} = \begin{cases} 1 & \text{if a depot is built,} \\ 0 & \text{otherwise,} \end{cases}$$

$$\delta_i = \begin{cases} 1 & \text{if customer } i \text{ is supplied from the depot,} \\ 0 & \text{otherwise,} \end{cases}$$

where $i = 1, 2, ..., n$.

At most $r(r < n)$ customers may be supplied from the depot if it is built. If the depot is not built, clearly nobody can be supplied from it.

The conditions above may be expressed by the constraint

$$\delta_1 + \delta_2 + \cdots + \delta_n - r\delta_{n+1} \leqslant 0. \tag{33}$$

This is obviously a generalization of the constraint (16) of Section 10.1.

It is convenient to express (33) with positive coefficients as

$$\delta_1 + \delta_2 + \cdots + \delta_n + r\delta_{n+1}' \leqslant r, \tag{34}$$

where

$$\delta_{n+1}' = 1 - \delta_{n+1}. \tag{35}$$

The minimal covers of (34) are

$$\{i, \ n+1\}, \qquad i = 1, 2, ..., n, \tag{36}$$

and all subsets of $\{1, 2, ...n\}$ such as

$$\{i_1, i_2, ..., i_{r+1}\} \tag{37}$$

containing $r + 1$ indices.

Covers (36) cannot be further extended.

All the covers (37) do extend to the same extended cover:

$$\{1, 2, ..., n, n + 1\}. \tag{38}$$

The minimal covers (36) and (37) in general are of a different size (if $r \neq 1$). Therefore (36) and (38) are all extensions of strong covers and give rise (after substituting $1 - \delta_{n+1}$ for δ'_{n+1}) to the constraints

$$\delta_i - \delta_{n+1} \leqslant 0, \qquad i = 1, 2, ..., n, \tag{39}$$

and

$$\delta_1 + \delta_2 + \cdots + \delta_n - \delta_{n+1} \leqslant r - 1. \tag{40}$$

These constraints do not necessarily all represent facets, but they are particularly restrictive constraints on the corresponding LP problem and include all the facets with coefficients 0 or 1. It would therefore be advantageous to append constraints (39) and (40) to the original constraint (33) in a model.

This way of obtaining particularly 'strong' extra constraints to add to an IP model could prove of value in the MARKET SHARING problem of Part 2.

Simplifying Collections of Constraints

So far we have described ways of simplifying individual constraints involving 0–1 variables. What we would ideally like to do would be to simplify the collection of all the constraints into a collection of constraints defining the convex hull of feasible integer points. It should be pointed out that simplifying constraints individually will not generally suffice although it may be computationally helpful towards the ultimate aim of solving the IP problem more easily. This is demonstrated by an example.

Example 5

Maximize $\quad\quad \delta_1 + 2\delta_2 + \delta_3$

subject to $\quad\quad 2\delta_1 + 3\delta_2 + 2\delta_3 \leqslant 3, \tag{41}$

$\quad\quad\quad\quad\quad \delta_1 + \delta_2 - 2\delta_3 \leqslant 0. \tag{42}$

$\delta_1, \delta_2, \delta_3$ are 0–1 variables.

The optimal solution to the associated LP problem is

$$\delta_1 = 0, \quad \delta_2 = \tfrac{3}{4}, \quad \delta_3 = \tfrac{3}{8}, \quad \text{giving an objective of } \tfrac{15}{8}.$$

If constraint (41) is replaced by the constraints representing its facets we obtain constraint (43) in the model below. Constraints (44) and (45) come from the two facets of (42). The simplified model is then:

Maximize $\quad \delta_1 + 2\delta_2 + \delta_3$

subject to $\quad \delta_1 + \ \delta_2 + \delta_3 \leqslant 1,$ $\qquad\qquad\qquad\qquad\qquad$ (43)

$\qquad\qquad\quad \delta_1 \qquad - \delta_3 \leqslant 0,$ $\qquad\qquad\qquad\qquad\qquad$ (44)

$\qquad\qquad\qquad\quad \delta_2 - \delta_3 \leqslant 0.$ $\qquad\qquad\qquad\qquad\qquad$ (45)

The optimal solution to the associated LP problem for this reformulated model is

$$\delta_1 = 0, \quad \delta_2 = \tfrac{1}{2}, \quad \delta_3 = \tfrac{1}{2}, \quad \text{giving an objective of } \tfrac{3}{2}.$$

Clearly simplifying constraints individually has not constrained the whole model sufficiently to guarantee an integer solution to the LP model although the objective value is closer to the integer optimum:

$$\delta_1 = 0, \quad \delta_2 = 0, \quad \delta_3 = 1, \quad \text{giving an objective of } 1.$$

Unfortunately no practical procedure is known for producing the convex hull of the feasible 0–1 points corresponding to a general collection of pure 0–1 constraints. In fact if such a computationally efficient procedure were known we could reduce all PIP problems to LP problems and dispense with PIP. Procedures of this sort do exist for special restricted classes of PIP problem. The best known is for the matching problem which was mentioned in Section 9.5. The main reference to the problem is Edmonds (1965).

Partial results exist enabling one to obtain some of the facets of the convex hull for some types of PIP problem. Hammer, Johnson, and Peled (1975) have a procedure for generating the facet constraints involving only coefficients 0 and 1 for a class of PIP problems they call 'regular'. Within this class of problems are the set covering problem and the knapsack problem.

Clearly by being able to cope with the knapsack problem they can also obtain the facets obtained by Balas for a single constraint. Apart from what has already been described none of these partial results seems as yet to give a valuable formulation tool for practical problems and they will not therefore be described further.

It should also be pointed out that procedures have been devised for doing the reverse of what we have described here. A collection of pure integer equality constraints can be progressively combined with one another to obtain a single equality constraint giving a knapsack problem. Bradley (1971) describes such a procedure. Unfortunately the resulting coefficients are often enormous. There is little interest in such a procedure if the corresponding LP problem is to be used as a starting point for solving the IP problem. The general effect of aggregating constraints in this way will be to weaken rather than restrict the corresponding LP problem. Chvatal and Hammer (1975) also describe a procedure for combining pure 0–1 inequality constraints.

Most of the discussion in this section has concerned adding further restrictions to an IP model in order to restrict the corresponding LP model. Such extra restrictions can be viewed in the context of cutting planes algorithms for IP. We are adding cuts to a model in order to eliminate some possible fractional solutions. Most algorithms which make use of cutting planes generate the extra constraints in the course of optimization. Our interest here, in a book on model building, is only in adding cuts to the initial model.

Discontinuous Variables

It is sometimes necessary to restrict a continuous variable to segments of continuous values, e.g.

$$x = 0 \quad or \quad a \leqslant x \leqslant b \quad or \quad x = c, \tag{46}$$

where $0 < a < b < c$.

A straightforward approach to follow is that described for disjunctive constraints in Section 9.4, where 0–1 variables are used to indicate each of the three (or more) possibilities. A constraint of type (3) in that section forces x to satisfy the condition.

There is an alternative formulation which has been suggested by Brearley (1975), following a more conventional formulation of a blending problem with logical restrictions by Thomas, Jennings, and Abbott (1978). This is

$$x = ay_1 + by_2 + c\delta_2, \tag{47}$$

$$\delta_1 + y_1 + y_2 + \delta_2 = 1, \tag{48}$$

where δ_1 and δ_2 are 0–1 integer variables and y_1 and y_2 are (non-negative) continuous variables.

Condition (46) can clearly be generalized or specialized. A common special case is that of a *semicontinuous* variable, i.e.

$$x = 0 \quad or \quad x \geqslant a \quad (a > 0). \tag{49}$$

In order to model this an upper bound (M) must be specified for x, giving the formulation

$$x = ay_1 + My_2, \tag{50}$$

$$\delta + y_1 + y_2 = 1, \tag{51}$$

where δ is a 0–1 variable and y_1 and y_2 are (non-negative) continuous variables.

An Alternative Formulation for Disjunctive Constraints

An alternative formulation for a *disjunction* of constraints has been given by

Jeroslow and Lowe (1984). In addition they construct a 'Theory of Mixed Integer Programming Representability' which begins to put the whole subject on systematic foundations. The use of Jeroslow's 'disjunctive formulations' has a considerable theoretical advantage as well as manifesting a practical advantage in large models. Computational experience is reported in Jeroslow and Lowe (1985).

A comprehensive discussion of the subject is given in the lecture notes of Jeroslow (1989).

Suppose we have a disjunction of constraints such as (1) in Section 9.4 where each R_k represents a set of constraints:

$$\sum_j a_{ijk} x_j \leqslant b_{ik}, \quad i = 1, 2, \ldots, m_k \tag{52}$$

We will suppose that each set of constraints (52) in this disjunction has a *closed* feasible region. If necessary this may be achieved by using known bounds on the quantities in the constraints as is also required in the conventional formulation. In fact even if the feasible region is not closed it is not always necessary to use such bounds in this new mode of formulation. The exact condition is given in Jeroslow and Lowe (1984).

Each variable x_j is split into separate variables x_{jk} with constraints:

$$x_j = x_{j1} + x_{j2} + \cdots + x_{jN} \tag{53}$$

The new variables replace the original variables in the set of constraints R_k to which they correspond giving constraints:

$$\sum_j a_{ijk} x_{jk} - b_{ik}\delta_k \leqslant 0, \quad i = 1, 2, \ldots, m_k \tag{54}$$

$$\sum_k \delta_k = 1 \tag{55}$$

where δ_k are 0–1 integer variables.

Constraint (55) forces exactly one δ_k to be 1 and the others to be zero. If δ_k is 0 then constraints (54) (having a closed feasible region) force the corresponding x_{jk} all to be zero. Hence for each j only one component x_{jk} can be non-zero making it, by constraint (53), equal to x_j and so guaranteeing the constraints corresponding to R_k.

It can be shown that if each set of constraints (52) is a *sharp* formulation of R_k then this resultant formulation of the disjunction is also sharp, i.e. the linear programming relaxation gives the convex hull of feasible integer solutions. If, for example, the variables in (52) are all continuous variables then the property holds.

In section 9.2 it was shown that logical conditions often can be specified in more than one way. A well-known result in Boolean Algebra is that any proposition can be expressed in a standard form known as *Disjunctive Normal*

Form which uses only the *and* (.), *or* ($\vee$) and *not* ($\sim$) connectives e.g.

$$(R_{11} . R_{12} ... R_{1m_1}) \vee (R_{21} . R_{22} ... R_{2m_2}) \vee ... \vee (R_{N1} . R_{N2} ... R_{Nm_N}) \quad (56)$$

where there is a disjunction of *clauses* each of which is made up of a *conjunction* of statements R_{ij} (some of which may be negated statements). Jeroslow suggests that it is generally better to express a model using this disjunctive normal form and then use his disjunctive formulation. It is theoretically possible to arrive at a sharp formulation for any IP this way taking account of the fact that any (bounded) integer variable represents a disjunction of possibilities e.g.

$$x = 0 \vee x = 1 \vee x = 2 \vee ... \vee x = m. \quad (57)$$

In practise the number of variables created by such a formulation can be prohibitively large since the disjunctive formulation splits variables into components in the manner described above. A compromise must generally be adopted which will not be sharp but is often tighter than a conventional formulation. In practice many simplifications of the resultant formulation are often possible (using for example a reduction procedure).

Two other observations of Jeroslow are worth making here. He points out that it is desirable, from the sharpness point of view, to apply the *and* connective before specifying an IP formulation. This is in contrast to creating IP formulations of components of a problem and then applying the *and* connective (i.e. putting all the resulting constraints together). This is because (in set notation)

$$\text{Con}(S \cap T) \subseteq \text{Con}(S) \cap \text{Con}(T) \quad (58)$$

where S and T are sets and *Con* is the operation of taking the convex hull.

It is also desirable to aim for formulations which are *hereditarily sharp*, i.e. when certain integer variables are fixed (by the branch and bound algorithm) the resulting submodels remain sharp.

10.3 Economic Information Obtainable by Integer Programming

We saw in Section 6.2 that in addition to the optimal solution values of an LP problem important additional economic information can also be obtained from such quantities as the shadow prices and reduced costs. The dual LP model was also shown to have an important economic interpretation in many situations. In addition a close relationship between the solution to the original model and its dual exist.

It is worth just briefly pointing out how the duality relationship fails in IP. Suppose we have an IP maximization problem P. Corresponding to P we have the LP problem P'. As long as P' is feasible and not unbounded we have a solvable dual problem Q'. From duality in LP we know that

$$\text{maximum objective of } P' = \text{minimum objective of } Q'.$$

By imposing extra integrality requirements on P' we obtain the IP problem P. Clearly since P is more constrained than P' we have

maximum objective of $P \leqslant$ maximum objective of P'
$$= \text{minimum objective of } Q'.$$

The minimum objective of Q' is the *smallest upper bound* we can obtain for the objective of P by a set of valuations on the constraints of P. This contrasts with the LP case where the dual values provide a *strict upper bound* (i.e. a bound that is obtained by the optimum) for the objective. In consequence the difference between the maximum objective value of P and the maximum objective of P' (or minimum objective of Q') is sometimes known as a *duality gap*. It can be regarded (rather loosely) as a measure of how inadequate any dual values will be when used as shadow prices.

In this section we attempt to obtain corresponding economic information from an IP model to that obtainable from an LP model. It will be seen that this information is much more difficult to come by in the case of IP and is, in some cases, rather ambiguous. In order to demonstrate the difficulties we will consider a 'product mix' problem where the variables in the model represent quantities of different products to be made and the constraints represent limitations on productive capacity. It is only meaningful to make integral numbers of each product.

Example 1

Maximize $12\gamma_1 + 5\gamma_2 + 15\gamma_3 + 10\gamma_4$

subject to
$$5\gamma_1 + \gamma_2 + 9\gamma_3 + 12\gamma_4 \leqslant 15, \tag{1}$$
$$2\gamma_1 + 3\gamma_2 + 4\gamma_3 + \gamma_4 \leqslant 10, \tag{2}$$
$$3\gamma_1 + 2\gamma_2 + 4\gamma_3 + 10\gamma_4 \leqslant 8, \tag{3}$$
$$\gamma_1, \gamma_2, \gamma_3, \gamma_4 \geqslant 0.$$

The γ_i are general integer variables.

The optimal integer solution is $\gamma_1 = 2$, $\gamma_2 = 1$, $\gamma_3 = 0$, and $\gamma_4 = 0$, giving an objective value of 29.

For comparison the optimal solution to the corresponding LP problem is $\gamma = 2\frac{2}{3}$, $\gamma_2 = 0$, $\gamma_3 = 0$, and $\gamma_4 = 0$, giving an objective value of 32.

In addition to the fractional solution of the LP problem we would be able to obtain answers to such questions as the following:

(Q1) What is the marginal value of increasing fully utilized capacities?

(Q2) How much should a non-manufactured product be increased in price to make it worth manufacturing?

We saw in Section 6.2 that the answers to Q1 came from the shadow prices on the corresponding constraints. These shadow prices represented valuations which could be placed on the capacities. Once these optimal valuations have been obtained the optimal manufacturing policy can be deduced by simple accounting. Moreover, the total valuation for all the capacities implied by these shadow prices is the same as the profit obtainable by the optimal manufacturing policy.

Unfortunately there are no such neat values which may be placed on capacities in the case of an IP model. For example, the capacity represented by constraint (1) is not fully used up in the IP optimal solution. In an LP problem if a constraint has slack capacity, as in this case, it represents a *free good* as described in Section 6.2 and has a zero shadow price. Such a constraint could be omitted from the LP model and the optimal solution would be unchanged. In this case constraint (1) cannot be omitted without changing the optimal solution. We would therefore like to give the constraint some economic valuation. This gives the first important difference that must exist between any valuations of constraints in IP and shadow prices in LP:

(A) If a constraint has positive slack it does not necessarily represent a free good and may therefore have a positive economic value.

Why this should be so is fairly easy to see since, although there is no virtue in slightly increasing the right-hand side value of 15 in constraint (1), there clearly is virtue in increasing it by at least 3 since we could then bring two of γ_3 into the solution in place of two of γ_1 and one of γ_2.

Even if we admit positive valuations on unsatisfied as well as satisfied capacities it may still be impossible to arrive at a method of decision making through pricing in a similar way to that described in Section 6.2 for LP. This is demonstrated by the following example.

Example 2

Maximize $4\gamma_1 + 3\gamma_2 + \gamma_3$

subject to $2\gamma_1 + 2\gamma_2 + \gamma_3 \leqslant 7,$ (4)

where $\gamma_1, \gamma_2, \gamma_3 \geqslant 0$ and take integer values.

The optimal solution is $\gamma_1 = 3$, $\gamma_2 = 0$, $\gamma_3 = 1$. We will attempt to find a valuation for the constraint which will produce this answer.

Suppose we give the constraint a 'shadow price' (or accounting value) of π, then to make γ_3 profitable we must have $\pi \leqslant 1$. This, however, implies $2\pi < 3$ making γ_2 also profitable. We know from the optimal solution that γ_3 is worth making but that γ_2 is not.

This example demonstrates a second difference between any economic valuation of constraints in IP in comparison with shadow prices in LP:

(B) For general IP problems no valuations will necessarily exist for the constraints which allow the optimal solution to be obtained in a similar manner to the LP case.

By 'constraints' in (B) we must as usual exclude the feasibility constraints $\gamma_i \geqslant 0$.

One way out of the dilemma posed by the IP model above is to obtain constraints representing the convex hull of feasible integer solutions. (For MIP models we would of course consider the convex hull of points with integer coordinates in the dimensions representing integer variables as mentioned in Section 10.1.) The model can then be treated as an LP problem and shadow prices obtained with desirable properties. Although a procedure for obtaining the convex hull of integer solutions is computationally often impractical, as discussed in the last section, it can be applied to certain models making useful economic information possible. This is demonstrated on a particular type of problem, the *shared fixed cost* problem, in Example 4 below. In spite of the general computational difficulties it is still worth considering this as a theoretical solution to our dilemma. For the purposes of explanation we have reformulated the IP model in Example 1 above, using constraints for the convex hull of feasible integer points. This gives the model below.

Example 3

Maximize $\qquad 12\gamma_1 + 5\gamma_2 + 15\gamma_3$

subject to $\qquad \gamma_1 + \qquad + \gamma_3 \leqslant 2,$ (5)

$\qquad\qquad\qquad \gamma_1 + \gamma_2 + \gamma_3 \leqslant 3,$ (6)

$\qquad\qquad\qquad 2\gamma_1 + \gamma_2 + 3\gamma_3 \leqslant 5,$ (7)

$\qquad\qquad\qquad\qquad\qquad \gamma_3 \leqslant 1,$ (8)

where $\gamma_1, \gamma_2, \gamma_3 \geqslant 0$ and take integer values. (When integer, γ_4 is clearly forced to be zero by constraint (3).)

The shadow prices on the new constraints are

constraint (5)	shadow price	2
constraint (6)	shadow price	0
constraint (7)	shadow price	5
constraint (8)	shadow price	0

N.B. Since Example 3 is degenerate there are alternative shadow prices, as explained in Section 6.2.

Unfortunately it is not clear how the new constraints (5), (6), (7), and (8) defining the convex hull of Example 1 can be related back to the original constraints (1), (2), and (3). It is therefore difficult to apply the shadow prices above to give meaningful valuations for the physical constraints of the original model. An attempt has been made to do this by Gomory and Baumol (1960). They apply a cutting planes algorithm to the IP model, successively adding constraints until an integer solution is obtained. Then shadow prices are obtained for the original constraints and for the added constraints. The shadow prices for the added constraints are imputed back to the original constraints from which they were derived. Unfortunately the valuations they obtain for the original constraints are not unique and depend on the way in which the cutting planes algorithm is applied. Also they have to include the feasibility conditions $\gamma_i \geqslant 0$ among their original constraints. As a result these constraints may end up being given non-zero economic valuations. In LP such valuations could be regarded as the reduced costs on the variables γ_i and no difficulty would arise. Variables with positive reduced costs would be out of the optimal solution. With IP using this procedure it would be perfectly possible for the feasibility condition $\gamma_i \geqslant 0$ to have non-zero economic values (suggesting that in some sense $\gamma_i \geqslant 0$ was a 'binding' constraint) and for γ_i to be in the optimal solution at a positive level. One way of justifying this would be to regard the economic valuation given to the feasibility constraint as a cost associated with the indivisibility of γ_i. Not only should γ_i be charged according to the use it makes of scarce capacities, it should also be charged an extra amount in view of the fact it can only come in integral quantities.

The fact that a constraint such as $\gamma_i \geqslant 0$ may have a non-zero valuation in the Gomory–Baumol system yet γ_i may not be at zero level is a special case of a more general difference between the Gomory–Baumol prices in IP and the shadow prices in LP:

(C) A free good as represented by a constraint in IP does not necessarily have a zero Gomory–Baumol price attached to it.

This difference is not as serious as it might first seem since a similar situation can happen in LP. We saw in Section 6.2 that with degeneracy there are alternate dual solutions, some of which may give non-zero shadow prices to (alternatively) redundant constraints. This also indicates that the problem on non-uniqueness in the Gomory–Baumol prices is not confined to IP. It clearly also happens, although to a much less serious extent, with degenerate problems in LP.

The exact way of obtaining limited economic information from a MIP model which is used quite widely in practice should be mentioned. This is simply to take this information from the LP subproblem at the node in the solution tree which gave the optimal integer solution. Such information may well be unreliable since the integer variables should only change by discrete amounts while the economic information results from the effect of marginal changes. Other integer variables (particularly 0–1 variables) will have become fixed by the bounds imposed in the course of evaluating the solution tree and it will not be possible to evaluate the effect of any changes on these variables.

A variation of this way of obtaining economic information from a MIP model is to 'fix' all integer variables at their optimal values and only consider the effect of marginal changes on the continuous variables. This procedure has something to recommend it since the integer variables usually represent major operating decisions. Given that these decisions have been accepted, the economic effects of marginal changes within the basic operating pattern may be of interest.

An example of the need to 'value' the constraints of a MIP model is provided by the TARIFF RATES (POWER GENERATION) problem in Part 2. The rates at which electricity is sold on different tariffs implicitly value the constraints. Different ways of doing this are discussed with the solution of the model in Part 4.

In spite of the difficulties in getting meaningful subsidiary economic information out of an IP model there are circumstances where useful information can be obtained by reformulation of the model. This is discussed by Williams (1981). We will illustrate this in the example below by reformulating a model using the ideas contained in Section 10.2. The problem considered involves *shared fixed costs* and is described by Rhys (1970), to whom these ideas are due.

Example 4

In the network of Figure 10.3 the nodes represent capital investments with the costs associated with them. The arcs represent money-making activities with the estimated revenues associated with them. To carry out any activity (arc) it is necessary to use both the resources represented by the nodes at either end of the arc. The problem is to share the capital investment (fixed) cost associated with a node in some optimal way among the activities associated with the arcs joining the node, e.g. how should the capital cost of node D be shared among the arcs AD, BD, CD, and DE? An illustrative way of viewing this problem is to think of the nodes as stations with the arcs as railways between those stations.

In order to show how the required economic information can arise through reformulating an IP model we will first consider a rather different problem.

Suppose we wish to decide which nodes (stations) to cut in order to make the

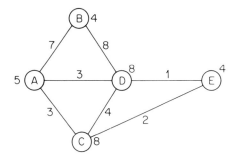

Figure 10.3

whole network (railway system) as profitable as possible. It must be borne in mind that cutting out a node (station) necessitates cutting out all the arcs (lines) leading into it. This problem can easily be formulated as an IP problem using the following 0–1 variables:

$$\delta_i = \begin{cases} 1 & \text{if node } i \text{ is kept,} \\ 0 & \text{if node } i \text{ is cut out;} \end{cases}$$

$$\delta_{ij} = \begin{cases} 1 & \text{if arc } (ij) \text{ is kept,} \\ 0 & \text{if arc } (ij) \text{ is cut;} \end{cases}$$

i, j, are A, B, C, D, and E.

The objective to be maximized is

$$- 5\delta_A - 4\delta_B - 8\delta_C - 8\delta_D - 4\delta_E + 7\delta_{AB} + 3\delta_{AC} + 3\delta_{AD} + 8\delta_{BD}$$
$$+ 4\delta_{CD} + \delta_{DE} + 2\delta_{CE}. \quad (9)$$

The conditions to be modelled are that certain acts require certain nodes, i.e.

$$\delta_{ij} = 1 \rightarrow \delta_i = 1, \ \delta_j = 1. \quad (10)$$

We saw in Section 10.1 that such a condition may be modelled two ways using either one or two constraints as

$$- \delta_i - \delta_j + 2\delta_{ij} \leqslant 0 \quad (11)$$

or

$$\begin{aligned} - \delta_i \quad &+ \ \delta_{ij} \leqslant 0, \\ - \delta_i + \ & \delta_{ij} \leqslant 0. \end{aligned} \quad (12)$$

The second formulation has the advantage that the model will be totally unimodular and can be solved as an LP problem yielding an integer optimal solution. Geometrically we have specified the convex hull of feasible integer points by the constraints (12). Since we now have an LP problem we obtain well defined shadow prices on the constraints. In this example the shadow prices have the following interpretation.

The shadow price on $- \delta_i + \delta_{ij} \leqslant 0$ is the amount of the capital cost of node i which should be met by revenue from arc (ij).

Similarly the shadow price on $- \delta_j + \delta_{ij} \leqslant 0$ is the amount of the capital cost of node j which should be met by revenue from arc (ij).

We have clearly found a way of sharing the capital costs of the nodes among the arcs. Should any activity not be able to meet the capital cost demanded of it, it should be cut out. This allocation of capital costs will be such as to lead to the most profitable network. Using the numbers given on the network in Figure 10.3 the following shadow prices result as shown in Table 10.1.

It will be seen that for example, node C will receive 3 from AC, node A will receive 1 from AC. Clearly are AC is no longer viable and must be cut. Applying similar arguments to all the other arcs we are left with the optimal network shown in Figure 10.4.

Table 10.1

Constraint	Shadow price
$-\delta_A + \delta_{AB} \leqslant 0$	3
$-\delta_B + \delta_{AB} \leqslant 0$	3
$-\delta_A + \delta_{AC} \leqslant 0$	1
$-\delta_C + \delta_{AC} \leqslant 0$	3
$-\delta_A + \delta_{AD} \leqslant 0$	1
$-\delta_D + \delta_{AD} \leqslant 0$	1
$-\delta_B + \delta_{BD} \leqslant 0$	1
$-\delta_D + \delta_{BD} \leqslant 0$	6
$-\delta_C + \delta_{CD} \leqslant 0$	5
$-\delta_D + \delta_{CD} \leqslant 0$	0
$-\delta_C + \delta_{CE} \leqslant 0$	0
$-\delta_E + \delta_{CE} \leqslant 0$	3
$-\delta_D + \delta_{DE} \leqslant 0$	1
$-\delta_E + \delta_{DE} \leqslant 0$	1

An interesting observation following from duality in LP is that dividing the capital costs of the nodes up in other ways among the arcs could not lead to a more profitable network and could well lead to a less profitable one.

It should have become apparent from all the discussion in this section that there is no generally satisfactory way of getting the subsidiary economic information from an IP model that often proves so valuable in the case of LP. This topic represents a considerable gap in mathematical programming theory. The subject is more fully discussed in Williams (1979).

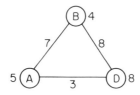

Figure 10.4

10.4   Sensitivity Analysis and the Stability of a Model

We saw in Section 6.3 that having built and solved an LP model it was very important to see how sensitive the answer was to changes in the data from which the model was constructed. Using ranging procedures on the objective and right-hand side coefficients some insight into this could be obtained. In addition it was shown how a model could, to some extent, be built in order to behave in a 'stable' fashion. Our considerations here are exactly the same as those in Section 6.3 only they concern IP models. As in the last section we will see that IP models present considerable extra difficulties. This section falls into two parts. Firstly we will consider ways of testing the sensitivity of the solution of an IP model. Secondly we will consider how models may be built in order that they may exhibit stability.

Sensitivity Analysis and Integer Programming

A theoretical way of doing sensitivity analysis on the objective coefficients of a model would be to replace the constraints by constraints representing the convex hull of feasible integer points. The model could then be treated as an LP model and objective ranging performed as described in Section 6.3.

For those PIP models where a reformulation easily yields the constraints for the convex hull this is fairly straightforward. Otherwise it is not a practical way of approaching the problem. Nor does it give a way of performing right-hand side ranging.

For MIP models solved by the branch and bound method a sensitivity analysis can be performed on the LP subproblem at the node giving the optimal integer solution. Alternatively the integer variables can be fixed at their optimal values and a sensitivity analysis performed on the continuous part of the problem. These approaches clearly have the same drawbacks as those apparent when using similar approaches to derive economic information from an IP model as described in Section 10.3.

The only really satisfactory method of sensitivity analysis in IP involves solving the model again with changed coefficients and comparing optimal solutions. Obviously the subsequent time to solve the model should be able to be reduced by exploiting the knowledge of the previous solution.

Building a Stable Model

In an LP model the optimal value of the objective function varies continuously as the right-hand side and objective coefficients are changed. In an IP model this may not happen. We consider the following very simple example.

Example 1

Maximize $\quad 40\delta_1 + 35\delta_2 + 15\delta_3 + 8\delta_4 + 9\delta_5$

subject to $\quad 8\delta_1 + 8\delta_2 + 5\delta_3 + 4\delta_4 + 3\delta_5 \leqslant 16.$ $\qquad(1)$

$\delta_1, \delta_2, \delta_3, \delta_4, \delta_5$ are 0–1 variables.

The optimal solution to this model is $\delta_1 = 1$ and $\delta_2 = 1$ giving an objective value of 75.

If, however, the right-hand side value of 16 is reduced by a small amount the optimal solution changes to $\delta_1 = 1$, $\delta_4 = 1$, and $\delta_5 = 1$ giving an objective value of 57.

The optimal value of the objective function is obviously not a continuous function of the right-hand side coefficient. In many practical situations this is unrealistic. Suppose constraint (1) represented a budgetary limitation and the 0–1 variables referred to capital investments. It is very unlikely that a small decrease in the budget would cause us radically to alter our plans. A more likely occurrence is that the budget would be stretched slightly at some increased cost or the cost of one of the capital investments would be trimmed slightly. It is important that if this is the case this should be represented in the model. As it stands the above example represents a poor model of the situation.

One way to remodel constraint (1) is to use the device described in Section 3.3 in order to allow constraints to be violated at a certain cost. A surplus (continuous) variable u is added into constraint (1) and given a cost (say 20) in the objective. This results in the model:

Maximize $\quad 40\delta_1 + 35\delta_2 + 15\delta_3 + 8\delta_4 + 9\delta_5 - 20u$

subject to $\quad 8\delta_1 + 8\delta_2 + 5\delta_3 + 4\delta_4 + 3\delta_5 - u \leqslant 16.$ $\qquad$ (2)

For a right-hand side of 16 the optimal solution is still $\delta_1 = \delta_2 = 1$, giving an objective value of 75.

If the right-hand side value of 16 is reduced slightly the effect of u will be to 'top the budget up' to 16 at a unit cost of 20. For example, if the right-hand side falls to $15\frac{1}{2}$, u will become $\frac{1}{2}$. We will retain the same optimal solution but the objective will fall by 10 to 65. As the right-hand side is further reduced the optimal value of the objective will continue gradually to fall until we reach a right-hand side value of $15\frac{1}{10}$. We will then have the solution $\delta_1 = 1$, $\delta_4 = 1$, and $\delta_5 = 1$ as an alternative optimum. If the right-hand side is further reduced we will transfer to this alternative optimum. It can be seen that this device of adding a surplus variable to the problem with a certain cost has two desirable effects on the model:

(i) The optimal objective value becomes a continuous function of the right-hand side coefficient.

(ii) The optimal solution values do not change 'suddenly' as the right-hand side coefficient changes. They are said to be 'semi-continuous' functions of the right-hand side.

In some applications we might wish to add a slack (continuous) variable v as well; giving v a cost in the objective (of say 8). This would result in the following model:

Maximize $\quad 40\delta_1 + 35\delta_2 + 15\delta_3 + 8\delta_4 + 9\delta_5 - 20u - 8v$

subject to $\quad 8\delta_1 + 8\delta_2 + 5\delta_3 + 4\delta_4 + 3\delta_5 - u + v = 16$ $\qquad$ (3)

This topic will not be pursued further here since it has been fully covered for LP problems in Section 6.3. It is important to notice, however, the desirability of forcing the optimal solution of an IP model to vary 'continuously' with the data coefficients. Clearly for many logical type constraints which appear in MIP models it is meaningless to use a device such as that above. There are

234

some classes of MIP model where the continuity property can be shown to hold without further reformulation. This subject is discussed more deeply by A. C. Williams (1989).

10.5 When and How to Use Integer Programming

In this section we try, very briefly, to summarize some of the points made in the preceding three chapters as a quick guide to using IP.

(1) If a practical problem has any of the characteristics described in Section 8.2 it is worth considering the use of an IP model.

(2) Before a decision is made to build an IP model an estimate should be made of the potential size. If the number of integer variables is more than a few hundred then, unless the problem has a special structure, it is probable that IP will be computationally too costly.

(3) A close examination of the structure of the IP model which would result from the problem is always worthwhile. Should the model be a PIP model and have a totally unimodular structure then LP can be used and models involving thousands of constraints and variables solved in a reasonable period of time. If the structure is a PIP model but not totally unimodular it is worth seeing if it can easily be transformed into a known totally unimodular structure, as described in Section 10.2. For MIP models or models where there is no apparent way of producing a unimodular structure it is often possible to constrain the corresponding LP problem more tightly. If it is apparent that the IP model will have one of the other special structures mentioned in Section 9.5, it is worth examining the literature and computational experience with the class of problem to get an impression of the difficulty.

(4) Before embarking on the full scale model it is worth building a model for a much smaller version of the problem. Experiments should be performed on this model to find out how easy it is to solve. If necessary, reformulations such as those described in Section 10.2 should be tried. Different solution strategies as mentioned in Section 8.3 should also be experimented with.

(5) If the problem appears too difficult to solve as an IP model after carrying out the above investigations some *heuristic* method will have to be used. Much literature exists on different heuristic algorithms for Operational Research problems but this topic is beyond the scope of this book. For an apparently difficult problem where an IP model still seems worthwhile it may also be worth some time being spent on a heuristic approach to get a fairly good, though probably not optimal solution. This good solution can then be exploited in the tree search as a cut-off value for the objective function as described in Section 8.3.

(6) Having built an IP model it is very important to use an intelligent solution strategy, using, if possible, one's knowledge of the practical problem. This has been mentioned briefly in Section 8.3 but is, in the main, beyond the

scope of a book on model building. An extremely good description of this subject is given by Forrest, Hirst, and Tomlin (1974).

Finally it should be pointed out that theoretical and computational progress in IP is being made all the time, making it possible to solve larger and more complex models.

CHAPTER 11

The Implementation of a Mathematical Programming System of Planning

11.1 Acceptance and Implementation

Most of this book has been concerned with the problems of formulating and interpreting the solution of mathematical programming models. There is, however, generally another phase to be gone through before the solution of a model influences the making of real decisions. This final phase is that of gaining acceptance for, and implementing the solution. Many people who have been involved with all the phases of formulating a model, solving it, interpreting the solution, gaining acceptance for the solution, and then implementing it have found the last two phases to be the most difficult. In some cases they may have stumbled fatally at this point. There are a number of lessons to be learnt from such experiences which will be considered in this chapter. Obviously the problem of acceptance and implementation will depend on the type of organization involved as well as the type of application. It is useful here to classify mathematical programming models for planning into short, medium, and long term planning models.

Short term planning models may be simply 'one off' models used to decide the answer to a specific question, e.g. do we build a new factory or not, what is the optimum design for this communications network? If these questions are unlikely to recur then there is generally little to be said about the acceptance and implementation. Either the solution produced by the model is used or it is not used. For other short term planning questions which do arise regularly at daily or weekly intervals there may be an implementation problem. Firstly it should be pointed out that in some cases a mathematical programming model may be applicable but unworkable. For example, a complicated distribution or job-shop scheduling problem may be essentially 'dynamic'. Changes may be taking place all the time, new orders may be coming in, and machines may be breaking down. It might be impossible to define a once and for all schedule. To adapt such a schedule to each change might involve a rerun of the model. Unless the changes were infrequent and the model comparatively quick to solve, such an approach would be impossible. In such cases special purpose adaptive (and probably non-optimal) quick decision rules would probably be used. Some short term decision problems which occur regularly can often be tackled through a mathematical programming model. Day to day blending problems, for example, may be of this nature. Sometimes fertilizer suppliers or food manufacturers run small linear programming models for individual orders or blends. In such cases acceptance of the method must have already been achieved. An organizational problem will also have had to be solved probably by automating the conversion of the data into a standard type of model for quick solution by a computer (probably through a terminal). The use of such short term operational models creates few other implementation problems since once accepted their use is fairly straightforward.

Medium term planning is usually considered to involve periods of a month up to one or two years. It is for these problems that mathematical programming has been most widely used to date. Once a medium term planning model has been implemented and is being used regularly, it may be incorporated into, or form a starting point for, a *longer term planning* model typically looking up to about six years ahead. The problems of getting acceptance of such models are similar but usually more acute in the case of longer term planning. Both will be considered together.

Much has been written on the more general problem of how to gain acceptance for and ensure the implementation of the results of any operational research study. A clear and useful account of the considerations which should be made is given by Rivett (1968). The main lesson to be learnt is to involve the potential decision makers in a model building project at an early stage. If they have lived with the problems of defining and building a model they will be much more likely to accept and understand its final use than if it is sprung on them at a late stage. Early involvement by top management can have its dangers. It is possible that the development of a model may get bogged down in detailed technical arguments between managers who would normally never be concerned with such technicalities. More seriously a model building project might be rejected at an early stage through disagreement over detail. These risks are, however, normally worth taking in comparison with the risk of rejection at the final hurdle. Involving top management will often be by no means easy. They will need to understand the potentialities of a mathematical programming model but will probably lack both detailed technical knowledge as well as detailed departmental knowledge of some aspects of their company. Some of this detail may well need to be incorporated into the model. The solution is probably to involve one or two such managers in the model building project as well as give regular presentations to the others. There is then of course another danger to be avoided. It is important not to oversell the model. If it is thought that the model will answer every question, then later, disillusion may be in store.

Many people have found that a new mathematical programming model has gained acceptance when the answers which it produces confirm a decision which has already been made. For example, an important investment decision may have been made in some other way. If the answer to the model confirms this, the ultimate regular use of mathematical programming may be assured.

It has already been suggested that sometimes the very exercise of building a model leads to the explicit recognition of relationships which were not realized before. In such circumstances the modelling exercise may be as valuable as the answers produced. When this happens the effect on management may well be to make the use of mathematical programming more acceptable.

The ultimate acceptance of a regular mathematical programming system of planning usually requires organizational changes which are considered in the next section.

A very full and useful description of the experiences in developing and gaining acceptance for a large long term planning mathematical programming model in British Petroleum is described by Stewart (1971).

An analysis of the factors which make for success or failure in implementing the results of corporate models is given by Harvey (1970). On the result of a survey he isolates the characteristics of both management and decision problems which lead to success or failure in the implementation of a model. Problems of implementation are also discussed very fully in the book by Miller and Starr (1960).

A perceptive analysis of three industrial problems where linear programming has yielded disappointing results is given by Corner (1979). He draws conclusions and presents advice on the basis of these experiences.

Finally, as was mentioned in Section 2.4, it seems quite likely that mathematical programming methods will be incorporated in much larger pieces of software known as *decision support systems*. The resultant systems will usually be tailor-made to specific applications. In this way much of the effort of model building will be transferred to the computer system. It will then be necessary to include model building expertise in the designing and writing of such systems.

11.2 The Unification of Organizational Functions

One of the virtues of a corporate planning model is that many interconnections between different departments and functions in an organization have to be represented explicitly. The obvious example is production and marketing. In many manufacturing industries these two functions are kept very separate. The result is sometimes a divergence of objectives. Production may be trying to satisfy orders with a reasonable level of productivity. Marketing may be trying to maximize the total volume of sales rather than concentrating on those that make the greatest contribution to profit. One of the greatest virtues of a product mix type of model is that it forces marketing to take account of production costs. The result is almost always a reduction in the range of products produced to those which can be produced most efficiently. In practice with this type of model the incorporation of the marketing function can present difficulties. As was suggested in Section 3.2 it may sometimes be politically more acceptable to first of all leave out the marketing aspect. A model is built simply to meet all market estimates at minimum production cost. When this type of model has come into regular use it can fairly easily be extended also to decide quantities to be marketed, taking into account their profit contributions. The marketing division of a company is often less able to quantify its data and more reluctant to accept the answers produced by a model. Indeed their individual objective may be at variance with that of the company. Stewart (1971) gives a case history of a linear programming model built for the Gas Council which was considered to be of little use for marketing.

In order to give an idea of the different company functions which can be incorporated in a mathematical programming model Figure 11.1 demonstrates how purchasing, operating, and planning functions can become involved in a model.

The model here is described by Williams and Redwood (1974) and takes in all the functions in the box enclosed by a dotted line. It is a multi-period, multi-brand model for aiding decisions of the purchase of edible oils on the commodity market and their blending together into foods. The involvement of different functions and departments in the building and use of a model such as this can force some degree of centralization on an organization. This aspect is considered in Section 11.3.

While the explicit recognition of interrelationships in an organization through a model is desirable, it usually makes extra coordination necessary for

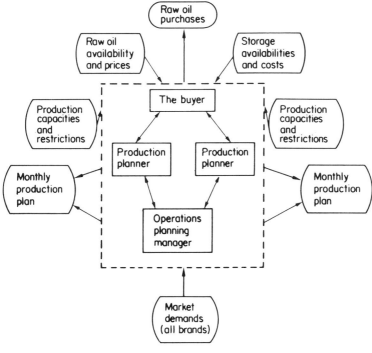

Figure 11.1

the supply of data to, and the use of a model. Often this requires the creation of a special job or even a small department. Such a coordinating role is often effectively done through the management accounting department. They are one of the few departments with an overview of the whole organization.

One of the, possibly contentious, results of decisions which may be reached through a corporate model should be recognized. Because such a model will have a corporate objective, this may conflict within the objectives of individual departments. It has already been pointed out that a marketing division may force them to reduce their product range and therefore their total volume in the interests of greater company profit. The disputes that may result in consequence are added reason for obtaining top management backing for this method of planning. In Section 4.1 it was demonstrated through a very simple example how a corporate objective could result in an individual factory having its individual profit reduced in the interests of overall company profit. Again the possible political implications are obvious.

Although there may be obvious difficulties in getting different departments to work more closely together, there can be advantages resulting from a planning model. The combination of a large amount of data and information in one computer model can lead to greater convenience. Each department can be given the relevant portions of a computer run. Problems of communication and incompatibility of information will be reduced in consequence. One of the by-products of a corporate model is usually greater contact between departments. Each department will want to know what information other departments have fed into the model, since this may affect the suggested plans for their own department.

The correct use of a multi-period model for planning has already been mentioned in Section 4.1. Such a model may well provide operating information for the current time period as well as provisional information for future periods. Such a model would generally be rerun at least once in each period, giving the same combination of operating information and planning information based on the best available future estimates which have been fed into the model.

11.3   Centralization versus Decentralization

A corporate model obviously brings into its orbit many aspects of an organization which might normally be separated into different divisions. Sometimes these divisions may be separated geographically. In some respects the greater centralization of planning which results may seem desirable. The small example of Section 4.1 demonstrated how individual factories in a company might produce sub-optimal plans when working independently. In the last section it was pointed out how the recognition of the interdependence of different departments in an organization often results from a model.

Although many of these features are to some degree desirable, when carried to excess they may be far from desirable. In fact the increasing disadvantages of greater and greater centralization have been a major factor in discouraging the continual growth in the size of mathematical programming models.

In theory, decomposition, which was discussed in Section 4.2, offers a way out by avoiding the need to include all the detail of an organization in one total model. Unfortunately the computational problems of using a decomposition method in general have not yet been fully resolved. At present it cannot be considered to be a sufficiently developed technique to be always usable in practice. Moreover, mathematical methods of decomposition do not always correspond to acceptable decentralized planning methods. This aspect of the subject has been discussed by Atkins (1974).

Stewart (1971) rather surprisingly suggests that the use of a long tern planning model in British Petroleum led to some degree of decentralization. In particular it was then possible for a division to obtain complete information before making a plan themselves rather than the information being restricted to head office. This enabled the division to take on more responsibility. On the other hand, the division now had to work within some centrally defined objective rather than choose its own objective. People now, however, felt that they were working to an independent system, in the form of a model, rather than being simply dictated to by head office. This, to some extent, made centralization more acceptable.

As was pointed out in Chapter 6, a wealth of information can be obtained from the solution to a linear programming model. For large corporate models this excess of information can create difficulties. It is very important to ensure that departments only get relevant information. Otherwise they can be submerged. The use of an automatic report writer as discussed in Section 6.5 is obviously desirable. Such a report writer can be designed to produce the information in different sections for the use of different departments.

It is necessary to strike a correct balance between the model builders, the contributors of data and the managers who use the results. There is a great danger, in a large organization, of them losing touch with one another. Relevant data may not be used at the right time and inaccurate results obtained. Ideally management will become accustomed to using a model on a 'what if…' basis. They will ask questions which the model builder will be able to answer quickly by new runs or post-optimal analysis.

The degree of centralization or decentralization which the use of a model should be allowed to impose on an organization must obviously depend very much on the organization and its ultimate objectives. In consequence few general guidelines can be given. The recognition of the problem of centralization is, however, important. It is interesting that mathematical programming is used quite widely in communist countries for national economic planning. In the west this is far less common. Models are usually limited to the level of individual companies.

11.4 The Collection of Data and the Maintenance of a Model

The collection of data is a major task in building a large mathematical programming model for the first time. Once this has been done the organization should be geared to providing and updating the data regularly. Inevitably much work will be involved in collecting suitable data. Coming from different departments it will often need to be standardized. Again such standardization and coordination will ultimately need to be the responsibility of a special person or department if the model is to be used regularly. As has already been pointed out a management accounting department is often a suitable place to which to entrust this responsibility.

The person entrusted with the regular collection and standardization of the data must be in a position where he is kept up to date with all changes. These changes will come from different departments. There may be marketing estimates, changes in productive capacity, technological changes in production processes, and changes in raw materials costs. Ensuring that all this information gets incorporated in the model and it remains an up-to-date representation is no mean task. It may sometimes be necessary to do preliminary processing of the data. For example, sales estimates may be the result of a regular forecasting exercise. This may require preliminary computation. It may be necessary to convert costing data to a suitable form, e.g. to ensure that only variable costs are used. With some packages it is now possible to prepare, manipulate and present the data though *spreadsheets*. The solutions are sometimes conveniently presented in this form also.

The use and regular updating of *data bases* to include all relevant statistical information is of value when used in conjunction with a mathematical programming model. Such data bases may also be used for other purposes as well within an organization. It is important, however, to ensure that their organization and design is compatible with the mathematical programming model used. Most commercial package programs for mathematical programming can be incorporated as part of a much larger computer software system (e.g. a *decision support system*) using a data base.

As with so many computer applications their use does not reduce the need for employees. Instead it changes the type of employee required and sometimes increases the total number of people. It should be obvious that the problems of collecting data and maintaining a model deserve considerable attention and effort if its use is to be effective. The gain should come from the wider range of policy options which can be considered as well as their greater reliability.

PART 2

CHAPTER 12

The Problems

There is no significance in the order in which the following 20 problems are presented. Some of them are easy to formulate and present no computational difficulties in solution. Others are more difficult in either one of these respects or both. It will be found that some of the problems can be solved with linear programming, others require integer programming or separable programming.

It is suggested that the reader attempts to formulate those problems which interest him before consulting the suggested formulations and solutions in Parts 3 and 4. If he has available a computer he may wish to use this on his model. Alternatively, he may attempt an intuitive (heuristic) approach to some of the problems using original methods of his own. He can compare his answer with the optimal one given in Part 4.

If the reader does wish to follow the recommended course of solving the models using a computer package he is strongly advised to use a matrix generator/language, as discussed in Sections 3.5 and 4.3. This enables him to concentrate on the *structure* of the model as well as facilitating error detection and greatly reducing data preparation.

In Section 3.5 some discussion has been given of XPRESS-MP's matrix generator language MP-MODEL. Further details of its use can be found in Ashford and Daniel (1992). Each of the formulations suggested in Part 3 has been modelled using MP-MODEL. Should the reader wish to obtain these formulations he should write to the author at the Faculty of Mathematical Studies, The University, Highfield, Southampton SO9 5NH, UK.

12.1   Food Manufacture

A food is manufactured by refining raw oils and blending them together. The raw oils come in two categories:

vegetable oils	VEG 1
	VEG 2
non-vegetable oils	OIL 1
	OIL 2
	OIL 3

Each oil may be purchased for immediate delivery (January) or bought on the future's market for delivery in a subsequent month. Prices now, and in the future's market are given below (in £/ton):

	VEG 1	VEG 2	OIL 1	OIL 2	OIL 3
January	110	120	130	110	115
February	130	130	110	90	115
March	110	140	130	100	95
April	120	110	120	120	125
May	100	120	150	110	105
June	90	100	140	80	135

The final product sells at £150 per ton.

Vegetable oils and non-vegetable oils require different production lines for refining. In any month it is not possible to refine more than 200 tons of vegetable oils and more than 250 tons of non-vegetable oils. There is no loss of weight in the refining process and the cost of refining may be ignored.

It is possible to store up to 1000 tons of each raw oil for use later. The cost of storage for vegetable and non-vegetable oil is £5 per ton per month. The final product cannot be stored. Nor can refined oils be stored.

There is a technological restriction of hardness on the final product. In the units in which hardness is measured this must lie between 3 and 6. It is assumed that hardness blends linearly and that the hardnesses of the raw oils are

VEG	1	$8 \cdot 8$
VEG	2	$6 \cdot 1$
OIL	1	$2 \cdot 0$
OIL	2	$4 \cdot 2$
OIL	3	$5 \cdot 0$

What buying and manufacturing policy should the company pursue in order to maximize profit?

At present there are 500 tons of each type of raw oil in storage. It is required that these stocks will also exist at the end of June.

Investigate how total profit and buying and manufacturing policy should change for different prices in the future's market. The price changes to be considered are an $x\%$ increase in vegetable oils and a $2x\%$ increase in non-vegetable oils in the February market. For March these increases are $2x\%$ and $4x\%$. These increases continue linearly upwards for the rest of the year. The policy changes necessary and their effect on total profit should be mapped out for different values of x (up to 20).

12.2 Food Manufacture 2

It is wished to impose the following extra conditions on the food manufacture problem:

(1) The food may never be made up of more than three oils in any month.
(2) If an oil is used in a month at least 20 tons must be used.
(3) If either of VEG 1 or VEG 2 are used in a month then OIL 3 must also be used.

Extend the food manufacture model to encompass these restrictions and find the new optimal solution.

12.3 Factory Planning

An engineering factory makes seven products (PROD 1 to PROD 7) on the following machines: four grinders, two vertical drills, three horizontal drills, one borer, and one planer. Each product yields a certain contribution to profit (defined as £/unit selling price minus cost of raw materials). These quantities (in £/unit) together with the unit production times (hours) required on each process are given below. A dash indicates that a product does not require a process.

	PROD 1	PROD 2	PROD 3	PROD 4	PROD 5	PROD 6	PROD 7
Contribution to profit	10	6	8	4	11	9	3
Grinding	0·5	0·7	—	—	0·3	0·2	0·5
Vertical drilling	0·1	0·2	—	0·3	—	0·6	—
Horizontal drilling	0·2	—	0·8	—	—	—	0·6
Boring	0·05	0·03	—	0·07	0·1	—	0·08
Planing	—	—	0·01	—	0·05	—	0·05

In the present month (January) and the five subsequent months certain machines will be down for maintenance. These machines will be:

January	1 grinder
February	2 horizontal drills
March	1 borer
April	1 vertical drill
May	1 grinder and 1 vertical drill
June	1 planer and 1 horizontal drill

There are marketing limitations on each product in each month. These are:

	1	2	3	4	5	6	7
January	500	1000	300	300	800	200	100
February	600	500	200	0	400	300	150
March	300	600	0	0	500	400	100
April	200	300	400	500	200	0	100
May	0	100	500	100	1000	300	0
June	500	500	100	300	1100	500	60

It is possible to store up to 100 of each product at a time at a cost of £0·5 per unit per month. There are no stocks at present but it is desired to have a stock of 50 of each type of product at the end of June.

The factory works a 6 day week with two shifts of 8 hours each day.

No sequencing problems need to be considered.

When and what should the factory make in order to maximize the total profit? Recommend any price increases and the value of acquiring any new machines.

N.B. It may be assumed that each month consists of only 24 working days.

12.4 Factory Planning 2

Instead of stipulating when each machine is down for maintenance in the factory planning problem, it is desired to find the best month for each machine to be down.

Each machine must be down for maintenance in one month of the six apart from the grinding machines, only two of which need be down in any six months.

Extend the model to allow it to make these extra decisions. How much is the extra flexibility of allowing down times to be chosen worth?

12.5 Manpower Planning

A company is undergoing a number of changes which will affect its manpower requirements in future years. Owing to the installation of new machinery, less unskilled, but more skilled and semi-skilled men will be required. In addition to this a downturn in trade is expected in the next year which will reduce the need for men in all categories. The estimated manpower requirements are (for the next three years) as follows:

	Unskilled	Semi-skilled	Skilled
Current strength	2000	1500	1000
Year 1	1000	1400	1000
Year 2	500	2000	1500
Year 3	0	2500	2000

The company wishes to decide its policy with regard to the following over the next three years:

(1) Recruitment
(2) Retraining
(3) Redundancy
(4) Short-time working.

There is a natural wastage of labour. A fairly large number of men leave during their first year. After this the rate is much smaller. Taking this into account, the wastage rates can be taken as below:

	Unskilled	Semi-skilled	Skilled
Less than one year's service	25%	20%	10%
More than one year's service	10%	5%	5%

There has been no recent recruitment and all men in the current labour force have been employed for more than one year.

Recruitment

It is possible to recruit a limited number of men from outside. In any one year the numbers which can be recruited in each category are:

Unskilled	Semi-skilled	Skilled
500	800	500

Retraining

It is possible to retrain up to 200 unskilled men a year to make them semi-skilled. This costs £400 a man. The retraining of semi-skilled men to make them skilled is limited to a number no more than one quarter of the skilled labour force at the time as some training is done on the job. To retrain a semi-skilled man in this way costs £500.

Downgrading of men to a lower skill is possible but 50% of such men leave, although it costs the company nothing. (This wastage is additional to the 'natural wastage' described above.)

Redundancy

If an unskilled man is declared redundant he is made a payment of £200. If a semi-skilled or skilled man is made redundant he is made a payment of £500.

Overmanning

It is possible to employ up to 150 more men over the whole company, than are needed but the extra costs per man per year are:

Unskilled	Semi-skilled	Skilled
£1500	£2000	£3000

Short-time Working

Up to 50 men in each category of skill can be put on short-time working. The cost of this (per man per year) is:

Unskilled	Semi-skilled	Skilled
£500	£400	£400

A man on short-time working meets the production requirements of half a man.

The company's declared objective is to minimize redundancy. How should they operate in order to do this?

If their policy were to minimize costs, how much extra would this save? Deduce the cost of saving each type of job each year.

12.6 Refinery Optimization

An oil refinery purchases two crude oils (crude 1 and crude 2). These crude oils are put through four processes: distillation, reforming, cracking, and blending, to produce petrols and fuels which are sold.

Distillation

Distillation separates each crude oil into fractions known as *light naphtha*, *medium naphtha*, *heavy naphtha*, *light oil*, *heavy oil*, and *residuum* according to their boiling points. Light, medium, and heavy naphthas have octane numbers of 90, 80, and 70 respectively. The fractions into which one barrel of each type of crude splits are given in the table:

	Light naphtha	Medium naphtha	Heavy naphtha	Light oil	Heavy oil	Residuum
Crude 1	0·1	0·2	0·2	0·12	0·2	0·13
Crude 2	0·15	0·25	0·18	0·08	0·19	0·12

N.B. There is a small amount of wastage in distillation.

Reforming

The naphthas can be used immediately for blending into different grades of petrol or can go through a process known as reforming. Reforming produces a product known as reformed gasoline with an octane number of 115. The yields of reformed gasoline from each barrel of the different naphthas are given below:

    1 barrel of light naphtha yields 0·6 barrels of reformed gasoline;
    1 barrel of medium naphtha yields 0·52 barrels of reformed gasoline;
    1 barrel of heavy naphtha yields 0·45 barrels of reformed gasoline.

Cracking

The oils (light and heavy) can either be used directly for blending into *jet fuel* or *fuel oil* or can be put through a process known as catalytic cracking. The catalytic cracker produces *cracked oil* and *cracked gasoline*. Cracked gasoline has an octane number of 105.

    1 barrel of light oil yields 0·68 barrels of cracked oil and 0·28 barrels of cracked gasoline;
    1 barrel of heavy oil yields 0·75 barrels of cracked oil and 0·2 barrels of cracked gasoline.

Cracked oil is used for blending *fuel oil* and *jet fuel*; cracked gasoline is used for blending *petrol*.

    Residuum can be used for producing either *lube-oil* or blending into *jet fuel* and *fuel oil:*

    1 barrel of residuum yields 0·5 barrels of lube-oil

Blending

Petrols (*Motor Fuel*)

There are two sorts of petrol, *regular* and *premium*, obtained by blending the naphtha, reformed gasoline, and cracked gasoline. The only stipulations concerning them are that regular must have an octane number of at least 84 and that premium must have an octane number of at least 94. It is assumed that octane numbers blend linearly by volume.

Jet Fuel

The stipulation concerning jet fuel is that its vapour pressure must not exceed 1 kilogram per square centimetre. The vapour pressures for light, heavy, and cracked oils and residuum are $1 \cdot 0$, $0 \cdot 6$, $1 \cdot 5$, and $0 \cdot 05$ kilograms per square centimetre respectively. It may again be assumed that vapour pressures blend linearly by volume.

Fuel Oil

To produce fuel oil, light oil, cracked oil, heavy oil, and residuum must be blended in the ratio 10:4:3:1.

There are availability and capacity limitations on the quantities and processes used:

(a) The daily availability of crude 1 is 20 000 barrels.
(b) The daily availability of crude 2 is 30 000 barrels.
(c) At most 45 000 barrels of crude can be distilled per day.
(d) At most 10 000 barrels of naphtha can be reformed per day.
(e) At most 8000 barrels of oil can be cracked per day.
(f) The daily production of lube oil must be between 500 and 1000 barrels.
(g) Premium motor fuel production must be at least 40% of regular motor fuel production.

The profit contributions from the sale of the final products are (in pence per barrel)

Premium petrol	700
Regular petrol	600
Jet fuel	400
Fuel oil	350
Lube-oil	150

How should the operations of the refinery be planned in order to maximize total profit?

12.7 Mining

A mining company is going to continue operating in a certain area for the next five years. There are four mines in this area but it can operate at most three in any one year. Although a mine may not operate in a certain year it is still necessary to keep it 'open', in the sense that royalties are payable, should it be operated in a future year. Clearly if a mine is not going to be worked again it can be closed down permanently and no more royalties need be paid. The yearly royalties payable on each mine kept 'open' are

Mine 1	£5m (5 million pounds)
Mine 2	£4m
Mine 3	£4m
Mine 4	£5m

There is an upper limit to the amount of ore which can be extracted from each mine in a year. These upper limits are:

Mine 1	2×10^6 tons
Mine 2	$2 \cdot 5 \times 10^6$ tons
Mine 3	$1 \cdot 3 \times 10^6$ tons
Mine 4	3×10^6 tons

The ore from the different mines is of varying quality. This quality is measured on a scale so that blending ores together results in a linear combination of the quality measurements, e.g. if equal quantities of two ores were combined the resultant ore would have a quality measurement half way between that of the ingredient ores. Measured in these units the qualities of the ores from the mines are given below:

Mine 1	$1 \cdot 0$
Mine 2	$0 \cdot 7$
Mine 3	$1 \cdot 5$
Mine 4	$0 \cdot 5$

In each year it is necessary to combine the total outputs from each mine to produce a blended ore of exactly some stipulated quality. For each year these qualities are

Year 1	$0 \cdot 9$
Year 2	$0 \cdot 8$
Year 3	$1 \cdot 2$
Year 4	$0 \cdot 6$
Year 5	$1 \cdot 0$

The final blended ore sells for £10 per ton each year. Revenue and expenditure for future years must be discounted at a rate of 10% per annum.

Which mines should be operated each year and how much should they produce?

12.8 Farm Planning

A farmer wishes to plan production on his 200 acre farm over the next five years.

At present he has a herd of 120 cows. This is made up of 20 heifers and 100 milk-producing cows. Each heifer needs $\frac{2}{3}$ acre to support it and each dairy cow 1 acre. A dairy cow produces an average of $1 \cdot 1$ calves per year. Half of these calves will be bullocks which are sold almost immediately for an average of £30 each. The remaining heifers can either be sold almost immediately for £40 or reared to become milk-producing cows at two years old. It is intended that all dairy cows be sold at 12 years old for an average of £120 each, although there will probably be an annual loss of 5% per year among heifers and 2% among dairy cows. At present there are 10 cows of each age from newborn to 11 years old. The decision of how many heifers to sell in the current year has already been taken and implemented.

The milk from a cow yields an annual revenue of £370. A maximum of 130 cows can be housed at the present time. To provide accommodation for each cow beyond this number will entail a capital outlay of £200 per cow. Each milk-producing cow requires $0 \cdot 6$ tons of grain and $0 \cdot 7$ tons of sugar beet per year. Grain and sugar beet can both be grown on the farm. Each acre yields $1 \cdot 5$ tons of sugar beet. Only 80 acres are suitable for growing grain. They can be divided into four groups whose yields are as follows:

$$
\begin{array}{llll}
\text{group 1} & 20 \text{ acres} & 1 \cdot 1 & \text{tons per acre} \\
\text{group 2} & 30 \text{ acres} & 0 \cdot 9 & \text{tons per acre} \\
\text{group 3} & 20 \text{ acres} & 0 \cdot 8 & \text{tons per acre} \\
\text{group 4} & 10 \text{ acres} & 0 \cdot 65 & \text{tons per acre}
\end{array}
$$

Grain can be bought for £90 per ton and sold for £75 per ton. Sugar beet can be bought for £70 per ton and sold for £58 per ton.

The labour requirements are:

each heifer	10 hours per year
each milk-producing cow	42 hours per year
each acre put to grain	4 hours per year
each acre put to sugar beet	14 hours per year

Other costs are:

each heifer	£50 per year
each milk-producing cow	£100 per year
each acre put to grain	£15 per year
each acre put to sugar beet	£10 per year

Labour costs for the farm are at present £4000 per year and provide 5500 hours labour. Any labour needed above this will cost £1·20 per hour.

How should the farmer operate over the next five years to maximize profit? Any capital expenditure would be financed by a 10 year loan at 15% annual interest. The interest and capital repayment would be paid in 10 equally sized yearly instalments. In no year can the cash flow be negative. Lastly, the farmer would not wish to reduce the total number of dairy cows at the end of the five year period by more than 50% nor increase by more than 75%.

12.9   Economic Planning

An economy consists of three industries: coal, steel and transport. Each unit produced by one of the industries (a unit will be taken as £1's worth of value of production) requires inputs from possibly its own industry as well as other industries. The required inputs as well as the manpower requirements (also measured in £) are given in Table 12.1. There is a time lag in the economy so that output in year $t + 1$ requires an input in year t.

Output from an industry may also be used to build productive capacity for itself or other industries in future years. The inputs required to give unit increases (capacity for £1's worth of extra production) in productive capacity are given in Table 12.2. Input from an industry in year t results in a (permanent) increase in productive capacity in year $t + 2$.

Stocks of goods may be held from year to year. At present (year 0) the stocks and productive capacities (per year) are given in Table 12.3 (in £m). There is a limited yearly manpower capacity of £470m.

It is wished to investigate different possible growth patterns for the economy over the next five years. In particular it is desirable to know the growth patterns which would result from pursuing the following objectives:

(i) Maximizing total productive capacity at the end of the five years while meeting an exogenous consumption requirement of £60m of coal, £60m of steel, and £30m of transport in every year (apart from year 0).

Table 12.1

Inputs (year t)	Outputs (year $t + 1$), production		
	Coal	Steel	Transport
Coal	0·1	0·5	0·4
Steel	0·1	0·1	0·2
Transport	0·2	0·1	0·2
Manpower	0·6	0·3	0·2

Table 12.2

Inputs (year t)	Output (year $t + 2$), productive capacity		
	Coal	Steel	Transport
Coal	0·0	0·7	0·9
Steel	0·1	0·1	0·2
Transport	0·2	0·1	0·2
Manpower	0·4	0·2	0·1

Table 12.3

	Year 0	
	Stocks	Productive capacity
Coal	150	300
Steel	80	350
Transport	100	280

(ii) Maximizing total production (rather than productive capacity) in the fourth and fifth years, but ignoring exogenous demand in each year.

(iii) Maximizing the total manpower requirement (ignoring the manpower capacity limitation) over the period while meeting the yearly exogenous demands of (i).

12.10 Decentralization

A large company wishes to move some of its departments out of London. There are benefits to be derived from doing this (cheaper housing, government incentives, easier recruitment, etc.) which have been costed. Also, however, there will be greater costs of communication between departments. These have also been costed for all possible locations of each department.

Where should each department be located so as to minimize overall yearly cost?

The company comprises five departments (A, B, C, D, E). The possible cities for relocation are Bristol and Brighton, or a department may be kept in London. None of these cities (including London) may be the location for more than three of the departments.

Benefits to be derived from each relocation are given below (in thousands of pounds per year):

	A	B	C	D	E
Bristol	10	15	10	20	5
Brighton	10	20	15	15	15

Communication costs are of the form $C_{ik}D_{jl}$, where C_{ik} is the quantity of communication between departments i and k per year and D_{jl} is the cost per unit of communication between cities j and l. C_{ik} and D_{jl} are given by the tables below:

	Quantities of communication C_{ik} (in thousands of units)				
	A	B	C	D	E
A		0·0	1·0	1·5	0·0
B			1·4	1·2	0·0
C				0·0	2·0
D					0·7

	Costs per unit of communication D_{jl} (in £)		
	Bristol	Brighton	London
Bristol	5	14	13
Brighton		5	9
London			10

12.11 Curve Fitting

A quantity y is known to depend upon another quantity x. A set of corresponding values has been collected for x and y and is presented in Table 12.4.

(1) Fit the 'best' straight line $y = bx + a$ to this set of data points. The objective is to minimize the sum of *absolute deviations* of each observed value of y from the value predicted by the linear relationship.
(2) Fit the 'best' straight line where the objective is to minimize the *maximum deviation* of all the observed values of y from the value predicted by the linear relationship.
(3) Fit the 'best' quadratic curve $y = cx^2 + bx + a$ to this set of data points using the same objectives as in (1) and (2).

Table 12.4

x	0·0	0·5	1·0	1·5	1·9	2·5	3·0	3·5	4·0	4·5	5·0	5·5	6·0	6·6	7·0
y	1·0	0·9	0·7	1·5	2·0	2·4	3·2	2·0	2·7	3·5	1·0	4·0	3·6	2·7	5·7

x	7·6	8·5	9·0	10·0
y	4·6	6·0	6·8	7·3

12.12 Logical Design

Logical circuits have a given number of inputs and one output. Impulses may be applied to the inputs of a given logical circuit and it will either respond by giving an output (signal 1) or will give no output (signal 0). The input impulses are of the same kind as the outputs, i.e. 1 (positive input) or 0 (no input).

In this example a logical circuit is to be built up of NOR gates. A NOR gate is a device with two inputs and one output. It has the property that there is positive output (signal 1) if and only if *neither* input is positive, i.e. both inputs have value 0. By connecting such gates together with outputs from one gate possibly being inputs into another gate it is possible to construct a circuit to perform any desired logical function. For example the circuit illustrated in Figure 12.1 will respond to the inputs A and B in the way indicated by the truth table.

A	B	Output
0	0	0
0	1	0
1	0	0
1	1	1

Figure 12.1

The problem here is to construct a circuit using the *minimum number* of NOR gates which will perform the logical function specified by the truth table in Figure 12.2. This problem, together with further references to it, is discussed in Williams (1974).

Inputs		Output
A	B	
0	0	0
0	1	1
1	0	1
1	1	0

Figure 12.2

'Fan-in' and 'fan-out' are not permitted. That is, more than one output from a NOR gate cannot lead into one input. Nor can one output lead into more than one input.

It may be assumed throughout that the optimal design is a 'subnet' of the 'maximal' net shown in Figure 12.3.

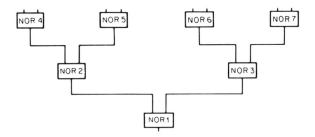

Figure 12.3

12.13 Market Sharing

A large company has two divisions D1 and D2. The company supplies retailers with oil and spirit.

It is desired to allocate each retailer to either division D1 or division D2. This division will be his supplier. As far as possible this division must be made so that D1 controls 40% of the market and D2 the remaining 60%. The retailers are listed below as M1 to M23. Each retailer has an estimated market for oil and spirit. Retailers M1 to M8 are in region 1; retailers M9 to M18 are in region 2; retailers M19 to M23 are in region 3. Certain retailers are considered to have good growth prospects and categorized as group A and the others are in group B. Each retailer has a certain number of delivery points as given below. It is desired to make the 40/60 split between D1 and D2 in each of the following respects:

(1) Total number of delivery points
(2) Control of spirit market
(3) Control of oil market in region 1
(4) Control of oil market in region 2
(5) Control of oil market in region 3
(6) Number of retailers in group A
(7) Number of retailers in group B

There is a certain flexibility in that any share may vary ± 5%. That is, the share can vary between the limits 35/65 and 45/55.

The primary aim is to find a feasible solution. If, however, there is some choice, then possible objectives are (i) to minimize the sum of the percentage deviations from the 40/60 split and (ii) to minimize the maximum such deviation.

Build a model to see if the problem has a feasible solution and if so find the optimal solutions.

The numerical data are given in Table 12.5.

Table 12.5

	Retailer	Oil market (10^6 gallons)	Delivery points	Spirit market (10^6 gallons)	Growth category
Region 1	M1	9	11	34	A
	M2	13	47	411	A
	M3	14	44	82	A
	M4	17	25	157	B
	M5	18	10	5	A
	M6	19	26	183	A
	M7	23	26	14	B
	M8	21	54	215	B
Region 2	M9	9	18	102	B
	M10	11	51	21	A
	M11	17	20	54	B
	M12	18	105	0	B
	M13	18	7	6	B
	M14	17	16	96	B
	M15	22	34	118	A
	M16	24	100	112	B
	M17	36	50	535	B
	M18	43	21	8	B
Region 3	M19	6	11	53	B
	M20	15	19	28	A
	M21	15	14	69	B
	M22	25	10	65	B
	M23	39	11	27	B

12.14 Opencast Mining

A company has obtained permission to opencast mine within a square plot 200 ft × 200 ft. The angle of slip of the soil is such that it is not possible for the sides of the excavation to be steeper than 45°. The company has obtained estimates for the value of the ore in various places at various depths. Bearing in mind the restrictions imposed by the angle of slip the company decides to consider the problem as one of the extracting of rectangular blocks. Each block has horizontal dimensions 50 ft × 50 ft and a vertical dimension of 25 ft. If the blocks are chosen to lie above one another, as illustrated in vertical section in Figure 12.4, then it is only possible to excavate blocks forming an

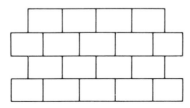

Figure 12.4

upturned pyramid. (In a three-dimensional representation Figure 12.4 would show four blocks lying above each lower block.)

If the estimates of ore value are applied to give values (in percentage of pure metal) for each block in the maximum pyramid which can be extracted then the following values are obtained:

Level 1
(surface)

1.5	1.5	1.5	0.75
1.5	2.0	1.5	0.75
1.0	1.0	0.75	0.5
0.75	0.75	0.5	0.25

Level 2
(25 ft depth)

4.0	4.0	2.0
3.0	3.0	1.0
2.0	2.0	0.5

Level 3
(50 ft depth)

12.0	6.0
5.0	4.0

Level 4
(75 ft depth)

6.0

The cost of extraction increases with depth. At successive levels the cost of extracting a block is:

Level 1	£3000
Level 2	£6000
Level 3	£8000
Level 4	£10 000

The revenue obtained from a '100% value block' would be £200 000. For each block here the revenue is proportional to ore value.

Build a model to help decide the best blocks to extract. The objective is to maximize revenue – cost.

12.15 Tariff Rates (Power Generation)

A number of power stations are committed to meeting the following electricity load demands over a day:

12 p.m. to 6 a.m.	15 000 megawatts
6 a.m. to 9 a.m.	30 000 megawatts
9 a.m. to 3 p.m.	25 000 megawatts
3 p.m. to 6 p.m.	40 000 megawatts
6 p.m. to 12 p.m.	27 000 megawatts

Table 12.6

	Minimum level	Maximum level	Cost per hour at minimum	Cost per hour per megawatt above minimum	cost
Type 1	850 MW	2000 MW	1000	2	2000
Type 2	1250 MW	1750 MW	2600	1·30	1000
Type 3	1500 MW	4000 MW	3000	3	500

There are three types of generating unit available. Twelve of type 1, ten of type 2, and five of type 3. Each generator has to work between a minimum and a maximum level. There is an hourly cost of running each generator at minimum level. In addition there is an extra hourly cost for each megawatt at which a unit is operated above minimum level. To start up a generator also involves a cost. All this information is given in Table 12.6 (with costs in £).

In addition to meeting the estimated load demands there must be sufficient generators working at any time to make it possible to meet an increase in load of up to 15%. This increase would have to be accomplished by adjusting the output of generators already operating within their permitted limits.

Which generators should be working in which periods of the day to minimize total cost?

What is the marginal cost of production of electricity in each period of the day; i.e. what tariffs should be charged?

What would be the saving of lowering the 15% reserve output guarantee; i.e. what does this security of supply guarantee cost?

12.16   Three-dimensional Noughts and Crosses

Twenty-seven cells are arranged in a $(3 \times 3 \times 3)$-dimensional array as shown in Figure 12.5.

Three cells are regarded as lying in the same line if they are on the same horizontal or vertical line or the same diagonal. Diagonals exist on each horizontal and vertical section and connecting opposite vertices of the cube. (There are 49 lines altogether.)

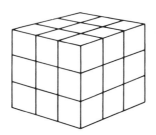

Figure 12.5

Given 13 white balls (noughts) and 14 black balls (crosses), arrange them, one to a cell, so as to minimize the number of lines with balls all of one colour.

12.17 Optimizing a Constraint

In an integer programming problem the following constraint occurs:

$$9x_1 + 13x_2 - 14x_3 + 17x_4 + 13x_5 - 19x_6 + 23x_7 + 21x_8 \leqslant 37.$$

All the variables occurring in this constraint are 0–1 variables, i.e. they can only take the value of 0 or 1.

Find the 'simplest' version of this constraint. The objective is to find another constraint involving these variables which is logically equivalent to the original constraint but which has the smallest possible absolute value of the right-hand side (with all coefficients of similar signs to the original coefficients).

If the objective were to find an equivalent constraint where the sum of the absolute values of the coefficients (apart from the right-hand side coefficient) were a minimum what would be the result?

12.18 Distribution

A company has two factories, one at Liverpool and one at Brighton. In addition it has four depots with storage facilities at Newcastle, Birmingham, London, and Exeter. The company sells its product to six customers C1, C2, ..., C6. Customers can be supplied from either a depot or from the factory direct (see Figure 12.6).

The distribution costs (wich are borne by the company) are known; they are given in Table 12.7 (in £ per ton delivered).

Figure 12.6

Table 12.7[a]

Supplied to	Supplier					
	Liverpool factory	Brighton factory	Newcastle depot	Birmingham depot	London depot	Exeter depot
Depots						
Newcastle	0·5	—				
Birmingham	0·5	0·3				
London	1·0	0·5				
Exeter	0·2	0·2				
Customers						
C1	1·0	2·0	—	1·0	—	—
C2	—	—	1·5	0·5	1·5	—
C3	1·5	—	0·5	0·5	2·0	0·2
C4	2·0	—	1·5	1	—	1·5
C5	—	—	—	0·5	0·5	0·5
C6	1·0	—	1·0	—	1·5	1·5

[a]A dash indicates the impossibility of certain suppliers for certain depots or customers.

Certain customers have expressed preferences for being supplied from factories or depots which they are used to. The preferred suppliers are

C1	Liverpool (factory)
C2	Newcastle (depot)
C3	No preferences
C4	No preferences
C5	Birmingham (depot)
C6	Exeter or London (depots)

Each factory has a monthly capacity given below which cannot be exceeded:

Liverpool	150 000 tons
Brighton	200 000 tons

Each depot has a maximum monthly throughput given below which cannot be exceeded:

Newcastle	70 000 tons
Birmingham	50 000 tons
London	100 000 tons
Exeter	40 000 tons

Each customer has a monthly requirement given below which must be met:

C1	50 000 tons
C2	10 000 tons
C3	40 000 tons
C4	35 000 tons

C5	60 000 tons
C6	20 000 tons

The company would like to determine:

(1) What distribution pattern would minimize overall cost?
(2) What the effect of increasing factory and depot capacities would be on distribution costs?
(3) What the effects of small changes in costs, capacities and requirements would be on the distribution pattern?
(4) Would it be possible to meet all customers preferences regarding suppliers and if so what would the extra cost of doing this be?

12.19 Depot Location (Distribution 2)

In the distribution problem there is a possibility of opening new depots at Bristol and Northampton as well as of enlarging the Birmingham depot.

It is not considered desirable to have more than four depots and if necessary Newcastle or Exeter (or both) can be closed down.

The monthly costs (in interest charges) of the possible new depots and expansion at Birmingham are given in Table 12.8 together with the potential monthly throughputs.

The monthly savings of closing down the Newcastle and Exeter depots are given in Table 12.9.

The distribution costs involving the new depots are given in Table 12.10 (in £ per ton delivered).

Which new depots should be built? Should Birmingham be expanded? Should Exeter or Newcastle be closed down? What would be the best resultant distribution pattern to minimize overall costs?

Table 12.8

	Cost (£1000)	Throughput (1000 tons)
Bristol	12	30
Northampton	4	25
Birmingham (expansion)	3	20

Table 12.9

	Saving (£1000)
Newcastle	10
Exeter	5

Table 12.10

	Supplier			
Supplied to	Liverpool factory	Brighton factory	Bristol depot	Northampton depot
New depots				
Bristol	0·6	0·4		
Northampton	0·4	0·3		
Customers				
C1			1·2	—
C2			0·6	0·4
C3	As given for		0·5	—
C4	distribution problem		—	0·5
C5			0·3	0·6
C6			0·8	0·9

12.20 Agricultural Pricing

The government of a country wants to decide what prices should be charged for its dairy products, milk, butter, and cheese. All these products arise directly or indirectly from the country's raw milk production. This raw milk is usefully divided into the two components of fat and dry matter. After subtracting the quantities of fat and dry matter which are used for making products for export or consumption on the farms there is a total yearly availability of 600 000 tons of fat and 750 000 tons of dry matter. This is all available for producing milk, butter, and two kinds of cheese for domestic consumption.

The percentage compositions of the products are given in Table 12.11.

For the previous year the domestic consumption and prices for the products are given in Table 12.12.

Price elasticities of demand, relating consumer demand to the prices of each product have been calculated on the basis of past statistics. The price elasticity E of a product is defined by

$$E = \frac{\text{percentage decrease in demand}}{\text{percentage increase in price}}.$$

Table 12.11

	Fat	Dry matter	Water
Milk	4	9	87
Butter	80	2	18
Cheese 1	35	30	35
Cheese 2	25	40	35

Table 12.12

	Milk	Butter	Cheese 1	Cheese 2
Domestic consumption (1000 tons)	4820	320	210	70
Price (£/ton)	297	720	1050	815

For the two makes of cheese there will be some degree of substitution in consumer demand depending on relative prices. This is measured by cross-elasticity of demand with respect to price. The cross elasticity E_{AB} from a product A to a product B is defined by

$$E_{AB} = \frac{\text{percentage increase in demand for A}}{\text{percentage increase in price of B}}.$$

The elasticities and cross-elasticities are given in Table 12.13 below.

The objective is to determine what prices and resultant demand will maximize total revenue.

It is, however, politically unacceptable to allow a certain price index to rise. As a result of the way this index is calculated this limitation simply demands that the new prices must be such that the total cost of last year's consumption would not be increased. A particularly important additional requirement is to quantify the economic cost of this political limitation.

Table 12.13

Milk	Butter	Cheese 1	Cheese 2	Cheese 1 to Cheese 2	Cheese 2 to Cheese 1
0·4	2·7	1·1	0·4	0·1	0·4

PART 3

CHAPTER 13

Formulation and Discussion of Problems

A suggested way of formulating each of the problems of Part 2 as a mathematical programming model is described. Each of these formulations is 'good' in the sense that it proved possible to solve the resultant model in a reasonable time on the computer system used. With some of the problems other formulations were tried only to show that computation times were prohibitive. It must be emphasized that although the formulations presented here are the best known to the author there are probably better formulations possible for some of the problems. Indeed one of the purposes of the latter part of this book is to present concrete problems which may help to advance the art of formulation.

All the models described here assume that a computer program is to be employed using one of the following algorithms:

(1) The revised simplex algorithm for linear programming problems.
(2) The branch and bound algorithm for integer programming problems.
(3) The separable extension to the revised simplex algorithm for separable programming problems.

It is these three algorithms that are most widely incorporated into commercial package programs.

For some of the problems more specialized algorithms might be more efficient. In practice the employment of such algorithms is often made difficult by the absence of efficient computer packages for handling large models. Where there is, however, obvious advantage to be gained from a specialized algorithm, this is pointed out in the discussion associated with the formulation description. This is particularly true where the model (or its dual) admits a network formulation. In such cases it should still, however, be possible to solve the model reasonably efficiently using one of the above three methods. Sometimes it is desirable to build a model in a particular way to suit a particular algorithm (particularly for integer programming problems). In the formulations here the models are all built on the assumption that one of the above three algorithms will be used.

Again, especially with integer programming models, it is often desirable to build a model with a particular branch and bound solution strategy in mind. When this is done the suggested strategy is explained.

272

Computational experience on a commercial system (XPRESS-MP) with the formulations suggested here is given with the solutions in Part 4.

13.1 Food Manufacture

Blending problems are frequently solved using linear programming. Linear programming has been used to find 'minimum cost' blends of fertilizer, metal alloys, clays, and many food products to name only a few. Applications are described in (for example) Fisher and Schruben (1953) and Williams and Redwood (1974).

The problem presented here has two aspects. Firstly it is a series of simple blending problems. Secondly there is a purchasing and storing problem. To understand how this problem may be formulated it is convenient to consider first the blending problem for only one month. This is the single-period problem which has already been presented as the second example in Section 1.2.

The Single-period Problem

If no storage of raw oils were allowed the problem of what to buy and how to blend in January could be formulated as follows:

Maximize

PROFIT $\quad -110x_1 - 120x_2 - 130x_3 - 110x_4 - 115x_5 + 150y$

subject to

VVEG $\quad x_1 + x_2 \leqslant 200,$

NVEG $\quad x_3 + x_4 + x_5 \leqslant 250,$

UHRD $\quad 8\cdot8x_1 + 6\cdot1x_2 + 2x_3 + 4\cdot2x_4 + 5x_5 - 6y \leqslant 0,$

LHRD $\quad 8\cdot8x_1 + 6\cdot1x_2 + 2x_3 + 4\cdot2x_4 + 5x_5 - 3y \geqslant 0,$

CONT $\quad x_1 + x_2 + x_3 + x_4 + x_5 - y = 0.$

The variables x_1, x_2, x_3, x_4, x_5 represent the quantities of the raw oils which should be bought respectively, i.e. VEG 1, VEG 2, OIL 1, OIL 2, and OIL 3. y represents the quantity of PROD which should be made.

The objective is to maximize profit which represents the income derived from selling PROD minus the cost of the raw oils.

The first two constraints represent the limited production capacities for refining vegetable and non-vegetable oils.

The second two constraints force the hardness of PROD to lie between its upper limit of 6 and its lower limit of 3. It is important to model these restrictions correctly. A frequent mistake is to model them as

$$8\cdot8x_1 + 6\cdot1x_2 + 2x_3 + 4\cdot2x_4 + 5x_5 \leqslant 6$$

and

$$8\cdot8x_1 + 6\cdot1x_2 + 2x_3 + 4\cdot2x_4 + 5x_5 \geqslant 3.$$

Such constraints are clearly dimensionally wrong. The expressions on the left have the dimension of hardness × quantity, whereas the figures on the right have the dimensions of hardness. Instead of the variables x_i in the above two inequalities expressions x_i/y are needed representing *proportions* of the ingredients rather than the absolute quantities x_i. When such replacements are made the resultant inequalities can easily be re-expressed in a linear form as the constraints UHRD and LHRD.

Finally it is necessary to make sure that the weight of the final product PROD is equal to the weight of the ingredients. This is done by the last constraint CONT which imposes this continuity of weight.

The single-period problems for the other months would be similar to that for January apart from the objective coefficients representing the raw oil costs.

The Multi-period Problem

The decisions of how to buy each month with a view to storing for use later can be incorporated into a linear programming model. To do this a 'multi-period' model is built. It is necessary, each month, to distinguish the quantities of each raw oil bought, used, and stored. These quantities must be represented by different variables. We suppose the quantities of VEG 1 bought, used, and stored in each successive month are represented by variables with the following names:

$$\text{BVEG 11,} \quad \text{BVEG 12,} \quad \text{etc.,}$$
$$\text{UVEG 11,} \quad \text{UVEG 12,} \quad \text{etc.,}$$
$$\text{SVEG 11,} \quad \text{SVEG 12,} \quad \text{etc.}$$

It is necessary to link these variables together by the relation

quantity stored in month $(t-1)$ + quantity bought in month t

$=$ quantity used in month t + quantity stored in month t

Initially (month 0) and finally (month 6) the quantities in store are constants (500). The relation above involving VEG 1 gives rise to the following constraints:

$$\text{BVEG 11} - \text{UVEG 11} - \text{SVEG 11} = -500,$$
$$\text{SVEG 11} + \text{BVEG 12} - \text{UVEG 12} - \text{SVEG 12} = 0,$$
$$\text{SVEG 12} + \text{BVEG 13} - \text{UVEG 13} - \text{SVEG 13} = 0,$$
$$\text{SVEG 13} + \text{BVEG 14} - \text{UVEG 14} - \text{SVEG 14} = 0,$$
$$\text{SVEG 14} + \text{BVEG 15} - \text{UVEG 15} - \text{SVEG 15} = 0,$$
$$\text{SVEG 15} + \text{BVEG 16} - \text{UVEG 16} = 500.$$

Similar constraints must be specified for the other five raw oils.

It may be more convenient to introduce variables SVEG 10, etc., and SVEG 16, etc., into the model and *fix* them at the value 500.

In the objective function the 'buying' variables will be given the appropriate raw oil costs in each month. The storage variables will be given the cost of £5 (or 'profit' of $-£5$). Separate variables PROD 1, PROD 2, etc., must be defined to represent the quantity of PROD to be made in each month. These variables will each have a profit of £150.

The resulting model will have the following dimensions as well as the single objective function:

$6 \times 5 = 30$ buying variables
$6 \times 5 = 30$ using variables
$5 \times 5 = 25$ storing variables
$\underline{6}$ product variables

Total 91 variables

$6 \times 5 = 30$ blending constraints (as in the single-period model)
$6 \times 5 = \underline{30}$ storage linking constraints

Total 60 constraints

It is also important to realize the use to which a model such as this might be put for medium term planning. By solving the model in January buying and blending plans could be determined for January together with provisional plans for the succeeding months. In February the model would probably be resolved with revised figures to give firm plans for February together with provisional plans for succeeding months up to and including July. By this means the best use is made of the information for succeeding months to derive an operating policy for the current month.

In order to investigate how the optimal solution changes with the increased prices in the future's market parametric programming can be used as described in Section 6.4. An additional expression is specified which is to be added to the objective function. For this model the expression is conveniently written as

$$x \sum_{t=2}^{6} (Ct \times \text{BVEG } 1t + Ct \times \text{BVEG } 2t + Dt \times \text{BOIL } 1t$$

$$+ Dt' \times \text{BOIL } 2t + Dt \times \text{BOIL } 3t.$$

The coefficients C and D take the following values:

$$C2 = -1, \quad D2 = -2,$$
$$C3 = -2, \quad D3 = -4,$$
$$C4 = -3, \quad D4 = -6,$$
$$C5 = -4, \quad D5 = -8,$$
$$C6 = -5, \quad D6 = -10.$$

As x is increased from 0 to 20 the composite objective function will take the desired forms and it will be possible to map out the changes in the optimal solution.

13.2   Food Manufacture 2

The extra restrictions stipulated are quite common in blending problems. It is often desired to: (i) limit the number of ingredients in a blend; (ii) rule out small quantities of one ingredient; and (iii) impose 'logical conditions' on the combinations of ingredients.

These restrictions cannot be modelled by conventional linear programming. Integer programming is the obvious way of imposing the extra restrictions. In order to do this it is necessary to introduce 0–1 integer variables into the problem as described in Section 9.2. For each 'using' variable in the problem a corresponding 0–1 variable will also be introduced. This variable will be used as an indicator of whether the corresponding ingredient appears in the blend or not. For example, corresponding to variable UVEG 11 a 0–1 variable DVEG 11 is introduced. These variables are linked together by two constraints. Supposing x_1 represents UVEG 11 and δ_1 represents DVEG 11 the following extra constraints are added to the model:

$$x_1 - 200\delta_1 \leqslant 0,$$
$$x_1 - 20\delta_1 \geqslant 0.$$

Since δ_1 is only allowed to take the integer values 0 and 1, x_1 can only be non-zero (i.e. VEG 1 in the blend in month 1) if $\delta_1 = 1$ and then it must be at a level of at least 20 tons. The constant 200 in the first of the above inequalities is a known upper limit to the level of UVEG 11 (the combined quantities of vegetable oils used in a month cannot exceed 200). Similar 0–1 variables and corresponding 'linkage' constraints are introduced for the other ingredients. Suppose x_2, x_3, x_4, and x_5 represent UVEG 21, UOIL 11, UOIL 21, and UOIL 31, then the following constraints and 0–1 variables are also introduced:

$$x_2 - 200\delta_2 \leqslant 0, \qquad x_2 - 20\delta_2 \geqslant 0,$$
$$x_3 - 250\delta_3 \leqslant 0, \qquad x_3 - 20\delta_3 \geqslant 0,$$
$$x_4 - 250\delta_4 \leqslant 0, \qquad x_4 - 20\delta_4 \geqslant 0,$$
$$x_5 - 250\delta_5 \leqslant 0, \qquad x_5 - 20\delta_5 \geqslant 0.$$

All these variables and constraints are repeated for all six months.

In this way condition 2 in the statement of the problem is automatically imposed. Condition 1 can be imposed by the constraint

$$\delta_1 + \delta_2 + \delta_3 + \delta_4 + \delta_5 \leqslant 3,$$

and the corresponding constraints for the other five months.

Condition 3 can be imposed in two possible ways. Firstly by the following single constraints,

$$\delta_1 + \delta_2 - 2\delta_5 \leqslant 0,$$

or by the pairs of constraints

$$\delta_1 - \delta_5 \leqslant 0,$$
$$\delta_2 - \delta_5 \leqslant 0.$$

There is computational advantage to be gained by using the second pair of constraints since they are 'tighter' in the continuous problem (see Section 10.1). Similar constraints are of course imposed for the other five months.

The model has now been augmented in the following way:

$$6 \times 5 = \underline{30} \quad \text{0–1 variables}$$

$$\text{Total} \quad 30 \quad \text{extra variables (all integer)}$$

$$2 \times 6 \times 5 = 60 \quad \text{linking constraints}$$
$$6 \quad \text{constraints for condition 1}$$
$$2 \times 6 = \underline{12} \quad \text{constraints for condition 3}$$

$$\text{Total} \quad 78 \quad \text{extra constraints}$$

It is also necessary to impose upper bounds of 1 on all the 30 integer variables.

There is probably advantage to be gained from the user specifying a priority order for the variables in order to control the tree search in the branch and bound algorithm. The six δ_5 variables (one for each month) were given priority in choosing branching variables.

13.3 Factory Planning

This example is typical of some very common applications of linear programming. The objective is to find the optimum 'product mix' subject to the production capacity and the marketing limitations. As with the food manufacture problem there are two aspects. Firstly there is the single-period problem then the extension to six months.

The Single-period Problem

If storage of finished products is not allowed, the model for January can be formuated as follows:

Maximize

PROFIT	$10x_1 +$	$6x_2 +$	$8x_3 +$	$4x_4 +$	$11x_5 +$	$9x_6 +$	$3x_7$	

subject to

GR	$0 \cdot 5x_1 +$	$0 \cdot 7x_2$			$+ 0 \cdot 3x_5$	$+ 0 \cdot 2x_6 +$	$0 \cdot 5x_7$	$\leqslant 1152$
VD	$0 \cdot 1x_1 +$	$0 \cdot 2x_2$		$+ 0 \cdot 3x_4$		$+ 0 \cdot 6x_6$		$\leqslant 768$
HD	$0 \cdot 2x_1$		$+ 0 \cdot 8x_3$				$+ 0 \cdot 6x_7$	$\leqslant 1152$
BR	$0 \cdot 05x_1 +$	$0 \cdot 03x_2$		$+ 0 \cdot 07x_4 +$	$0 \cdot 1x_5$		$+ 0 \cdot 08x_7$	$\leqslant 384$
PL			$0 \cdot 01x_3$		$+ 0 \cdot 05x_5$		$+ 0 \cdot 05x_7$	$\leqslant 384$
Market	500	1000	300	300	800	200	100	
(upper bounds)								

where GR, VD, HD, BR, and PL stand for, respectively, grinding, vertical drilling, horizontal drilling, boring and planing.

The variables x_i represent the quantities of PROD i to be made.

The single-period problems for the other months would be similar apart from different market bounds, and different capacity figures for the different types of machine.

The Multi-period Problem

It is necessary to distinguish each month the quantities of each product manufactured from the quantities sold and held over in storage. These quantities must be represented by different variables. Suppose the quantities of PROD 1 manufactured, sold, and held over in successive months are represented by variables with the following names:

$$\text{MPROD 11, \quad MPROD 12, \quad etc.,}$$
$$\text{SPROD 11, \quad SPROD 12, \quad etc.,}$$
$$\text{HPROD 11, \quad HPROD 12, \quad etc.}$$

It is necessary to link these variables together by the relation

quantity held in month $(t - 1)$ + quantity manufactured in month t

= quantity sold in month t + quantity held in month t

Initially (month 0) there is nothing held but finally (month 6) there are 50 of each product held: This relation involving PROD 1 gives rise to the following constraints:

$$\text{MPROD 11} - \text{SPROD 11} - \text{HPROD 11} = 0,$$
$$\text{HPROD 11} + \text{MPROD 12} - \text{SPROD 12} - \text{HPROD 12} = 0,$$
$$\text{HPROD 12} + \text{MPROD 13} - \text{SPROD 13} - \text{HPROD 13} = 0,$$
$$\text{HPROD 13} + \text{MPROD 14} - \text{SPROD 14} - \text{HPROD 14} = 0,$$
$$\text{HPROD 14} + \text{MPROD 15} - \text{SPROD 15} - \text{HPROD 15} = 0,$$
$$\text{HPROD 15} + \text{MPROD 16} - \text{SPROD 16} = 50,$$

Similar constraints must be specified for the other six products.

It may be more convenient to define also variables HPROD 16, HPROD 26, etc., and 'fix' them at the value 50.

In the objective function the 'selling' variables will be given the appropriate 'unit profit' figures and the 'holding' variables coefficients of $-0 \cdot 5$.

The resulting model has the following dimensions:

$$6 \times 7 = 42 \quad \text{manufacturing variables}$$
$$6 \times 7 = 42 \quad \text{selling variables}$$
$$6 \times 7 = \underline{42} \quad \text{holding variables}$$
$$\text{Total} \quad 126 \quad \text{variables}$$

$$6 \times 5 = \quad 30 \quad \text{capacity constraints}$$
$$6 \times 7 = \underline{\ 42\ } \quad \text{monthly linking constraints}$$
$$\text{Total} \quad 72 \quad \text{constraints}$$

In addition there are market bounds on the seven products in each month and the bounds on the holding quantities in each month. This gives a total of 84 upper bounds.

13.4 Factory Planning 2

The extra decisions which this problem requires over the factory planning problem requires the use of integer programming. This is a clear case of extending a linear programming model by adding integer variables with extra constraints.

It is convenient to number the different types of machine as below:

Type 1 Grinders
Type 2 Vertical drills
Type 3 Horizontal drills
Type 4 Borer
Type 5 Planer

Extra Variables

Integer variables γ_{it} are introduced with the following interpretations:

γ_{it} = number of machines of type i down from maintenance in month t;

$$\text{for } i = \begin{cases} 4, 5 & \gamma_{it} \text{ will have upper bounds of 1,} \\ 1, 2 & \gamma_{it} \text{ will have upper bounds of 2,} \\ 3 & \gamma_{it} \text{ will have upper bounds of 3.} \end{cases}$$

There are 30 such integer variables.

Revised Constraints

The machining capacity constraints in the original model must be changed since capacity will now depend on the values of γ_{it}. For example, the grinding capacity in month t will now be (in hours)

$$1536 - 384\gamma_{it}.$$

There will be similar expressions representing the capacities of other machines. The integer variables γ_{it} can be transferred to the left-hand side of the inequalities. As a result the single-period model for January would become:

Maximize

PROFIT $10x_1 + 6x_2 + 8x_3 + 4x_4 + 11x_5 + 9x_6 + 3x_7$

subject to

GR	$0 \cdot 5\ x_1 + 0 \cdot 7\ x_2$ $0 \cdot 3\ x_5 + 0 \cdot 2x_6 + 0 \cdot 5\ x_7 + 384\gamma_{11}$	$\leqslant 1536,$
VD	$0 \cdot 1\ x_1 + 0 \cdot 2\ x_2 + 0 \cdot 3\ x_4 + 0 \cdot 6x_6 + 384\gamma_{21}$	$\leqslant 768,$
HD	$0 \cdot 2\ x_1 + 0 \cdot 8\ x_3 + 0 \cdot 6\ x_7 + 384\gamma_{31}$	$\leqslant 1152,$
BR	$0 \cdot 05x_1 + 0 \cdot 03x_2 + 0 \cdot 07x_4 + 0 \cdot 1\ x_5 + 0 \cdot 08x_7 + 384\gamma_{41}$	$\leqslant 384,$
PL	$0 \cdot 01x_3 + 0 \cdot 05x_5 + 0 \cdot 05x_7 + 384\gamma_{51}$	$\leqslant 384.$

The upper market bounds would still apply together with upper bounds on the new integer variables.

The extension to a multi-period model would be similar to that described from the original problem.

It is necessary to ensure that each machine (apart from the grinders) is down for maintenance once in six months. This is achieved by the following constraints:

$$\sum_{t=1}^{6} \gamma_{it} = \begin{cases} 2 & \text{for} \quad i = 1, 2, \\ 3 & \text{for} \quad i = 3, \\ 1 & \text{for} \quad i = 4, \\ 1 & \text{for} \quad i = 5. \end{cases}$$

The new model therefore has five extra constraints.

Clearly the solution to the original problem implies a feasible (though probably non-optimal) solution to the new problem. The optimal objective value obtained there can usefully be used as a cut-off value in the tree search.

An alternative formulation is possible using a 0–1 variable to indicate for *each* machine whether it is down for maintenance in a particular month or not. Such a formulation would have more variables and suffer the drawback, mentioned in Section 10.1, of producing equivalent alternate solutions in the tree search.

13.5   Manpower Planning

A number of applications of linear programming to manpower planning have been published. Selected references are Davies (1973), Price and Piskor (1972), who apply goal programming, and Vajda (1975).

In order to formulate the problem presented here it will be assumed that everything happens on the first day of each year. Clearly this assumption is far from the truth. It is necessary to make some such assumption as it is only possible to represent quantities at discrete points of time if linear programming is to be applied.

On the first day of each year the following changes will take place simultaneously:

(1)   Men will be recruited into all categories.

(2) A certain proportion of these will leave immediately (less than one year's service).
(3) A certain proportion of last year's labour force will leave (more than one year's service).
(4) A certain number of men will be (simultaneously) retrained.
(5) A certain number of men will be declared redundant.
(6) A certain number of men will be put on short time.

Variables

Strength of Labour Force

t_{SKi} = number of skilled men employed in year i,
t_{SSi} = number of semi-skilled men employed in year i,
t_{USi} = number of unskilled men employed in year i.

Recruitment

u_{SKi} = number of skilled men recruited in year i,
u_{SSi} = number of semi-skilled men recruited in year i,
u_{USi} = number of unskilled men recruited in year i.

Retraining

v_{USSSi} = number of unskilled men retrained to semi-skilled in year i,
v_{SSSKi} = number of semi-skilled men retrained to skilled in year i,

Downgrading

v_{SKSSi} = number of skilled men downgraded to semi-skilled in year i,
v_{SKUSi} = number of skilled men downgraded to unskilled in year i,
v_{SSUSi} = number of semi-skilled men downgraded to unskilled in year i.

Redundancy

w_{SKi} = number of skilled men made redundant in year i,
w_{SSi} = number of semi-skilled men made redundant in year i,
w_{USi} = number of unskilled men made redundant in year i.

Short-time Working

x_{SKi} = number of skilled men on short-time working in year i,
x_{SSi} = number of semi-skilled men on short-time working in year i,
x_{USi} = number of unskilled men on short-time working in year i.

Overmanning

y_{SKi} = number of superfluous skilled men employed in year i,

y_{SSi} = number of superfluous semi-skilled men employed in year i,

y_{USi} = number of superfluous unskilled men employed in year i.

Constraints

Continuity

$$t_{SKi} = 0 \cdot 95 t_{SKi-1} + 0 \cdot 9 u_{SKi} + 0 \cdot 95 v_{SSSKi} - v_{SKSSi} - v_{SKUSi} - w_{SKi},$$

$$t_{SSi} = 0 \cdot 95 t_{SSi-1} + 0 \cdot 8 u_{SSi} + 0 \cdot 95 v_{USSSi} - v_{SSSKi} + 0 \cdot 5 v_{SKSSi} - v_{SSUSi} - w_{SSi},$$

$$t_{USi} = 0 \cdot 9 t_{USi-1} + 0 \cdot 75 u_{USi} - v_{USSSi} + 0 \cdot 5 v_{SKUSi} + 0 \cdot 5 v_{SSUSi} - w_{USi}.$$

Retraining Semi-skilled Men

$$v_{SSSKi} - 0 \cdot 25 t_{SKi} \leqslant 0.$$

Overmanning

$$y_{SKi} + y_{SSi} + y_{USi} \leqslant 150.$$

Requirements

$$t_{SKi} - y_{SKi} - 0 \cdot 5 x_{SKi} = 1000, 1500, 2000 \ (i = 1, 2, 3),$$

$$t_{SSi} - y_{SSi} - 0 \cdot 5 x_{SSi} = 1400, 2000, 2500 \ (i = 1, 2, 3),$$

$$t_{USi} - y_{USi} - 0 \cdot 5 x_{USi} = 1000, 500, \ \ 0 \ \ \ (i = 1, 2, 3),$$

Initial Conditions

The initial conditions are $t_{SK0} = 1000$, $t_{SS0} = 1500$, $t_{US0} = 2000$.

Some variables have upper bounds. These are (for $i = 1, 2, 3$):

Recruitment	Short-time working	Retraining
$u_{SKi} \leqslant 500$	$x_{SKi} \leqslant 50$	$v_{USSSi} \leqslant 200$
$u_{SSi} \leqslant 800$	$x_{SSi} \leqslant 50$	
$u_{USi} \leqslant 500$	$x_{USi} \leqslant 50$	

To minimize *redundancy* the objective function is

$$\sum_i (w_{SKi} + w_{SSSi} + w_{USi}).$$

To minimize *cost* the objective function is

$$\sum_i (400v_{\text{USS}i} + 500v_{\text{SSSK}i} + 200w_{\text{US}i} + 500w_{\text{SS}i} + 500w_{\text{SK}i}$$

$$+ 500x_{\text{US}i} + 400x_{\text{SS}i} + 400x_{\text{SK}i} + 1500y_{\text{US}i} + 2000y_{\text{SS}i}$$

$$+ 3000y_{\text{SK}i})$$

This formulation has 24 constraints and 60 variables as well as simple upper bounds on 21 variables.

With most packages it is convenient to incorporate both objectives into the model as 'non-constraint' rows. It is then possible to optimize both objectives within one computer run by means of the control program. In some packages it is possible to form a composite objective through the control program, taking a certain linear combination of the original objectives. Alternatively, one of the objectives can be made a constraint. For a model such as this, with only two objectives, the most efficient way of investigating their effect is to treat one as a constraint and to perform parametric programming on its right-hand side.

13.6   Refinery Optimization

The petroleum industry is the major user of linear programming models. This is a very small version of a typical application. Generally the models used will consist of thousands of constraints, linking together possibly more than one oil refinery, giving a structured model as described in Section 4.1. The application of linear programming in the petroleum industry is described by Manne (1956).

Variables

In view of the many different sorts of variables in a model of this sort it is convenient to use mnemonic names in this description of the formulation. The following variables are used to represent quantities of the materials (measured in barrels):

CRA	Crude 1
CRB	Crude 2
LN	Light naphtha
MN	Medium naphtha
HN	Heavy naphtha
LO	Light oil
HO	Heavy oil
R	Residuum

LNRG	Light naphtha used to produce reformed gasoline
MNRG	Medium naphtha used to produce reformed gasoline
HNRG	Heavy naphtha used to produce reformed gasoline
RG	Reformed gasoline
LOCGO	Light oil used to produce cracked oil and cracked gasoline
HOCGO	Heavy oil used to produce cracked oil and cracked gasoline
CG	Cracked gasoline
CO	Cracked oil
LNPMF	Light naphtha used to produce premium motor fuel
LNRMF	Light naphtha used to produce regular motor fuel
MNPMF	Medium naphtha used to produce premium motor fuel
MNRMF	Medium naphtha used to produce regular motor fuel
HNPMF	Heavy naphtha used to produce premium motor fuel
HNRMF	Heavy naphtha used to produce regular motor fuel
RGPMF	Reformed gasoline used to produce premium motor fuel
RGRMF	Reformed gasoline used to produce regular motor fuel
CGPMF	Cracked gasoline used to produce premium motor fuel
CGRMF	Cracked gasoline used to produce regular motor fuel
LOJF	Light oil used to produce jet fuel
HOJF	Heavy oil used to produce jet fuel
RJF	Residuum used to produce jet fuel
COJF	Cracked oil used to produce jet fuel
RLBO	Residuum used to produce lube-oil
PMF	Premium motor fuel
RMF	Regular motor fuel
JF	Jet fuel
FO	Fuel oil
LBO	Lube-oil

There are 36 such variables.

Constraints

Availabilities

The limited availability of the crude oils gives simple upper bounding constraints:

$$CRA \leqslant 20\,000,$$
$$CRB \leqslant 30\,000.$$

Capacities

The distillation capacity constraint is

$$CRA + CRB \leqslant 45\,000.$$

The reforming capacity constraint is

$$LNRG + MNRG + HNRG \leqslant 10\,000.$$

The cracking capacity constraint is

$$LOCGO + HOCGO \leqslant 8000.$$

The stipulation concerning production of lube-oil gives the following lower and upper bounding constraints:

$$LBO \geqslant 500,$$
$$LBO \leqslant 1000.$$

Continuities

The quantity of light naphtha produced depends on the quantities of the crude oil used, taking into account the way in which each crude splits under distillation. This gives

$$-0 \cdot 1CRA - 0 \cdot 15CRB + LN = 0.$$

Similar constraints exist for MN, HN, LO, HO, and R.

The quantity of reformed gasoline produced depends on the quantities of the naphthas used in the reforming process. This gives the constraint

$$-0.6LNRG - 0 \cdot 52MNRG - 0 \cdot 45\,HNRG + RG = 0.$$

The quantities of cracked oil and cracked gasoline produced depend on the quantities of light and heavy oil used. This gives the constraints

$$-0 \cdot 68LOCGO - 0 \cdot 75HOCGO + CO = 0,$$

$$-0 \cdot 28LOCGO - 0 \cdot 2HOCGO + CG = 0.$$

The quantity of lube-oil produced (and sold) is $0 \cdot 5$ times the quantity of residuum used. This gives

$$-0 \cdot 5RLBO + LBO = 0.$$

The quantities of light naphtha used for reforming and blending are equal to the quantities available. This gives

$$-LN + LNRG + LNPMF + LNRMF = 0.$$

Similar constraints exist for MN and HN.

The quantities of light oil used for cracking and blending are equal to the quantities available.

For the blending of fuel oil the proportion of light oil is *fixed* at 10/18. Therefore separate variables have not been introduced for this proportion since it is determined by the variable LO. This gives

$$-LO + LOCGO + LOJF + 0 \cdot 55FO = 0.$$

Similar constraints exist for HO, CO, and R, also involving *fixed proportions* of FO, and for CG and RG.

The quantity of premium motor fuel produced is equal to the total quantity of its ingredients. This gives

$$- LNPMF - MNPMF - HNPMF - RGPMF - CGPMF + PMF = 0$$

Similar constraints exist for RMF and JF.

Premium motor fuel production must be at least 40% of regular motor fuel production, giving

$$PMF - 0 \cdot 4RMF \geqslant 0.$$

Qualities

It is necessary to stipulate that the octane number of premium motor fuel does not drop below 94. This is done by the constraint

$$- 90LNPMF - 80MNPMF - 70HNPMF - 115RGPMF - 105CGPMF$$
$$+ 94PMF \leqslant 0.$$

There is a similar constraint for RMF.

For jet fuel we have the constraint imposed by vapour pressure. This is

$$- LOJF - 0 \cdot 6HOJF - 1 \cdot 5COJF - 0 \cdot 05RJF + JF \geqslant 0.$$

This model has 29 constraints together with simple bounds on three variables.

Some comment should be made concerning the blending of fuel oil where the ingredients (light, heavy, and cracked oil and residuum) are taken in *fixed* proportions. Here it might be preferable to think of the production of FO as an *activity*. It is common in the oil industry to think in terms of activities rather than quantities. In Section 3.4 *modal formulations* are discussed where activities represent the extreme *modes* of operation of a process. Here we have a special case of this of a process with one mode of operation. The level of this activity then fixes the proportions of the ingredients, in a case such as this, automatically.

Objective

The only variables involving a profit (or cost) are the final products. This gives an objective (in £) to be maximized of

$$7PMF + 6RMF + 4JF + 3 \cdot 5FO + 1 \cdot 5LBO.$$

13.7   Mining

This problem has a combinatorial character. In each year a choice of up to three out of the four possible mines must be chosen for working. There are 15 ways of doing this each year, giving a total of 15^5 possible ways of working over five years. For larger problems with, say, 15 mines being considered over 20 years the number of possibilities will be astronomic. By using integer programming, with the branch and bound method, only a fraction of these possibilities need be investigated.

0–1 variables are introduced to represent decisions whether to work or not to work a particular mine in a certain year. The different sorts of variables are described below.

Variables

$$\delta_{it} = \begin{cases} 1 & \text{if mine } i \text{ is worked in year } t, \\ 0 & \text{otherwise.} \end{cases}$$

There are 20 such 0–1 integer variables.

$$\gamma_{it} = \begin{cases} 1 & \text{if mine } i \text{ is 'open' in year } t \text{ (i.e. royalities are payable)} \\ 0 & \text{otherwise.} \end{cases}$$

There are 20 such 0–1 integer variables.

$$x_{it} = \text{output from mine } i \text{ in year } t \text{ (millions of tons).}$$

There are 20 such continuous variables

$$q_t = \text{quantity of blended ore produced in year } t \text{ (millions of tons).}$$

There are five such continuous variables.
In total there are therefore 65 variables of which 40 are integer.

Constraints

$$x_{it} - M_i \delta_{it} \leqslant 0 \text{ for all } i, t.$$

M_i is the maximum yearly output from mine i. This constraint implies that if mine i is not worked in year t there can be no output from it in that year. There are 20 such constraints.

$$\sum_{i=1}^{4} \delta_{it} \leqslant 3 \text{ for all } t.$$

This constraint allows no more than three mines to be worked in any year. There are five such constraints.

$$\delta_{it} - \gamma_{it} \leqslant 0 \text{ for all } i, t.$$

According to this constraint, if mine i is 'closed' in year t it cannot be worked in that year. There are 20 such constraints.

$$\gamma_{it+1} - \gamma_{it} \leqslant 0 \quad \text{for all } i, t < 5.$$

This forces a mine to be closed in all years subsequent to that in which it is first closed. There are 16 such constraints.

$$\sum_{i=1}^{4} Q_i x_{it} - P_t q_t = 0 \text{ for all } t.$$

Q_i is the quality of the ore from mine i and P_t the quality required in year t. There are five such blending constraints.

$$\sum_{i=1}^{4} x_{it} - q_t = 0 \text{ for all } t.$$

This constraint ensures that the tonnage of blended ore in each year equals the combined tonnage of the constituents. There are five such constraints.

In total there are 71 constraints

Objective

The total profit consists of the income from selling the blended ore minus the royalties payable. This is to be maximized. It can be written

$$- \sum_{\substack{i=1,4 \\ t=1,5}} R_{it} \gamma_{it} + \sum_{t=1,5} I_t q_t.$$

R_t is the royalty payable on mine i in year t discounted at a rate of 10% per annum. I_t is the selling price of each ton of blended ore in year t discounted at a rate of 10% per annum. The advantage of this formulation of the problem over an alternative one is discussed by Williams (1978).

There would seem to be advantage in this model in working mines early in the hope that they may be closed permanently later. In addition the discounting of revenue gives an advantage to working mines early. The suggested solution strategy is therefore to branch on the variables δ_{it} giving priority to low values of t.

13.8 Farm Planning

This problem is based on that of Swart, Smith, and Holderby (1975). By only considering five years the model can be kept reasonably small but inevitably much of the realism is lost.

There are a number of different ways of formulating this problem. In the formulation suggested here a large number of variables are introduced whose values are effectively fixed by the constraints of the model. These variables represent the numbers of cows of different ages in each year. For example the number of cows of ages 1, 2, etc., in year 1 will be determined by the initial numbers of cows given in year 0. Similarly the numbers of cows of ages 2, 3, etc., in year 2 will be fixed. It would therefore be possible to calculate the values of all these variables and not introduce them into the model. While this would make for a more compact model it would not be as easy to understand.

Nor does it seem worthwhile to carry out manual calculation best done by a computer. The most satisfactory course of action is to REDUCE or PRESOLVE the model in order to determine the *fixed* values of these variables. Experience with doing this is reported with the solution in Part 4.

Variables

x_{it} = number of tons of grain grown on group i land in year t
y_t = number of tons of sugar beet grown in year t
z_t = number of tons of grain bought in year t
s_t = number of tons of grain sold in year t
u_t = number of tons of sugar beet bought in year t
v_t = number of tons of sugar beet sold in year t
l_t = extra labour recruited in year t (in units of 100 hours)
m_t = capital outlay in year t (in units of £200)
n_t = number of heifers sold at birth in year t
q_{jt} = number of cows of age j years in year t
r_t = number of cows of age 0 in year t
p_t = profit in year t
i = 1, 2, 3, 4; t = 1, 2, 3, 4, 5; j = 1, 2, ..., 12.

(A variable n_6 is also defined to allow heifers to be sold at the beginning of the sixth year.)

As with other planning models it is necessary to consider discrete intervals of time and assume changes occur once in each interval. In this case we assume changes occur once each year.

Constraints

Continuity

$$q_{1,t+1} = 0 \cdot 95 r_t \quad \text{for} \quad t = 1, 2, 3.$$
$$q_{2,t+1} = 0 \cdot 95 q_{1t} \quad \text{for} \quad t = 1, 2, 3.$$
$$q_{j+1,t+1} = 0 \cdot 98 q_{jt} \quad \text{for all } j > 1, \quad t = 1, 2, 3.$$

$$r_t = \frac{1 \cdot 1}{2} \sum_{j=2,11} q_{jt} - n_t \text{ for all } t.$$

Initial Conditions (Fixed Variables)

$$q_{j1} = 9 \cdot 5 \text{ for } j = 1, 2.$$
$$q_{j1} = 9 \cdot 8 \text{ for } j = 3, 4, ..., 12.$$

Accommodation

$$r_t + \sum_{j=1,11} q_{jt} \leqslant 130 + \sum_{k \leqslant t} m_k \text{ for all } t.$$

Grain Consumption

$$\sum_{j=2,11} q_{jt} \le \frac{1}{0\cdot 6}\left(\sum_{i=1,4} x_{it} + z_t - s_t\right) \text{ for all } t.$$

Sugar Beet Consumption

$$\sum_{j=2,11} q_{it} \le \frac{1}{0\cdot 7} (y_t + u_t - v_t) \text{ for all } t.$$

Grain Growing

$$x_{1t} \le 1\cdot 1 \times 20 \text{ for all } t,$$
$$x_{2t} \le 0\cdot 9 \times 30,$$
$$x_{3t} \le 0\cdot 8 \times 20,$$
$$x_{4t} \le 0\cdot 65 \times 10,$$

Acreage

$$\frac{1}{1\cdot 1} x_{1t} + \frac{1}{0\cdot 9} x_{2t} + \frac{1}{0\cdot 8} x_{3t} + \frac{1}{0\cdot 65} x_{4t} + \frac{1}{1\cdot 5} y_t + \frac{2}{3} r_t$$

$$+ \frac{2}{3} q_{1t} + \sum_{j=2,11} q_{jt} \le 200 \text{ for all } t$$

Labour (in 100 hours)

$$0\cdot 1 r_t + 0\cdot 1 q_{1t} + 0\cdot 42 \sum_{j=2,11} q_{jt}$$

$$+ 0\cdot 04\left(\frac{1}{1\cdot 1} x_{1t} + \frac{1}{0\cdot 9} x_{2t} + \frac{1}{0\cdot 8} x_{3t} + \frac{1}{0\cdot 65} x_{4t}\right)$$

$$+ \frac{0\cdot 14}{1\cdot 5} y_t \le 55 + l_t \text{ for all } t.$$

End total

$$\sum_{j=2,11} q_{j5} \le 175,$$

$$\sum_{j=2,11} q_{j5} \ge 50.$$

(This constraint may be specified by a *range* of 125 on the previous constraint.)

Profit

$$p_t = 30 \times \frac{1 \cdot 1}{2} \sum_{j=2,11} q_{jt}$$

$+ 40n_t$ (selling heifers) $+ 120q_{12}t$ (selling 12-year-old cows)

$+ 370 \sum_{j=2,11} q_{jt}$ (selling milk) $+ 75s_t$ (selling grain)

$+ 58v_t$ (selling sugar beet) $- 90z_t$ (buying grain)

$- 70u_t$ (buying sugar beet) $- 120l_t - 4000$ (labour) $- 50r_t$

$- 50q_{1t}$ (heifer costs) $- 100 \sum_{j=2,11} q_{jt}$ (dairy cow costs)

$- 15\left(\dfrac{1}{1 \cdot 1} x_{1t} + \dfrac{1}{0 \cdot 9} x_{2t} + \dfrac{1}{0 \cdot 8} x_{3t} + \dfrac{1}{0 \cdot 65} x_{4t}\right)$ (grain costs)

$- \dfrac{10}{1 \cdot 5} y_t$ (sugar beet costs) $- 39 \cdot 71 \sum_{k \leqslant t} m_k$ (capital costs) for all t.

(The annual repayment on a £200 loan is £39·71.)

Profit Can Never be Negative

$$p_t \geqslant 0 \text{ for all } t.$$

(The main effect of this constraint is to limit capital expenditure to cash available.)

Objective Function

In order to make capital expenditure as 'costly' in latter years as in former ones it is necessary to take account of repayments beyond the five years. This gives an objective function (to be maximized):

$$\sum_{t=1,5} p_t - 39 \cdot 71 \sum_{t=1,5} (4 + t)m_t.$$

The costs incurred by the repayments beyond the five years must be credited back when the final profit over the five years is obtained.

This model has 84 constraints and 130 variables.

13.9   Economic Planning

The model resulting from this problem is a dynamic Leontief model of the type mentioned in Section 5.2. A rather similar model has been considered by Wagner (1957).

Variables

x_{it} = total output of industry i in year t (i = C (coal), S (steel), T (transport), (t = 1, 2, ..., 5),

s_{it} = stock level of industry i at the beginning of year t,

y_{it} = extra productive capacity for industry i becoming effective in year t (t = 2, 3, ..., 6).

Constraints

Total Input

$$\sum_{j=1,3} c_{ij} x_{jt+1} + \sum_{j=1,3} d_{ij} y_{jt+2} \leqslant x_{it} + s_{it} - s_{it+1} - \text{exogenous demand for}$$

$$\text{industry } i \text{ for all } i, t$$

(s_{i0} are initial stocks given), where c_{ij} and d_{ij} are the input/output coefficients in the first three rows of Tables 12.1 and 12.2 respectively in the statement of the problem.

Manpower

$$0 \cdot 6 x_{Ct+1} + 0 \cdot 3 x_{St+1} + 0 \cdot 2 x_{Tt+1} + 0 \cdot 4 y_{Ct+2} + 0 \cdot 2 y_{St+2} + 0 \cdot 1 y_{Tt+2}$$

$$\leqslant 470 \text{ for all } t.$$

Productive Capacity

$$x_{it} \leqslant \text{initial capacity} + \sum_{l \leqslant t} y_{il} \text{ for all } i, t.$$
$$\text{of } i \text{ (year 0).}$$

In order to build a realistic model it is necessary to think beyond the end of the five year period. To ignore exogenous demand in the sixth and subsequent years would result in no inputs being accounted for in the fifth year. We therefore assume that exogenous demand remains constant up to and beyond year 5, the stock level remains constant, and that there is no increase in productive capacity after year 5. In order to find the inputs to each industry in year 5 we simply have to solve a *static Leontief model*:

$$\sum_{j} c_{ij} x_j = x_i - \text{endogenous demand for industry } i \qquad \text{for all } i.$$

x_i is the (static) output from industry i in year 5 and beyond.

This set of three equations gives lower limits to the variables, giving

$$x_C \geqslant 116 \cdot 4,$$
$$x_S \geqslant 105 \cdot 7,$$
$$x_T \geqslant 92 \cdot 3.$$

In the total output constraint above x_{it} will be set greater than or equal to these values for $t \geqslant 6$. y_{it} will be set to 0 for $t \geqslant 6$.

Objective Function

(i) Maximize

$$\sum_{\substack{i \\ l \leqslant 5}} y_{il}$$

(ii) Maximize

$$\sum_{\substack{i \\ t = 4,5}} x_{it}$$

(Exogenous demand is set to 0 with this objective.)
(iii) Maximize

$$\sum_{t} (0 \cdot 6 x_{Ct+1} + 0 \cdot 3 x_{St+1} + 0 \cdot 2 x_{Tt+1} + 0 \cdot 4 y_{Ct+2} + 0 \cdot 2 y_{St+2} + 0 \cdot 1 y_{Tt+2}).$$

(The manpower constraint is ignored with this objective.)

This model has 45 variables and 42 constraints.

13.10   Decentralization

This is a modified form of the quadratic assignment problem described in Section 9.5. Methods of solving such problems are described by Lawler (1974). The problem presented here is based on the problem described by Beale and Tomlin (1972). They treat their problem by linearizing the quadratic terms and reducing the problem to a 0–1 integer programming problem. We adopt the same approach here.

Variables

$$\delta_{ij} = \begin{cases} 1 & \text{if department } i \text{ is located in city } j(i = \text{A, B, C, D, E, } j = \text{L} \\ & \text{(London), S (Bristol), G (Brighton)),} \\ 0 & \text{otherwise.} \end{cases}$$

There are 15 such 0–1 variables.

$$\gamma_{ijkl} = \begin{cases} 1 & \text{if } \delta_{ij} = 1 \text{ and } \delta_{kl} = 1, \\ 0 & \text{otherwise.} \end{cases}$$

γ_{ijkl} is only defined for $i < k$ and $C_{ik} \neq 0$. There are 54 such 0–1 variables.

Constraints

Each department must be located in exactly one city. This gives the constraints

$$\sum_j \delta_{ij} = 1 \text{ for all } i.$$

There are five such constraints. These constraints can be treated as special ordered sets of type 1 as described in Section 9.3.

No city may be the location for more than three departments. This gives the constraints

$$\sum_j \delta_{ij} \leqslant 3 \text{ for all } j.$$

There are three such constraints.

Using the variables δ_{ij} together with the two types of constraint above, we could formulate a model with an objective function involving some quadratic terms $\delta_{ij}\delta_{kl}$. Instead these terms are replaced by the $0-1$ variables γ_{ijkl} giving a linear objective function. It is, however, necessary to relate these new variables to the δ_{ij} variables correctly. To do this we model the relations

$$\gamma_{ijkl} = 1 \rightarrow \delta_{ij} = 1, \ \delta_{kl} = 1$$

and

$$\delta_{ij} = 1, \ \delta_{kl} = 1 \rightarrow \gamma_{ijkl} = 1.$$

Following the discussion in Section 9.2 the first conditions can be achieved by the following constraints:

$$\gamma_{ijkl} - \delta_{ij} \leqslant 0 \text{ for all } i, j, k > i, l,$$
$$\gamma_{ijkl} - \delta_{kl} \leqslant 0 \text{ for all } i, j, k > i, l.$$

There are 108 such constraints.

The second conditions are achieved by the constraints

$$\delta_{ij} + \delta_{kl} - \gamma_{ijkl} \leqslant 1 \text{ for all } i, j, k > i, l.$$

There are 54 such constraints.

Objective

The objective is to minimize

$$-\sum_{i,j} B_{ij}\delta_{ij} + \sum_{\substack{i,j,k,l \\ i<k}} C_{ik} D_{jl} \gamma_{ijkl},$$

where B_{ij} is the benefit to be gained from locating department i in city j as given in Part 2 (for $j = $ L (London), $B_{ij} = 0$). C_{ik} and D_{ji} are given in the tables in Part 2, Section 12.10.

This model has 162 constraints and 69 variables (all $0-1$).

In order to illustrate some features of the matrix generator language MP-MODEL discussed in Section 3.5, this formulation is presented below in the MP-MODEL language.

```
MODEL    DECENT
LET NDEPTS  = 5
LET NCITIES = 3
TABLES
        BENEFIT(NDEPTS,NCITIES)
        DIST(NCITIES,NCITIES)
        COMM(NDEPTS,NDEPTS)
DATA
        BENEFIT(1,1)    =    10,   10,   0
        BENEFIT(2,1)    =    15,   20,   0
        BENEFIT(3,1)    =    10,   15,   0
        BENEFIT(4,1)    =    20,   15,   0
        BENEFIT(5,1)    =    5,    15,   0
        DIST(1,1)       =    5,    14,   13
        DIST(2,1)       =    14,   5,    9
        DIST(3,1)       =    13,   9,    10
        COMM(1,1)       =    0,    0,    1.0,  1.5,  0.0
        COMM(2,1)       =    0,    0,    1.4,  1.2,  0.0
        COMM(3,1)       =    0,    0,    0.0,  0.0,  2.0
        COMM(4,1)       =    0,    0,    0.0,  0.0,  0.7

VARIABLES
        D(NDEPTS,NCITIES)
        G(NDEPTS,NCITIES,NDEPTS,NCITIES)


CONSTRAINTS
        TCOST:-SUM(I=1:NDEPTS,J=1:NCITIES-1) BENEFIT(I,J)*D(I,J)      &
              +SUM(I=1:NDEPTS,J=1:NCITIES,K=I+1:NDEPTS,L=1:NCITIES)   &
                  (COMM(I,K)*DIST(J,L))*G(I,J,K,L)                    $

        DEPT(I=1:NDEPTS):  SUM(J=1:NCITIES) D(I,J) = 1
        CITY(J=1:NCITIES): SUM(I=1:NDEPTS)  D(I,J) < 3
        LOGA(I=1:NDEPTS-1,J=1:NCITIES,K=I+1:NDEPTS,L=1:NCITIES):      &
            G(I,J,K,L) < D(I,J)
        LOGB(I=1:NDEPTS-1,J=1:NCITIES,K=I+1:NDEPTS,L=1:NCITIES):      &
            G(I,J,K,L) < D(K,L)
        LOGC(I=1:NDEPTS-1,J=1:NCITIES,K=I+1:NDEPTS,L=1:NCITIES):      &
            D(I,J) + D(K,L) - G(I,J,K,L) < 1

BOUNDS
        D(I=1:NDEPTS,J=1:NCITIES) .BV.
        G(I=1:NDEPTS,J=1:NCITIES,K=I+1:NDEPTS,L=1:NCITIES) .BV.

GENERATE
```

Beale and Tomlin formulate their model much more compactly. As a consequence, the corresponding linear programming problem is much less constrained than it might be (see Section 10.1). They then expand some of the constraints, although not to the extent that has been done here. Use is then made of the branching strategy to avoid expanding other constraints.

13.11   Curve Fitting

This is an application of the goal programming type of formulation discussed in Section 3.3. Each pair of corresponding data values (x_i, y_i) gives rise to a constraint. For (1) and (2) these constraints are

$$bx_i + a + u_i - v_i = y_i, \qquad i = 1, 2, ..., 19.$$

x_i and y_i are constants (the given values); b, a, u_i, and v_i are variables. u_i and v_i give the amounts by which the values of y_i proposed by the linear expression differ from that observed. It is important to allow a and b to be 'free' variables, i.e. they can be allowed to take negative as well as positive values.

In case (1) the objective is to minimize

$$\sum_i u_i + \sum_i v_i.$$

This model has 19 constraints and 40 variables.

In case (2) it is necessary to introduce another variable z together with 38 more constraints:

$$z - u_i \geqslant 0, \qquad z - v_i \geqslant 0, \qquad i = 1, 2, \ldots, 19.$$

The objective, in this case, is simply to minimize z. This minimum value of z will clearly be exactly equal to the maximum value of v_i and u_i.

In case (3) it is necessary to introduce a new (free) variable c into the first set of constraints to give

$$cx_i^2 + bx_i + a + u_i - v_i = y_i, \qquad i = 1, 2, \ldots, 19.$$

The same objective functions as in (1) and (2) will apply.

It is much more usual in statistical problems to minimize the sum of squares of the deviations as the resultant curve often has desirable statistical properties. There are, however, some circumstances in which a sum of absolute deviations is acceptable or even more desirable. Moreover, the possibility of solving this type of problem by linear programming makes it computationally easy to deal with large quantities of data.

Minimizing the maximum deviation has certain attractions from the point of view of presentation. The possibility of a single data point appearing a long way off the fitted curve is minimized.

13.12 Logical Design

In order to simplify the formulation the optimal circuit can be assumed to be a subnet of the maximum shown in Figure 13.1.

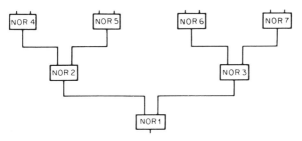

Figure 13.1

The following 0–1 integer variables are used:

$$s_i = \begin{cases} 1 & \text{if NOR gate } i \text{ exists, } i = 1, 2, ..., 7, \\ 0 & \text{otherwise;} \end{cases}$$

$$t_{i1} = \begin{cases} 1 & \text{if external input } A \text{ is an input to gate } i, \\ 0 & \text{otherwise;} \end{cases}$$

$$t_{i2} = \begin{cases} 1 & \text{if external input } B \text{ is an input to gate } i, \\ 0 & \text{otherwise;} \end{cases}$$

x_{ij} is the output from gate i for the combination of external input signals specified in the jth row of the truth table.

The following constraints are imposed.

A NOR gate can only have an external input if it exists. These conditions are imposed by the constraints

$$s_i - t_{i1} \geqslant 0, \qquad s_i - t_{i2} \geqslant 0, \qquad i = 1, 2, ..., 7.$$

If a NOR gate has one (or two) external inputs leading into it, only one (or no) NOR gates can feed into it. These conditions are imposed by the constraints:

$$s_j + s_k + t_{i1} + t_{i2} \leqslant 2, \qquad i = 1, 2, 3,$$

where j and k are the two NOR gates leading into i in Figure 13.1.

The output signal from NOR gate i must be the correct logical function (NOR) of the input signals into gate i if gate i exists. Let α_{1j} (a constant) be the value of the external input signal A in the jth row of the truth table. Similarly α_{2j} corresponds to the external input signal B. These conditions give

$$\begin{aligned} x_{jl} + x_{il} &\leqslant 1, \\ x_{kl} + x_{il} &\leqslant 1, \end{aligned} \qquad i = 1, 2, 3;$$

$$\begin{aligned} \alpha_{1l}t_{i1} + x_{il} &\leqslant 1, \\ \alpha_{2l}t_{i2} + x_{il} &\leqslant 1, \end{aligned} \qquad i = 1, 2, ..., 7;$$

$$\alpha_{1l}t_{i1} + \alpha_{2l}t_{i2} + x_{il} - s_i \geqslant 0, \qquad i = 4, 5, 6, 7;$$

$$\alpha_{1l}t_{i1} + \alpha_{2l}t_{i2} + x_{jl} + x_{kl} + x_{il} - s_i \geqslant 0, \qquad i = 1, 2, 3.$$

The above six classes of constraints are defined for $l = 1, 2, ..., 4$, where j and k are the NOR gates leading into gate i in Figure 13.1. Since the α_{ij} are constants, some of the above constraints are redundant for particular values of l and may be ignored.

For NOR gate 1 the x_{1l} variables are fixed at the values specified in the truth table, i.e.

$$x_{11} = 0, \qquad x_{12} = 1, \qquad x_{13} = 1, \qquad x_{14} = 0.$$

If there is an output signal of 1 from a particular NOR gate for any combination of the input signals, then that gate must exist.

$$s_i - x_{il} \geqslant 0, \qquad i = 1, 2, ..., 7, \qquad l = 1, 2, 3, 4.$$

In order to avoid a trivial solution containing no NOR gates it is necessary to impose a constraint such as

$$s_1 \geqslant 1.$$

The objective is to minimize $\sum_i s_i$.

This model has 154 constraints and 49 variables (all 0–1), including the four fixed variables. The redundant constraints are included in this total.

13.13 Market Sharing

This problem can be formulated as an integer programming model where each of the 23 retailers is represented by a 0–1 variable δ_i. If $\delta_i = 1$ retailer i is assigned to division D1. Otherwise he is assigned to division D2. Slack and surplus variables can be introduced into each constraint to provide the required objective which is to minimize the sum of the proportionate deviations from the desired 'goals' of the 40/60 splits. For example in the oil market in region 3 we have a total market of 100 (10^6 gallons). In order to split this 40/60 we have the constraint

$$6\delta_{19} + 15\delta_{20} + 15\delta_{21} + 25\delta_{22} + 39\delta_{23} + y_1 - y_2 = 40.$$

y_1 and y_2 are slack and surplus variables which are given a cost of $0 \cdot 01$ in the first objective function. y_1 and y_2 are also given simple upper bounds of 5. The other 'goal' constraints can be treated in a similar fashion.

In order to define the second 'minimax' objective we need to introduce a variable z together with the constraints

$$z - \frac{y_i}{w_i} \geqslant 0$$

for all slack and surplus variables y_i, where w_i is the total quantity for the 40% goal constraint with which y_i is associated. The second objective is then simply to minimize z.

The resultant model has 18 constraints and 36 variables of which 23 are 0–1.

As it stands this model is a correct representation of the problem but could prove difficult to solve since one feasible integer solution need bear no resemblance to another one. In consequence the tree search for the optimal integer solution could be fairly random. As the results in Section 14.13 suggest, this model did prove difficult to solve optimally. One approach to reformulating the problem is to replace some of the constraints by 'facet' constraints in the manner described in Section 10.2. For example the goal constraint above is equivalent to

$$6\delta_{19} + 15\delta_{20} + 15\delta_{21} + 25\delta_{22} + 39\delta_{23} \geqslant 35,$$
$$6\delta_{19} + 15\delta_{20} + 15\delta_{21} + 25\delta_{22} + 39\delta_{23} \leqslant 45.$$

The first of these constraints can be augmented by the following constraints obtained from strong covers:

$$\delta_{20} \qquad + \delta_{22} + \delta_{23} \geqslant 1,$$
$$\delta_{21} + \delta_{22} + \delta_{23} \geqslant 1,$$
$$\delta_{19} \qquad + \delta_{22} + \delta_{23} \geqslant 1,$$
$$\delta_{20} + \delta_{21} \qquad + \delta_{23} \geqslant 1.$$

The second of the constraints can be augmented by the constraints

$$\delta_{20} \qquad + \delta_{23} \leqslant 1,$$
$$\delta_{21} + \qquad + \delta_{23} \leqslant 1,$$
$$\delta_{22} + \delta_{23} \leqslant 1,$$
$$\delta_{19} + \delta_{20} \qquad + \delta_{22} + \delta_{23} \leqslant 2,$$
$$\delta_{19} \qquad + \delta_{21} + \delta_{22} + \delta_{23} \leqslant 2.$$
$$\delta_{20} + \delta_{21} + \delta_{22} + \delta_{23} \leqslant 2.$$

All the other constraints could be treated in a similar fashion. Unfortunately the number of such 'facet' constraints derivable from each of the goal constraints for (1) and (2) in the statement of the problem in Section 12.13 proved prohibitively large. There are, however, a large but manageable number which can be derived from (3) and (4) together with those above for (5)). In total the number of such constraints turned out to be 228. They were enumerated in a trivial amount of time on a microcomputer using the method described in Section 10.2.

It is still necessary to retain the original constraints, with their slack and surplus variables providing an objective function, since we are only adding in some of the 'facet' constraints for each goal constraint.

Unfortunately this augmented formulation proved difficult to solve largely as a result of its increased size.

A third possibility is to replace some of the goal constraints by *single* tighter constraints. How this may be done for a general 0–1 constraint is described by Bradley, Hammer, and Wolsey (1974). An example of such a single constraint simplification is provided by the problem OPTIMIZING A CONSTRAINT, in this book.

The three goal constraints for (3), (4), and (5) in Section 12.13 can be written as three pairs of constraints:

$$9\delta_1 + 13\delta_2 + 14\delta_3 + 17\delta_4 + 18\delta_5 + 19\delta_6 + 23\delta_7 + 21\delta_8 \leqslant 60,$$
$$9\delta_1 + 13\delta_2 + 14\delta_3 + 17\delta_4 + 18\delta_5 + 19\delta_6 + 23\delta_7 + 21\delta_8 \geqslant 46;$$
$$9\delta_9 + 11\delta_{10} + 17\delta_{11} + 18\delta_{12} + 18\delta_{13} + 17\delta_{14} + 22\delta_{15} + 24\delta_{16} + 36\delta_{17} + 43\delta_{18} \leqslant 96,$$
$$9\delta_9 + 11\delta_{10} + 17\delta_{11} + 18\delta_{12} + 18\delta_{13} + 17\delta_{14} + 22\delta_{15} + 24\delta_{16} + 36\delta_{17} + 43\delta_{18} \geqslant 75;$$
$$6\delta_{19} + 15\delta_{20} + 15\delta_{21} + 25\delta_{22} + 39\delta_{23} \leqslant 45,$$
$$6\delta_{19} + 15\delta_{20} + 15\delta_{21} + 25\delta_{22} + 39\delta_{23} \geqslant 35.$$

Using the method referenced above it is possible to give six constraints which have equivalent sets of 0–1 solutions but are 'tighter' in a *linear programming* sense. These are

$$5\delta_1 + 7\delta_2 + 8\delta_3 + 9\delta_4 + 10\delta_5 + 10\delta_6 + 13\delta_7 + 12\delta_8 \leqslant 33,$$

$$2\delta_1 + 3\delta_2 + 3\delta_3 + 4\delta_4 + 4\delta_5 + 4\delta_6 + 5\delta_7 + 5\delta_8 \geqslant 11,$$

$$8\delta_9 + 8\delta_{10} + 13\delta_{11} + 14\delta_{12} + 14\delta_{13} + 13\delta_{14} + 17\delta_{15} + 19\delta_{16} + 28\delta_{17} + 34\delta_{18} \leqslant 75,$$

$$8\delta_9 + 8\delta_{10} + 14\delta_{11} + 15\delta_{12} + 15\delta_{13} + 14\delta_{14} + 18\delta_{15} + 20\delta_{16} + 30\delta_{17} + 36\delta_{18} \geqslant 63;$$

$$\delta_{19} + 2\delta_{20} + 2\delta_{21} + 3\delta_{22} + 4\delta_{23} \leqslant 5,$$

$$\delta_{19} + 2\delta_{20} + 2\delta_{21} + 3\delta_{22} + 5\delta_{23} \geqslant 5.$$

Each of these constraints is the equivalent one, to the corresponding one above, which has smallest right-hand side coefficient. These tighter constraints were derived in a trivial amount of time using linear programming. Details of the method are described with the example, OPTIMIZING A CONSTRAINT, in Section 13.17.

It is still necessary to retain the original constraints with their slack and surplus variables needed in the objective function. This reformulation proved the most successful. Computational experience is given with the solution in Section 14.13.

13.14 Opencast Mining

This problem can be formulated as a pure 0–1 programming problem by introducing 0–1 variables δ_i and numbering the blocks:

$$\delta_i = \begin{cases} 1 & \text{if block } i \text{ is extracted,} \\ 0 & \text{otherwise} \end{cases}$$

If a block is extracted then the four blocks above it must also be extracted. Suppose, for example, that the numbering were such that blocks 2, 3, 4, and 5 were directly above 1. The condition could then be imposed by the four constraints

$$\delta_2 - \delta_1 \geqslant 0,$$
$$\delta_3 - \delta_1 \geqslant 0,$$
$$\delta_4 - \delta_1 \geqslant 0,$$
$$\delta_5 - \delta_1 \geqslant 0.$$

Similar constraints can be imposed for all other blocks (apart from those on the surface).

The objective is to maximize

$$\sum_i p_i \delta_i,$$

where

$$p_i = \text{profit from block } i \text{ (revenue} - \text{cost of extraction).}$$

This formulation has the extremely important property described in Section 10.1. Each constraint contains one coefficient $+1$ and one coefficient -1. This guarantees a *totally unimodular matrix*. If the model is solved as a continuous linear programming model, the optimal solution will be integer automatically. There is therefore no need to use, computationally much more costly, integer programming.

This property makes it possible to solve much larger versions of this problem in a reasonable amount of time. As described in Section 10.1 the dual of this linear programming model is a network flow problem and could be solved very efficiently by a specialized network flow algorithm (see Williams, 1982).

The model has 56 constraints and 30 variables. Each variable has an upper bound of 1.

13.15 Tariff Rates (Power Generation)

This problem is based on a model described by Garver (1963). The following formulation is suggested here.

Variables

n_{ij} = number of generating units of type i working in period j

(where $j = 1, 2, 3, 4,$ and 5 are the five periods of the day listed in the question);

s_{ij} = number of generators of type i started up in period j,

x_{ij} = total output rate from generators of type i in period j.

x_{ij} are continuous variables; n_{ij} and s_{ij} are general integer variables.

Constraints

Demand must be met in each period:

$$\sum_j x_{ij} \geqslant D_j \text{ for all } j,$$

where D_i is demand given in period j.

Output must lie within the limits of the generators working:

$$x_{ij} \geqslant m_i n_{ij} \text{ for all } i \text{ and } j,$$

$$x_{ij} \leqslant M_i n_{ij} \text{ for all } i \text{ and } j,$$

where m_i and M_i are the given minimum and maximum output levels for generators of type i.

The extra guaranteed load requirement must be able to be met without starting up any more generators:

$$\sum_i M_i n_{ij} \geqslant \frac{115}{100} D_j \text{ for all } j.$$

The number of generators started in period j must equal the increase in number:

$$s_{ij} \geqslant n_{ij} - n_{ij-1} \text{ for all } i \text{ and } j,$$

where n_{ij} is number of generators started in period j (when $j = 1$ period $j - 1$ is taken as 5).

In addition all the integer variables have simple upper bounds corresponding to the total number of generators of each type.

Objective Function (to be Minimized)

$$\text{Cost} = \sum_{i,j} C_{ij}(x_{ij} - m_i n_{ij}) + \sum_{i,j} E_{ij} n_{ij} + \sum_{i,j} F_i s_{ij},$$

where C_{ij} are costs per hour per megawatt above minimum level multiplied by the number of hours in the period. E_{ij} are costs per hour for operating at minimum level multiplied by the number of hours in the period. F_i are start-up costs.

This model has a total of 55 constraints and 30 simple upper bounds. There are 45 variables of which 30 are general integer variables.

13.16   Three-dimensional Noughts and Crosses

This 'pure' problem is included since it typifies the combinatorial character of quite a lot of integer programming problems. Clearly there are an enormous number of ways of arranging the balls in the three-dimensional array. Such problems often prove difficult to solve as integer programming models. There is advantage to be gained from using a heuristic solution first. This solution can then be used to obtain a cut-off value for the branch and bound tree search as described in Section 8.3. A discussion of two possible ways of formulating this problem is given in Williams (1974). The better of those formulations is described here.

Variables

The cells are numbered from 1 to 27. It is convenient to number sequentially row by row and section by section. Associated with each cell a 0−1 variable δ_j is introduced with the following interpretation:

$$\delta_j = \begin{cases} 1 & \text{if cell } j \text{ contains a black ball,} \\ 0 & \text{if cell } j \text{ contains a white ball.} \end{cases}$$

There are 27 such 0−1 variables.

There are 49 possible lines in the cube. With each of these lines we associate a 0–1 variable γ_i with the following interpretations:

$$\gamma_i = \begin{cases} 1 & \text{if all the balls in the line } i \text{ are of the same colour,} \\ 0 & \text{if there are a mixture of colours of ball in line } i. \end{cases}$$

There are 49 such 0–1 variables.

Constraints

We wish to ensure that the values of the variables γ_i truly represent the conditions above. In order to do this we have to model the condition

$$\gamma_i = 0 \rightarrow \delta_{i1} + \delta_{i2} + \delta_{i3} \geqslant 1 \quad \text{and} \quad \delta_{i1} + \delta_{i2} + \delta_{i3} \leqslant 2,$$

where $i1$, $i2$, and $i3$ are the numbers of the cells in line i.

This condition can be modelled by the constraints

$$\delta_{i1} + \delta_{i2} + \delta_{i3} - \gamma_i \leqslant 2,$$
$$\delta_{i1} + \delta_{i2} + \delta_{i3} + \gamma_i \geqslant 1,$$
$$i = 1, 2, \ldots, 49.$$

In fact these constraints do not ensure that if $\gamma_i = 1$ all balls will be of the same colour in the line. When the objective is formulated it will be clear that this condition will be guaranteed by optimality.

In order to limit the black balls to 14 we impose the constraint

$$\sum_j \delta_j = 14.$$

There are a total of 99 constraints.

Objective

In order to minimize the number of lines with balls of a similar colour we minimize

$$\sum_i \gamma_i.$$

In total this model has 99 constraints and 76 0–1 variables.

13.17 Optimizing a Constraint

A procedure for simplifying a single 0–1 constraint has been described by Bradley, Hammer, and Wolsey (1974). We adopt their procedure of using a linear programming model. It is convenient to consider the constraint in a standard form with positive coefficients in descending order of magnitude.

This can be achieved by the transformation:

$$y_1 = x_7, \quad y_2 = x_8, \quad y_3 = 1 - x_6, \quad y_4 = x_4,$$
$$y_5 = 1 - x_3, \quad y_6 = x_5, \quad y_7 = x_2, \quad y_8 = x_1$$

giving:

$$23y_1 + 21y_2 + 19y_3 + 17y_4 + 14y_5 + 13y_6 + 13y_7 + 9y_8 \leqslant 70$$

We wish to find another, equivalent constraint of the form:

$$a_1y_1 + a_2y_2 + a_3y_3 + a_4y_4 + a_5y_5 + a_6y_6 + a_7y_7 + a_8y_8 \leqslant a_0$$

The a_i coefficients become variables in the linear programming model. In order to capture the total logical import of the original constraint we search for subsets of the indices known as 'roofs' and 'ceilings'. 'Ceilings' are 'maximal' subsets of the indices of the variables for which the sum of the corresponding coefficients does not exceed the right-hand side coefficient. Such a subset is maximal in the sense that no subset properly containing it, or to the left in the implied lexicographical ordering can also be a ceiling. For example the subset $\{1, 2, 4, 8\}$ is a ceiling, $23 + 21 + 17 + 9 \leqslant 70$ but any subset property containing it (e.g. $\{1, 2, 4, 7, 8\}$) or to the 'left' of it (e.g. $\{1, 2, 4, 7\}$) is not a ceiling. 'Roofs' are 'minimal' subsets of the indices for which the sum of the corresponding coefficients exceeds the right-hand side coefficient. Such a subset is 'minimal' in the same sense as a subset is 'maximal'. For example $\{2, 3, 4, 5\}$ is a roof. $21 + 19 + 17 + 14 > 70$ but any subset properly contained in it (e.g. $\{3, 4, 5\}$) or to the 'right' of it (e.g. $\{2, 3, 4, 6\}$ is not a roof.

If $\{i_1, i_2, ..., i_r\}$ is a 'ceiling' the following condition among the new coefficients a_i is implied:

$$a_{i1} + a_{i2} + \cdots a_{ir} \leqslant a_0$$

If $\{i_1, i_2, ..., i_r\}$ is a 'roof' the following condition among the new coefficients a_i is implied:

$$a_{i1} + a_{i2} + \cdots a_{ir} \geqslant a_0 + 1$$

It is also necessary to guarantee the ordering of the coefficients. This can be done by the series of constraints:

$$a_1 \geqslant a_2 \geqslant a_3 \geqslant \cdots \geqslant a_8$$

If these constraints are given together with each constraint corresponding to a roof or ceiling then this is a sufficient set of conditions to guarantee that the new 0–1 constraint has exactly the same set of feasible 0–1 solutions as the original 0–1 constraint.

In order to pursue the first objective we minimize $a_0 - a_3 - a_5$ subject to these constraints.

For the second objective we minimize $\displaystyle\sum_{i=1}^{8} a_i$.

For this example the set of ceilings is

$\{1, 2, 3\}, \{1, 2, 4, 8\}, \{1, 2, 6, 7\}, \{1, 3, 5, 6\}, \{2, 3, 4, 6\}, \{2, 5, 6, 7, 8\}$

The set of roofs is

$\{1, 2, 3, 8\}, \{1, 2, 5, 7\}, \{1, 3, 4, 7\}, \{1, 5, 6, 7, 8\}, \{2, 3, 4, 5\}, \{3, 4, 6, 7, 8\}$

The resultant model has 19 constraints and nine variables.

If the constraint were to involve *general integer* rather than 0–1 variables, then we could still formulate the simplification problem in a similar manner after first converting the constraint to one involving 0–1 variables in the way described in Section 10.1. It is, however, necessary to ensure, by extra constraints in our LP model, the correct relationship between the coefficients in the simplified 0–1 form. How this may be done is described in Section 10.2.

13.18 Distribution

This problem can be regarded as one of finding the minimum cost flow through a network. Such network flow problems have been extensively treated in the mathematical programming literature. A standard reference is Ford and Fulkerson (1962). Specialized algorithms exist for solving such problems and are described in Ford and Fulkerson (1962), Jensen and Barnes (1980), Glover and Klingman (1977), and Bradley (1975).

It is, however, always possible to formulate such problems as ordinary linear programming models. Such models have the total unimodularity property described in Section 10.1. This property guarantees that the optimal solution to the LP problem will be integer as long as the right-hand side coefficients are integer.

We choose to formulate this problem as an ordinary LP model in order that we may use the standard revised simplex algorithm. There would be virtue in using a specialized algorithm. The special features of this sort of problem which make the use of a specialized algorithm worthwhile also, fortunately, make the problem fairly easy to solve as an ordinary LP problem. Sometimes, however, when formulated in this way the resultant model is very large. The use of a specialized algorithm then also becomes desirable as it results in a compact representation of the problem. As the example presented is very small, such considerations do not arise here.

The factories, depots, and customers will be numbered as below:

Factories	1	Liverpool
	2	Brighton
	1	Newcastle
Depots	2	Birmingham
	3	London
	4	Exeter
Customers	C1	to C6

Variables

$$x_{ij} = \text{quantity sent from factory } i \text{ to depot } j,$$
$$i = 1, 2, \quad j = 1, 2, 3, 4;$$
$$y_{ik} = \text{quantity sent from factory } i \text{ to customer } k,$$
$$i = 1, 2, \quad k = 1, 2, ..., 6;$$
$$z_{jk} = \text{quantity sent from depot } j \text{ to customer } k,$$
$$j = 1, 2, 3, 4, \quad k = 1, 2, ..., 6.$$

There are 44 such variables.

Constraints

Factory Capacities

$$\sum_{j=1}^{2} x_{ij} + \sum_{k=1}^{6} y_{ik} \leqslant \text{capacity}, \qquad i = 1, 2.$$

Quantity into Depots

$$\sum_{i=1}^{2} x_{ij} \leqslant \text{capacity}, \qquad j = 1, 2, 3, 4$$

Quantity out of Depots

$$\sum_{k=1}^{6} y_{jk} = \sum_{i=1}^{2} x_{ij}, \qquad j = 1, 2, 3, 4.$$

Customer Requirements

$$\sum_{i=1}^{2} y_{ik} + \sum_{j=1}^{4} z_{jk} = \text{requirement}, \qquad k = 1, 2, ..., 6.$$

The capacity, quantity and requirement figures are given with the statement of the problem in Part 2.

There are 16 such constraints.

Objectives

The first objective is to minimize cost. This is given by

$$\sum_{\substack{i=1 \\ j=1}}^{\substack{i=2 \\ j=4}} c_{ij} x_{ij} + \sum_{\substack{i=1 \\ k=1}}^{\substack{i=2 \\ k=6}} d_{ik} y_{ik} + \sum_{\substack{j=1 \\ k=1}}^{\substack{j=4 \\ k=6}} e_{jk} z_{jk},$$

where the coefficients c_{ij}, d_{ik}, and e_{jk} are given with the problem in Part 2.

The second objective will take the same form as that above, but this time the c_{ij}, d_{ik}, and e_{jk} will be difined as below:

$$d_{ik} = \begin{cases} 0 & \text{if customer } k \text{ prefers factory } i, \\ 1 & \text{otherwise} \end{cases}$$

$$e_{ik} = \begin{cases} 0 & \text{if customer } k \text{ prefers depot } j, \\ 1 & \text{otherwise} \end{cases}$$

$$c_{ij} = 0 \quad \text{for all } i, j.$$

This objective is to be minimized.

13.19 Depot Location (Distribution 2)

The linear programming formulation of the distribution problem can be extended to a *mixed integer* model to deal with the extra decisions of whether to build or close down depots. Extra 0–1 integer variables are introduced with the following interpretations:

$$\delta_1 = \begin{cases} 1 & \text{if the Newcastle depot is retained,} \\ 0 & \text{otherwise;} \end{cases}$$

$$\delta_2 = \begin{cases} 1 & \text{if the Birmingham depot is expanded,} \\ 0 & \text{otherwise;} \end{cases}$$

$$\delta_4 = \begin{cases} 1 & \text{if the Exeter depot is retained} \\ 0 & \text{otherwise;} \end{cases}$$

$$\delta_5 = \begin{cases} 1 & \text{if a depot is built at Bristol,} \\ 0 & \text{otherwise;} \end{cases}$$

$$\delta_6 = \begin{cases} 1 & \text{if a depot is built at Northampton,} \\ 0 & \text{otherwise;} \end{cases}$$

In addition extra continuous variables x_{i5}, x_{i6}, z_{5k}, and z_{6k} are introduced to represent quantities sent to and from the new depots.

The following constraints are added to the model.

If a depot is closed down or not built then nothing can be supplied to it or from it:

$$\sum_{i=1}^{2} x_{ij} \leqslant T_j \delta_j,$$

where T_j is the capacity of depot j.

From Brimingham the quantity supplied to and from the depot must lie within the extension:

$$\sum_{i=1}^{2} x_{i2} \leqslant 50 + 20\delta_2.$$

There can be no more than four depots (including Birmingham and

London):
$$\delta_1 + \delta_4 + \delta_5 + \delta_6 \leqslant 2.$$

In the objective function the new x_{ij} and z_{jk} variables are given their appropriate costs. The additional expression involving the δ_j variables is added to the objective function:

$$10\delta_1 + 3\delta_2 + 5\delta_4 + 12\delta_5 + 4\delta_6 - 15.$$

This model has 21 constraints and 65 variables (five are integer and 0–1).

13.20   Agricultural Pricing

This problem is based on that described by Louwes, Boot, and Wage (1963).

Let x_M, x_B, x_{C1}, and x_{C2} be the quantities of milk, butter, cheese 1, and cheese 2 consumed (in thousands of tons) and p_M, p_B, p_{C1}, and p_{C2} their respective prices (in £1000 per ton).

The limited availabilities of fat and dry matter give the following two constraints:

$$0 \cdot 04 x_M + 0 \cdot 8 \ x_B + 0 \cdot 35 x_{C1} + 0 \cdot 25 x_{c2} \leqslant 600,$$
$$0 \cdot 09 x_M + 0 \cdot 02 x_B + 0 \cdot 3 \ x_{C1} + 0 \cdot 4 \ x_{C2} \leqslant 750.$$

The price index limitation gives (measured in £1000)

$$4 \cdot 82 p_M + 0 \cdot 32 p_B + 0 \cdot 21 p_{C1} + 0 \cdot 07 p_{c2} \leqslant 1 \cdot 939.$$

The objective is to maximize $\sum_i x_i p_i$.

In addition the x variables are related to the p variables through the price elasticity relationships:

$$\frac{dx_M}{x_M} = -E_M \frac{dp_M}{p_M}, \qquad \frac{dx_B}{x_B} = -E_B \frac{dp_B}{p_B},$$

$$\frac{dx_{C1}}{x_{C1}} = -E_{C1} \frac{dp_{C1}}{p_{C1}} + E_{C1C2} \frac{dp_{C2}}{p_{C2}}, \qquad \frac{dx_{C2}}{x_{C2}} = -E_{C2} \frac{dx_{C2}}{p_{C2}} + E_{C2C1} \frac{dp_{C1}}{p_{c1}}.$$

These differential equations can easily be integrated to give the x variables as expressions involving the p variables. If these expressions are substituted in the above constraints and the objective function, non-linearities are introduced into the first two constraints as well as the objective function. The non-linearities could be separated and approximated to by piecewise linear functions as described in Section 7.4.

In order to reduce the number of non-linearities in the model, the relationships implied by the differential equations above can be approximated to by the linear relationships:

$$\frac{x_M - \bar{x}_M}{\bar{x}_M} = -E_M \frac{p_M - \bar{p}_M}{\bar{p}_M}, \qquad \frac{x_B - \bar{x}_B}{\bar{x}_B} = -E_B \frac{p_B - \bar{p}_B}{\bar{p}_B},$$

$$\frac{x_{C1} - \bar{x}_{C1}}{\bar{x}_{C1}} = -E_{C1} \frac{p_{C1} - \bar{p}_{C1}}{\bar{p}_{C1}} + E_{C1C2} \frac{p_{C2} - \bar{p}_{C2}}{\bar{p}_{C2}},$$

308

$$\frac{x_{C2} - \bar{x}_{C2}}{\bar{x}_{C2}} = -E_{C2}\frac{p_{C2} - \bar{p}_{C2}}{\bar{p}_{C2}} + E_{C2C1}\frac{p_{C1} - \bar{p}_{C1}}{\bar{p}_{C1}}.$$

$\bar{x}$ and $\bar{p}$ are the known quantities consumed with their prices for the previous year. The approximation can be regarded as warranted if the resultant values of x and p do not differ significantly from $\bar{x}$ and $\bar{p}$.

Using the above relationships to substitute for the x variables in the first two constraints and the objective function gives the model:

Maximize
$$-6492p_M^2 - 1200p_B^2 - 220p_{C1}^2 - 34p_{C2}^2 + 53p_{C1}p_{C2}$$
$$+ 6748p_M + 1184p_B + 420p_{C1} + 70p_{c2}$$

subject to
$$260p_M + 960p_B + 70\cdot25p_{C1} - 0\cdot6\ p_{C2} \geqslant 782,$$
$$584p_M + 24p_B + 55\cdot2\ p_{C1} + 5\cdot8\ p_{C2} \geqslant 35,$$
$$4\cdot82p_M + 0\cdot32p_B + 0\cdot21p_{C1} + 0\cdot07p_{C2} \leqslant 1\cdot939.$$

In addition it is necessary to represent explicitly the non-negativity conditions on the x variables. These give

$$p_M \leqslant 1\cdot039, \qquad p_B \leqslant 0\cdot987,$$
$$220p_{C1} - 26p_{C2} \leqslant 420,$$
$$-27p_{C1} + 34p_{C2} \leqslant 70.$$

This is a *quadratic programming model* as there are quadratic terms in the objective function. Special algorithms exist for obtaining a, possibly, *local optimum* such as that of Beale (1959). In order to solve the model with a standard package (if this does not have a quadratic programming facility) we can convert it into a separable form and approximate the non-linear terms by piecewise linear expressions.

In order to put this model into a separable form it is necessary to remove the term $p_{C1}p_{C2}$. This may be done by introducing a new variable q together with the constraint

$$p_{C1} - p_{C2} - 0\cdot194q = 0.$$

(It is important to allow q to be negative, if necessary, by incorporating it in the model as a 'free' variable.)

The objective function can then be written in the separable form (a sum of non-linear functions of *single* variables):

$$-6491p_M^2 - 1200p_B^2 - 193\cdot5p_{C1}^2 - 7\cdot5p_{C2}^2 - q^2 + 6748p_M + 1184p_B$$
$$+ 420p_{C1} + 70p_{C2}.$$

This transformation also demonstrates that the model is *convex* (as described in Section 7.2). Using a piecewise linear approximation to the non-linearities, there is therefore no danger of obtaining a local optimum with separable programming. In fact it is sufficient to use the conventional simplex algorithm. This will enable one to obtain a true (global) optimum.

The solution given in Part 4 is based on grids where p_i, q and p_i^2 and q^2 are defined in intervals of $0 \cdot 05$. It is only necessary to define the grids within the possible ranges of values which p_i and q can take. These ranges can be found by examining the constraints of the model or using liner programming to successively maximize and minimize the individual variables p_i and q subject to the constraints.

PART 4

CHAPTER 14

Solutions to Problems

Optimal solutions to the problems presented in Part 2 are given here. The main purpose in giving the solutions is to allow the reader to check solutions he may have obtained to the same problems. All the solutions given here result from the formulations presented in Part 3. Sometimes alternative optimal solutions are possible, as described in Section 6.2, although the optimal value of the objective function will be unique.

If the reader obtains a different solution to a problem from that given here he should attempt to validate his solution using the principles described in Section 6.1. In many cases it is realistic to take the solution given here to represent the current operating pattern in the situation being modelled. The different solution obtained can then be validated relative to this solution.

All the solutions presented here were obtained by solving the model formulated in Part 3 using the XPRESS-MP package MP-OPT running on a 33 MHz 486 PC. Full details of this package are given in the reference manual. For linear programming models the MAXIMISE or MINIMISE command was used and for the integer programming models this was followed by the GLOBAL command. More sophisticated integer programming solution strategies are possible. Their implementation requires reference to the manual. The purpose of this book is to concentrate on *model building*. Therefore experimentation with different solution strategies has not been attempted, although it would almost certainly result in a more efficient computation of the solutions.

For the linear and separable programming models the number of iterations taken to solve the models are given. These provide a fairly good indication of the computational difficulty. With integer programming models the number of nodes needed to complete the solution tree, and so obtain and prove optimality, is given.

14.1 Food Manufacture

The optimal policy is given in Table 14.1

The profit (income from sales−cost of raw oils) derived from this policy is £107 843. This figure includes storage costs for the last month.

There are alternative optimal solutions.

313

Table 14.1

	Buy	Use	Store
January	Nothing	22·2 tons VEG 1 177·8 tons VEG 2 250 tons OIL 3	477·8 tons VEG 1 322·2 tons VEG 2 500 tons OIL 1 500 tons OIL 2 250 tons OIL 3
February	250 tons OIL 2	200 tons VEG 2 250 tons OIL 3	477·8 tons VEG 1 122·2 tons VEG 2 500 tons OIL 1 750 tons OIL 2
March	Nothing	159·3 tons VEG 1 40·7 tons VEG 2 250 tons OIL 2	318·5 tons VEG 1 81·5 tons VEG 2 500 tons OIL 1 500 tons OIL 2
April	Nothing	159·3 tons VEG 1 40·7 tons VEG 2 250 tons OIL 2	159·3 tons VEG 1 40·7 tons VEG 2 500 tons OIL 1 250 tons OIL 2
May	500 tons OIL 3	159·3 tons VEG 1 40·7 tons VEG 2 250 tons OIL 2	500 tons OIL 1 500 tons OIL 3
June	659·3 tons VEG 1 540·7 tons VEG 2 750 tons OIL 2	159·3 tons VEG 1 40·7 tons VEG 2 250 tons OIL 2	500 tons each oil (stipulated)

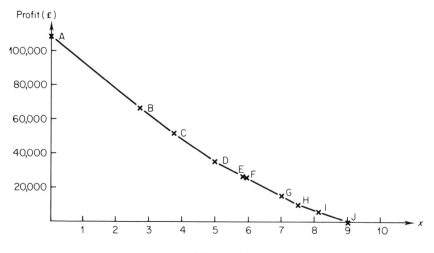

Figure 14.1

Table 14.2. Changes in optimal policy

	Value of parameter	Total profit (£)	Change in policy
A	0	107 843	Use OIL 2 in January Use OIL 2 in February *Cease to:* Use OIL 3 in January Buy OIL 3 in May
B	2·73	66 870	Use OIL 1 in June
C	3·75	51 593	Use OIL 3 in March Store OIL 2 in May *Cease to:* Use OIL 3 in February
D	5	35 343	Use VEG 1 in February Buy OIL 3 in March Use OIL 3 in April Buy VEG 1 in May Use OIL 3 in May *Cease to:* Use OIL 2 in March Use OIL 2 in April Buy OIL 2 in June
E	5·81	27 398	Buy OIL 1 in February Use OIL 2 in March *Cease to:* Store VEG 1 in April Use OIL 3 in May
F	5·93	26 231	*Cease to:* Use VEG 2 in June
G	7	15 768	Buy VEG 1 in January
H	7·5	10 907	Buy OIL 3 in January Store VEG 1 in April *Cease to:* Buy OIL 3 in March Buy VEG 1 in May
I	8·125	6 354	Use OIL 1 in April Use OIL 1 in May *Cease to:* Use VEG 2 in April Use VEG 2 in May
J	9	695	Buy VEG 2 in January Store VEG 1 in May *Cease to:* Buy VEG 2 in June

As would be expected, the optimal total profit progressively gets smaller as the parameter x increases. The optimal profit for increasing values of x is shown on the graph in Figure 14.1. When x reaches the value of 9·14 the optimal profit becomes negative and the graph is not continued beyond this point. Within certain ranges the optimal buying, manufacturing, and storing policies will remain the same (although the levels of these activities will change). The points at which changes in the optimal policy occur are marked B, C, D, etc. A represents the optimal solution using the original objective. As pointed out, however, above, there are alternative optimal solutions with this objective. When parametric programming is performed a change occurs to one of these alternative optimal solutions at A. The policy changes to effect this are given at A together with the policy changes at B, C, D, etc., in Table 14.2.

The total time to obtain the optimal solution together with the parametric run on the objective was 1 second. Some 56 iterations were needed to reach the optimum with the original objective and a further 34 iterations for the parametric run.

14.2   Food Manufacture 2

Table 14.3

	Buy			Use			Store		
January	Nothing			85·2	tons VEG	1	414·8	tons VEG	1
				114·8	tons VEG	2	385·2	tons VEG	2
				250	tons OIL	3	500	tons OIL	1
							500	tons OIL	2
							250	tons OIL	3
February	190	tons OIL	2	200	tons VEG	2	414·8	tons VEG	1
				230	tons OIL	2	185·2	tons VEG	2
				20	tons OIL	3	500	tons OIL	1
							460	tons OIL	2
							230	tons OIL	3
March	580	tons OIL	3	85·2	tons VEG	1	329·6	tons VEG	1
				114·8	tons VEG	2	70·4	tons VEG	2
				250	tons OIL	3	500	tons OIL	1
							460	tons OIL	2
							560	tons OIL	3
April	Nothing			155	tons VEG	1	174·6	tons VEG	1
				230	tons OIL	2	70·4	tons VEG	2
				20	tons OIL	3	500	tons OIL	1
							230	tons OIL	2
							540	tons OIL	3
May	Nothing			230	tons OIL	8	19·6	tons VEG	1
				20	tons OIL	3	70·4	tons VEG	2
							500	tons OIL	1
							520	tons OIL	3
June	480·4	tons VEG	1	200	tons VEG	2	500 tons		
	629·6	tons VEG	2	230	tons OIL	2	each oil		
	730	tons OIL	2	20	tons OIL	3	(stipulated)		

This model proved hard to solve. The optimal solution found is given in Table 14.3.

The profit (income from sales – cost of raw oils) derived from this policy is £100 279. There are alternative, equally good, solutions. This solution was obtained after 645 nodes. A total of 2007 nodes were examined to prove optimality. The whole run took 43 seconds.

14.3 Factory Planning

The optimal policy is given in Table 14.4.

This policy yields a total profit of £93 715.

Information on the value of acquiring new machines can be obtained from the *shadow prices* on the appropriate constraints. The value of an extra hour in the particular month when a particular type of machine is used to capacity is given below:

	Machines used to capacity	Value
January	Grinders	£8·57
February	Horizontal drills	£0·625
March	Borer	£200[a]

[a]The borer is not in use in March. This figure indicates the high value of putting it into use. As explained in Section 6.2 these figures only give the *marginal value* of increases in capacity and can only therefore be used as indicators. Further investigation can usefully be done by using parameteric programming.

This model was solved in 60 iterations and less than 1 second.

Table 14.4

	Manufacture		Sell		Hold	
January	500	PROD 1	500	PROD 1		
	888·6	PROD 2	888·6	PROD 2		
	382·5	PROD 3	300	PROD 3	82·5	PROD 3
	300	PROD 4	300	PROD 4		
	800	PROD 5	800	PROD 5		
	200	PROD 6	200	PROD 6		
February	700	PROD 1	600	PROD 1	100	PROD 1
	600	PROD 2	500	PROD 2	100	PROD 2
	117·5	PROD 3	200	PROD 3	100	PROD 5
	500	PROD 5	400	PROD 5	100	PROD 7
	300	PROD 6	300	PROD 6		
	250	PROD 7	150	PROD 7		

(*Continued*)

318

Table 14.4   (*cont.*)

	Manufacture		Sell		Hold	
March	400	PROD 6	100	PROD 1	Nothing	
			100	PROD 2		
			100	PROD 5		
			400	PROD 6		
			100	PROD 7		
April	200	PROD 1	200	PROD 1	Nothing	
	300	PROD 2	300	PROD 2		
	400	PROD 3	400	PROD 3		
	500	PROD 4	500	PROD 4		
	200	PROD 5	200	PROD 5		
	100	PROD 7	100	PROD 7		
May	100	PROD 2	100	PROD 2	100	PROD 3
	600	PROD 3	500	PROD 3	100	PROD 5
	100	PROD 4	100	PROD 4	100	PROD 7
	1100	PROD 5	1000	PROD 5		
	300	PROD 6	300	PROD 6		
	100	PROD 7				
June	550	PROD 1	500	PROD 1	50 of every	
	550	PROD 2	500	PROD 2	product	
	350	PROD 4	50	PROD 3	(stipulated)	
	550	PROD 6	300	PROD 4		
			50	PROD 5		
			500	PROD 6		
			50	PROD 7		

14.4   Factory Planning 2

There are a number of alternative optimal maintenance schedules. One such is to put the following machines down for maintenance in the following months:

January	—
February	one vertical drill, one horizontal drill
March	one grinder, two horizontal drills
April	one grinder, one borer, one planer
May	one vertical drill
June	—

This results in the production and marketing plans shown in Table 14.5.
These plans yield a total profit of £108 855.
There is therefore a gain of £15 140 over the six months by seeking an optimal maintenance schedule instead of the one imposed in the FACTORY PLANNING solution.

This solution was obtained in 191 nodes. The optimal objective value of £93 715 for the factory planning solution was used as an objective cut-off since this clearly corresponds to a known integer solution. A total of 3320 nodes were needed to prove optimality. Total run time was 39 seconds.

Table 14.5

	Manufacture		Sell		Hold	
January	500	PROD 1	500	PROD 1	Nothing	
	1000	PROD 2	1000	PROD 2		
	300	PROD 3	300	PROD 3		
	300	PROD 4	300	PROD 4		
	800	PROD 5	800	PROD 5		
	200	PROD 6	200	PROD 6		
	100	PROD 7	100	PROD 7		
February	600	PROD 1	600	PROD 1	Nothing	
	500	PROD 2	500	PROD 2		
	200	PROD 3	200	PROD 3		
	400	PROD 5	400	PROD 5		
	300	PROD 6	300	PROD 6		
	150	PROD 7	150	PROD 7		
March	400	PROD 1	300	PROD 1	100	PROD 1
	700	PROD 2	600	PROD 2	100	PROD 2
	100	PROD 3			100	PROD 3
	100	PROD 4			100	PROD 4
	600	PROD 5	500	PROD 5	100	PROD 5
	400	PROD 6	400	PROD 6		
	200	PROD 7	100	PROD 7	100	PROD 7
April	Nothing		100	PROD 1	Nothing	
			100	PROD 2		
			100	PROD 3		
			100	PROD 4		
			100	PROD 5		
			100	PROD 7		
May	100	PROD 2	100	PROD 2	Nothing	
	500	PROD 3	500	PROD 3		
	100	PROD 4	100	PROD 4		
	1000	PROD 5	1000	PROD 5		
	300	PROD 6	300	PROD 6		
June	550	PROD 1	500	PROD 1	50	PROD 1
	550	PROD 2	500	PROD 2	50	PROD 2
	150	PROD 3	100	PROD 3	50	PROD 3
	350	PROD 4	300	PROD 4	50	PROD 4
	1150	PROD 5	1100	PROD 5	50	PROD 5
	550	PROD 6	500	PROD 6	50	PROD 6
	110	PROD 7	60	PROD 7	50	PROD 7

14.5 Manpower Planning

With the objective of minimizing redundancy the optimal policies to pursue
are given below:

Recruitment

	Unskilled	Semi-skilled	Skilled
Year 1	0	0	0
Year 2	0	649	500
Year 3	0	677	500

Retraining and Downgrading

	Unskilled to semi-skilled	Semi-skilled to skilled	Semi-skilled to unskilled	Skilled to unskilled	Skilled to semi-skilled
Year 1	200	256	0	0	168
Year 2	200	80	0	0	0
Year 3	200	132	0	0	0

Redundancy

	Unskilled	Semi-skilled	Skilled
Year 1	445	0	0
Year 2	164	0	0
Year 3	232	0	0

Short-time Working

	Unskilled	Semi-skilled	Skilled
Year 1	50	50	50
Year 2	50	0	0
Year 3	50	0	0

Overmanning

	Unskilled	Semi-skilled	Skilled
Year 1	130	18	0
Year 2	150	0	0
Year 3	150	0	0

These policies result in a total redundancy of 842 over the three years. The total cost of pursuing these policies is £1 438 383.

In order to obtain this total cost it is important to recognize that there are alternative solutions and we should choose that with minimum cost.

If the objective is to minimize cost the optimal policies are those given below:

Recruitment

	Unskilled	Semi-skilled	Skilled
Year 1	0	0	55
Year 2	0	800	500
Year 3	0	800	500

Retraining and Downgrading

	Unskilled to semi-skilled	Semi-skilled to skilled	Semi-skilled to unskilled	Skilled to unskilled	Skilled to semi-skilled
Year 1	0	0	25	0	0
Year 2	142	105	0	0	0
Year 3	96	132	0	0	0

Redundancy

	Unskilled	Semi-skilled	Skilled
Year 1	812	0	0
Year 2	258	0	0
Year 3	354	0	0

Short-time Working

	Unskilled	Semi-skilled	Skilled
Year 1	0	0	0
Year 2	0	0	0
Year 3	0	0	0

Overmanning

	Unskilled	Semi-skilled	Skilled
Year 1	0	0	0
Year 2	0	0	0
Year 3	0	0	0

These policies cost £498 677 over the three years and result in a total redundancy of 1424 men. Again alternative solutions should be considered if necessary to ensure that this redundancy is the minimum possible for this (minimum) level of cost.

Clearly minimizing costs instead of redundancy saves £939 706, but results in 582 extra redundancies.

The cost of saving each job (when minimizing redundancy) could therefore be regarded as £1615.

With the objective of minimizing cost the model was solved in 26 iterations. This solution was then used as a starting solution to solve the model with the objective of minimizing redundancy. This took a further 3 iterations. The whole run took less than 1 second.

14.6 Refinery Optimization

The optimal solution results in a profit of £211 365.

The optimal values of the variables defined in Part 3 are given below:

CRA	15 000	MNPMF	3 537
CRB	30 000	MNRMF	6 962
LN	6 000	HNPMF	0
MN	10 500	HNRMF	2 993
HN	8 400	RGPMF	1 344
LO	4 200	RGRMF	1 089
HO	8 700	CGPMF	1 936
R	5 550	CGRMF	0
LNRG	0	LOJF	0
MNRG	0	HOJF	4 900
HNRG	5 407	RJF	4 550
RG	2 433	COJF	5 706
LOCGO	4 200	RLBO	1 000
HOCGO	3 800	PMF	6 818
CG	1 936	RMF	17 044
CO	5 706	JF	15 156
LNPMF	0	FO	0
LNRMF	6 000	LBO	500

This solution was obtained in 18 iterations and less than 1 second. There are alternative optimal solutions.

14.7 Mining

The optimal solution is as follows: work the following mines in each year

Year 1	Mines 1, 3, 4
Year 2	Mines 2, 3, 4
Year 3	Mines 1, 3

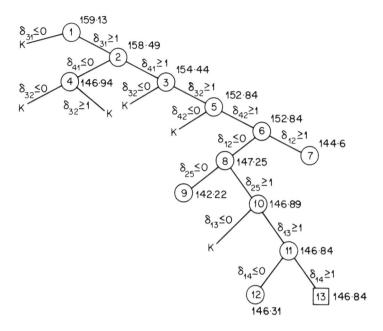

Figure 14.2

| | Year 4 | Mines 1, 2, 4 |
| | Year 5 | Mines 1, 2, 3 |

Keep every mine open each year apart from mine 4 in year 5.
Produce the following quantities of ore (in millions of tons) from each mine
every year:

	Mine 1	Mine 2	Mine 3	Mine 4
Year 1	2·0	—	1·3	2·45
Year 2	—	2·5	1·3	2·2
Year 3	1·95	—	1·3	—
Year 4	0·12	2·5	—	3·0
Year 5	2·0	2·17	1·3	—

Produce the following quantities of blended ore (in millions of tons) each
year:

Year 1	5·75
Year 2	6·00
Year 3	3·25
Year 4	5·62
Year 5	5·47

This solution results in a total profit of £146·84m. It was obtained (and proved) in 13 nodes using an objective cut-off of 140·0. The total run time was less than 1 second. The solution tree is given here in Figure 14.2 and was obtained using the priority order of variables for branching described with the formulation in Part 3.

The same model was used to produce the solution tree given in Section 8.3 as an illustration of the branch and bound method. There the solution strategy involved giving priority to the integer variables with highest objective coefficient. Using that less intelligent strategy, which takes no account of the physical meaning of the model required 25 nodes to obtain the above solution. A total of 32 nodes were required to prove optimality. The total run time was again less than 1 second.

14.8 Farm Planning

The optimal plan results in a total profit of £121 719 over the five years. Each year's detailed plan should be as follows:

Year 1   Grow 22 tons of grain on group 1 land
Grow 91 tons of sugar beet
Buy 37 tons of grain
Sell 23 tons of sugar beet
Sell 31 heifers (leaving 23)

The profit on the year will be £21 906.

Year 2   Grow 22 tons of grain on group 1 land
Grow 94 tons of sugar beet
Buy 35 tons of grain
Sell 27 tons of sugar beet
Sell 41 heifers (leaving 12)

The profit on the year will be £21 888.

Year 3   Grow 22 tons of grain on group 1 land
Grow 3 tons of grain on group 2 land
Grow 98 tons of sugar beet
Buy 38 tons of grain
Sell 25 tons of sugar beet
Sell 57 heifers (leaving none)

The profit on the year will be £25 816.

Year 4   Grow 22 tons of grain on group 1 land
Grow 115 tons of sugar beet
Buy 40 tons of grain
Sell 42 tons of sugar beet
Sell 57 heifers (leaving none)

The profit on the year will be £26 826.

Year 5   Grow 22 tons of grain on group 1 land
Grow 131 tons of sugar beet
Buy 33 tons of grain
Sell 67 tons of sugar beet
Sell 51 heifers (leaving none)

The profit on the year will be £25 283.

Only in year 1 does accommodation limit the total number of cows. No investment should be made in further accommodation.

At the end of the five year period there will be 92 dairy cows.

This solution was obtained in 39 iterations and 1 second.

14.9 Economic Planning

With the first objective (maximizing total productive capacity in year 5) the growth pattern shown in Table 14.6 results in a total productive capacity of £2142m in year 5. Quantities are in £m.

With the second objective (maximizing total production in the fourth and fifth years) the growth pattern shown in Table 14.7 results in a total output of £2619m in those years.

With the third objective (maximizing manpower requirements) the growth pattern shown in Table 14.8 results in a total manpower usage of £2450m.

The first objective obviously results in effort being concentrated on building

Table 14.6

	Year 1	Year 2	Year 3	Year 4	Year 5
Coal capacity	300	300	300	489	1512
Steel capacity	350	350	350	350	350
Transport capacity	280	280	280	280	280
Coal output	260·4	293·4	300	17·9	166·4
Steel output	135·3	181·7	193·1	105·7	105·7
Transport output	140·7	200·6	267·2	92·3	92·3
Manpower requirement	270·6	367	470	150	150
End of the year					
Coal stock	0	0	0	148·4	0
Steel stock	0	0	0	0	0
Transport stock	0	0	0	0	0

Table 14.7

	Year 1	Year 2	Year 3	Year 4	Year 5
Coal capacity	300	430·5	430·5	430·5	430·5
Steel capacity	350	350	350	359·4	359·4
Transport capacity	280	280	280	519·4	519·4
Coal output	184·8	430·5	430·5	430·5	430·5
Steel output	86·7	153·3	182·9	359·4	359·4
Transport output	141·3	198·4	225·9	519·4	519·4
Manpower requirement	344·6	384·2	470	470	150
End of the year					
Coal stock	31·6	16·4	0	0	0
Steel stock	11·5	0	0	0	176·5
Transport stock	0	0	0	0	0

Table 14.8

	Year 1	Year 2	Year 3	Year 4	Year 5
Coal capacity	300	316	320	366	859·4
Steel capacity	350	350	350	350	350
Transport capacity	280	280	280	280	280
Coal output	251·8	316	319·8	366·3	859·4
Steel output	134·8	179	224·1	223·1	220
Transport output	143·6	181·7	280	279·1	276
Manpower requirement	281·1	333·2	539·7	636·8	659·7
End of the year					
Coal stock	0	0	0	0	0
Steel stock	11	0	0	0	0
Transport stock	4·2	·0	0	0	0

up capacity in the coal industry. This happens because the production of extra coal capacity uses comparatively little output from the other industries.

With the second objective more effort is put into the transport industry. This results, in part, from the fact that transport uses less manpower than other industries.

With the third objective the coal industry is again boosted in view of its heavy manpower requirement.

With the first objective the model was solved in 27 iterations. A further 18 iterations were required to optimize the second objective. The third objective needed a further 18 iterations. The total run took 1 second.

14.10   Decentralization

The optimal solution is

> locate departments A and D in Bristol;
> locate departments B, C, and E in Brighton

This results in a yearly benefit of £80 000 but communications costs of £65 100. It is interesting to note that communication costs are also reduced by moving out of London in this problem since they would have been £78 000 if each department had remained in London.

The net yearly benefit (benefits less communication costs) is therefore £14 900.

This solution was obtained (and proved) in 2 seconds and 33 nodes.

14.11   Curve Fitting

(1) The 'best' straight line which minimizes the *sum of absolute deviations* is

$$y = 0 \cdot 6375x + 0 \cdot 5812.$$

This is line 1 shown in Figure 14.3. The sum of absolute deviations resulting from this line is $11 \cdot 46$.

(2) The 'best' straight line which minimizes the *maximum absolute deviation* is

$$y = 0 \cdot 625x - 0 \cdot 4.$$

This is line 2 shown in Figure 14.3. The maximum absolute deviation resulting from this line is $1 \cdot 725$. (Points $(3 \cdot 0, 3 \cdot 2)$, $(5 \cdot 0, 1 \cdot 0)$, and $(7 \cdot 0, 5 \cdot 7)$ all have this absolute deviation from the line.) In constrast line 1 allows point $(5 \cdot 0, 1 \cdot 0)$ to have an absolute deviation of $2 \cdot 77$. On the other hand, although line 2 allows no point to have an absolute deviation of more than $1 \cdot 725$, the sum of absolute deviations is $19 \cdot 95$ compared with the $11 \cdot 47$ resulting from line 1.

(3) The 'best' quadratic curve which minimizes the *sum of absolute deviations* is

$$y = 0 \cdot 0337x^2 + 0 \cdot 2945x + 0 \cdot 9823.$$

This is curve 1 shown in Figure 14.4. The sum of absolute deviations resulting from this curve is $10 \cdot 45$.

(4) The 'best' quadratic curve which minimizes the *maximum absolute deviation* is

$$y = 0 \cdot 125x^2 - 0 \cdot 625x + 2 \cdot 475.$$

This is curve 2 shown in Figure 14.4. The maximum absolute deviation resulting from this curve is $1 \cdot 475$. (Points $(0 \cdot 0, 1 \cdot 1)$, $(3 \cdot 0, 3 \cdot 2)$, $(5 \cdot 0, 1 \cdot 0)$, and $(7 \cdot 0, 5 \cdot 7)$ all have this absolute deviation from the curve.)

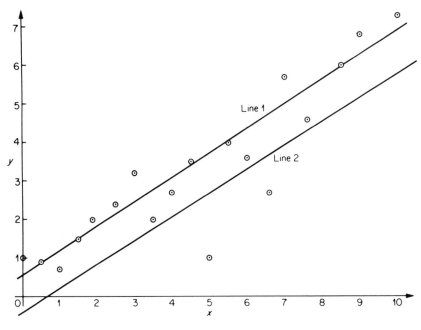

Figure 14.3

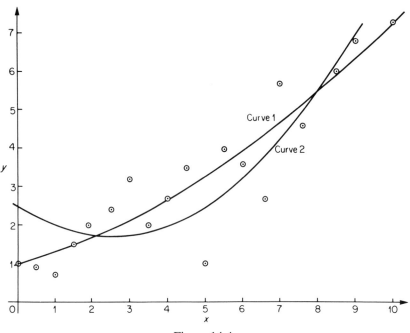

Figure 14.4

The optimal solution to (1) was obtained in 48 iterations. A further 32 iterations were needed to obtain the optimal solution to (2). The run time was 1 second.

The optimal solutions to (3) were obtained in 78 iterations, followed by a further 50 iterations. The run time was 1 second.

14.12   Logical Design

The optimal solution is shown in Figure 14.5. There are, of course, symmetric alternatives.

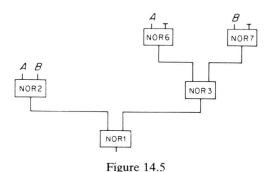

Figure 14.5

This solution was obtained in 10 nodes using an ADDCUT of $-0 \cdot 999$. The total run time was less than 1 second.

14.13   Market Sharing

This model proves difficult to solve optimally although a feasible solution is comparatively easy to obtain. Using the original formulation with no extra constraints a feasible solution was found after 21 nodes by minimizing the sum of percentage deviations. This solution gave a sum of percentage deviations of $8 \cdot 49$ with the maximum such deviation being $3 \cdot 73\%$ (the Region 3 OIL goal). The best solution obtained in this run was after 360 nodes with a sum of percentage deviations of $4 \cdot 53$, the maximum such deviation being $2 \cdot 5\%$ (the DELIVERY POINTS goal). After a total of 1995 nodes and 31 seconds the search was completed.

Minimizing the maximum percentage deviation produced a feasible solution after 37 nodes. This solution gave a maximum deviation of $2 \cdot 5\%$ (the OIL in region 3 goal). The sum of percentage deviations was $8 \cdot 82$. This was proved to be the optimal solution after 3158 nodes and 71 seconds.

The second formulation was obtained by adding 228 'facets' for the OIL goals in the three regions. The increased size of this model drastically reduced the number of nodes which could be explored in a given time. After 10 seconds with the objective of minimizing the sum of percentage deviations, 75 nodes had been explored with a minimum sum of percentage deviations of 11·28 obtained at node 61. The maximum deviation associated with this solution was 2·77% (the SPIRITS goal). When the objective was to minimize the maximum deviation, 36 nodes were explored in 10 seconds with no feasible solution being found.

The most successful formulation was the third one, where six single 'tighter' constraints, logically equivalent to the six constraints implied by the OIL goals in the three regions, were added. With the objective of minimizing the sum of percentage deviations a feasible solution was obtained after 35 nodes. The sum of percentage deviations was 8·83 and the maximum deviation was 2·5% (in the GROWTH prospects goals). This run was terminated after 394 nodes and 10 seconds with no other feasible solutions being found.

With the objective of minimizing the maximum deviation a feasible solution was found after 44 nodes with a maximum deviation of 3·15% (in the SPIRITS goal). The associated sum of percentage deviations was 12·14. A better solution was found at node 200 with a maximum deviation of 2·5% (in the GROWTH prospects goals). The associated sum of percentage deviations was 9·7. No better solutions were found after 10 seconds and 303 nodes.

With hindsight it is possible to observe that the minimax objective cannot be reduced below 2·5% since the slack variable in the GROWTH goal cannot be less than 0·2, given a right-hand side of 3·2. Therefore the slack in this constraint was *fixed* at 0·2 and the surplus at 0. The third formulation of the problem was then rerun in order to minimize the sum of percentage deviations. At node 681 the optimal integer solution was found where the sum of percentage deviations was 7·806. The solution was proved optimal after 889 nodes. Total run time was 17·4 seconds. This optimal solution allocates the following retailers to D1:

M1, M2, M3, M4, M11, M16, M18, M21, M22.

All other retailers are to be assigned to division D2.

14.14 Opencast Mining

The optimal solution is to extract the shaded blocks shown below. This results in a profit of £17 500.

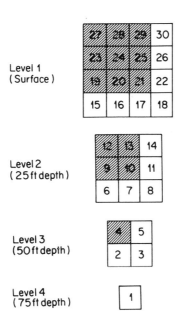

This solution was obtained in 28 iterations and less than 1 second.

14.15 Tariff Rates (Power Generation)

The following generators should be working in each period giving the following outputs:

Period 1	12 of type 1,	output	10 200 MW
	3 of type 2,	output	4 800 MW
Period 2	12 of type 1,	output	16 000 MW
	8 of type 2,	output	14 000 MW
Period 3	12 of type 1,	output	11 000 MW
	8 of type 2,	output	14 000 MW
Period 4	12 of type 1,	output	21 250 MW
	9 of type 2,	output	15 750 MW
	2 of type 3,	output	3 000 MW
Period 5	12 of type 1,	output	11 250 MW
	9 of type 2,	output	15 750 MW

The total daily cost of this operating pattern is £988 540.

Deriving the marginal cost of production from a mixed integer programming model such as this encounters the difficulties discussed in Section 10.3. We could adopt the approach of fixing the integer variables at the optimal integer values and obtaining this economic information from the resulting linear programming model. The marginal costs then result from any changes within the optimum operating pattern, i.e. without altering the numbers of different types of generator working in each period (although their levels of operation could vary).

The marginal costs of production per hour are then obtained from the shadow prices on the demand constraints (divided by the number of hours in the period). These give

Period 1   £1·3 per megawatt hour
Period 2   £2   per megawatt hour
Period 3   £2   per megawatt hour
Period 4   £2   per megawatt hour
Period 5   £2   per megawatt hour

With this method of obtaining marginal valuations there will clearly be no values associated with the reserve output guarantee constraints since all the variables have been fixed in these constraints.

As an alternative to using the above method of obtaining marginal valuations on the constraints, we could take the shadow prices corresponding to the continuous optimal solution. In this model this solution (the continuous optimum) does not differ radically from the integer optimum. It gives the following operating pattern which is clearly unacceptable in practice because of the fractional number of generators working:

Period 1	12 of type 1,	output 10 200 MW
	2·75 of type 2,	output 4 800 MW
Period 2	12 of type 1,	output 15 200 MW
	8·46 of type 2,	output 14 800 MW
Period 3	12 of type 1,	output 10 200 MW
	8·46 of type 2,	output 14 800 MW
Period 4	12 of type 1,	output 21 250 MW
	9·6 of type 2,	output 16 800 MW
	1·3 of type 3,	output 1 950 MW
Period 5	12 of type 1,	output 10 200 MW
	9·6 of type 2,	output 16 800 MW

The resulting objective value (cost) is £985 164.

The shadow prices on the demand constraints imply the following marginal cost of production:

Period 1   £1·76 per megawatt hour
Period 2   £2   per megawatt hour
Period 3   £1·79 per megawatt hour
Period 4   £2   per megawatt hour
Period 5   £1·86 per megawatt hour

In this case we can obtain a meaningful valuation for the 15% reserve output guarantee from the shadow prices on the appropriate constraints. The only non-zero valuation is on the constraint for period 4. This indicates that the cost of each guaranteed hour is £0·042. The ranges on the right-hand side coefficient of this constraint indicates that the 15% output guarantee can change between 2% and 52% with the marginal cost of each extra hour being £0·042.

The optimal solution was obtained (and proved) in less than 1 second and 29 nodes.

14.16   Three-dimensional Noughts and Crosses

The minimum number of lines of the same colour is four. There are many alternative solutions, one of which is given in Figure 14.6, where the top, middle, and bottom sections of the cube are given. Cells with black balls are shaded.

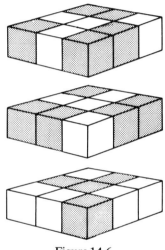

Figure 14.6

This solution was obtained in 15 nodes using an ADDCUT of $-0·999$. A total of 1367 nodes were needed to prove optimality. The total run time was 48 seconds.

14.17   Optimizing a Constraint

The 'simplest' version of this constriant (with minimum right-hand side coefficient) is

$$6x_1 + 9x_2 - 10x_3 + 12x_4 + 9x_5 - 13x_6 + 16x_7 + 14x_8 \leqslant 25.$$

This is also the equivalent constraint with the minimum sum of absolute values of the coefficients.

This solution was obtained in 16 iterations. The total run time was less than 1 second.

334

14.18   Distribution

The minimum cost distribution pattern is shown in Figure 14.7 (with quantities in thousands of tons).

There is an alternative optimal solution in which the 40 000 tons from Brighton to Exeter come from Liverpool instead.

This distribution pattern costs £198 500 per month.

Depot capacity is exhausted at Birmingham and Exeter. The value (in reducing distribution costs) of an extra ton per month capacity in these depots is £0·20 and £0·30 respectively.

This distribution pattern will remain the same as long as the unit distribution costs remain within certain ranges. These are given below (for routes which are to be used):

Route	Cost range
Liverpool to C1	$-\infty$ to 1·5
Liverpool to C6	$-\infty$ to 1·2
Brighton to Birmingham	$-\infty$ to 0·5
Brighton to London	0·3 to 0·8
Brighton to Exeter	$-\infty$ to 0·2
Birmingham to C2	$-\infty$ to 1·2
Birmingham to C4	$-\infty$ to 1·2
Birmingham to C5	0·3 to 0·7
London to C5	0·3 to 0·8
Exeter to C3	0 to 0·5

Depot capacities can be altered within certain limits. For the not fully utilized depots of Newcastle and London changing capacity within these limits has no effect on the optimal distribution pattern. For Birmingham and Exeter the effect on total cost will be £0·2 and £0·3 per ton per month within the limits. Outside certain limits the prediction of the effect requires resolving the problem. The limits are:

Depot	Capacity range
Birmingham	45 000 to 105 000 tons
Exeter	40 000 to 95 000 tons

N.B. All the above effects of changes are only valid if *one* thing is changed at a time within the permitted ranges. Clearly the above solution does not satisfy the customer preferences for suppliers.

By minimizing the second objective it is possible to reduce the number of goods sent by non-preferred suppliers to a customer to a minimum. This was done and revealed that it is impossible to satisfy all preferences. The best that could be done resulted in the distribution pattern shown in Figure 14.8, where

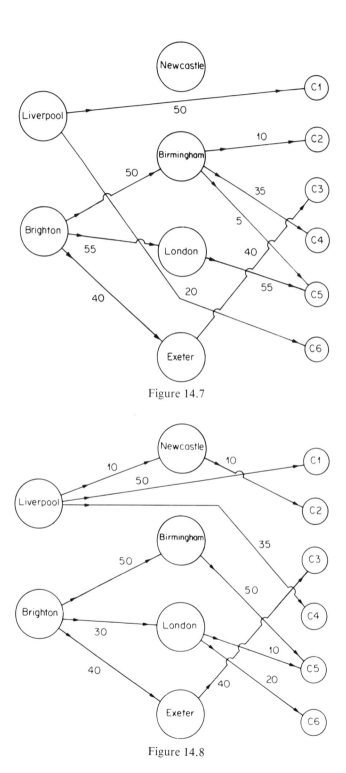

Figure 14.7

Figure 14.8

customer C5 receives 10 000 tons from his non-preferred depot of London. This is the minimum cost such distribution pattern. (There are alternative patterns which also minimize the number of non-preferences but which cost more). The minimum cost here is £246 000, showing that the extra cost of satisfying more customers preferences is £47 500.

The solution with the first objective was obtained in 19 iterations. Six more iterations were needed to obtain the solution which minimized non-preferences. The total run time was 1·32 seconds.

14.19 Depot Location (Distribution 2)

The minimum cost solution is to close down the Newcastle depot and open a depot in Northampton. The Birmingham depot should be expanded. The total monthly cost (taking account of the saving from closing down Newcastle) resulting from these changes and the new distribution pattern is £174 000. Figure 14.9 shows the new distribution pattern (with quantities in thousands of tons).

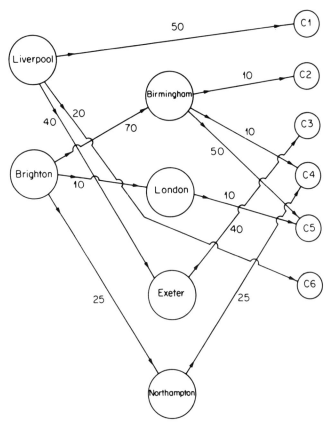

Figure 14.9

This solution was obtained in 40 iterations. The continuous optimal solution was integer. Therefore no tree search was necessary. Total run time was less than 1 second.

14.20 Agricultural Pricing

The optimal prices are

Milk	£304 per ton
Butter	£667 per ton
Cheese 1	£889 per ton
Cheese 2	£1064 per ton

The resultant yearly revenue will be £1992m. It is straightforward to calculate the yearly demands which will result from these prices. They are

Milk	4 775 000 tons
Butter	383 000 tons
Cheese 1	252 000 tons
Cheese 2	57 000 tons

The economic cost of imposing a constraint on the price index can be obtained from the shadow price on the constraint. For this example this shadow price in the optimal solution indicates that each £1 by which the new prices are allowed to increase the cost of last year's consumption would result in an increased revenue of £0·62.

This solution was obtained in 44 iterations and less than 1 second.

References

Agarwala, R., and G. C. Goodson, (1970), A linear programming approach to designing an optimum tax package, *Opl Res.*, **21**, 181–192.

Ashford, R. W., and R. C. Daniel, (1992), Some lessons in solving practical integer programs, *J. Opl Res. Soc.*, **43**, 425–433.

Atkins, D., (1974), Managerial decentralisation and decomposition in mathematical programming, *Opl Res. Q.*, **25**, 615–624.

Aucamp, D. C., and D. I. Steinberg, (1982), The computation of shadow prices in linear programming, *J. Opl Res. Soc.*, **33**, 557–565.

Babayer, D. A., (1975), Mathematical models for optimal timing of drilling on multilayer oil and gas fields, *Mgmt Sci.*, **21**, 1361–1369.

Balas, E., (1965), An additive algorithm for solving linear programs with zero-one variables, *Ops Res.*, **13**, 517–546.

Balas, E., (1975), Facets of the knapsack polytope, *Math. Prog.*, **8**, 146–164.

Balas, E, and M. W. Padberg, (1975), On the set covering problem II, *Ops Res.*, **23**, 74–90.

Balm, I. R., (1980), LP applications in Scottish agriculture, *J. Opl Res. Soc.*, **31**, 387–392.

Bass, F. M., and R. T. Lonsdale, (1966), An exploration of linear programming in media selection, *J. Marketing Res.*, **3**, 179–188.

Baston, V. J. D., M. K. Rahmouni, and H. P. Williams, (1991), The practical conversion of linear programmes to network flow models, *Eur. J. Opl Res.*, **50**, 325–335.

Beale, E. M. L., (1959), On quadratic programming, *Naval Res. Logist. Q.*, **6**, 227–243.

Beale, E. M. L., (1968), *Mathematical Programming in Practice*, Pitman, London.

Beale, E. M. L., (1975), Some uses of mathematical programming systems to solve problems that are not linear, *Opl Res. Q.*, **26**, 609–618.

Beale, E. M. L., (1980), Branch and bound methods for numerical optimisation of non-convex functions, in M. M. Barritt and D. Wishart (Eds), *COMPSTAT 80: Proceedings in Computational Statistics*, pp. 11–20, Physica Verlag, Wien.

Beale, E. M. L., G. C. Beare, and P. B. Tatham, (1974), The DOAE reinforcement and redeployment study: a case study in mathematical programming, in P. L. Hammer and G. Zoutendijk (Eds), *Mathernatical Programming in Theory and Practice*, North-Holland, Amsterdam.

Beale, E. M. L., P. A. B. Hughes, and R. E. Small, (1965), Experiences in using a decomposition program, *Comp. J.*, **8**, 13–18.

Beale, E. M. L., and J. A. Tomlin, (1969), Special facilities in a general mathematical programming system for non-convex problems using ordered sets of variables, in J. Lawrence (Ed.), *Proceedings of the 5th International Conference on Operations, Research*, Tavistock, London.

Beale, E. M. L., and J. A. Tomlin, (1972), An integer programming approach to a class of combinatorial problems, *Math. Prog.*, **1**, 339–344.

Beard, C. N., and C. T. McIndoe, (1970), The determination of the least cost mix of transport aircraft, ships and stockpiled material to provide British forces with adequate strategic mobility in the future, in E. M. L. Beale (Ed.), *Applications of Mathematical Programming Techniques*, English University Press, London.

Benders, J. F., (1962), Partitioning procedures for solving mixed-variable programming problems, *Numer. Math.*, **4**, 238–252.

Bixby, R. E., and W. H. Cunningham, (1980), Converting linear programmes to network problems, *Math. Op. Res.*, **5**, 321–357.

Bradley, G. H., (1971), Transformation of integer programs to knapsack problems, *Discrete Math.*, **1**, 29–45.

Bradley, G. H., (1975), Survey of deterministic networks *AIIE Trans.*, **7**, 222–234.

Bradley, G. H., P. L. Hammer, and L. Wolsey, (1974), Coefficient reduction for inequalities in 0–1 variables, *Math. Prog.*, **7**, 263–282.

Brearley, A. L., (1975), An investigation into the effects of different algorithmic heuristics on different formulations of the paint blending problem, Working Paper 27, School of Industrial and Business Studies, Unversity of Warwick, UK.

Brearley, A. L., G. Mitra, and H. P. Williams, (1975), Analysis of mathematical programming problems prior to applying the simplex algorithm, *Math. Prog.*, **8**, 54–83.

Buchanan, J. T., and K. I. M. McKinnon, (1987), An animated interactive modelling system for decision support, in G. Rand (Ed.), *Proceedings of IFORS 87*, North Holland, Amsterdam.

Catchpole, A. R., (1962), An application of LP to integrated supply problems in the oil industry, *Opl Res. Q.*, **13**, 163–169.

Charnes, A., and W. W. Cooper, (1959), Chance constrained programming, *Mgmt Sci.*, **6**, 73–79.

Charnes, A., and W. W. Cooper, (1961a), Multicopy traffic models, in R. Herman (Ed.), *Theory of Traffic Flow*, Elsevier, Amsterdam.

Charnes, A., and W. W. Cooper, (1961b), *Management Models and Industrial Applications of Linear Programming*, Wiley, New York.

Charnes, A., W. W. Cooper, J. K. Devon, D. B. Learner, and W. Reinecke (1968), A goal programming model for media planning, *Mgmt Sci.*, **14**, B431–B436.

Charnes, A., W. W. Cooper, R. J. Niehaus, and D. Sholtz, (1975), A model and a program for manpower management and planning, Graduate School of Industrial Administratlon Reprint No. 383, Carnegie Mellon University.

Charnes, A., W. W. Cooper, and E. Rhodes, (1978), Measuring the efficiency of decision making units, *Eur. J. Opl Res.*, **2**, 429–444.

Cheshire, M. K., K. I. M. McKinnon, and H. P. Williams (1984), The efficient allocation of private contractors to public works, *J. Opl Res. Soc.*, **35**, 705–709.

Christofides, N., (1975), *Graph Theory, An Algorithmic Approach*, Academic Press London.

Chvatal, V., and P. L. Hammer, (1975), Aggregation of inequalities in integer programmmg, Paper presented at Workshop on Integer Programming, Bonn, September.

Corner, L. J., (1979), Linear programming: some unsuccessful applications, *OMEGA*, **7**, 257–262.

Crowder, H., E. L. Johnson, and M. W. Padberg, (1983), Solving large-scale zero-one linear programming problems, *Opl Res.*, **31**, 803–834.

Daniel, R. C., (1973), Phasing out capital equipment, *Opl Res. Q.*, **24**, 113–116.

Daniel, R. C., (1978), Reducing computational effort in solving a hard integer programme, in Publication no. 25 of the Association for Computing Machinery, Special Interest Group on Mathematical Programming (SIGMAP), pp. 39–44.

Danzig, G. B., (1951), Application of the simplex method to a transportation problem in T. C. Koopmans (Ed.), *Activity Analysis of Production and Allocation*, Wiley, New York.

Dantzig, G. B., (1955), Optimal solution of a dynamic Leontief model with substitution, Rand Report RM-1281-1, The Rand Corporation, Santa Monica, California.

Dantzig, G. B., (1963), *Linear Programming and Extensions*, Princeton University Press, Princeton, New Jersey.

Dantzig, G. B., (1969), A hospital admission problem, Technical Report No. 69-15, Stanford University, California.

Dantzig, G. B., (1970), Large scale linear programs—a survey, Paper presented to the 7th International Symposium on Mathematical Programming, The Hague, Netherlands.

Davies, G. S., (1973), Structural control in a graded manpower system, *Mgmt Sci.*, **20**, 76–84.

Day, R. E., (1984), *MAGIC: User's Guide*, Department of Business Studies, University of Edinburgh, Edinburgh.

Dempster, M., (1980), *Stochastic Programming*, Academic Press, London.

Dijkstra, E. W., (1959). A note on two problems in connection with graphs, *Numer. Math.*, **1**, 269–271.

Dorfman, R. P. A., P. A. Samuelson, and R. M. Solow, (1958), *Linear Programming and Economic Analysis*, McGraw-Hill, New York.

Duffin, R. J., E. L. Peterson, and C. Zener, (1968), *Geometric Programming: Theory and Application*, Wiley, New York.

Dyson, R. G., (1980), Maximin programming, fuzzy linear programming and multicriteria decision making, *J. Opl Res. Soc.*, **31**, 263–267.

Edmonds, J., (1965), Maximum matching and a polyhedron with 0–1 vertices, *J. Res. Nat. Bur. Stds*, **69B**, 125–130.

Eilon, S., C. D. T. Watson-Gandy, and N. Christofides, (1971), *Distribution Management: Mathematical Modelling and Practical Analysis*, Griffin, London.

Eisemann, K., (1957), The trim problem, *Mgmt Sci.*, **3**, 279–284.

Engel, J. F., and M. R. Warshaw, (1964), Allocating advertising dollars by linear programming, *J. Advertising Res.*, **5**, 42–48.

Fabian, T., (1967), Blast furnace production planning—a linear programming example, *Mgmt Sci.*, **14**, B1–B27.

Fanshel, S., and E. S. Lynes, (1964), Economic power generation using linear programming, *AIEE Trans. Power Apparatus Systems*, **83**, 347–356.

Feuerman, M., and H. Weiss, (1973), A mathematical programming model for test construction and scoring, *Mgmt Sci.*, **19**, 961–966.

Fisher, W. D., and L. W. Schruben, (1953), Linear programming applied to feedmixing under different price conditions, *J. Farm Econ.*, **35**, 471–483.

Fokkens, B., and M. Puylaert, (1981), A linear programming model for daily harvesting operations at the large-scale grain farm of the Ijsselmeerpolders Development Authority, *J. Opl Res. Soc.*, **32**, 535–548.

Ford, L. R., and D. R. Fulkerson, (1956), Solving the transportation problem, Rand Report RM-1736, The Rand Corporation, Santa Monica, California.

Ford, L. W., and D. R. Fulkerson, (1962), *Flows in Networks*, Princeton University Press, Princeton, New Jersey.

Forrest, J. J. H., J. P. H. Hirst, and J. A. Tomlin, (1974), Practical solution of large mixed integer programming problems with UMPIRE, *Mgmt Sci.*, **20**, 736–773.

Fourer, R., (1983), Modelling languages versus matrix generators for linear programming, *Ass. Comp. Manufact. Trans. Math. Software*, **9**, 143–183.

Garfinkel, R. S., and G. L. Nemhauser, (1970), Optimal political districting by implicit enumeration techniques, *Mgmt Sci.*, **16**, B495–B508.

Garfinkel, R. S., and G. L. Nemhauser, (1972), *Integer Programming*, Wiley, New York.

Garver, L. L., (1963), Power scheduling by integer programming, *IEEE Trans. Power Apparatus and Systems*, **81**, 730–735.

Geoffrion, A. M., (1969), An improved implicit enumeration approach for integer programming, *Ops Res.*, **17**, 437–454.

Geoffrion, A. M., and R. E. Marsten, (1972), Integer programming: a framework and state-of-the-art survey, *Mgmt Sci.*, **18**, 465–491.

Gilmore, P. C., and R. E. Gomory, (1961), A linear programming approach to the cutting stock problem part I, *Ops Res.*, **9**, 849–859.

Gilmore, P. C., and R. E. Gomory, (1963), A linear programming approach to the cutting stock problem part II, *Ops Res.*, **11**, 863–888.

Gilmore, P. C., and R. E. Gomory, (1965), Multistage cutting stock problems of two and more dimensions, *Ops Res.*, **13**, 94–120.

Glassey, R., and V. Gupta, (1974), A linear programming analysis of paper recycling, *Mgmt Sci.*, **21**, 392–408.

Glen, J. J., (1980), A parametric programming method for beef cattle ration formulation, *J. Opl Res. Soc.*, **31**, 689–698.

Glen, J. J., (1988), A mixed integer programming model for fertilizer policy evaluation, *Eur. J. Opl Res.*, **35**, 165–171.

Glover, F., J. Hultz, D. Klingman, and J. Stutz, (1978), Generalized Networks: A fundamental computer-based planning tool, *Mgmt Sci.*, **24**, 1209–1220.

Glover, F., and J. M. Mulvey, (1980), Equivalence of the 0–1 integer programming problem to discrete generalized and pure networks, *Ops Res.*, **28**, 829–835.

Glover, F., and D. Klingman, (1977), Network applications in industry and government, *AIIE Trans.*, **9**, 363–376.

Gomory, R. E., (1958), Outline of an algorithm for integer solutions to linear programs, *Bull. Am. Math. Soc.*, **64**, 275–278.

Gomory, R. E., and W. J. Baumol, (1960), Integer programming and pricing, *Econometrica*, **28**, 521–550.

Granot, F., and P. L. Hammer, (1972), On the use of Boolean functions in 0–1 programming, *Meth. Ops Res.*, **12**, 154–184.

Greenberg, H., (1986), A natural language discourse model to explain linear programming models, *Technical Report*, University of Colorado, Denver, USA.

Greenberg, H., C. Lucas, and G. Mitra, (1987), Computer assisted modelling and analysis of linear programming problems; towards a unified framework, *IMA J. Maths Mgmt*, **1**, 251–266.

Hammer, P. L., and U. N. Peled, (1972), On the maximisation of a pseudo-Boolean function, *J. Ass. Comp. Mach.*, **19**, 262–282.

Hammer, P. L., E. L. Johnson, and U. N. Peled, (1975), Facets of regular 0–1 polytopes, *Math. Prog.*, **8**, 179–206.

Hammer, P. L., and S. Rudeanu, (1968), *Boolean Methods in Operations Research and Related Areas*, Springer-Verlag, Berlin.

Harvey, A., (1970), Factors making for implementation success and failure, *Mgmt Sci.*, **16**, B312–B321.

Held, M., and R. M. Karp, (1971), The travelling salesman problem and minimum spanning trees, *Math. Progr.*, **1**, 6–25.

Heroux, R. L., and W. A. Wallace, (1973), Linear programming and financial analysis of the new community development process, *Mgmt Sci.*, **19**, 857–872.

Hitchcock, F. L., (1941). Distribution of a product from several sources to numerous localities, *J. Math. Phys.*, **20**, 224–230.

Ho, J. K., and E. Loute, (1981), An advanced implementation of the Dantzig–Wolfe decomposition algorithm for linear programming, *Math. Prog.*, **20**, 303–326.

IBM (1979), *Mathematical Programming System Extended/370 (MPSX/370), Program Reference Manual*, Form number SH19-1095, IBM Corporation, New York.

Jack, W., (1985), An interactive graphical approach to linear financial models, *J. Opl Res. Soc.*, **36**, 367–382.

342

Jeffreys, M., (1974), Some ideas on formulation strategies for integer programming problems so as to reduce the number of nodes generated by a branch and bound algorithm, Working Paper 74/2, Wootton, Jeffreys and Partners, London.

Jensen, P. A., and J. W. Barnes, (1980), *Network Flow Programming*, Wiley, New York.

Jeroslow, R., (1985), An extension of mixed-integer programming models and techniques to some database and artificial intelligence settings, *Research Report*, Georgia Institute of Technology, Atlanta, Georgia, USA.

Jeroslow, R., (1987), Representability in mixed integer programming, *Discrete Appl. Math.*, **17**, 223–243.

Jeroslow, R., (1989), Logic-based decision support: Mixed integer model formulation, *Annals of Discrete Mathematics 40*, North-Holland, Amsterdam.

Jeroslow, R. G., and J. K. Lowe, (1984), Modelling with integer variables, *Math. Prog. Studies*, **22**, 167–184.

Jeroslow, R. G., and J. K. Lowe, (1985), Experimental results with the new techniques for integer programming formulations, *J. Opl Res. Soc.*, **36**, 393–403.

Jones, W. G., and C. M. Rope, (1964), Linear programming applied to production planning—a case study, *Opl Res. Q.*, **15**, 293–302.

Kalvaitis, R., and A. G. Posgay, (1974), An application of mixed integer programming in the direct mail industry, *Mgmt Sci.*, **20**, 788–792.

Karwan, M. H., V. Lotfi, J. Telgen, and S. Zionts, (1983), *Redundancy in Mathematical Programming: A State of the Art Survey*, Springer-Verlag, New York.

Khodaverdian, E., A. Brameller, and R. M. Dunnett, (1986), Semi-rigorous thermal unit commitment for large scale electrical power systems, *IEE Proc.*, **133**, 157–164.

Knolmayer, G., (1982), Computational experiments in the formulation of linear product-mix and non-convex production-investment models, *Comp. Ops Res.*, **9**, 207–219.

Kraft, D. H., and T. W. Hill, (1973), The journal selection problem in a university library system, *Mgmt Sci.*, **19**, 613–626.

Kuhn, H. W., (1955), The Hungarian method for the assignment problem, *Naval Res. Logist. Q.*, **2**, 83–97.

Land, A. H., and S. Powell, (1979), Computer codes for problems of integer programming, in P. L. Hammer, E. L. Johnson and B. H. Korte (Eds) *Annals of Discrete Mathematics 5: Discrete Optimization*, pp. 221–269, North-Holland, Amsterdam.

Lasdon, L. S., (1970), *Optimization Theory for Large Systems*, Macmillan, New York.

Lawler, E., (1974), The quadratic assignment problem: a brief review, Paper presented at an Advanced Study Institute on Combinatorial Programming, Versailles, France, September.

Lawler, E. L., J. K. Lenstra, A. H. G. Rinnooy Kan, and D. B. Shmoys, (1985), (Eds), *The Travelling Salesman Problem*, Wiley, Chichester.

Lawrence, J. R., and A. D. J. Flowerdew, (1963), Economic models for production planning, *Opl Res. Q.*, **14**, 11–30.

Leontief, W., (1951), *The Structure of the American Economy, 1919–1931*, Oxford University Press, New York.

Lilien, G. L., and A. G. Rao, (1975), A model for manpower management, *Mgmt Sci.*, **21**, 1447–1457.

Lockyer, K. G., (1967), *An Introduction to Critical Path Analysis*, Pitman, London.

Loucks, O. P., C. S. Revelle, and W. R. Lynn, (1968), Linear programming models for water pollution control, *Mgmt Sci.*, **14**, B166–B181.

Louwes, S. L., J. C. G. Boot, and S. Wage, (1963), A quadratic programming approach to the problem of the optimal use of milk in the Netherlands, *J. Farm Econ.*, **45**, 309–317.

Lucas, C., and G. Mitra, (1988), Computer assisted mathematical programming (modelling) system: CAMPS, *Comp. J.*, **31**, 364–375.

McColl, W. H. S., (1969), Management and operations in an oil company, *Opl Res. Q.*, **20** (conference issue), 64–65.

McDonald, A. G., G. C. Cuddeford, and E. M. L. Beale, (1974), Mathematical models of the balance of care, *Brit. Med, Bull.*, **30**, 262–270.

McKinnon, K. I. M., and H. P. Williams, (1989), Constructing integer programming models by the predicate calculus, *Ann. OR*, **21**, 227–246.

Manne, A., (1956), *Scheduling of Petroleum Refinery Operations*, Harvard Economic Studies 48, Harvard University Press, Cambridge, Mass.

Markland, R. E., (1975), Analyzing multi-commodity distribution networks having milling-in-transit features, *Mgmt Sci.*, **21**, 1405–1416.

Markowitz, H., (1959), *Portfolio Section*, Wiley, New York.

Mathematical Programming Study 9: Mathematical Programming in Use, (1975), North Holland, Amsterdam.

Mathematical Programming Study 20: Applications, (1982), North-Holland, Amsterdam.

Meyer, M., (1969), Applying linear programming to the design of ultimate pit limits, *Mgmt Sci.*, **16**, B121–B135.

Meyer, R. R., (1975), Integer and mixed-integer programming models: general properties, *J. Optimization Theory Appl.* **16**, 191–206.

Miercort, F. A., and R. M. Soland, (1971), Optimal allocation of missiles against area and point defences *Ops Res.*, **19**, 605–617.

Miller, C. E., (1963), The simplex method for local separable programming, in R. L. Graves and P. Wolfe (Eds), *Recent Advances in Mathematical Programming*, pp. 89–110, McGraw-Hill, New York.

Miller, D. W., and M. K. Starr, (1960), *Executive Decisions and Operations Research*, Prentice-Hall, Englewood Cliffs, New Jersey.

Mitra, G., (1973), Investigation of some branch-and-bound strategies for the solution of mixed integer linear programs, *Math. Prog.*, **4**, 155–170.

Muckstadt, J. A., and S. Koenig, (1977), An application of Lagrangian relaxation to scheduling in power generation systems, *Opl Res.*, **25**, 387–403.

Müller-Merbach, H., (1978), Entwurf von input-output-Modellen, *Proz. Ops Res.*, **7**, 521–531.

Murtagh, B. A., (1981), *Advanced Linear Programming: Computation and Practice*, McGraw-Hill, New York.

Nemhauser, G. L., and L. A. Wolsey, (1988), *Integer and Combinatorial Optimization*, Wiley, New York.

Orchard-Hays, W., (1969), *Advanced Linear Programming Computing Techniques*, McGraw-Hill, New York.

Orden, A., (1956), The transhipment problem, *Mgmt Sci.*, **2**, 276–285.

Padberg, M. W., (1974), Perfect zero–one matrices, *Math. Prog.*, **6**, 180–196.

Price, W. L., and W. G. Piskor, (1972), The application of goal programming to manpower planning, *Information*, **10**, 221–231.

Redpath, A. T., and D. H. Wright, (1981), Optimization procedures for computerised therapy planning, in G. Burger (Ed.), *Treatment Planning for External Beam Therapy with Neutrons* (Supplement to *Strahlentherapie*, Vol. 77), pp. 54–59, Urban and Schwarzenberg, München.

Revelle, C., F. Feldmann, and W. Lynn, (1969), An optimization model of tuberculosis Epidemiology, *Mgmt Sci.*, **16**, B190–B211.

Rhys, J. M. W., (1970), A selection problem of shared fixed costs and network flows, *Mgmt Sci.*, **17**, 200–207.

Riley, V., and S. I. Gass, (1958), *Bibliography on Linear Programming and Related Techniques*, Johns Hopkins University Press, Baltimore, Maryland.

344

Rivett, B. H. P., (1968), *Concepts of Operational Research*, Watts, London.

Rose, C. J., (1973), Management science in the developing countries: a comparative approach to irrigation feasibility, *Mgmt Sci.*, **20**, 423–438.

Rosen, J. B., (1964), Primal partitioning programming for block diagonal matrices, *Numer. Math.*, **6**, 250–260.

Royce, N. J., (1970), Linear programming applied to the production planning and operation of a chemical process, *opl Res. Q.*, **21**, 61–80.

Salkin, G., and J. Kornbluth, (1973), *Linear programming in Financial Planning and Accounting*, Haymarket Publishing, London.

Shapiro, J. F., (1979), *Mathematical Programming: Structures and Algorithms*, Wiley, New York.

Smith, D., (1973), *Linear Programming Models in Business*, Polytech Publishers, Stockport, UK.

Souder, W. E., (1973), Analytical effectiveness of mathematical models for R & D project Section, *Mgmt Sci.*, **19**, 907–923.

Spath, H., W. Gutgesell, and G. Grun, (1975), Short term liquidity management in a large concern using linear programming, in H. M. Salkiin and J. Saha (Eds), *Studies in Linear Programming*, North-Holland/American Elsevier, Amsterdam.

Srinivason, V., (1974), A transshipment model for cash management decisions, *Mgmt Sci.*, **20**, 1350–1363.

Stanley, E. D., D. Honig, and L. Gainen, (1954), Linear programming in bid evaluation, *Naval Res. Logist. Q.*, **1**, 48–54.

Stewart, R., (1971), *How Computers Affect Management*, Pan Books, London.

Stone, R., (1960), *Input/Output and National Accounts*, OECD, Paris.

Sutton, D. W., and P. A. Coates, (1981), On-line mixture calculation system for stainless steel production by BSC stainless: the least through cost mix system (LTCM), *J. Opl Res. Soc.*, **32**, 165–169.

Swart, W., C. Smith, and T. Holderby, (1975), Expansion planning for a large dairy farm, in H. M. Salkin, and J. Saha (Eds), *Studies in Linear Programming*, North Holland/American Elsevier, Amsterdam.

Thanassoulis, E., R. G. Dyson, and M. J. Foster, (1987), Relative efficiency assessments using data envelopment analysis: an application to data on rates departments, *J. Opl Res. Soc.*, **5**, 397–411.

Thomas, G. S., J. C. Jennings, and P. Abbott, (1978), A blending problem using integer programming on-line, *Math. Prog. Study* **9**, 30–42.

Tomlin, J. A., (1966), Minimum-cost multicommodity network flows, *Ops Res.*, **14**, 45–51.

Vajda, S., (1975), Mathematical aspects of manpower planning, *Opl Res. Q.*, **26**, 527–542.

Van Roy, T. J., and L. A. Wolsey, (1984), Solving mixed integer programs by automatic reformulation, *Core Discussion Paper No. 8432*, Center for Operations Research and Econometrics, Université Catholique de Louvain, Belgium.

Veinott, A. F., and H. M. Wagner, (1962), Optimal capacity scheduling—I, *Ops Res.*, **10**, 518–532.

Wagner, H. M., (1957), A linear programming solution to dynamic Léontief type models, *Mgmt Sci.*, **3**, 234–254.

Wardle, P. A., (1965), Forest management and operational research, *Mgmt Sci.*, **11**, B260–B270.

Warner, D. M., and J. Prawda, (1972), A mathematical programming model for scheduling nursing personnel in a hospital, *Mgmt Sci.*, **9**, 411–422.

Williams, A. C., (1989), Marginal values in mixed integer linear programming, *Math. Prog.*, **44**, 67–75.

Williams, H. P., (1974), Experiments in the formulation of integer programming problems, *Math. Prog. Study*, **2**, 180–197.

Williams, H. P., (1977), Logical problems and integer programming, *Bull. Inst. Math. Appl.*, **13**, 18–20.

Williams, H. P., (1978), The reformulation of two mixed integer programming problems, *Math. Prog.*, **14**, 325–331.

Williams, H. P., (1979), The economic interpretation of duality for practical mixed integer programming models in A. Prekopa (Ed.), *Survey of Mathematical Programming,* North-Holland, Amsterdam.

Williams, H. P., (1981), Reallocating the cost of dependent decisions, *Appl. Econ.*, **13**, 89–98.

Williams, H. P., (1982), Models with network duals, *J. Opl Res. Soc.*, **33**, 161–169.

Williams, H. P., (1987), Linear and integer programming applied to the propositional calculus, *Int. J. Syst. Res. Inform. Sci.*, **2**, 81–100.

Williams, H. P., and A. C. Redwood, (1974), A structured linear programming model in the food industry, *Opl Res. Q.*, **25**, 517–527.

Wilson, E. J. G., and R. J. Willis, (1983), Scheduling of telephone betting operators—a case study, *J. Opl Res. Soc.* **33**, 999–1006.

Wolsey, L. A., (1975), Faces for a linear inequality in 0–1 variables, *Math. Prog.*, **8**, 165–178.

XPRESS-MP Reference Manual, (1993), Dash Associates, Blisworth House, Church Lane, Blisworth, Northants NN7 3BX, UK.

Young, W., J. G. Ferguson, and B. Corbishley, (1963), Some aspects of planning in coal mining, *Opl Res. Q.*, **14**, 31–45.

.

Author Index

348

Subject Index

Decision Processes and Modelling ...

MARKOV DECISION PROCESSES
Doug J White, University of Manchester, UK
The purpose of this book is to provide a basic text covering some of the fundamentals involved in the manner in which Markov decision problems may be properly formulated, and solutions determined. It provides a sound foundation for the study of Markov decision processes at a moderate mathematical level.
0471 93627 8   Published 1993   £39.95

THE CRAFT OF DECISION MODELLING
Patrick Rivett, University of Sussex, UK
Despite the multitude of texts written in the area of models for decision making there remains a rift between sophisticated theory and practical application. Patrick Rivett provides an extensive and varied discussion which brings the two areas together.

Based on a lifetime's experience, the book deals with the construction of models for decision making and the scientific analysis or consequence of decisions in complex situations. Richly illustrated with case studies, all taken from real life situations, the author illustrates the principles of good practice and the evolution of the subject area.
0471 93962 5   Published 1994   £24.95

MULTICRITERIA DECISION-AID
Philip Vincke, University Libre De Bruxelles, Belgium
This book presents the foundations, models and methods of multicriteria decision aid, a discipline which has seen considerable development over the past ten years in the world of applied mathematics.
0471 93184 5   Published 1993   £39.95

(prices correct at time of going to press but subject to change, please contact the New York office for prices in the USA)

All titles available from your bookseller or direct from the publisher

JOHN WILEY & SONS LTD, BAFFINS LANE, CHICHESTER, SUSSEX, PO19 1UD, UK
Tel: (+)1243 779777 Fax: (+)1243 775878
JOHN WILEY & SONS INC, 605 THIRD AVENUE, NEW YORK NY 10158-0012, USA
Tel: (212) 850 6000 Fax: (212) 850 6088